Haim Genizi

AMERICAN APATHY
The Plight of Christian Refugees from Nazism

HAIM GENIZI

AMERICAN APATHY

THE PLIGHT
OF CHRISTIAN REFUGEES FROM NAZISM

BAR-ILAN UNIVERSITY PRESS

ISBN 965-226-037-1

©

Copyright Bar-Ilan University
Ramat-Gan

Printed in Israel, 1983
at "Menachem" Press, Jerusalem

*To the Memory
of my parents
Sima and Jacob
Genizi (Günsberger)*

CONTENTS

PREFACE

Despite the increasing flow of books and articles published in recent years on the subject of American apathy toward Jewish refugees during the Nazi era, the contribution of non-Jewish relief organizations to the alleviation of the refugee problem in general, and the plight of non-Jewish refugees in particular, has been largely neglected. Christians who fled Nazi-dominated countries on account of political, religious or racial persecution, constituted almost a third of the refugees who reached American shores. As a result of the Nazi racial decrees, not only Jewish converts to Christianity but even Christians born of Christian parents were, in certain cases, considered Jews, and persecuted as such. While these non-Aryan Christians constituted the largest group of non-Jewish refugees, many "pure" Aryans, trade-union leaders, Socialists, Communists and pacifists had to flee because of political reasons. Clergymen and men of letters, too, who refused to suppress their consciences were persecuted, and many of them preferred exile in a democratic country to a regime of tyranny in their homeland.

It is the purpose of this study to survey the activities of agencies such as the American Committee for Christian Refugees, the Catholic Committee for Refugees, the American Friends Service Committee, the Unitarian Service Committee, the International Migration Service and the International Rescue and Relief Committee. These bodies were either set up for the purpose of helping

Christian refugees or, being long-established agencies, formed special refugee committees for that purpose. We shall examine the American Christian community's attitude toward Aryan and non-Aryan Christians and the scope of the actual help given by it to them. To this end we shall describe in some detail how these Christian relief organizations were founded and how they operated and were financed. We shall also explore "non-sectarian" relief agencies, among others the National Coordinating Committee, the Emergency Committee in Aid of Displaced Foreign Physicians, the Emergency Committee in Aid of Displaced German Scholars, the U.S. Committee for the Care of European Children and Self-help for German Refugees. This will enable us to determine the measure and success of interfaith partnership and cooperation in relation to the subject of our research.

The term "refugees from Nazism" is generally used here to embrace people who were forced to emigrate from Nazi-ruled territories on account of their political views, religious beliefs or racial origin. Although that definition excludes other categories of refugees, such as Spanish Loyalists, displaced persons, or victims of World War II, to whom American agencies extended relief, we see no reason to refrain from mentioning in our study such humanitarian activity undertaken by any of the relief agencies discussed.

I am indebted to various persons for the help extended to me in the writing of this book. The late Mr. Zosa Szajkowski of YIVO, Institute of Jewish Research, first drew my attention to the relatively unexplored field of my study. My thanks are due to many librarians and archivists for their unfailing courtesy and helpfulness. I am particularly grateful to the following: Mr. William B. Liebmann, curator of James McDonald and Herbert H. Lehman papers at the School of International Affairs, Columbia University; Dr. Irene Jones, archivist of the National Council of Churches of Christ in America; Mr. Edmund Cummings of Migration and Refugee Services, and the Rev. Lydio Tomasy of the Center for Migration Studies, both of the U.S. Catholic Conference; Mr. Marek Web, archivist of YIVO; Mrs. Elizabeth Norris, librarian of the National Board of YWCA; Mrs. Rosa Kleipfisz, archivist of the Joint Distribution Committee; Mrs. Ruth Rauch of the American Jewish Committee's Record Center; Mr. J. R. Sutters, archivist of the American Friends Service Committee's Collection in Philadelphia; and finally to the librarians of the Franklin D. Roosevelt Library, Hyde Park, N.Y.; the National Archives, Washington D.C.; the archives of the YMCA National Board in New York, and the International Social Service in New York City.

The editors of *Bar-Ilan Annual, Bar-Ilan Studies In History, Proceedings of the Seventh World Congress of Jewish Studies,* the *Wiener Library Bulletin, Yad Vashem Studies* and *Yalkut Moreshet,* have kindly granted me permission to use articles of my own, which have appeared in these publications. Grants from the Research Committee of Bar-Ilan University and from the Israel National Academy of Sciences helped me to prepare the manuscript for publication.

My special thanks are due to Professor Avrom Saltman and Dr. Zwi Bacharach of Bar-Ilan University, and to Professor John S. Conway of the University of British Columbia, who read the manuscript and made valuable suggestions; to Professor D. Sperber, Chairman, Publications Committee, and to Mrs. M. Drory, Director of Bar-Ilan University Press, who saw the book through the press, with efficiency, devotion and skill. Mr. Julius Kopelowitz devoted time and energy to the linguistic and stylistic improvement of the study, which was typed by Mrs. Zipora Berger. My deepest debt is to my wife, Elisheva, whose patience and understanding have made this book possible. Above all, I pray to the Almighty to make me worthy of His mercy in granting my family and myself deliverance from the Holocaust and allowing us to build a new home in Israel.

Haim Genizi

LIST OF ABBREVIATIONS

Abbreviations used for organizations and archival sources are listed below. The locations of archival collections may be found in the Bibliography.

ACCR		American Committee for Christian Refugees
ACVAFS		American Council of Voluntary Agencies for Foreign Service
AFSC		American Friends Service Committee
	GF	General Files
	MF	Minutes Files
	FS	Foreign Service Files
	RS	Refugee Service Files
	C & O	Committees and Organizations
AJC		American Jewish Committee
ARC		American Red Cross
CC		The Catholic Committee for Refugees
CWS		Church World Service
ERC		Emergency Rescue Committee
FCC		Federal Council of Churches of Christ in America
FDRL		Franklin D. Roosevelt Library
	OF	Official Files
	PF	Personal Files

GJCA		German Jewish Children's Aid
HIAS		Hebrew Immigrant Aid Society
HICEM		HIAS+JCA, Emigdirect Immigration Agency
HMC		Home Missions Council
ICO		International Catholic Office for Refugee Affairs
IGC		Intergovernmental Committee
IMS		International Migration Service
IRA		International Relief Association
IRC		International Red Cross
IRRC		International Rescue and Relief Committee
ISS		International Social Service
JCA		Jewish Colonization Association
JDC		American Jewish Joint Distribution Committee
MP		James G. McDonald Papers
	GC	General Correspondence Files
	H	High Commissioner for Refugees Files
	P	President's Advisory Committee Files
NA		National Archives
NCC		National Coordinating Committee for Aid to Refugees and Emigrants Coming from Germany
NCWC		National Catholic Welfare Conference
NRS		National Refugee Service
NWF		National War Fund
OFRRO		Office of Foreign Relief and Rehabilitation Operations
OSE		*Oeuvre de Secours aux Enfants*
PAC		President's Advisory Committee on Political Refugees
RRT		Refugee Relief Trustees
RSARO		Representation in Spain of American Relief Organizations
UJA		United Jewish Appeal
UNRRA		United Nations Relief and Rehabilitation Administration
USC		Unitarian Service Committee

US Com.   United States Committee for the Care of European
            Children
WIL   Women's International League for Peace and Free-
            dom
WRB   War Refugee Board
WRS   War Relief Services of NCWC
YIVO   Institute for Jewish Research
YMCA   Young Men's Christian Association
YWCA   Young Women's Christian Association

1

GERMANY, 1933—1938 : DISCRIMINATION AND EMIGRATION

The refugee problem in the 1930s was the outcome of the Nazis' systematic policy of racial, political and religious persecutions. As a totalitarian regime, the Nazis crushed their political rivals and challenged Church independence. Jews, Aryans and non-Aryan Christians were victims of legal discrimination, expropriations and terror. These persecutions led to an increasing flow of Jewish and Christian refugees out of Germany.

A striking feature of the Nazi Jewish policy was that despite its central role in Nazi thought and propaganda, it was not planned in advance. At least through 1938 there was no master plan for anti-Jewish legislation.[1] The "destruction process", as Raul Hilberg has termed a series of anti-Jewish administrative measures, was "a step by step operation".[2]

---

1 In spite of Shaul Esh's assertion. See Esh, "Master Plan for Nazi Legislation Against the Jews", *Studies in the Holocaust and Contemporary Jewry* (Jerusalem, 1973), pp. 142—147 (Hebrew); Uwe D. Adam, "An Overall Plan for Anti-Jewish Legislation in the Third Reich?", *Yad Vashem Studies*, 11 (1976), pp. 33—41.

2 Raul Hilberg, *The Destruction of the European Jews* (Chicago: Quadrangle, 1961), p. 31; see Karl A. Schleunes, "Nazi Policy

Prerequisite to discriminatory anti-Jewish legislation was a clear definition of the term "Jew". However, only a few months in power, Hitler preferred the less racial term of "non-Aryan" to "Jew". On April 7, 1933 the Reichstag adopted the "Restoration of the Professional Civil Service Law" that dismissed non-Aryans from governmental posts. The term "non-Aryan descent" was defined in the decree of April 11, 1933 as follows:

> A non-Aryan is one who is descended from non-Aryan, particularly Jewish, parents or grandparents. It suffices if one parent or grandparent is non-Aryan. This pertains especially when one parent or one grandparent belonged to the Jewish faith.[3]

The effect of the Civil Service decree was more comprehensive than it at first seemed, because bankers, lawyers, railroad and hospital workers were also included in the "Civil Service" framework. Several decrees were enacted between 1933 and 1935 which drove non-Aryans out of medicine, law, schools, universities and the arts.[4]

Although the main intention was to eliminate "Jewish influence", using the comprehensive term of "non-Aryans", the laws disqualified numerous Christians who had had no connection with the Jewish community. One has to bear in mind that in the course of the 19th and 20th centuries not a few German Jews had been converted to Christianity. Even more numerous were the intermarriages between Jews and German Catholics or Protestants, whose children were brought up as Christians. In certain cases even the "grandfather clause" was not acceptable. In the law of Septem-

---

Toward German Jews, 1933—1938" (Unpublished Ph.D. dissertation, the University of Minnesota, 1966), p. 118.

3   James G. McDonald, *The Letter of Resignation of James G. McDonald, High Commissioner for Refugees (Jewish and Other) Coming from Germany, Addressed to the Secretary General of the League of Nations* (London, December 27, 1935), *Annex*, pp. 3—4.

4   Schleunes, "Nazi Policy", pp. 127—138.

ber 29, 1933, for example, only those in whose veins no Jewish blood had run since 1800 were entitled to hold land.[5]

In 1935, when Hitler felt himself strong enough to announce the rearmament of Germany, thus openly defying the Versailles Treaty, he decided on a tougher policy against the Jews. In the Nuremberg decrees of September 15, 1935, the racial term of "Jewish blood" was openly used. The essence of that document was in Article 2, which stated that "only he is a citizen, who is a national of German or cognate blood and has shown by his behavior that he is willing and fit loyally to serve the German people and the Reich". The "Law for the Protection of German Blood and Honor", as it was eventually called, prohibited marriages and extramarital relations between "Jews and citizens of the state with German or related blood".[6] Many "pure" Aryans lost their status on account of their non-Aryan spouse. While many families were broken up because of this law, which was backed by strong social pressure, there were numerous couples who became refugees, preferring exile to separation. Thus, Aryans with a Jewish spouse joined the category of Christian refugees.[7] Further definition was needed to differentiate between a full Jew, a half Jew and three-quarter Christian. The "First Supplementary Decree to the Reich Citizenship Law" of November 14, 1935 divided the non-Aryans into two categories: Jews and *Mischlinge*.[8]

After the definition came the stage of expropriation. In a series of inconsistent and even contradictory laws and regulations, the Nazis launched a campaign to free the German economy from "Jewish dominance". Jews and non-Aryan Christians were dis-

---

5 McDonald, *Letter of Resignation, Annex*, p. 4
6 *Ibid.*, pp. 1—2; Hilberg, *Destruction of European Jews*, p. 46; Schleunes, "Nazi Policy", p. 168.
7 McDonald, *Letter of Resignation, Annex*, pp. 24—25.
8 *Mischlinge* were persons whose blood was a mixture from Jewish and Aryan races. See Hilberg's summary of the different categories, *Destruction of European Jews*, p. 53.

missed from their jobs, driven out of their businesses and professions, deprived of their financial status and eventually became victims of starvation. Through the so-called "Aryanization", Jews were forced to transfer their businesses into German hands. While until 1938 this procedure was "voluntary", after that it became compulsory.[9]

In addition to the enactments themselves, that deprived non-Aryans not only of their economic status but of their civil rights as well, one has to bear in mind the unlawful methods employed to suppress non-Aryan influence. Those classified as "non-Aryan" were subjected to constant intimidation, harassment, violence and terror. They could rely for the protection of their rights neither on the police nor on the courts.

The Nazi hope, that through dismissal, Aryanization, boycott and terror, Jewish influence would soon be excluded from German life, vanished in certain SS circles. Gradually it became evident that both the boycott of April 1, 1933 as well as the slow process of Aryanization were a failure from the Nazi point of view. Emigration was then suggested as the new path to the solution of the Jewish problem.

As early as the summer of 1934 a secret SS memorandum entitled "Situation Report — Jewish Question", suggested that Heinrich Himmler, the SS leader and head of the Gestapo, consider mass Jewish emigration. The report supported the Zionists because they had promoted emigration to Palestine; stressed the need for unity of different Jewish organizations; encouraged youth movements; supported Jewish self-awareness and endorsed vocational training for prospective emigrants.[10] By 1935 these recommendations had gradually been implemented. Encouragement of Jewish emigration became the official line of the Third Reich. *West German Beobachter*, the official National Socialist organ, stated on August 21, 1935: "There is another way recommended

9 *Ibid.*, pp. 54—105; Schleunes, "Nazi Policy", pp. 176—224.
10 Schleunes, "Nazi Policy", pp. 233—238.

by every German and available to every Jew. It is 'Emigrate! Emigrate!'"[11]

Thus emigration became the panacea to the Jewish problem. The discriminatory law, accompanied by physical violence — which intended to make life for non-Aryans, particularly Jews, unbearable in Germany — eventually forced them to leave the country. But Jewish emigration from Germany declined annually from 37,000 in 1933 to 23,000 in 1934, and to 21,000 in 1935. Through 1938 only 150,000 out of 500,000 German Jews left the country.[12] This was considered by the Nazis to be a failure, particularly in view of Germany's successes in 1936 on other fronts, such as the occupation of the demilitarized Rhine Zone, the Olympic Games in Berlin and the foundation of the Berlin-Rome axis. In view of these developments a more drastic approach to emigration was under consideration. Indeed, 1938 was a fateful, or a crucial year, and the turning-point in the Nazi treatment of the solution of the Jewish problem.[13] Forced mass emigration replaced the orderly procedure which had operated between 1933 and 1938 on a strictly legal basis. The responsibility for emigration was transferred from the Reich Office of Migration to the Gestapo. Unrealistic mass emigration plans were promoted, such as the Syria scheme, the Ecuador and later the Madagascar projects. Arthur Prinz, the manager of the German Jewish Relief Association, stated that "a mass emigration to Ecuador would indeed have led to a solution of the Jewish problem by the annihilation of the Jews concerned".[14]

In June 1938 the policy of forced emigration was actually im-

11   McDonald, *Letter of Resignation, Annex*, p. 33.
12   Werner Rosenstock, "Exodus, 1933—1939: A Survey of Jewish Emigration from Germany", *Leo Baeck Institute Yearbook*, 1 (London, 1956), p. 377.
13   Shaul Esh, "Between Discrimination and Extermination: the Fateful Year, 1938", *Yad Vashem Studies*, 2 (1958), pp. 84—85; Joseph Tenenbaum, "The Crucial Year", 1938", *ibid.*, pp. 49—77.
14   Arthur Prinz, "The Role of the Gestapo in Obstructing and Promoting Jewish Emigration", *Yad Vashem Studies*, 2 (1958), p. 209.

plemented. In the so-called June Operation, 1500 "anti-social" elements were arrested and imprisoned in concentration camps. The Gestapo allowed their release only when satisfactory arrangements had been made for their immediate emigration. In December 1938 there were 30,000 detainees whose release from the concentration camps was conditional upon their immediate departure from the country.[15] With the annexation of Austria in March, 1938, Adolf Eichmann established in Vienna a Central Office, which had complete control over emigration. Within half a year Eichmann sent abroad one quarter of Austria's Jewry (50,000).[16]

SS authorities helped and cooperated with relief agencies in order to promote emigration. The Jewish *Hilfsverein* and Pastor Gruber's Büro in Berlin, as well as the Protestant Swedish International Mission in Vienna, received governmental support in several phases of the emigration procedure.[17] However, the Gestapo's attitude toward Jewish and non-Aryan emigration was "inconsistent, unclear and torn between two opposing trends", observed Arthur Prinz. While the authorities were eager to get rid of the Jews, to make Germany *Judenrein*, no efforts were made to remove the obstacles that lay before emigrants. Furthermore, Nazi anti-Jewish propaganda only increased opposition in foreign countries to the absorption of immigrants.[18] A circular of the German Foreign Office, of January 25, 1939, summed up that approach: "The poorer and therefore the more burdensome the immigrant Jews to the country absorbing them, the stronger that country will react and the more favorable will the effect be in the interest of German propaganda".[19]

15   *Ibid.*, pp. 208, 211.
16   Schleunes, "Nazi Policy", pp. 272—273.
17   Peter W. Ludlow, "The Refugee Problem in the 1930s: The Failure and Successes of Protestant Relief Programmes", *English Historical Review*, 90 (July 1975), p. 598.
18   Prinz, "The Role of the Gestapo", pp. 208—209.
19   Quoted in Gerald Reitlinger, *The Final Solution: The Attempt to Exterminate the Jews in Europe, 1939—1945*, 2nd, revised and augmented ed. (London: Vallentine, Mitchell, 1968), p. 11.

How did non-Aryan Christians cope with their plight? Hundreds of thousands of non-Aryan Christians were affected by the racial legislation. Many lost their public posts, were stripped of their rights as citizens and were expelled from Germany's cultural life. Not only recently evangelized people but even Christians born of Christian parents were, in certain cases, considered as Jews and persecuted as such. In certain respects the plight of non-Aryan Christians was worse than that of the Jews. It was a stunning psychological blow for many of them, who had always regarded themselves as loyal sons of the Church and the homeland, suddenly to be told that they belonged to an inferior race.[20] They had nowhere to go to receive moral and psychological comfort or financial support. Unlike the Jews, the non-Aryan Christians had no established institutions. The governmental charges against them were so absurd, so lacking in foundation, that they could not serve as a common denominator uniting these people.

The multiplicity of the laws and decrees differentiating between Aryans and Jews further complicated the situation. Legally it was not always clear where the rights of semi-Aryans ended. While an editor or a farmer had to prove his racial purity back to the year 1800, a reporter, for example, was only required to trace back to his grandparents. A 50% Jew enjoyed, at least theoretically, greater privileges than a full Jew, such as the right to marriage with an Aryan.[21] That situation, which differentiated between a 75% Christian and a 25% Christian, hampered the creation of an atmosphere of group-belonging. Hence, they were unable to imitate the Jewish example of establishing schools for their children who had been expelled from public schools. The lack of homogeneity and unity in non-Aryan Christian circles also precluded the maintenance of any separate cultural life

20 Isabel Lundberg, "Who Are These Refugees?", *Harper's Magazine*, 182 (Jan. 1941), pp. 164—172.
21 Dorothy Thompson, "Refugees: A World Problem", *Foreign Affairs*, 16 (April 1938), p. 384.

among them. The only culture they knew was the one from which they had been ostracized.[22]

Protestant and Catholic priests who had some Jewish ancestry protested against the racial laws that forced them out of their homeland. "We are Germans and we want to remain Germans", they declared proudly.[23] They established an organization called "Reich Confederation of Christian-Jewish Citizens and non-Aryans", that would speak in the name of millions of non-Aryans and provide them with spiritual as well as material aid.[24] The German press sharply criticized the new body. "The foundation of this society", wrote the *Westfaelische Landeszeitung*, "is fresh evidence of the fact that Jews, like evil weeds, everlasting, seek new places for their parasitic activities with any and all means, under all sorts of guises".[25]

The heads of the Reich Confederation of Christian-Jewish Citizens claimed to represent two and a half million non-Aryan German Christians. Their exact number, however, is controversial. Because of the unclear legal position that governed the matter, as well as the Nazi inability to examine the genealogical record of every German, it is difficult today to reach any definite conclusion as to the number of non-Aryan Christians.

The estimate, including Austrian non-Aryan Christians, ranged between one and a half million to three million.[26] In spite of their

22 Walter Kotschnig, "Christian Untouchables", November 20, 1935: 8 pp. ms. The article, which was written by Kotschnig, was intended to be published, probably signed by McDonald, in an American periodical to advance the appeal of the American Christian Committee for Refugees. See Kotschnig to Olive Sawyer, December 5, 1935 (McDonald papers, the School of International Affairs, Columbia University, New York City, the files of the High Commissioner. Hereinafter cited, MP:H).
23 *The New York Times*, November 4, 1933.
24 *Ibid.*; see also the editorial, November 6, 1933.
25 *Ibid.*, March 20, 1934.
26 Thompson, "Refugees", *Foreign Affairs*, 16 (April 1938), p. 384; "Evian Conference", *The Christian World*, 147 (August 1938), p. 619; Kotschnig, "Christian Untouchables", p. 4 (MP:H).

difficult position, proportionally only a small number of non-Aryan Christians left Germany. There were only a few agencies to help them, such as the Quakers, Pastor Gruber's Büro in Berlin, the Swedish Mission in Vienna and the Non-Aryan Applicants for Emigration. The latter, which consisted of baptized Jews and half Jews, was organized by an Upper Silesian named Aris for the purpose of promoting their emigration. Aris gained the Ecuador Government's permission for a grand-scale immigration. But because of the climate and other conditions in that country, nothing came out of that venture.[27]

Besides refugees, who left Germany on account of racial persecution, there were "pure" Aryan political leaders whose lives were in jeopardy. Totalitarianism would not tolerate political rivalry. A decree of July 14, 1933 declared the National Socialist Party as the sole political entity in the Reich. For continuing their personal political activities, people were arrested, tortured and sent to concentration camps. Hence, thousands of pacifists, liberals, Social Democrats and Communists fled Germany.[28] Union leaders and labor activists had to do likewise. In June 1934 the International Federation of Trade Unions, one of the first non-Jewish agencies that provided help to Christian refugees, assisted 1200 of its most needy members in Holland, Belgium, the Saar Basin and Czechoslovakia.[29]

Another stratum of Aryan Christians that was reduced to the status of refugee was that of intellectuals, professors, authors and artists. Men of letters, like Thomas Mann, preferred exile in a

27 Prinz, "The Role of the Gestapo, p. 209. On other Christian relief organizations in the Reich, such as Pastor H. Gruber's Büro and Pastor Hedenquist's Swenska Israelmission in Vienna, see below, p. 30.
28 Frank Ritchie, "German Refugees and American Christians", 5 pp. ms. (The papers of the American Friends Service Committee, General File, 1935, Committees and Organizations: at AFSC Archives, Philadelphia. The papers hereinafter cited, AFSC:GF, C & O.)
29 André Wurfbain to James McDonald, June 5, 1934: "Non-Jewish Refugees from Germany", n.d. (MP:H).

democratic country to a regime of tyranny in their homeland. While some of them left the country voluntarily, many others — including university professors — were dismissed from their positions, thus losing their economic as well as social status.[30] In spite of the relatively small number of intellectuals among the refugees, their fame and standing lent them importance as molders of world opinion.

In addition to racial, political and intellectual refugees, the Nazi suppression of the German churches forced thousands of priests to leave the country. Although Hitler and other Nazi leaders were indifferent to religion, they understood the need to provide the people with belief and religious symbols. Furthermore, their opposition to atheism partially derived from their hostility to Communists, who were regarded as heretics. In that way, by exploiting the emotionalism of the masses, by deceiving the intelligentsia and by opposing Communism, the Nazis posed as advancing the cause of religion. They kept the traditional religious principles but changed the original meaning, transposing them to the State and to the Party. So the Nazis utilized religion as a powerful political instrument to bind the people to the regime.[31]

The Church's political influence and social prestige were not less dangerous to the Reich than their power over the souls of the believers. The Catholic Center party was a thorn in the flesh of the Reich leaders. The social status of Protestant circles that constituted the powerful and influential elite also contributed to antagonism.[32]

His first target was the political power of the Catholics, namely

---

30 See press release of the High Commission for Refugees, July 7, 1934: "7500 Academic and Kindred Refugees from Germany" (MP:H).

31 John S. Conway, *The Nazi Persecution of the Churches, 1933—1945* (London, 1968), pp. 141—157; see also Johan M. Snoek, *The Grey Book* (Assen, 1969), pp. iv—v.

32 Frederick O. Bonkovsky, "The German State and Protestant Elites", *The German Church Struggle and the Holocaust*, ed. Franklin H. Littell and Hubert G. Locke (Detroit: Wayne State University Press, 1974), pp. 124—147.

the Center party and the Bavarian People's party. In the Concordat, reached in July 1933 between F. von Papen, deputy Chancellor and Cardinal Pacelli, Papal Secretary of State, the German demand for non-politicization of the church and its priests was accepted. Pacelli, on the other hand, secured the continuity of religious activities by Catholic institutions, such as the Catholic Action.[33] The armistice between the Reich and the Catholic Church did not last long. After the destruction of its political base came the turn of the Church's religious influence. The Nazis were determined to limit the Church's authority in the dioceses and in the congregations. There was, however, no uniform or constant application of pressure. One may distinguish between three "waves" of suppression. If, in the first stage, 1933—1934, the purpose was to eliminate the political power of the Catholics, the second stage, in 1935, was aimed against the authority of local communities. The third "wave" was intended to destroy the reputation of the priests, by means of charges against their moral behavior. There were intervals during these campaigns at times when the Reich needed Catholic support, as was the case at the time of the Olympic Games in 1936.[34]

Thus, religious persecution was one of the factors in the flight of Catholics from Germany. The stream of Catholic refugees increased after the annexation of Austria in March 1938, since Catholics constituted the great majority of that country's population. In 1938 the number of Catholic refugees who turned for help to the American Catholic Committee grew fivefold.[35] According to a survey prepared in July 1938 by George N. Shuster, editor of

33   *The New York Times*, July 9, 1933.
34   F. I. Murphy, "The American Christian Press and Pre-War Hitler's Germany, 1933—1939" (Unpublished Ph.D. dissertation, the University of Florida, 1970), p. 111; see also *The New York Times*, November 13, 1933.
35   *Report of the Committee for Catholic Refugees from Germany, Covering the Period from January 1, 1937 to September 30, 1938*, p. 5. (The archives of the National Catholic Welfare Conference, Staten Island, New York. Hereafter, NCWC.)

Commonweal, the influential Catholic periodical in the United States, there were approximately 5000—7000 Catholic refugees in Europe who needed immediate help.[36]

What was the reaction of the Catholic Church in Germany to that onslaught? Several Catholic bishops had apprehended the danger in the Nazi ideology even before Hitler assumed power. Already in 1931 Adolf Cardinal Bertram, Archbishop of Breslau and president of the German bishops, had begun to warn against false Nazi Messiahs who preached racism and extreme nationalism.[37] The Vatican, which was aware of constant violations of the Concordat, protested from time to time against the suppression of the Church. Pope Pius XI voiced his opposition to the dismissal of non-Aryan Catholics.[38] The annual conference of the German bishops in Fulda adopted mild resolutions criticizing Nazi intervention in Church affairs and the limitations placed on its authority. However, the bishops were silent on the racial laws.[39]

The Vatican's reaction was a little stronger. When the Reich disregarded Pacelli's protests, Pius XI issued, in March 1937, an encyclical, called *Mit Brennender Sorge* ('with burning anxiety'), which called upon Catholics to reject racism and nationalism.[40] These protests failed, however, to change the Reich's policy, partly because of their mild and irresolute character. A noted exception was the forceful criticism of euthanasia in 1941. That was an example of what the Church could accomplish by vigorous and well-coordinated protests. But as far as the general line was

---

36 *Ibid.* See also the mimeographed "Report" of the Committee for Catholic Refugees from Germany, covering the period January 1, 1937—November 30, 1937, Table I (NCWC).

37 Conway, *Nazi Persecution of the Churches*, pp. 6—7.

38 *The New York Times*, December 24, 1933; February 14, 15, 1934.

39 The Committee for Catholic Refugees, *Report, Covering the Period January 1, 1937—September 30, 1938*, p. 2; "German Catholic Bishops Protest Curbs on Church", *Christian Century*, 58 (July 23, 1941), p. 924.

40 Pinchas E. Lapide, *The Last Three Popes and the Jews* (Souvenir Press, 1967), p. 110.

concerned, the Catholic establishment refrained from any concerted pressure of organized struggle for reversal of the anti-Church policy. Only a few courageous individuals dared to voice criticism publicly, such as Michael Cardinal von Faulhaber, Archbishop of Munich and Clement Cardinal Graf von Galen, Bishop of Münster.[41]

How can the failure of German Catholic officialdom to effectively oppose the Nazis be explained? Three major factors served to bind the Church to support of the Reich: mutual hostility to Communism, the Concordat and, finally, the Church's tradition that tended to strengthen nationalism. The Nazi propaganda succeeded in presenting the restrictions on Church authority as an essential step toward uniting the nation in its struggle against the Bolshevik enemy. The Nazi crusade against the "Red Danger" turned Catholics into the Nazi allies. The Concordat, that had never been officially revoked despite actually having been breached by the Nazis, symbolized the ideological anti-Communist partnership. How could a faithful Catholic view the Third Reich as an unlawful regime when the Vatican had signed a treaty with it? Disbandment of Catholic organizations, as well as steps taken against Church leaders, were explained as measures for the non-politicization of the Church, a principle to which even the Holy See had subscribed. The Church's tradition of support for German nationalism prevented it from attacking Hitler. The bells of the churches rang when the Nazis marched into Vienna. Patriotic preaching from the pulpit, particularly during World War II, stifled any serious effort at insurrection. Feelings of duty, of loyalty to the homeland and to the existing regime, were deeply rooted in the German character. Centuries of Lutheran teaching to obey temporal authority exerted its influence even upon Catholics.[42]

41 *The New York Times*, January 2, 1934; Editorial, January 3, 1934; Joachim Remak (ed.), *The Nazi Years: A Documentary History* (Prentice Hall, 1969), pp. 98—99.
42 Gordon C. Zahn, "Catholic Resistance?", *German Church Struggle*, pp. 207—214.

Furthermore, serious physical obstacles stood in the way of organized Church opposition, such as efficient and brutal police, courts
that disregarded the individual's rights, governmental regulations
that outlawed oppositionist organizations, and lack of free means
of communication. Uprising under these conditions required great
personal courage, a quality displayed by only a few Catholic
bishops at that time.[43]

One should not disregard the consideration of the Catholic
hierarchy to safeguard the existing interests of the Church. It was
apprehensive that opposition to the regime would seriously hamper
the status of religion in the country. Priority went to the fundamental needs of the Church rather than to personal moral values.
In the clash of values it was incumbent upon Church leaders to
decide "according to the spirit of their doctrine and tradition",
stated the late Shaul Esh, the historian of the Holocaust. Following
that reasoning, Esh concluded that the Catholic Church in Germany "had no other alternative".[44]

The Protestant Church in Germany was consigned to an even
gloomier fate than that of the Catholic Church. While Hitler was
compelled to take the Vatican's worldwide influence into consideration, many Nazis regarded the Protestant Church as "their"
church and, since the latter was of a national character, they did
not hesitate to intervene in its affairs. The establishment of a State
Church, independent of world synods outside Germany, perfectly
suited Hitler's purpose of subjecting the Church to the authority
of the State. Through orders and directives Ludwig Mueller, an
army chaplain and a devoted Nazi, seized control of the Lutheran

---

43   Mary Alice Gallin, *German Resistance to ... Hitler: Ethical and
       Religious Factors* (Washington D.C.: The Catholic University of
       America Press, 1961), pp. 198—202.
44   Shaul Esh, *Studies in the Holocaust and Contemporary Jewry* (Jeru-
       salem, 1973), pp. 218—219 (Hebrew).

Church. He suppressed freedom of preaching and forbade any criticism of the regime.[45]

That approach, as well as the dictatorial methods of Bishop Mueller, met with growing resistance in the Evangelical Church. The one and a half million members of the Confessing Church, led by Martin Niemöller, represented the most remarkable expression of organized opposition from the Church. Nevertheless, even that group confessed in 1945 to not doing enough. "We accuse ourselves for not witnessing more courageously, for not praying more faithfully, for not believing more joyously and for not loving more ardently", read the "Confession of Faith" which was adopted in Stuttgart. It is remarkable that there was no mention of not fighting anti-Semitism more boldly.[46]

Hans Kerrl, the minister in charge of Church affairs in Germany, made strenuous efforts to stifle the opposition of the Confessing Church. Strong measures were employed. Niemöller was arrested along with other leaders, and the Gestapo dispersed church meetings, taking participants into custody. In November 1937, 700 priests were imprisoned.[47]

One of the products of the Confessing Church was Pastor H. Gruber's Büro, which was founded in the summer of 1936. It was, probably, the most important Protestant relief agency in Germany that undertook the difficult task of helping non-Aryan Protestants to emigrate. Since the Büro was connected with the Confessing Church rather than with the official Reich-Church, it had a most ambivalent relationship during the short and troubled period of its existence. Due to Gruber's ability to establish working relations with the different sections of the German Protestant churches on the one hand, and with several European church organizations on the other hand, his agency was able to provide help to a growing number of non-Aryan Christians. In April 1939 Gruber's Büro

---

45 *The New York Times*, Editorial, January 13, 1934; Conway, *Nazi Persecution of Churches*, pp. 34—36, 46—48.
46 Conway, *Nazi Persecution of Churches*, p. 332.
47 *Ibid.*, pp. 208—212.

employed thirty paid workers and took care of 100—130 daily
visitors. According to a conservative estimate, by 1940 his office
had helped 1100 people to emigrate.[48]

The Swenska Israelmission in Vienna, under the directorship of
Pastor Hedenquist, was another relief organization that provided
help to victims of Nazi persecution. After the annexation of Austria
and after *Kristallnacht* (November 10, 1938), the financial sources
of the Swedish Mission increased. Consequently, it assisted thousands of non-Aryan Protestants with relief and other kinds of help.
Approximately 3000 of them left the Reich due to the assistance
of Hedenquist's Mission.[49]

Most of the Protestants, however, were not as brave and as conscientious as Niemöller, Gruber and Hedenquist. The overwhelming majority accepted the new regime and surrendered to Mueller's
demands. The reasons for Protestant obedience were not far
removed from those motivating the Catholics: support of the
Fatherland, both in its effort to break the chains of the Versailles
arrangements during the 1930s and in its fight during the war; the
traditional Lutheran trend to obey the existing ruler; sympathy
for the ideas of "positive Christianity"; and finally the notion that
the Reich constituted a barrier against Communist expansion.
Resistance to the regime, especially during the war, was considered as treason. Hence the forceful methods employed during
the 1940s against conscientious clergymen who wanted to follow
their own inclinations.[50]

Thus, the persecution of the Churches in Germany was the

48 Ludlow, "Refugee Problem", *English Historical Review*, 90 (July
    1975), pp. 600—602.
49 *Ibid.*, pp. 597—599.
50 Conway, *Nazi Persecution of the Churches*, pp. 322—334; see the
    secret memorandum, "Not for Publication", "Note on the Situation
    of the Church in Europe", n.d. p. 5. (The papers of the Federal
    Council of Churches of Christ in America, Box 163, in the archives
    of Presbyterian Historical Society. Hereafter, FCC.)

outcome of political nihilism and ideological fanaticism of Nazi Germany. The supremacy of the State over religion and the uncompromising measures of totalitarianism led to antagonism between the Church and the State. Every manifestation of opposition was cruelly crushed. Indeed, thousands of Aryan priests and laymen escaped from Germany and later from Austria. However, since the neighboring countries refused to issue work permits or to allow them permanent residence, thousands of "pure" Aryan Christian refugees were desperately in need of help.[51]

The reaction to regulations that endangered the Church set the pattern for the attitude of Church leaders toward the Nazi annihilation of Jews, racial decrees and persecution of the Socialist and Communist leadership. Intervention on behalf of the members of other faiths was regarded as a political step, an area that the Church was forbidden to enter. The conspiracy of silence and marked lack of reference to Jews in much of the internal church correspondence and in many decisions, nevertheless, clearly pointed to an anti-Semitic overtone in the religious leadership's reluctance to intervene on behalf of Jews, as Gordon C. Zahn has suggested. Even protests concerning discrimination against non-Aryan Christian priests and mixed couples were virtually unknown before the winter of 1941.[52]

There was little or no recognition by the majority of Catholics and Protestants that they had obligations to their co-religionists. The St. Raphael's Society and the Büro of Pastor Gruber were forced to turn to foreign sources because of the poor response at home. While the former turned to the Vatican and requested the intervention of the American Catholic hierarchy, the latter relied on Protestant agencies in Holland, Geneva and London. In light

---

51 See the confidential report of A. Freudenberg to Samuel Cavert, December 9, 1942 (FCC papers, Box 3); Freudenberg to Henry Smith Leiper, July, 3, 1940 (*ibid.*, Box 11).

52 Zahn, "Catholic Resistance?", *German Church Struggle and the Holocaust*, p. 226; Conway, *Nazi Persecution of Churches*, pp. 265–266.

of the failure of the German authorities to desist from their policies of discrimination and enforced emigration, and in face of the failure of the German Churches to take sufficiently energetic measures to counteract such practices, an increasingly large number of observers abroad recognized the need for the refugee problem to be tackled on an international scale, rather than be left to private philanthropic or church agencies.

2

THE LEAGUE OF NATIONS AND THE REFUGEE PROBLEM, 1933–1935

The Nazi policy of discrimination and enforced emigration led to a growing flow of non-Aryan refugees. Out of 80,000 refugees who left Germany during the period 1933—1935, 15,000 were non-Jewish.[1] Strict immigration regulations in most of the countries denied refugees a permanent haven. Many of them were in a particularly desperate situation, scattered in temporary shelters in Western European countries, awaiting the help of their co-religionists. Jewish organizations in America and Europe rushed to help them. Nevertheless, in the light of the international scope of the refugee problem, many looked to the League of Nations for leadership. The League had some experience in dealing with the refugees of World War I. Dr. Fridtjof Nansen, the Norwegian polar explorer, serving as High Commissioner for Refugees (1921–30), had managed to resettle hundreds of thousands of White

---

1 Frank Ritchie, "German Refugees and American Christians", pp. 3—4 (AFSC, GF, 1935, C&O); Norman Bentwich, "Aryan and non-Aryan Refugees from Germany", n.d. 4 pp. ms. (MP: General Correspondence=GC); see also *Catholic World*, 147 (August 1938), p. 619; McDonald, *Letter of Resignation, Annex*, pp. 33—34.

Russians, Greeks, Turks and Bulgarians, among others. The Nansen Office had secured jobs and helped the refugees financially until final settlement was found for them. Furthermore, it had created an identity card for stateless persons, the "Nansen Passport", which was recognized by over fifty nations. Shortly after the death of Dr. Nansen in 1930, the League — predicting the end of the refugee problem within seven years — decided to disband the Nansen Office in 1938.[2]

With the flight of growing numbers of refugees to the states bordering on Germany, the Dutch representative called upon the members of the League to institute a new High Commission for German Refugees. The unique situation of the German refugees called for an organization separate from the Nansen Office. While the latter dealt with refugees whom the war had made homeless, the former was supposed to help people who were forced to leave their country in peacetime. During the 1930s the worldwide economic depression made the task of the new High Commissioner much more difficult than that of Dr. Nansen, since countries were now even more reluctant to admit refugees. The Jewish leaders had been particularly anxious that the German refugees would not be under the authority of the Nansen Office, but that a separate organization would take care of them. A High Commissioner specially nominated by the League for refugees coming from Germany would be "the first recognition by the League that an event affecting Jewry had become a world problem and the value of such recognition is ... great and may be ... useful as a precedent in the future", as Sir Osmond E. d'Avigdor Goldsmid, the British Jewish leader, wrote to Felix M. Warburg.[3]

The member states of the League, especially those who had

2   Louise W. Holborn, "The League of Nations and the Refugee Problem", *Annals of the American Academy of Political and Social Science*, 203 (May 1939), pp. 124—126, 131—132.
3   Sir Osmond E. d'Avigdor Goldsmid to Felix M. Warburg, September 11, 1934 (Felix Warburg papers, Box 317, at the American Jewish Archives, Cincinnati, Ohio).

considerable numbers of refugees, responded positively to the Dutch proposal. They, too, were eager to transfer the burden of refugees to the High Commissioner. As McDonald complained to Felix Warburg, the former chairman of the American Jewish Joint Distribution Committee, the countries "from the beginning tried to use the High Commission merely as an instrument to rid themselves of their refugees".[4]

The main objection to this plan came not from the host countries, who hoped to exploit the new Commissioner and so solve their problems, but rather from Germany who threatened to veto the proposal as an intervention in her internal affairs. To overcome the German opposition a compromise had been worked out, under which the High Commission became an autonomous organization separated from the League, both financially and administratively, and responsible to a newly-established Governing Body and not to the League Council. To emphasize this separation, its headquarters were set up in Lausanne, not Geneva. The division between the League and the High Commission hampered work on behalf of the German refugees, as the new High Commissioner, James Grover McDonald (1886–1964), later complained.[5] Although Germany withdrew from the League in the same month that he was nominated (October 1933), no effort was made by the member states to change the High Commission's autonomous status.

At Geneva, the candidacy of an American citizen was encouraged. The League of Nations Secretariat, always looking for ways to enlist U.S. cooperation, hoped that an American High Commissioner would attract American money for refugee work. The name of James McDonald as a possible candidate had been welcomed by Jewish and Gentile groups in the United States.

James Grover McDonald first became interested in international

---

4   James McDonald to Felix Warburg, August 6, 1934 (MP: GC).
5   "Talk of McDonald delivered over the facilities of NBC", October 11, 1935 (MP: H); Norman Bentwich, *Wanderer Between the Two Worlds* (London 1941), p. 233.

affairs as a college student of political science. While a graduate student at Harvard, he began to teach history and political science at Harvard and Radcliffe, later returning to his Alma Mater, Indiana University, as an assistant professor. He eventually served as Chairman of the American Foreign Policy Association for fifteen years (1918–33). In this capacity he tried to bring about a better understanding of international relations in the United States. In order to learn at firsthand the political situation in Europe after the rise of Hitler, he toured several European countries, including Germany, during the summer and autumn of 1933, and was able to discuss international affairs with Hitler himself. Despite these political activities and his membership of the editorial staff of *The New York Times*, at heart he always remained a teacher. Since he felt that his own generation had brought destruction on the world, he pinned his hopes on the young people, only to be sickened with world affairs by World War II and the Holocaust.

Although an idealist by nature, he was forced by the situation to become a realist. He was a devout Christian and humanist, a patient resourceful man, reliable and straighforward, who fought for the cause in which he believed, rather than standing on his personal dignity. These traits, along with his deep concern about the fate of the refugees, gained him the respect of Jews and Gentiles alike. Through personal friendship with the banker Felix M. Warburg, the founder and honorary chairman of the American Jewish Joint Distribution Committee (JDC), he made contacts with Jewish leaders and philanthropic organizations. Thus, his acquaintance with international affairs and his interest in an humane attitude toward the refugees led Henry Morgenthau Sr. to propose, in the name of the American Jewish Committee as well as the JDC, that Secretary of State Cordell Hull should support McDonald's candidacy as High Commissioner for Refugees.[6]

6 Barbara McDonald Stewart, "The United States Government Policy on Refugees from Nazism, 1933—1940" (Unpublished Ph.D. dissertation, Columbia University, 1969), pp. iii—v; Felix M. Warburg to Cyrus Adler, October 14, 1933 (Warburg papers, Box 305); Warburg

His political views, however, were not entirely satisfactory to some of the Jewish leaders in Great Britain. There were some hesitations because he was considered "somewhat too sympathetic to Germany". He had, for example, while not remaining entirely silent, tempered criticism of the Nazis because he hoped to become Ambassador to Berlin. Chaim Weizmann, the Zionist leader, considered McDonald an "extraordinarily ambitious man", who would use the post of High Commissioner only as a stepping stone to his future career. The choice of the British Jewish leaders, including Weizmann, was Lord Robert Cecil, a British statesman who would be able to command universal authority, a merit that — according their opinion — McDonald did not possess.[7]

Nevertheless, McDonald's proviso that he would accept the appointment only if it were endorsed by American and British Jewry, brushed aside any Jewish objections. The President of the Council of the League, fearful of any further reflection, nominated McDonald on October 26, 1933 as High Commissioner for Refugees Coming from Germany, after he had received the approval of prominent American Christians.[8]

What was the attitude of the Roosevelt Administration toward the nomination of an American citizen as High Commissioner? Apparently, McDonald was not the favorite son of the State Department. He did not belong to the Administration, although he was eager to be part of it. When Cordell Hull suggested a list

to Lewis Strauss, October 26, 1933; Morgenthau to Cordell Hull, October 8, 1933 (*ibid.*, Box 303); James McDonald, *My Mission in Israel* (New York, 1951), p. xiii.

7 Chaim Weizmann to Arthur Ruppin, November 21, 1933 (Weizmann archives, Rechovot, 7/1/1); Stewart, "U.S. Government Policy", pp. 110—112; McDonald to President Roosevelt, May 3, 1934 (MP:GC); "Remarks of McDonald on the Occasion of Presentation of the American Hebrew Award", January 3, 1935 (MP:H).

8 Raymond B. Fosdick of the Rockefeller Foundation contributed to McDonald's nomination. "Note by the Secretary General", October 13, 1933; Fosdick to Sweetser, October 16, 1933 (MP:H).

of distinguished persons to President Roosevelt as possible candidates, McDonald's name was not on it.[9] In view of American opposition to any involvement in the League's affairs, the passive attitude of the State Department was not surprising. The Department was not consulted as to the establishment of the High Commission, but was merely asked to send a representative to the Governing Body. The fact that the new organization was not an integral part of the League facilitated the American decision in favor of a nominal participation. Nevertheless, the State Department considered the High Commission a European institution whose task was to solve the problems of European refugees. Since the United States had a clear restrictionist policy, she was reluctant to contribute to the solution of this problem, and accordingly nominated a private citizen, Joseph P. Chamberlain, a professor of international law, as an unbriefed representative to the Governing Body.[10] As to the selection of James McDonald for the post, Secretary of State Cordell Hull admitted that although he had prior knowledge of his candidacy and had no objection to McDonald's nomination, the Department had had no part in the process of selection.[11] This policy of non-participation in the High Commission's activities was to be a source of frustration to McDonald during the years to come.

As one who had closely observed the international situation and increasingly strict immigration regulations, McDonald must have been aware of the difficulties facing the High Commissioner. Nevertheless, it seems that he underestimated the anti-alien, especially the anti-Semitic, forces in the world. He saw in the office of the High Commission an opportunity "to play a helpful part in cre-

9   Yehuda Bauer, *My Brother's Keeper: A History of the American Jewish Joint Distribution Committee, 1929—1939* (Philadelphia, 1974), p. 142.

10 Cordell Hull to the Secretary General of the League of Nations, October 25, 1933 (MP:GC); William Phillips to Joseph P. Chamberlain, November 19, 1933, February 21, 1935 (MP:H).

11 *The New York Times*, October 27, 1933.

ating more humane relations between Jewish and non-Jewish folk at home and abroad . . . . It is primarily because of this desire and because I think the High Commission offers the best opportunity for me to serve this purpose that I am prepared to go on".[12]

Apart from the laudable goal of creating an atmosphere of better understanding between Jews and Gentiles, McDonald faced more immediate problems, such as the organization of the administration of the High Commission and the need to finance it. The refugees, scattered in the countries neighboring Germany, needed temporary shelters, food, clothing, blankets, medical treatment and schools. It was to be one of McDonald's most time-consuming efforts to persuade developing and under-populated countries to provide final settlements for refugees. Meanwhile, and until such colonization projects could become effective, the High Commissioner tried to obtain from the countries represented in the Governing Body an agreement to honor the civil status of refugees and to issue them with work permits. The defense of stateless persons and recognition of an international passport for them were also among the subjects of negotiation between McDonald and the host countries. No easier was the task of calling on Nazi Germany to adopt an organized and humane system of emigration; to honor, for example, the rights to a pension, to social security and compensation for dismissal.

As a matter of fact, it was not the task of the High Commissioner to campaign for financial help or to provide food and medical care for the refugees, but rather to "coordinate and stimulate the activities" of existing international and national agencies.[13] For this purpose the Governing Body and the Advisory Council had been established. Whilst the former was the forum for representatives of states, the latter included private refugee organizations. The Governing Body met twice a year under the chairmanship of Lord Robert Cecil, who courageously attacked Nazi atrocities, the apa-

12   McDonald to Felix Warburg, August 16, 1934 (MP:GC).
13   Bentwich, *Wanderer Between the Two Worlds*, p. 236.

thetic attitude of the international community and the unwillingness of countries to accept refugees. He warned that the fate of Christian civilization was at stake, but his was a lone voice. Governments were "only incidentally or even casually interested in the human problems of the refugees", and their primary concern was politics, as McDonald complained to Lord Cecil. That the Governing Body was, according to its own chairman, "useless", seems, however, to have been partly McDonald's fault.[14] He failed to stir its members to action. He never criticized them publicly, although they were "nondescript diplomatists, who knew little, cared little and wanted to do as little as possible about the cause", as Bentwich observed.[15] Providing refugees with a uniform document of identity and travel was one of the Governing Body's few achievements. Although it was not as effective as the Nansen Passport, the document did grant some measure of security to the stateless persons wandering through the countries of Europe.[16]

McDonald hoped that through the Governing Body he would be able to exert influence at least upon the member states. But he failed to secure their cooperation. They flatly rejected any suggestion that they should contribute to the budget of the High Commission, which, since it did not belong to the League, was supposed to cover its own expenses. McDonald applied to the member countries for a "symbolic" annual participation of $10,000, but in vain. He was especially eager to enlist the United States for a "token contribution", hoping to persuade other countries to follow the American lead. The State Department, however, anticipating "very savage attack both on world entanglement and on the Jews", decided to make no appropriation "until the other

---

14   McDonald to Lord Cecil, January 16, 1935; Lord Cecil to McDonald, February 7, 1935 (MP:GC).
15   Bentwich, *Wanderer Between the Two Worlds*, p. 236.
16   Louise W. Holborn, "The League of Nations and the Refugee Problem", *Annals of the American Academy of Political and Social Science*, 203 (May 1939), p. 133.

Powers have acted".[17] With the American refusal, the whole scheme
of government help to the High Commission collapsed.

After failing to secure financial contribution from member
countries, McDonald turned to Jewish and non-Jewish private
organizations. Moreover, he was unable to enlist the financial
support of such humanitarian agencies as the American Red
Cross and the American Friends Service Committee. Admiral
Grayson of the American Red Cross rejected McDonald's appeal
for a token participation. Though he sympathized with the refugee
problem, Grayson considered his refusal "not a matter of choice
but of necessity".[18] While the Quakers in Europe, especially the
British Friends, organized and maintained refugee shelters and
relief work in Paris, Vienna and Prague, the American Quakers
were unenthusiastic. Bentwich and McDonald were disappointed
by their apathetic attitude in 1934—1935. Only after 1938 did the
American Friends Service Committee become a major refugee
organization in America.[19]

The Jewish Joint Distribution Committee, the Jewish Colonization Association and the Jewish Agency for Palestine were the
main supporters of the High Commission. While these bodies
contributed tens of thousands of dollars annually, the Quakers
donated a mere £125 in 1935, the National Christian Appeal for
German Refugees contributed £189 and the International Christian Appeals sent only £100 to the High Commission.[20] Officially,

17   Chamberlain to McDonald, February 5, 1935; Phillips to Chamber-
     lain, February 1, 1935 (MP:H).
18   Bentwich to McDonald, November 4, 1933, May 24, 1935 (MP:GC).
19   Bentwich to McDonald, May 7, 1935; McDonald to Bentwich, June
     21, 1935 (MP:GC). See below, Chapter 3.
20   Joseph P. Chamberlain, "Report of the Governing Body of the High
     Commission for Refugees", n.d. (MP:GC). In 1935 the JDC con-
     tributed $25,000; The American Palestine Campaign gave $10,000;
     McDonald (Lewis Strauss) $10,000, and JCA and the British Central
     Fund contributed £3500. High Commission, Report on Accounts for
     December 31, 1935 (MP:H). Bentwich to McDonald, January 13, 1936
     (MP: GC).

McDonald contributed his annual salary of $15,000, but this was
a secret donation from Jewish sources.[21] To be sure, these contributions were intended to cover only the administrative expenses
of the High Commission. The actual relief for the refugees was
to come from private organizations. McDonald opposed the idea
of initiating a separate appeal for relief, believing that the High
Commissioner should not be engaged simultaneously in an independent campaign and in actual relief work.[22]

Jewish organizations were anxious not only to support the
High Commission but also to participate in its decisions. Norman
Bentwich, McDonald's deputy and one of the leaders of British
Jewry, proposed to append a small committee, representing the
Jewish agencies, to the Governing Body. The High Commissioner,
however, rejected this, arguing that the Governing Body consisted
only of representatives of States and not of private organizations.
To utilize the agencies' help and to coordinate refugee activities,
McDonald decided to establish an Advisory Council. In the framework of this Council, Jewish and Gentile organizations from many
countries met to discuss the immediate problems of the refugees,
such as the problem of passports for stateless persons, or resettlement projects. The Jewish groups which participated included
the JDC, JCA, the Jewish Agency for Palestine, the American
Jewish Committee, the American Jewish Congress, B'nai B'rith,
Agudat Israel, and the English and French Communities. Other
organizations included the Universal Christian Council for Life
and Work, the Society of Friends, the European Office for Inter-
Church Aid, the International Federation of Trade Unions, the
International Students Service, the International Migration Service
and the Emergency Committee for Aid to German Scholars. Al-

21 Lewis Strauss donated $10,000 every year for that purpose. Strauss
     to McDonald, February 27, 1934; McDonald to Bentwich, May 28,
     1934. (MP:GC)
22 See McDonald's "Statement" from December 5, 1933 (MP:H); Memo-
     randum by André Wurfbain, "The Task of the High Commissioner
     Towards the Financing of Relief", n.d. (MP:H).

though the Advisory Council met from time to time and made some helpful suggestions, it seems that because it was such a large body, consisting of so many different organizations, it was not a real help to the High Commissioner. McDonald hoped to establish through the Council a standing executive committee that would take care of the German refugees. Instead, he faced rivalry and friction. He was called upon to be the "Peace" Commissioner to mediate between the organizations, especially between the Jewish ones. The Jewish internal fights were "baffling to an untutored Gentile", as Bentwich remarked. Therefore, the Advisory Council probably provided not much more than "moral support" for McDonald's efforts.[23]

Although McDonald's responsibility was for German refugees, he also devoted himself to caring for refugees from other countries. He frequently visited camps and temporary shelters in France, Holland, Belgium, Czechoslovakia and Poland. But he was mainly interested in the constructive solution of the refugee problem through colonization, rather than in relief work in refugee centers. He wanted to modify the status of the individuals from that of "refugee" to "immigrant" and "settler". To this end, he called the members of the Advisory Council to agree "on constructive programs for the liquidation of the relief work through permanent establishment".[24] This program became "most urgent" in the light of the "dangerous psychosis" concerning refugees in France and

23   Bentwich, "Notes on the Relations of the Office of a High Commissioner for Refugees . . . with Other Organizations", n.d. (MP:H). James N. Rosenberg questioned the advisability of the original plan to establish two separate sectarian councils, one for Jewish and the other for non-Jewish organizations. Rosenberg to McDonald, November 28, 1933 (MP:GC); "List of Organizations represented on Advisory Council of High Commission", July 12, 1934 (MP:H); Bentwich, *Wanderer Between the Two Worlds*, p. 234; McDonald to Bentwich, August 15, 1934 (MP:GC).

24   High Commissioner for the Members of the Advisory Council, "Summary of the Meeting of the Advisory Council of the High Commission, held in Paris", June 18, 1934 (MP:H).

in other countries. Anti-alien feelings increased in February 1934, when thousands of refugees fled to France after the annexation of the Saar Basin to Germany. Norman Bentwich was struck by the anti-refugee atmosphere in Paris. His report was of "immediate importance" for McDonald and gave impetus to colonization projects.[25]

The High Commission received plans "for every known and unknown corner of the world", as Bentwich recalled. People did not realize that it was impossible to settle thousands of refugees on empty land. The planners proved to have more knowledge of geography than of colonization, proposing to send immigrants to Angola, New Mexico, South-West Africa, North China, Alaska, Ecuador and North Australia, among other places. More practical were the schemes of settlement in Latin America. The governments of the Dominican Republic, Argentina and Cuba were ready to accept a certain number of immigrants. However, they were mainly interested in farmers and skilled workers and most of the refugees, Jewish and non-Jewish, did not meet that criterion. McDonald and his associates traveled widely to find permanent settlements. He conducted lengthy negotiations with the Argentinian authorities concerning the possibility of Catholic immigration to that country. Any settlement project demanded too much money for the refugee agencies to consider tackling the problem.[26]

To overcome that difficulty the foundation of a "permanent instrument for colonization and settlement" had been suggested. In April 1934 Felix M. Warburg discussed with McDonald and with Jewish leaders the establishment of the Refugee Economic Corporation, intended to operate under the auspices of the High Commissioner. The original plan of the Corporation was very ambitious. Warburg and Paul Baerwald, chairman of the Joint Distribution Committee, proposed to collect more than 10 million

25   Bentwich to McDonald, February 26, 1934; McDonald to Bentwich, February 27, 1934 (MP:H); Bentwich, *Wanderer Between the Two Worlds*, p. 327.
26   Bentwich to Felix Warburg, August 22, 1934 (MP:GC).

dollars from Jewish and non-Jewish sources. But this grandiose project "quickly dwindled in its ambitions", as Bentwich recalled. Arguments between the contributors and the organizations led to delays. After two years of red tape, the Corporation was launched with a fund of one and a half million dollars, but with no basic plan of action. Eventually the Refugee Economic Corporation supported the settlements in the Dominican Republic and financed retraining programs in several refugee camps. McDonald hoped to present the Corporation as a High Commission success and an American contribution to the constructive solution of the refugee problem. One may wonder, however, whether the delay and limited achievement of the Refugee Economic Corporation should be added to McDonald's credit.[27]

To avoid an uncontrollable flood of refugees, McDonald negotiated with European countries for the systematization of immigration. Among others he met Eduard Beneš, the future President of Czechoslovakia, the Polish foreign minister and officials in Denmark and Latvia. McDonald's most notable failure, however, was his effort to treat with German authorities. In spite of the fact that he carefully refrained from condemning the Nazis, he was *persona non grata* in Germany. During his visit there in 1934 no official was prepared to meet him. Only the legal advisor at the foreign office was "available", but he insisted on discussing refugee matters solely with Norman Bentwich, McDonald's deputy. In short, the Nazis preferred a Jew, Bentwich, to the "Aryan" High Commissioner for Refugees.[28]

When his personal channels with the Germans were closed,

---

27 Confidential Preliminary Draft of the Refugee Rehabilitation Committee, April 18, 1934; Warburg to McDonald, April 25, 1934; Bentwich to McDonald, August 10, 1934 (MP:GC); Stewart, "U.S. Government Policy", pp. 132—133; Bentwich, *My Seventy Seven Years: An Account of My Life and Times, 1883—1960* (Philadelphia, 1961), p. 132.

28 Bentwich, *My Seventy Seven Years*, p. 134; Stewart, "U.S. Government Policy", p. 121.

McDonald tried to use the services of the American ambassador to Berlin. He asked William E. Dodd to discuss with German authorities the rights of the refugees to compensation and pension. The Department of State agreed to McDonald's proposal, on condition that Sir Eric Phipps, the British Ambassador, should join Dodd in the negotiations. The two diplomats, who undertook the assignment halfheartedly to say the least, dropped the matter after one meeting with a German official. They decided to postpone the negotiation to a more appropriate time — which never arrived.[29]

As a matter of fact, Ambassador Dodd was critical of McDonald from the beginning. He doubted the wisdom and efficiency of the activities of the High Commissioner, considering that a representative of American Jewry might achieve more with the German authorities through quiet diplomacy than did McDonald through his press releases and public statements. He especially attacked McDonald's behavior, writing:

> Any man who would take a big salary for such a service, all from people who give the money for the relief of suffering fellows, is not apt to appeal strongly to other givers, and McDonald has shown so much self-esteem on different occasions that I fear these traits have become too well known in Berlin official circles.[30]

Since McDonald and Dodd were rivals in 1933 for the ambassadorship to Berlin, Dodd's criticism should be treated with caution. Nevertheless, this critical attitude toward McDonald was by no means unique. A visitor to a French refugee camp reported in the summer of 1934 that, "Everywhere I heard bitter complaints of the High Commissioner's work; criticism of his drawing so large a salary with such little actual results in his endeavors".[31] In a letter to the editor of *The New York Times* of March 4, 1934,

29   Stewart, "U.S. Government Policy", p. 141.
30   William E. Dodd Jr. and Martha Dodd (eds.), *Ambassador Dodd's Diary, 1933—1938* (New York, 1941), pp. 145—146.
31   Cited in Stewart, "U.S. Government Policy", p. 161.

Karl Brandt charged McDonald with "inaction", asking: "what has he done, what does he intend to do and when?". One could say that Brandt, as an outsider, was probably not familiar with the facts. But Jay Pierrepont Moffat, of the State Department, had firsthand knowledge of the situation. After a lunch with McDonald, Moffat "reluctantly reached the conclusion that in spite of high sounding titles . . . the actual accomplishments to date of the High Commissioner were perilously close to nil".[32] Furthermore, McDonald's "high-sounding title" raised false hopes among the refugees. In some places he was regarded as the Messiah, and these exaggerated hopes sometimes did real harm, for which he was attacked.[33]

More fundamental was the criticism by Jewish leaders in Britain and France. At a meeting of the German Jewish Emigration Council in London, E. L. Rawson reported on the "dissatisfaction at the lack of initiative and poor efforts of the High Commissioner".[34] Max Gottschalk of HICEM also thought that McDonald did not serve "any useful purpose" except "as a symbol of international interest in the problem".[35]

In spite of Jewish criticism of McDonald's poor achievements, the continuation of his work was essential to the Jewish leadership. Felix M. Warburg cabled Sir Osmond d'Avigdor-Goldsmid, the Anglo-Jewish leader, in September 1934:

> Am informed that JCA (and) French representatives desire McDonald's resignation and do not even want to continue expense Commissioner's budget . . . . In our opinion Mc-

32 *The New York Times*, March 24, 1934; Moffat Diary, March 5, 1934 (Houghton Library, Harvard University, Cambridge, Mass.).
33 Bentwich, *Wanderer Between the Two Worlds*, p. 235.
34 Cited in Zosa Szajkowski, "Relief for German Jewry: Problems of American Involvement", *American Jewish Historical Quarterly*, 62 (Dec. 1972), p. 122.
35 Bentwich, "Note of a Talk with Dr. Gottschalk", October 13, 1934 (MP:GC).

Donald's resignation would probably result in collapse of entire Governing Body and would be serious blow to Jewish cause throughout the world.[36]

Sir Osmond d'Avigdor-Goldsmid was indeed "rather disappointed with McDonald's absence of achievements". Moreover, McDonald took credit for relief work actually rendered by Jewish organizations, which irritated Sir Osmond. Nevertheless, his appointment had been the first recognition by the League that the refugee problem was an international matter. This recognition, according to d'Avigdor-Goldsmid, was so important that the Jews should make "further sacrifices in order to maintain McDonald and his staff".[37]

It seems that dissatisfaction was mutual. McDonald complained that the Jewish refugee organizations constantly attacked the High Commission, "for failure to do what it never undertook to do". This criticism could be ignored "if the work were being adequately done by the private organizations", argued McDonald, which was certainly not the case.[38] Obviously these accusations did not make life easier for McDonald, but one should not overstress the point. In spite of their inadequate work, the JDC, JCA, HIAS and other refugee agencies carried the main burden of relief for Jewish and sometimes Christian refugees. They not only covered the High Commission's administrative expenses, but their leaders, such as Felix Warburg, James N. Rosenberg, Paul Baerwald, Sir Osmond d'Avigdor-Goldsmid and Norman Bentwich were among McDonald's few confidants, and he frequently consulted them.

36 Felix Warburg to Sir Osmond d'Avigdor-Goldsmid, September 5, 1934 (Warburg papers, Box 316).
37 Goldsmid to Warburg, September 11, 1934 (Warburg papers, Box 317). Along the same lines James N. Rosenberg wrote to Felix Warburg, that in case of McDonald's resignation "it is vital that the failure shall not be placed on Jewish shoulders". Rosenberg to Warburg, July 30, 1934 (*ibid.*, Box 318).
38 McDonald to Warburg, August 16, 1934 (MP:GC).

The legal rather than the humanitarian approach of the member governments to the refugee issue was the pretext for their refusal to change the visa regulations. Only countries that had received considerable number of refugees showed any interest in the High Commission's activities, but this was merely to exploit it as an instrument to get rid of their refugees. France, for example, was convinced that the High Commissioner's only task should be colonization: rapid evacuation of the refugees from the host countries. Such an obstructive attitude on the part of most governments made the life of the refugees in the neighboring countries of Germany very difficult.[39]

Both Great Britain and France were beyond McDonald's influence. In spite of Norman Bentwich's good connections in the Foreign Office, Britain blocked every effort to include immigration to Palestine within the High Commissioner's Mandate. As to the regulations concerning refugees and the question of British financial aid to the budget of the Commission, McDonald cautioned Bentwich not to press too vigorously, because "unless Great Britain is willing to take the initiative, or at any rate support the initiative of some other power, nothing will be done".[40] One may question this over-cautious attitude to governments whose approach to the refugee problem was, as McDonald observed, dictated by "brutal considerations of expediency and political advantage".[41] Even after the rejection of his appeal for a symbolic contribution, he still believed that it would be unwise to put pressure on the member states, maintaining that it "would have been to invite a definite declination, whereas now, having raised it, we are in a position to follow it up vigorously... in the hope of securing affirmative action from at least three of the Governments".[42]

39 Ibid.; Bentwich to McDonald, February 26, 1934 (MP:H).
40 McDonald to Bentwich, March 10, 1935 (MP:GC); The New York Times, November 27, 1933.
41 McDonald to James Rosenberg, September 18, 1934 (MP:GC).
42 McDonald to Sir Osmond d'Avigdor-Goldsmid, September 28, 1934 (MP:H).

Although none of the countries reacted positively, McDonald failed "to follow it up vigorously". Norman Bentwich bore witness that McDonald "was prepared to talk in undiplomatic language",[43] but it seems that he did not use that capacity frequently. While privately he strongly condemned the attitude of various countries, he refused to criticize them publicly. On January 3, 1935, when receiving the American Hebrew Award as the American who had done the most for Jewry during that year, he decided to break his silence, attacking the ideology and practices of the Nazi regime. But he failed to condemn the member states for their refusal to help refugees. American unwillingness to support the High Commission was not mentioned at all. Nor did he threaten to resign in protest at the lack of cooperation, probably because of Jewish requests to remain.[44] Even in his *Letter of Resignation* as High Commissioner, on December 27, 1935, the member states were not the main target of his attack. Only shortly before he left office did he dare to condemn publicly "the callous indifference of some of the diplomats", that was so marked "as to make one almost despair of adequate action from Governments".[45] It might be argued that no criticism would have moved the independent states to take action on behalf of refugees. But it was surely worth trying "to press it vigorously".

Indeed, much of the work of the High Commissioner was disappointing. In August 1934, deeply frustrated, he complained to Felix M. Warburg:

43 Bentwich, *My Seventy Seven Years*, p. 131.
44 Warburg personally urged him to "avoid conditioning continuance work on large relief moneys" and promised him the support of private organizations, even without governmental contributions. Cable, Warburg to McDonald, September 6, 1934 (MP:GC); "Remarks of McDonald on the Occasion of the Representation of the American Hebrew Award", January 3, 1935 (MP:H).
45 "Talk of McDonald Delivered over the Facilities of NBC", October 11, 1935 (MP:H).

My own position sometimes seems to me unbearable. But I have no intention to surrender. Only a failure of the essential supplies for the work itself could drive me to confess to the world that I had been mistaken in my faith that in a great crisis *a way could be found* through the generosity of Jew and Christian. I still have hope that that faith will be justified.[46]

Only after his failure to receive moral and financial support did McDonald reconsider the function of the High Commission. The intensified persecutions in Germany now gave a new dimension to the refugee problem, a heavy burden which only the League of Nations was competent to carry. McDonald gradually arrived at the conclusion that the Commission should be reorganized under the direct leadership of the League. Accordingly, he discussed with the Governing Body a proposal to establish a "central League organization" to tackle the refugee crisis. While the new centralized institution would treat the political and legal aspects of the issue, the work of settlement would be carried on by private agencies. Among the advantages of the plan, agreed to by Lord Cecil and the Governing Body, was that it did not require additional contributions from the member states.[47] McDonald rejected the argument that Nazi persecutions were a domestic issue with which no government could properly interfere. In a personal letter to Eleanor Roosevelt he wrote: "I wonder how long the Governments of the world can continue to act on the assumption that everything which is taking place in Germany and

46 McDonald to Warburg, "Personal and Confidential", August 17, 1934 (MP:GC).
47 McDonald asked Warburg's "frank opinion as to whether or not the High Commission should endeavor to redefine its function". August 16, 1934 (MP:GC); see also High Commission for Refugees, "Proposals for a Central League Organization for Refugees", May 1935; "The Governing Body of the High Commission in its Session on July 17, 1935" (MP:H).

the threat implicit in present developments are matters purely of German domestic concern?''. He called on the Roosevelt Administration "to take the initiative in protesting against the prevailing violations of elementary civil and religious rights in Germany".[48]

Although Whitehall rejected the plan, Lord Cecil did manage to persuade the Norwegian Government to adopt the proposal to centralize the refugee issue under the League's auspices. When the Sub-committee of the League's Sixth Committee rejected the Norwegian proposition, Cecil, chairman of the Governing Body, suggested to McDonald "joint resignation".[49]

But McDonald's wish to give up his post was in no respect the outcome of the rejection of his proposal to transfer the High Commission to the League. Rather, he decided to suggest this plan because he wanted to withdraw from his post. As early as September 1934 he had planned the date of his resignation for November 1, 1935. It was not a decision hastily adopted out of despair, but a carefully-outlined plan, which he stubbornly refused to change. "You know my feeling that the refugee job is never really finished, and that therefore one should plan to liquidate our organization on a definite date, leaving the remnants of the task to other organizations", he wrote in a confidential letter to Joseph P. Chamberlain.[50] Though he promised Jewish leaders not to make public his decision to resign, he firmly stated that he would not yield to Jewish pressure in this case.[51]

Why then did McDonald resign? It was certainly not as a protest against the Nuremberg decrees, which were discussed in his letter of resignation to the Secretary General of the League of Nations and to which a long Annex was devoted. In fact he had decided upon the liquidation of the High Commission a full year before the

48 McDonald to Eleanor Roosevelt, July 24, 1935 (MP:GC).
49 Lord Cecil to McDonald, May 17, September 10, 24, 1935 (MP:GC).
50 McDonald to Chamberlain, January 20, 1935 (MP:GC).
51 McDonald to Sir Osmond d'Avigdor-Goldsmid, September 28, October 12, 1934 (MP:H); McDonald to Felix Warburg, September 9, 1935 (MP:GC).

promulgation of the Nuremberg Laws on September 15, 1935.[52] Barbara Stewart has rightly maintained that American failure to give more tangible evidence of support to the High Commission was one of the main reasons.[53] Perhaps, too, Norman Bentwich was correct in saying that the failure of the negotiations with South American countries concerning refugee settlements contributed to McDonald's decision to end his tour of duty at the end of 1935.[54] Why, then, did he not mention these causes in his letter of resignation? How could he awaken the conscience of the world if he did not spell out the apathy of governments to the refugee problem? It was, after all, his disappointment with the lack of cooperation from member states that was the main reason for his resignation.

In addition, McDonald had personal reasons for his retirement. He was tired, physically as well as mentally. The long periods of separation from his family, the exhausting journeys and transatlantic crossings and his emotional involvement with the fate of the victims of persecution, led him in January 1935 to ask Professor Chamberlain to help him secure a professorship of international affairs at Columbia University.[55]

Originally, McDonald had intended to send the Secretary General only a short letter of resignation, without making it public. When James N. Rosenberg learned of his intention, he proposed that if McDonald was leaving anyway, it should be "with a big bang" that would rouse the nations to take, through the League, more effective steps against German atrocities. With McDonald's approval, the American Jewish Committee sent the historian Dr. Oscar I. Janowsky and Melvin M. Fagen, an expert on refugee matters, to Europe. They were commissioned to compose a detailed report of the "continued violation by the German Govern-

---

52 James McDonald, *Letter of Resignation*.
53 Stewart, "U.S. Government Policy", p. 159.
54 Bentwich, *Wanderer Between the Two Worlds*, pp. 256—257.
55 McDonald to Chamberlain, January 20, 1935 (MP:GC); see also Stewart, "U.S. Government Policy", p. 160.

ment of universally recognized moral and judicial principles". The second aim of the proposed report was to bring the Jewish refugee problem before the League by depicting the grave situation of the refugees. It was hoped to arouse the enlightened nations to intervention, as had been the case in similar cases in the past.[56] Thus, the Report, which later was to be called the "Letter of Resignation", was in reality the creation of the American Jewish Committee rather than that of McDonald. Moreover, the latter was reluctant, at one stage, to associate himself too closely with it. Melvin M. Fagen complained that "there will be no, or little connection between his resignation and the document which we have drawn up".[57] Rosenberg, who inspired the project, was anxious to include details about the oppression of Catholics in Germany along with a description of anti-Protestant persecutions. But McDonald rejected the suggestion, because "the material is not as satisfactory as I should like to have it". Rosenberg was so eager to see the publication of the report that he tried to persuade McDonald not to wait for a political occasion. On August 6, 1935 he urged McDonald: "Let your voice be a lone one crying in the wilderness", without consideration of political consequences. Had McDonald listened to Rosenberg's advice, he would have missed the opportunity to publicize and attack the racial laws of Nuremberg which were still to come. The report was aimed to be "a reasoned statement to avoid denunciation". Janowsky and Fagen intentionally wrote it in a moderate, factual tone, leaving the reader to judge and evaluate the facts.[58] This moderate tone was eventually

---

56 Memorandum by M. M. Fagen, "Luncheon with James N. Rosenberg, James G. McDonald, M. M. Fagen, Joseph Chamberlain, Morris R. Cohen and Oscar I. Janowsky", June 20, 1935 (AJC, Refugees, 1933–35); "The Refugee Problem as the Result of National Socialist Policies", n.d.; Fagen to Morris Waldman, July 8, 1935 (MP:H).

57 Fagen to Waldman, November 16, 1935 (AJC, Refugees, 1933–35).

58 McDonald to Rosenberg, November 7, 12, 1935 (MP:H); Rosenberg to McDonald, August 6, 1935 (MP:GC); Rosenberg to Janowsky and Fagen, October 7, 1935 (MP:H).

accepted by McDonald, and Lord Cecil also promised to sign. Cecil, however, decided not to be associated with the report. As a statesman deeply involved in British politics, he considered that he could not go so far.[59]

While McDonald agreed with everything that his *Letter of Resignation* said, some of the sources of his frustration during his two years of work as High Commissioner did not find public expression. He was glad to leave the post in which he had met nothing but criticism and disappointment, instead of understanding and cooperation. He was only sorry to lay down the work at the moment "when the forces of evil seemed to have reached the climax of their power for destruction", as he wrote to Felix M. Warburg.[60]

In the *Letter of Resignation*, published in London on December 27, 1935, McDonald maintained that the position of German refugees had changed so drastically since he had been appointed as High Commissioner in 1933, that "a reconsideration by the League of Nations of the entire situation is essential". Since the separation of the High Commission from the League had hampered its effectiveness from the beginning, McDonald called for the transfer of its authority to the League. He clearly distinguished between the humanitarian task of helping the refugees and securing jobs and shelter for them, and the political efforts to solve the problem at its source. While private organizations, Christian and Jewish, could tackle the philanthropic side of the situation, the political aspect was clearly the function of the League.

> But in the new circumstances it will not be enough to continue the activities on behalf of those who flee from the Reich. Efforts must be made to remove or mitigate the causes which create German refugees. This could not have

---

59 McDonald to d'Avigdor-Goldsmid, July 23, 1935; McDonald to Rosenberg, November 7, 1935 (MP:H).
60 McDonald to Felix Warburg, October 10, 1935 (MP:GC).

> been any part of the work of the High Commissioner's of-
> fice; nor, presumably, can it be a function of the body to
> which the League may decide to entrust future administration
> activities on behalf of the refugees. It is a political function,
> which properly belongs to the League itself.

The developments in Germany demanded "a fresh collective
action", which only the League, with its moral authority, was able
to tackle. The member states, through the international organization, should call "for friendly but firm intercession with the German Government, by all pacific means". As mentioned, McDonald
strongly believed that the German persecutions were not an
internal German affair. In such a case, "considerations of diplomatic correctness must yield to those of common humanity". He
closed his statement by pleading for world opinion to act through
the League to avert catastrophe.[61]

The *Letter of Resignation* was published between Christmas and
New Year's Eve in order to achieve maximum public attention,
and it dominated the editorial pages of the press in the democratic
countries for several weeks. Even the detailed discussion of the
anti-Jewish legislation annexed to the statement was printed in
full by several leading newspapers. In the short run it seemed as
if the "Letter" had achieved its purpose and aroused the conscience of the world. The response in England, France, and the
United States was so extraordinary that the *Nation* considered
McDonald's departure from his post as his "most effective act
of his two years' service; more effective, perhaps, than the whole
period of heartbreaking labor".[62]

Enthusiasm, however, soon faded and no practical action was
taken by governments to change the course of German policy
toward non-Aryans.

---

61   McDonald, *Letter of Resignation*, pp. v—x.
62   See, "Repercussions of McDonald's Letter of Resignation", 8 pp.
      (MP:P); *The Nation*, 142 (January 15, 1936), p. 61.

Was McDonald's performance as High Commissioner a failure? It would certainly appear that the chief aims of the High Commission itself were not achieved. It was unable to raise a substantial sum of money, and failed to find permanent haven for the refugees. No improvement had been made in the legal status of stateless persons, and no successful contact had been made with the German authorities to control the flood of emigration. What was McDonald's part in this failure?

It is true that the lion's share of the responsibility should go to the member states of the League and to the United States. In a decade of economic depression and political appeasement toward Germany, other nations were unwilling to tear down their barriers of anti-alien legislation, especially when the great majority of the refugees were Jewish. It is also true that neither Christians nor even Jews grasped the full gravity of the situation. However, the question still remains open, whether another High Commissioner, probably a tougher one, could have negotiated more successfully with the Germans, or would have obtained better access to foreign governments.

The results of McDonald's efforts certainly fell short of expectations. McDonald himself considered his two years' effort as High Commissioner a failure.[63] Part of the disappointment was probably due to the exaggerated hopes raised. As Norman Bentwich expressed it, "I worked with a High Commissioner who was expected to be a Messiah".[64] McDonald was certainly no Messiah. Nor did he emerge as a person of great stature. Although he had high morals and proved in his own way that Christian idealism was not dead, he never fought strongly enough to get his way. He was too cautious in negotiation with governments and, in particular, refrained from attacking the American restrictionist policy. Even his resignation was not the result of purely moral considerations. But can McDonald be blamed for lack of courage

---

63 Rosenberg to McDonald, November 16, 1935 (MP: GC).
64 Bentwich, *Wanderer Between the Two Worlds*, p. 235.

in fighting for Jewish refugees, when Jewish leaders and organizations themselves tried to avoid clashing with governmental regulations?

As to the League, its Council decided on January 23, 1936 to include the High Commission in that body's activities. With McDonald's resignation, the autonomous institution of the High Commission for Refugees ceased to exist, along with its Governing Body. The new High Commissioner, Sir Neill Malcolm, in contrast to his predecessor, was a League official and obtained the financial help of the body to which he was responsible. But this development was not the realization of McDonald's wish, since the Secretary General was clearly anxious to reduce the action of the High Commissioner to the narrowest and strictest interpretation by the Council. Malcolm's budget was too small to enable him to act effectively and he was not permitted to receive contributions from private organizations. Bentwich considered this "a complete break in the continuity of the work". Sir Neill confined his activities mainly to the political and juridical fields, and planned to convene an intergovernmental committee to discuss and secure legal defense for stateless persons. Neither coordination of work by private agencies nor relief fell within the new High Commissioner's authority.[65]

Thus failed the hope that the refugee problem be tackled on an international scale. The member states' refusal to shoulder the burden of responsibility for that humane issue increased the suffering of thousands of homeless people who were wandering through Western Europe. When it became clear that the support of the League of Nations failed to materialize, a small group of Americans, Jews as well as Christians, realized that a more effective response from the United States and its multitude private organizations was called for.

65   Lord Cecil to Joseph Chamberlain, January 31, 1936; Bentwich to
     McDonald, February 21, 1936 (MP: GC); André Wurfbain to the
     members of the Advisory Council of the High Commission, January
     30, 1936 (MP:H).

3

AMERICA AND THE REFUGEES:
THE PRESIDENT'S ADVISORY COMMITTEE
ON POLITICAL REFUGEES

Thousands of German refugees who had fled to neighboring countries and were living in miserable conditions were waiting for a visa that would offer an opportunity to begin a new life in a democratic country. Many pinned their hopes on the United States. But the "Nation of Immigrants" was reluctant to admit refugees. A restrictionist immigration policy that severely limited the number of immigrants permitted to enter the United States had been put into effect as early as 1924. Fixed quotas were established for each country of origin and the total number of immigrants allowed to enter America in one year was 153,744. Since very few immigrants came from England and Ireland — the countries with the largest quotas — more than half of the total number of entry visas were not taken up. In addition, administrative restrictions were introduced. Thus, for example in September 1930, in the midst of the economic crisis, President Herbert Hoover instructed U.S. consuls abroad not to grant visas to persons "likely to become a public charge" (LPC clause). This restrictionist policy, which the Roosevelt Administration continued

without meaningfully altering it, was so rigidly enforced that it
severely limited the number of refugees admitted as immigrants.

Accordingly, the U.S. immigration policy became the target of
Jewish and Christian protests. Institutions and individuals urged
the Administration to relax its regulations and permit the entry
of Jewish and non-Aryan refugees. A group of Protestant pastors,
headed by Harry Emerson Fosdick of the Riverside Drive Church,
sent a petition to President Roosevelt, asking for liberalization of
the immigration laws. The American Civil Liberties Union sent
an appeal to the White House, signed by Lillian D. Wald, William
Allen Neilson, Oswald Garrison Villard and Samuel M. Cavert,
among others, urging to direct a more lenient approach to the
issue of visas for refugees.[1]

Probably the most publicized appeal to the Administration was
the petition sent to President Roosevelt in January 1934 by the
Committee of Ten, chaired by Mrs. Carrie Chapman Calt. Accompanied by a detailed survey of American immigration policy, the
petition asked President Roosevelt to grant asylum to refugees
under the existing immigration laws. The Committee's practical
request was to instruct American consuls abroad to treat cases of
religious and political refugees more sympathetically. Thus, the
Committee, acting on Jewish advice, called neither for abandonment of the quota system, nor for change of the existing laws. Its
only request was that the official quota be filled by a more lenient
interpretation of the LPC clause.[2]

---

1 Harry Emerson Fosdick to Franklin D. Roosevelt, November 27,
   1933. (F.D. Roosevelt Library, Official File, 133a, Hyde Park, N.Y.
   The papers hereafter cited, FDRL, OF.) *The New York Times*, September 11, 1933.

2 Committee of Ten to President Roosevelt, January 24, 1934; Committee of Ten, *Asylum for Refugees Under Our Immigration Laws*,
   n.d. pp. 6—7; see the confidential memorandum "For the Information of the Executive Committee of the American Jewish Committee", March 12, 1934. (The archives of the American Jewish Committee, New York City. Hereafter, AJC.)

Indeed, leaders of American Jewry adamantly refused to support a resolution for the recall of Hoover's directive concerning the LPC clause. Jewish organizations naturally were not happy with the restrictionist policy. Nevertheless, they considered it a mistake to encourage congressional debates on the refugee issue: "...we have refrained from taking any steps in this direction", explained Morris Waldman of the AJC, "because we have been advised that there is the danger that some of the members of Congress may voice views which will give encouragement to the Hitlerites. You appreciate that, unless speeches in Congress are all anti-Hitler, a debate is likely to do more harm than good".[3]

In April 1938, Emanuel Celler, Democratic Congressman of New York, introduced a bill (H.R. 10013) which sought to exempt religious or political refugees from some of the provisions of the immigration laws. Celler's bill was to have been fortified by one of Samuel Dickstein, which proposed the utilization of the unused quotas of other countries for 1938, and the relaxation of the LPC clause. The scheduled hearings of the Celler–Dickstein bills caused agitation in Jewish circles. Jewish and Christian agencies that were concerned with the fate of refugees met to discuss the issue. Among those participating in the conference were representatives of the American Jewish Committee, the American Jewish Congress, the FCC, HIAS, the International Migration Service, the National Catholic Welfare Conference and the National Committee of Jewish Women. The conference expressed the unanimous opinion that "efforts to secure such legislation at the present time will be distinctly unwise", because they were likely to embarrass the State Department in its negotiations preceding the Evian Conference. Read Lewis, chairman of the meeting, sent a letter to Dickstein on behalf of the organizations represented, expressing the unanimous request "to find some way of indefinitely post-

---

3 Cyrus Adler to Samuel Dickstein, March 27, 1933 (AJC, Immigration); *The New York Times*, March 30, 1933; Morris Waldman to Joseph I. Brody, May 16, 1933 (AJC, Germany).

poning the hearings". They believed that "public discussion of bills to break down, or change, present quota restrictions is bound to let loose a flood of bitter anti-alien and anti-Jewish agitation which will intensify inter-group antagonism in the United States".[4]

The Jewish press also adopted the strategy of a mute bystander. Whilst Jewish papers loudly publicized the need to help Jewish refugees in Europe, they kept a discreet silence in regard to the restrictionist U.S. immigration policy. Whereas Great Britain had been attacked for closing the gates of Palestine to refugees, no such criticism was aimed publicly at the Roosevelt Administration. In retrospect, David S. Wyman's reproach seems justified: "it is not difficult to be critical of the strategy of muting the refugee issue. Because that approach . . . appears to have been defeatist". Christian leaders and agencies imitated the Jewish policy of evading the immigration aspect of the refugee issue. Among others, James McDonald and Joseph P. Chamberlain, as well as the American Committee for Christian Refugees and the American Friends Service Committee, declined to discuss publicly the Administration's restrictionist policy. Thus, in the end, Jews and Christians alike contributed to the postponement of the hearings of the Celler–Dickstein bills.[5]

An exception to this general approach was the Wagner–Rogers Bill, which proposed to grant 20,000 entry visas to refugee children during the years 1939—1940. Church leaders, Christian orga-

4   Emanuel Celler to Cyrus Adler, April 5, 1938; Harry Schneiderman to Cyrus Adler, April 7, 1938; Read Lewis to Samuel Dickstein, April 6, 1938 (AJC, Refugees).

5   Wyman, *Paper Walls*, pp. 23—25; James McDonald to Mrs. Jacob Riis, November 28, 1938 (MP:P=the files of the President's Advisory Committee on Political Refugees); Joseph Chamberlain to Cecilia Razovsky, July 10, 1936; Joseph Hyman to Paul Baerwald, November 12, 1937. (The archives of the Jewish Joint Distribution Committee, NCC papers, New York City. Hereafter, JDC.) ACCR, *Newscast*, 2 (Jan. 1942), 3; Harry Schneiderman to Morris Waldman, April 5, 1938 (AJC, Immigration).

nizations and editorials enthusiastically supported the bill. The *Churchman* urged that no stone be left unturned to secure passage of the bill. The Federal Council of Churches appealed to President Roosevelt "to express sympathy through special treatment of the young, robbed of country, homes and parents...". The American Friends Service Committee, the American Committee for Christian Refugees, the Young Women's Christian Association, and even the National Catholic Welfare Conference were in favor of that legislation. In spite of this widespread Christian backing, restrictionist and anti-Semitic forces in Congress were able to block the passage of this humanitarian initiative.[6]

Pro-refugee circles had to combat three major forces in order to win the support of rank and file Christians, namely: unemployment, nativism and anti-Semitism. The anti-alien feelings that swept over America during the 1930s were partly attributable to the Depression. When millions of people were unemployed there was no room for newcomers, was the national consensus. Employers were accused of preferring cheap immigrant labor to native American. Furthermore, refugees, it was said, created a charitable problem which added to the relief burden of the public. Resentment against refugees intensified after 1935 with minor relaxations of the restrictive immigration regulations. Coinciding with the increased flow of refugees was a new wave of economic recession in the United States. From the summer of 1937 onwards, unemployment increased steadily from 7.5 million to 10 million in 1939. Only World War II basically altered the situation. Soon the alien-baiting took the form of "mass hysteria". "The mere mention of the word 'refugee' seems to be sufficient these days to send shivers

6 76th Congress, 1st Session: Senate Joint Resolution, 64; Circular, Non-sectarian Committee for German Refugee Children, March 31, 1939 (German Jewish Children's Aid papers=GJCA at YIVO, folder 109); "Do You Care?", *Churchman* (May 1, 1939), 9; *The New York Times*, January 10, 1939; NCWC, "News Service", March 6, 1939 (NCWC papers, Box 80). For the Wagner-Rogers Bill, see below, pp. 321—323.

down the spines of certain people", attested Bernard W. Levmore in 1939. Old restrictionist circles, such as the Junior Order of United American Mechanics and the American Legion, that had been fighting immigration for decades, now gained a much wider following.[7]

Immigrants were accused of being "Communist agitators". It was part of a bigoted American outcry that "every Socialist is a Jew", and "all radicals are Jews", as William Seagle summarized the anti-Jewish arguments. Precisely that was the accusation of William Dudley Pelley, the leader of the anti-Semitic Silver Shirts Legion. He argued that the "seven million refugees", who had invaded the country, were part of a Jewish-Communist conspiracy to occupy the Federal Government.[8]

In spite of concerted efforts of Jewish and some Christian bodies to refute these charges, they continued to circulate. A combination of strong isolationist and nativist feelings served to reinforce the regular nativist groups in their opposition to opening the country's gates to foreign influence. Under the slogan of "100% Americanism" they wanted not only to stop immigration, but also that aliens be kept under close observation and even deported. Rumors about hordes of illegal immigrants pouring by their thousands into the country were effectively circulated and exploited by these circles.[9]

7   Wyman, *Paper Walls*, pp. 56, 94—97; *The New York Times*, March 26, 1938; Bernard W. Levmore, "A Stimulus for American Industry: Non-Professional Refugees", *Annals of American Academy of Political and Social Science*, 203 (May 1939), p. 162.

8   *Defender Magazine*, 13 (Jan. 1939), p. 16; William Seagle, "All Radicals Are Jews", *The Nation*, 135 (Oct. 5, 1932), p. 307; Harold Lavine, "Fifth Column Literature", *Saturday Review of Literature*, 22 (Sep. 14, 1940), pp. 3—4; (William Dudley Pelley), *What Every Congressman Should Know* (Asheville, 1938).

9   "Deportation of Aliens", *Hearings Before a Sub-Committee, U.S. Senate*, 76th Congress, 1st Session (March 1939), pp. 64—66; *Congressional Record*, 84, Part 4; 76th Congress, 1st Session, p. 3629.

How many refugees actually reached American shores? For a better understanding of the magnitude of the refugee problem it is important to clarify the approximate number of refugees admitted to the United States during the Hitler era. Moreover, in view of the oft-heard argument that almost all of the refugees were Jewish, it is necessary to establish the number of Christians among them. There are, however, a number of factors which make it difficult to determine the exact number of refugees who reached American shores during the stated period. Principal among these is the fact that the U.S. Immigration and Naturalization Service made no distinction between an immigrant and a refugee, recognizing only the former. Thus, little direct information is to be had from official publications as to the number of immigrants who held the status of refugees. For our purpose here, the term "refugee" is used as defined by the Intergovernmental Conference on Political Refugees at Evian, namely, that refugees are persons "who must emigrate on account of their political opinions, religious beliefs or racial origin".[10]

Anti-Semitic and restrictionist circles purposely exaggerated the number of newcomers. They gloomily depicted a "European invasion", with millions of illegal immigrants invading the country. Adding to the confusion is the fact that State Department officials gave exaggerated figures to prove the humanitarian approach of the Administration. Cordell Hull estimated that 600,000 refugees were admitted between 1933—1945, while Breckinridge Long, Assistant Secretary of State, attested that up to November 1943, 580,000 refugees reached America.[11]

Maurice R. Davie, the sociologist, took a more balanced approach. Seeking to distinguish between an immigrant and a refu-

---

10 "The Final Resolution of the Evian Conference", July 1938, *Foreign Relations of the United States, 1938* (Washington, D.C., 1955), I, pp. 755—756.

11 Cordell Hull, *The Memoirs of Cordell* Hull (New York, 1948), II, p. 1538; James McDonald to Breckinridge Long, December 31, 1943 (MP:P).

gee, he suggested recognizing as refugees all the permanent U.S. immigrants who had left Germany since 1933. Likewise, that all European immigrants — except those from England, Ireland, Iceland, Portugal, Spain, Switzerland, Sweden and Turkey — who reached the United States after 1937, be regarded as refugees. According to Davie, 243,862 permanent immigrants in the category of refugees entered the country between June 1933 and June 1944.[12] Still another problem was to ascertain how many refugees held temporary visas. Almost 200,000 visitors or temporary residents came to America from German-ruled territories, of which the great majority later returned to their countries of origin. Still, 15,000 of them asked the Immigration and Naturalization Service to renew their temporary visas time and again. It would not be unreasonable to count them as refugees who tried to settle in America. In addition, 1000 refugees arrived at the Oswego camp in New York. Thus, Davie concluded that, altogether, some 266,000 refugees entered the country up to June 1944.[13]

David S. Wyman, the historian, has adopted Davie's count, with some modifications. He excluded the victims of the Spanish Civil War, as well as most of the Italian immigrants, since they were not refugees from Nazism. On the other hand, he suggested the inclusion of 5016 refugees who arrived in 1944—1945, whom Davie did not count. In that way Wyman reached a maximum of 250,518 refugees. Maximum, because Davie's count included European refugees from June 1937 onwards, despite the fact that Austria was annexed in 1938, Czechoslovakia and Poland were occupied in 1939, West European countries were overrun by German forces in 1940 and the Balkans were occupied in 1940—1941.[14]

Wyman's account seems reasonable, i.e., a total of approximately a quarter of a million refugees reached the United States

12   Maurice R. Davie, *Refugees in America* (New York, 1947), pp. 22—27.
13   *Ibid.*, pp. 26—27.
14   Wyman, *Paper Walls*, pp. 218—219.

from German-occupied countries. How many of them were Christians? There are several obstacles to a definite answer. Out of bitter experience in Germany and being aware of the growing American anti-Semitism, many refugees preferred to hide their Jewish origin. There were also atheists and people without religious attachment who refused to subscribe to any faith. Hence, the number of Jews who entered the country was higher than was reported by the Immigration and Naturalization Service. The deletion of the term "Hebrew" from the Service's questionnaire, due to cancellation of the need to state one's religious identification, was another obstacle to the determination of the exact number of Jewish refugees. This was ordered by the Labor Department in response to the protests of Paul Richman of B'nai B'rith, so that after January 1944 immigrants were no longer required to list their religion, but only their nationality. The leaders of the American Jewish Committee were not happy with that change. It removed not only the most reliable source of information as to Jewish immigration, but also seriously hampered the chances of effectively refuting public misconceptions arising from exaggerated figures of Jewish refugees. The AJC refrained from requesting the withdrawal of the last directive. However, as a temporary measure Jewish organizations relied upon the information provided in the questionnaire of shipping companies, which every immigrant was required to fill out, including, in the case of Jews, the fact of "Hebrew" affiliation.[15]

Lack of accurate official data enabled interested groups to distort the facts, as was often done in tendentious publications. The widespread notion that the great majority of the refugees were Jewish, encouraged certain anti-alien circles, both Catholic and Protestant, to minimize — if not to disregard — the existence of non-Jewish refugees.[16] Just as unsympathetic elements tried to

---

15   H. Schneiderman to Dr. Slawson, March 15, 1944 (AJC, Immigration, 1940—1944).

16   Bruce M. Mohler to T.F. Mulholland, May 25, 1934 (NCWC, Box 82).

dismiss the problem of Christian refugees, so friends of the new-comers tended to emphasize the importance of the issue by pro-viding exaggerated data of Christian refugees. Frank Ritchie, exe-cutive secretary of the American Committee for Christian Refu-gees, maintained that half the refugees were Christians. In Novem-ber 1938 the National Convention of the Family Welfare Associa-tion of America adopted a resolution in the same sense, that "contrary to popular impression, 50% of the refugees now are non-Jewish". The Refugee Committee of the Young Women's Christian Association gave a like report. One source even main-tained that there were more potential Christian refugees than Jews.[17]

Jewish organizations like the AJC and the JDC, despite their anxiety to refute public misconceptions about most of the refugees being Jewish, refrained from exaggerations and published only accurate, well-checked facts. The data that the AJC provided to Christian organizations came from the reports of the Immigration and Naturalization Service of the Labor Department, just as all other published informations came from a reliable source. Thus, when Clarence Pickett of the American Friends Service Commit-tee stated on a radio program in 1938 that about one-third of all refugees from Germany were Christians, he relied upon AJC's information which stated that 30.7% of the refugees of 1937/8 were non-Jews.[18]

The estimate of James McDonald, High Commissioner for Refugees in December 1935, was considerably lower, namely, that 15—20% of the refugees were Christians. Norman Bentwich, his

---

17   *The New York Times*, November 18, 1938; YWCA, Report of the
      Secretary, Committee on Refugees, November-December, 1940 (YWCA
      archives, roll 99, Immigration, Refugees); Hope B. Newman to Mc-
      Donald, December 16, 1938 (MP:P).
18   Henry Levy to Frank N. Trager, April 5, 25, 1939 (AJC, Refugees);
      AFSC: "Refugee Facts"; Henry S. Leiper, "Those German Refu-
      gees", *Current History*, 50 (May 1939), pp. 19—22; YWCA, "Meet
      the Refugees"; "Refugees At War Time".

deputy, reckoned that 15% of the refugees were non-Aryan Christians. If we add to this figure the Aryan refugees who had to flee from Germany, Bentwich's account would also put the total of non-Jewish refugees at close to 20%[19] While McDonald and Bentwich dealt with the period 1934/5, the AJC's data related to 1938/9. Therefore, the two positions were not necessarily contradictory. Moreover, the Nazi regime during the first years of its rule concentrated on the persecutions of Jews and Communists, so obviously the number of Jewish refugees was high. Later, however, with the enforcement of the racial laws against non-Aryans, with the assault on the Churches in 1936—1937 and the annexation of Austria, the proportion of non-Jewish refugees increased, as the YWCA's Refugee Committee reported.[20]

The AJC campaigned to downplay the impact of Jewish refugee immigration by comparing their number with the total number of immigrants, not only refugees, admitted to the country. It was explained that only in 1939—1940, the peak period of Jewish immigration from Germany, did the number of Jews exceed that of non-Jews, reaching 52% of the total immigration. In 1933 Jewish immigration was only 10% and, in 1943, one-fifth of the total.[21] The Immigration and Naturalization Service reported that during the decade of June 1933—June 1943, 476,930 immigrants entered the United States, of whom 165,756 were Jews.[22] Lyman C. White gave a closely similar account. He considered that between 1933—1945, 574,152 immigrants entered the country, of whom 175,528 were Jewish.[23] Another estimate was that of Solo-

19 James McDonald, *Letter of Resignation, Annex*, p. 34; Norman Bentwich to William Paton, March 15, 1934 (MP:H).
20 YWCA, Report of the Secretary, Committee on Refugees, November–December, 1940 (YWCA, Roll 99).
21 Schneiderman to Fred Lazarus, December 14, 1943 (AJC, Immigration, 1940—1944).
22 See Henry Feingold, *Politics of Rescue*, p. 328, n. 2.
23 Lyman C. White, *300,000 New Americans: The Epic of Modern Immigrant-Aid Service* (New York, 1957), *Annex* A, p. 397.

mon Dingol, who calculated in 1944 that the Jewish immigration up to June 1943 numbered 157,927 souls.[24] The different estimates show no basic variation and the picture that emerged is clear. Up to June 1943 the number of Jewish refugees was between 157,927 and 168,128. Jewish immigration to the United States during the Hitler regime reached an aggregate of 30—35% of the total immigration. Thus, for every Jewish immigrant there were two non-Jewish newcomers.[25]

The situation would naturally be different if the proportion of Jews to Christians is calculated not out of the total immigration from all countries, but out of the refugees who came from Nazi-dominated countries. Davie reached the conclusion that 80—83% were Jewish refugees,[26] which approximates to McDonald's estimates of 15—20% Christian refugees. Davie admitted, however, that his figure was probably too high, because Jewish relief agencies were more efficient than Christian organizations, hence, more Jewish refugees were registered and in a more accurate manner. Donald P. Kent, who wrote a study on intellectuals among the refugees, concluded that "the number of Jewish persons among the refugees would seem to fall somewhere between 75 and 80%, with the latter figure probably being more accurate".[27] Kent took into consideration McDonald's position (80—85%) and Davie's account (83%). He also relied on the reports of the Immigration Service, that between 1933—1941 76% of the German-Austrian immigrants were Jewish. However, as already mentioned, McDonald's estimation was valid only for 1934—1935 and Davie

24 Solomon Dingol, "How Many Refugees from Nazi Persecution were Admitted to the United States?" *Rescue*, 1 (Feb. 1944), pp. 1, 11—12; Davie also estimated that between 1933—1943, 157,473 Jewish refugees were admitted to the country. Davie, *Refugees in America*, p. 34.
25 Up to June 1945, according to White, 175,528 Jewish refugees entered the country. After the deduction of 7400 people who arrived during the years 1943—1945, White's figures, up to June 1943, are 168,128.
26 Davie, *Refugees in America*, p. 36.
27 Donald Paterson Kent, *The Refugee Intellectual: the Americanization of the Immigrants of 1933—1941* (New York, 1953), p. 17.

also admitted that the number of Christians should probably be higher. Kent's estimate is incomplete, since he took into consideration only Germans and Austrians, disregarding refugees from other European countries.

As a starting point we have accepted Wyman's point of view that the total number of refugees from Nazism who reached American shores between 1933—1945 was 250,518. As the Jewish refugees totaled between 173,156 and 165,327, the number of Christians was between 74,990 and 85,191.[28] Thus, Christians represented 30—34% of the refugees. Davie himself stated in 1945 that 67.6% of the refugees were Jewish. i.e., 32.4% of them were Christians.[29] In other words, the estimate that approximately 30% of the refugees admitted to the United States during the Holocaust period were Christians should be considered a fair and realistic one.

The American people, however, whose apathetic attitude toward refugees was widespread, were reluctant to face the facts. Leaders, as well as followers, Jewish and Christian, failed to grasp the gravity of the situation. James G. McDonald, High Commissioner for Refugees, was one of the few Americans who clearly and early on understood the danger of the Nazi threat. He was espe-

28 The figures of the Immigration and Naturalization Service up to June 1943 were 165,756 Jews. If we add 2400 who entered in 1944, and 5000 in 1945, we reach a total of 173,156 refugees. White, *300,000 New Americans*, p. 397; Feingold, *Politics of Rescue*, p. 328; Dingol, *Rescue*, 1 (Feb. 1944), pp. 1, 11—12; Dingol's estimate of the number of Jews who entered the country up to June 1943 was 157,927. With the addition of 7400 refugees who arrived during 1943—1945, the result is 165,327 Jews. If we deduct that figure from 250,518 of the total number of refugees, the result is 85,191 Christian refugees.

29 Maurice R. Davie and S. Koening, *The Refugees are now Americans* (1945), pp. 10—11. According to Herbert A. Strauss, who concentrated on Jews coming from Germany, not counting refugees coming from other Nazi-occupied countries, 130,000 Jews were admitted to the United States during the Nazi era. See Strauss (ed.), *Jewish Immigrants of the Nazi Period in the U.S.A.*, Vol. I (New York, 1978), p. xxii.

cially shocked by the lack of an adequate response from the Jewish leadership. "How under these circumstances Jewish leaders of intelligence dare plan as though the worst were over is beyond my comprehension", he complained in July 1934.[30] More than a year later, when the situation deteriorated after the publication of the racial Nuremberg decrees, he expressed his disappointment to James N. Rosenberg of the JDC as follows:

> ... what does surprise me and depress me terribly is the failure of the Christian world to sense what is involved for it in these developments. Only less depressing, however, is the failure of the Jewish world to respond adequately. Faced as they are by the first grave breach in the walls of emancipation so painfully erected during the past century and a half, one would have supposed that the Jewish leaders in every part of the world would have acted as if they realized that they are facing the gravest crisis in the history of Jews in modern times. But except for a few individuals here and there, and except for the leaders of the Zionists, who... you must admit have the courage of their convictions — there has been no response anywhere proportionate to the need.[31]

Certainly McDonald was right in criticizing American Jewry, whose response was indeed insufficient. Many Jews believed that it was more important to fulfill their responsibilities to their American brethren than to help refugees in Europe. Furthermore, philanthropists and welfare workers were reluctant to give up their long-established local activities for another, even if greater, need. The traditional differences, bordering on hostility, between Jews from Eastern Europe and Jews of German origin were also a cause of friction which prevented united action on behalf of

30 McDonald to Liebman, July 28, 1934; see also McDonald to James Rosenberg, July 28, 1934 (MP:GC).
31 McDonald to Rosenberg, November 7, 1935 (MP:H).

German Jewry. Probably the most important obstacle to the centralization of Jewish refugee work was the strong rivalry between the Jewish organizations. The American Jewish Joint Distribution Committee and the American Jewish Committee, for example, opposed collaboration with the Zionists. A confidential memorandum summarized the problem for McDonald: "The greatest difficulty will, of course, be to get the Jewish groups to work together".[32]

Whilst it was true that the Jews did not respond "adequately", the apathy of the Christian community toward refugees was alarming. McDonald outspokenly criticized their failure to undertake moral responsibility for the refugees. "I am shocked at the apparent lack of concern on the part of many Christian leaders for the victims of persecution conducted by those who call themselves Christians", he complained to Henry Smith Leiper of the Federal Council of Churches.[33]

McDonald was not the only one, though the most important and influential, who tried to persuade Christians "to realize their responsibility and act accordingly". Harry Emerson Fosdick, pastor of Riverside Drive Church in New York, complained that "it has been almost impossibly difficult to arouse the Christian conscience of this country, to make Christian people shoulder practical responsibility concerning it".[34] Lord Cecil, chairman of the Governing Body of the High Commission, argued that at stake were even more than Christian values. Along with James McDonald, he wondered how Christians could be blind to vital interests

---

32 The authors of this memorandum, who were aware of the delicate situation, added: "Better not leave this memo around". MSW and EMW to JGM (McDonald), December 23, 1933; see Zosa Szajkowski, "The Attitude of American Jews to Refugees from Germany in the 1930s", *American Jewish Historical Quarterly*, 61 (Dec. 1971), pp. 101—143; McDonald to Esther G. Ogden, September 28, 1933; McDonald to Bentwich, January 11, 1935 (MP:H).

33 McDonald to Henry Smith Leiper, November 30, 1933 (MP:GC).

34 Harry Emerson Fosdick, "Modern Christian German Martyrs" (American Committee for Christian Refugees, n.d. (*c.* 1934) (AJC:ACCR).

which were "fundamental to Civilization itself".[35] Parkes Cadman, former president of the Federal Council of Churches, also called on Christians to share the responsibility for their co-religionists "on broad humanitarian grounds".[36]

Unfortunately, these calls failed to stir the American Christian community. Mrs. John H. Randall of the Women's International League for Peace and Freedom lamented, as late as 1944, that "the voice of Christian America has not yet spoken in unmistakable accents of moral leadership".[37] Samuel Cavert, Frank Ritchie, Henry Smith Leiper and Joseph Chamberlain sided with Leslie B. Moss of the FCC, who kept asking in December 1942: "How much do Christians really care?". On the answer to that question, according to Moss, "may well depend the future of the Church, and perhaps of Civilization itself".[38]

The apathetic and sometimes hostile attitude of the American community toward the admittance of refugees from Nazism was clearly reflected in the Roosevelt Administration's approach. One has to bear in mind the tremendous difficulties that the Administration faced to rehabilitate the nation's economy. The President surrendered to restrictionist elements in Congress in order to gain their support for his New Deal program. Furthermore, in the light of growing anti-Semitism in the country, Roosevelt was reluctant to identify himself with an unpopular issue. Consequently, the

35   "Remarks of McDonald at the Dinner of the Anglo-Palestinian Club", October 21, 1935 (MP:H).
36   S. Parkes Cadman to James McDonald, "For Your Information", June 18, 1934 (MP:GC).
37   Mrs. John H. Randall, "The Voice of Thy Brother's Blood: An Eleventh-Hour Appeal to All Americans" (Washington, D.C.: Women's International League for Peace and Freedom, 1944), p. 16 (Joseph Chamberlain papers, p. 1729, YIVO).
38   Leslie B. Moss, "Do Christians Really Care?", December 1942 (3 pp. ms. Moss papers, FCC archives, Box 143). See also Cadman to McDonald, June 7, 1934 (MP: GC); H. S. Leiper, "The State of the Church", *Advance* (July 26, 1934), p. 332; Frank Ritchie, Letter to the Editor of *The New York Times*, November 12, 1938.

refugee problem received low priority in administrative considerations. As David Wyman has pointed out: "... United States refugee policy... was essentially what the American people wanted".[39]

In November 1935, after the publication of the Nuremberg racial decrees, President Roosevelt yielded to the pressures of Herbert H. Lehman, governor of New York, and James McDonald, and conceded minor relaxations of the immigration regulations. He instructed U.S. consuls abroad to grant refugees "the most... favorable treatment possible under the laws". With the increase of Nazi persecutions, the consular officers were directed further to ease the procedure for reviewing applications. Accordingly, the number of German immigrants grew by 20% in 1936 and by 78% in the following year.[40] With the exception of these measures, through 1938 Roosevelt was reluctant to intervene on behalf of refugees.

The annexation of Austria to the Reich on March 13, 1938, which was followed by brutal persecutions of Jews and political opponents, focused world attention on the refugee problem. To confront the crisis, President Roosevelt proposed that 32 European and Latin American States meet in a conference in order to facilitate the emigration of refugees and to establish an Intergovernmental Committee to work toward an overall solution of the refugee problem. In order to secure cooperation, the invitation stressed that "no country would be expected to receive greater numbers of emigrants than is permitted by its existing legislation". Nor would the states be expected to finance the refugee projects, since these would continue to be the burden of private organiza-

39 Wyman, *Paper Walls*, p. 213.
40 Herbert H. Lehman to President Roosevelt, November 1, 1935; Roosevelt to Lehman, November 13, 1935 (FDRL, OF 133); Avra Warren in "Deportation of Aliens", Hearings Before a Sub-Committee, U.S. Senate, 76th Congress, 1st Session (March 21—22—23, 1939), p. 71. In 1935 there were 5436 German immigrants, in 1936 their number rose to 6538 and in the following year it reached 11,648.

tions.[41] These reservations, as well as other declarations, clearly indicated the United States' reluctance to emerge as patron of the refugees. As Assistant Secretary of State George S. Messersmith admitted: "little positive action can be expected".[42]

In spite of such reservations, Roosevelt's step was a significant departure from the passive role he had played hitherto. It was the first time since Hitler's rise to power that the United States had assumed leadership in this subject, a position that contrasted with the indifference shown toward the High Commission for Refugees.

As a part of the preparations for the coming Evian refugee conference, President Roosevelt invited nine distinguished individuals to the White House "to undertake a preliminary consideration" for establishing an American advisory committee which would serve as an intermediary between the Intergovernmental Committee and the American refugee organizations. Trying to obscure the Jewish character of the refugee problem, the White House and the State Department emphasized the non-sectarian basis of the advisory committee by nominating representatives of Protestant, Catholic and Jewish organizations. The racial and religious character of the persecutions, which was the only cause for the Jewish emigration, was also carefully obscured by using the vague and sometimes misleading term: "political refugees".[43]

41   U.S. Department of State, *The Foreign Relations of the United States,* 1938, I, pp. 740—741, March 23, 1938; see also Roosevelt to Myron C. Taylor, April 26, 1938 (FDRL, OF/3186).

42   Minutes of the Second Meeting of the President's Advisory Committee on Political Refugees (=PAC), May 19, 1938 (MP:P); see also Sumner Welles' Memorandum to the President, April 11, 1938 (FDRL, OF/3186).

43   Roosevelt to McDonald, April 8, 1938 (MP:P); Roosevelt to Basil Harris, April 18, 1938 (FDRL, OF/3186). As to the meaning of "political refugees", McDonald explained that "Our government is interpreting 'political refugees' in the broadest sense of the term — that is, to include any persons forced into exile by the political policies of their governments". McDonald to Norman Bentwich, April 22, 1938 (MP:GC).

A study of the President's Advisory Committee reveals an accurate picture of the President's, as well as the State Department's, attitude toward the refugee problem. This agency therefore deserves close examination.

The President's Advisory Committee on Political Refugees eventually included five Protestants,[44] three Catholics [45] and two Jews.[46] The proportion of Gentiles and Jews on the PAC was the opposite of the proportion among the immigrants. It seems, however, that this fact did not bother Jewish organizations and nobody criticized it. Furthermore, some leaders, like James N. Rosenberg of the JDC, were enthusiastic, hoping that the PAC "may lead (to) some great non-sectarian undertaking".[47]

For the post of chairman of the PAC the Administration's first choice was Hamilton Fish Armstrong. But the editor of the prestigious *Foreign Affairs* preferred international relations to relief.

---

44 The Protestants were Hamilton Fish Armstrong, the editor of *Foreign Affairs*; James McDonald; Samuel McCrea Cavert, general secretary of the Federal Council of Churches of Christ; James M. Speers, vice-president of the Presbyterian Board of the Foreign Missions and Professor Joseph P. Chamberlain, chairman of the National Coordinating Committee.

45 The Catholics were Joseph F. Rummel, Archbishop of New Orleans and chairman of the Committee for Catholic Refugees from Germany; Basil Harris, vice-president of the U.S. Lines, and Louis Kenedy, president of the National Council of Catholic Men.

46 The two Jews were Paul Baerwald, chairman of the JDC, and Rabbi Stephen S. Wise, president of the American Jewish Congress. FDR to Basil Harris, April 18, 1938 (FDRL, OF/3186); Bernard M. Baruch and Henry Morgenthau Sr. had been originally selected as the representatives of the Jews, but they declined to serve. It was poor judgment to nominate them because they had never been active in Jewish life. Furthermore, Baruch openly opposed in the White House meeting on April 13, 1938 to let refugees come to America. See, Bauer, *My Brother's Keeper*, p. 232; Stewart, "U.S. Government Policy", p. 285.

47 James N. Rosenberg to Joseph Rosen, May 2, 1938 (JDC, Refugees, General).

So, James McDonald was elected as chairman.[48] Why was Mc-
Donald of all members of the Committee selected as chairman?
Naturally, his position as former High Commissioner for Refugees
made him one of the few American Gentiles who possessed firsthand knowledge of the international scope of the refugee crisis.
However, one may detect an additional reason for McDonald's
selection. The Administration was reluctant to become too deeply
involved in the solution of the refugee problem. Since the United
States neither contributed financially to the cause, nor showed
any readiness to absorb more Nazi victims, she naturally would
refrain from nominating a strong, ambitious and authoritative
person to such a position. McDonald's performance as High Commissioner was not impressive and, despite his personal efforts, his
chief aims remained unattained. Thus, the State Department could
show its concern for the refugee problem by choosing a man of
some importance as the head of the PAC, but not one powerful
enough to endanger or embarrass its restrictionist policy.[49]

Indeed, President Roosevelt himself shared this ambivalent attitude toward "his" Committee. He had convened that body, which
carried the ambitious title of "The President's Advisory Committee", in order that he "might have the benefit of the counsel of
men comprehensively representative", as McDonald later explained.[50] But during its eight years' activity, the President refrained from inviting the members of the PAC to the White House
on his own initiative, nor sought the Committee's advice on refugee
matters. On several occasions the President forgot about the very
existence of "his" Committee. On the other hand, the Committee
served Roosevelt well by easing pressure on him. When criticized
for his apathy toward the fate of the refugees, he could refer to
the PAC as the address of such complaints. Robert T. Pell, vice-
director of the Intergovernmental Committee and a member of

48   Armstrong to Roosevelt, April 26, 1938 (FDRL, OF/3186); Minutes
     of the Second Meeting of the PAC, May 19, 1938 (MP:P).
49   See above, pp. 57—58.
50   McDonald's memorandum to Jules E. Kohn, n.d. (c. 1945) (MP:P).

the staff of the State Department, considered that the White House's disregard of the Committee was "most unfortunate" because it might be very helpful to the President. "As it is he has offended some of the members who have come to feel that their names were being used but not their services", remarked Pell.[51]

Initially, the PAC was meant to serve as an intermediary between the IGC and the refugee agencies, and to coordinate the refugee work in America. Later, however (in 1941), it received a new function: to act in an "advisory liaison capacity" between the State Department and the social service agencies. Ultimately, its most important task was to serve as a watchdog for the interest of refugees against the increasing restrictionist approach of the State Department.[52]

But the PAC did retain several important channels of activity. McDonald's position as chairman enabled him to discuss refugee matters with the highest authorities, including the President and the Secretary of State. How successful was he in this task?

Although the Advisory Committee was nominated by the President and worked closely with the State Department, it did not receive financial support from the government. Its budget was entirely covered by Jewish organizations, specifically by the American Jewish Congress and the JDC.[53] Archbishop Rummel, chairman of the Committee for Catholic Refugees and a member of the PAC, was "surprised ... and a little troubled" by the fact that such a non-sectarian body was supported solely by Jewish groups. He agreed with Myron C. Taylor, U.S. representative to the Evian Conference, that the Committee's expenses should come

---

51 Feingold, *Politics of Rescue*, p. 26. Quoted in Stewart, "U.S. Government Policy", p. 564.

52 Roosevelt to Harris, April 18, 1938 (FDRL, OF/3186); McDonald to Sumner Welles, August 8, 1941; Minutes of the 49th Meeting of the PAC, August 7, 1941 (MP:P).

53 In 1940, for example, the PAC's expenses were $ 13,052 while its income from Jewish sources was $ 13,500 (Wise contributed $ 7500 and the JDC gave $ 6000). George Warren to McDonald, January 18, 1941 (MP:P).

from governmental sources. But George Messersmith made it clear that the PAC should not expect any contribution from the Administration. Consequently, the Committee had "never more than a skeleton staff", as McDonald remarked.[54]

Shortly after its foundation the PAC was busy screening re- settlement proposals. The increase of Nazi terror on the one hand, and the rising barriers to refugees in Western countries on the other, moved the U.S. and the British governments to consider colonization in under-developed countries in Latin America and Africa. By December 1938, the Committee had already handled about fifty plans.[55] President Roosevelt showed personal interest in several resettlement projects. He was especially eager to estab- lish a Jewish homeland in Angola, although experts, like Isaiah Bowman (the president of Johns Hopkins University), explained the futility of such endeavors. It seems that the Administration's enthusiasm for colonization there was a direct consequence of the distance of that locality from the United States. While the President dismissed practical plans for resettlement in U.S. terri- tories, such as Hawaii, Alaska and the Virgin Islands, he was inter- ested in establishing a new refugee colony in South-West Africa, to be named "the United States of Africa".[56]

After scrutinizing the flood of plans, the most promising appeared to be the Dominican Republic resettlement project. In March 1939 a survey commission sponsored by the PAC investigated President Trujillo's offer to accept 50,000 to 100,000 agricultural settlers into the Dominican Republic. The Agro-Joint, under the energetic leadership of James N. Rosenberg, undertook to orga-

54 McDonald to Myron C. Taylor, November 11, 1938; Minutes of the 2nd Meeting of the PAC, May 19, 1938; McDonald to Kohn, n.d. (c. 1945) (MP:P).

55 McDonald to Frederick P. Keppel, November 21, 1938; Report on the Special Meeting of the PAC, December 8, 1938 (MP:P).

56 See Roosevelt to Harold Ickes, December 18, 1940 (FDRL, OF/3186); Feingold, *Politics of Rescue*, pp. 102—109; Wyman, *Paper Walls*, pp. 57—61.

nize and even to finance the project. Sosua was selected as the site of the colony, which President Roosevelt hoped would be "the forerunner of many similar projects in other countries".[57] Early optimism gradually diminished when the prospective settlers met with transportation problems as well as administrative and financial obstacles. By June 1942 the Sosua colony contained less than 500 inhabitants.[58] Considering the long months of effort which it had taken for the PAC to find a permanent haven for the victims of Nazism, one may agree with Henry L. Feingold, the historian, that "despite a great deal of talk and activity, resettlement played virtually no role in actually rescuing refugees".[59]

With the failure of the resettlement plans, long-run solutions gave way to the need to find temporary shelters for the victims of the war. Especially acute was the situation of refugee children in un-Occupied France. The PAC supported the Wagner-Rogers Bill.[60] The Committee also appealed to Under Secretary of State, Sumner Welles, to intervene on behalf of thousands of refugee children in France who were in danger of deportation.[61]

McDonald unsuccessfully appealed to the State Department,

57 Quoted in Feingold, *Politics of Rescue*, p. 112; Warren to the members of PAC, December 19, 1939; April 25, 1940 (MP:P). See also Saul S. Friedman, *No Haven for the Oppressed: United States Policy Toward Jewish Refugees, 1938—1945* (Detroit, 1973), pp. 61—62.
58 See Wyman, *Paper Walls*, pp. 61—62; Feingold, *Politics of Rescue*, pp. 111—113; Stewart, "U.S. Government Policy", pp. 472—475.
59 Feingold, *Politics of Rescue*, p. 117.
60 The PAC to the President, June 13, 1940 (Joseph Chamberlain papers, at YIVO, New York City, p. 119); McDonald to Samuel Dickstein, June 6, 1939 (MP:P). For a detailed discussion of the Wagner-Rogers Bill, see below, pp. 321—323.
61 Memorandum for the members of the PAC, by McDonald, Warren and Baerwald, August 13, 1942; Cable, Sumner Welles to McDonald, October 2, 1942; McDonald and Warren to Welles, December 1, 1942; Minutes of the 57th meeting of the PAC, March 9, 1943 (MP:P); Katheryn Close, *Transplanted Children, A History* (New York, 1953), p. 26. For the tragic failure of the rescue of refugee children in France, see below, pp. 325—326.

time and again, to intervene on behalf of refugees. He suggested
the linking of a U.S. grant of wheat to Spain to a Spanish agreement to issue transit visas to refugees in France and Portugal. He
complained about the anti-Semitic attitude of American consuls
in Europe.[62] He tried to help refugees overcome the tremendous
difficulties of obtaining passage to the United States during the
war years.

The development of war in Europe meaningfully changed the
immigration situation. In June 1941 the American consuls left the
countries which had been occupied by Axis powers, so that visas
were unattainable from those countries. Furthermore, even before
the Japanese attack on Pearl Harbor, American individuals and
organizations who worked on behalf of the refugees were forced
to leave Nazi-occupied countries.

These events strongly affected the home front as well. The support of supplies of war material to the Allies in 1940—1941 and
the American military preparedness significantly increased the
production of the war industry. Consequently, the economic situation improved, and prosperity replaced decade-long depression.
The end of unemployment, however, did not decrease anti-alien
sentiments. On the contrary, the war situation aroused xenophobia
in America. Restrictionist forces successfully argued that admission of refugees would endanger national security, with every
immigrant considered a potential spy. President Roosevelt, echo-
ing the spy hysteria, warned in May 1940: "We know of new
methods of attack, the Trojan horse, the fifth column that betrays
a nation unprepared for treachery. . . . With all that we must and
will deal vigorously".[63]

62 McDonald to Cordell Hull, January 23, 1941; McDonald to Sumner
    Welles, January 25, 1941; Welles to McDonald, February 4, 1941,
    February 14, 1939. See McDonald to the State Department, August 9,
    1938 (NA, 123C 62/474); February 7, 1939 (NA, 811, 111 Refugees/29).
    See also the strictly confidential report of Jay Allen from Lisbon,
    November 15, 1940 (MP:P). Wyman, *Paper Walls*, pp. 155—168.
63 *The New York Times*, May 26, 1940.

With the entry of the United States into the war in December 1941 the prospects of immigration receded even more. The Enemy Alien Act of December 1941 further aggravated the position and the low morale of the refugees. The very notion that the victims of Nazism would be discriminated against in America on account of possible loyalty to Germany was a frustrating experience.

With the occupation of southern France by the Germans in November 1942, Lisbon became the single gateway to freedom, and a natural place for charity activities. Thousands of refugees were stranded there and desperately tried to find some kind of transportation. The PAC urged Roosevelt to use the Maritime Commission to return two ships, the *Washington* and the *Manhattan*, to service in order to help bring refugees out of Lisbon and Marseilles. Permission, however, was refused. Governmental refusal to provide ships for refugees was generally based on the war effort argument ; i.e., the issue was not sufficiently important to permit the hampering of the war effort. According to David S. Wyman, the deportation of Viennese Jews to Poland was recommended "directly after the American government decided against increasing shipping capacity between Lisbon and New York".[64] Thus, the U.S. entry into the war drastically reduced the refugees' chances of reaching American shores and necessitated the reorganization of refugee aid operations in the United States and abroad.

McDonald's position was a delicate one. Although his protests, suggestions and demands did not meet with understanding, he refused to criticize the government publicly. Only once did he threaten to resign, when he felt that the Committee was stripped of its functions. President Roosevelt, rejecting actual colonization projects in the Virgin Islands, envisaged the mass immigration of ten to twenty million refugees after the war. Therefore, he

64   McDonald to Robert M. Lovett, May 27, 1941; Cable, McDonald and Warren to the President, March 18, 1941 (MP:P); Wyman, *Paper Walls*, p. 154.

demanded of the PAC in November 1939 that "more imaginative engineering studies be pressed vigorously in larger areas".[65] McDonald, who was strongly opposed to diverting the Committee's energy into such a vague and bombastic assignment, "frankly raised the question", at the PAC's meeting, "whether the Committee had outlived its usefulness", and suggested recommending that the President appoint another group of technical experts to carry out inquiries for mass settlement.[66] Under Secretary of State, Sumner Welles, alarmed by McDonald's intention to resign because of the "present status of the Committee", sent Robert T. Pell of the State Department to iron out the differences. Pell assured McDonald that the PAC "had the complete confidence of the President and the State Department and that there was every desire on the part of both that the Committee should continue its work along present lines".[67] Thus McDonald won his way. Pressure on the White House in a specific issue sometimes bore fruit. The rescue of intellectuals and political leaders was a case in point.

On June 18, 1940 Hamilton Fish Armstrong called the attention of the President to the cases of outstanding intellectuals, political leaders and labor activists who were in immediate danger in France. He asked for emergency measures to save the lives of these prominent leaders. The President reacted promptly. On his orders, the State Department cabled American consuls in Lisbon, Marseilles and Bordeaux "to give immediate consideration" to persons named in Armstrong's list.[68] Breckinridge Long of the State Department complained that soon committees "were springing up on every hand", each with its own list and already con-

65   Warren to the members of the PAC, November 6, 1939 (MP:P).
66   Minutes of the 34th meeting of the PAC, May 15, 1940 (MP:P).
67   Robert T. Pell to McDonald, May 8, 1940; Minutes of the 34th meeting of the PAC, May 15, 1940 (MP:P).
68   H. F. Armstrong to Marguerite Le Hand (FDR's secretary), June 18, 1940 (FDRL, OF/3186); Armstrong to Breckinridge Long, June 21, 1940 (MP:P); Edwin M. Watson (FDR's secretary) to Armstrong, June 29, 1940 (FDRL, OF/3186).

demning the Administration "of favoring one side or the other".[69]

To make some order out of this confusing situation, the President's Advisory Committee took over the responsibility of screening the lists that had been submitted to the State Department. By this undertaking the PAC's function and activities drastically changed. Instead of examining futile colonization plans, the Committee now devoted its energy to the actual rescue of distinguished persons. Consequently, its work expanded. During the coming weeks the Committee examined the files of 567 refugees and made recommendations to the State Department.[70]

Breckinridge Long, Assistant Secretary of State for Special Problems and responsible for the Visa Division, who suspected almost every immigrant of being a German agent,[71] seized the opportunity to impose further restrictions on the method of scrutiny. On September 8, 1940 he asked the President "to modify the procedure" that had been agreed upon with the PAC. He complained that "a very large number of persons", who had been approved by the Committee, "have had records of activity abroad" not desirable to the United States. Furthermore, many of them did not fall into the category of intellectual leaders or were not in imminent danger. He argued that the interests of national defense called for "a more careful examination" of the refugees abroad. Therefore, he recommended that the consular officers in Europe should be left "some latitude of judgment", and that the PAC recommendations would not be mandatory. With Roosevelt's approval, Hull notified McDonald that the power of decision of issuing emergency visitor visas was taken out of the PAC's respon-

69 *Foreign Relations of the United States*, 1940, II, pp. 232—233.
70 Meeting in the office of the Acting Secretary of State, July 26, 1940 (NA, 811.111 Refugees/348); McDonald and Warren to Sumner Welles and Robert H. Jackson, July 31, 1940 (MP:P); see McDonald to Franklin Roosevelt, October 8, 1940 (FDRL, OF/3186); Warren to Long, August 14, 1940; McDonald to Long, August 30, 1940 (MP:P).
71 Israel, Fred L. (ed.), *The War Diary of Breckinridge Long* (Lincoln, Nebraska, 1966), pp. 114—115, 154, 174, 216.

sibility and was returned to the hands of the consuls abroad, who were able to delay their verdict as long as they wished.[72]

Long's accusations nearly provoked a mass resignation of the Committee. McDonald was "so wrought up" about the situation that he asked in the name of the PAC for an interview with the President, as Eleanor Roosevelt attested.[73] McDonald complained to Hull in a frank letter about fundamental changes that the Department had made in the agreement of July 26, "unilaterally and without notice to us". Such an act was not only an "embarrassment" to the members of the Committee, but an impugning of their good faith. The alterations of the procedure were aimed "to defeat the purpose which the President has repeatedly expressed ...". He therefore suggested a "return to the basis for admission previously worked out". The dispute between the State Department and the PAC was personified in the clash between McDonald and Long. The former accused the latter of noncooperation and obstruction. Before McDonald left a meeting with Sumner Welles and Long, he accused Long of having "a superlative ego and a vindictive mentality".[74]

The long-awaited conference with the President was a disappointment to the friends of refugees. Roosevelt was impatient with McDonald's complaints and explanations. As a matter of fact, he

72 Long to Franklin Roosevelt, September 18, 1940; Cordell Hull to McDonald, September 19, 1940 (FDRL, OF/3186); Long, *War Diary*, pp. 130—131, 144, 154, 161. Long outlined in a memorandum his delaying tactics as follows: "We can delay and effectively stop for a temporary period of indefinite length the number of immigrants into the United States. We could do this by simply advising our consuls to put every obstacle in the way and to resort to various administrative devices which would postpone and postpone the granting of the visas". Long to Adolf A. Berle and James C. Dunn, June 26, 1940. Quoted in Feingold, *Politics of Rescue*, p. 142.

73 *PM*, February 11, 1941, p. 7; E. R. (Eleanor Roosevelt) to FDR, September 28 (1940) (FDRL, OF/3186).

74 McDonald and Warren to Cordell Hull, September 24, 1940; see also McDonald's detailed letter to Roosevelt, October 8, 1940 (FDRL, OF/3186); Long, *War Diary*, p. 134.

did not allow McDonald to present his case. One of the participants recalled that "a very cordial Roosevelt spun a succession of stories. Whenever McDonald tried to confront the President with the refugee issue, Roosevelt would be reminded of something else and another anecdote would result. This entertainment continued until the half hour was up . . .".[75] The outcome of the interview was typically Rooseveltian. He left the PAC, the Justice and State Departments to work out a compromise. One may agree with Long's statement that he found the President's directive "in full accord" with his own point of view.[76]

As a shrewd politician, Roosevelt more or less supported the the restrictionist attitude of the State Department on the one hand, and gave encouraging hints to the PAC on the other. McDonald learned with relief that the President realized that the members of his Committee "have throughout been motivated solely by two considerations, our obligations to our consciences and our loyalty to him".[77] One may wonder how McDonald could reconcile these two obligations, since on several occasions they were contradictory.

Infuriated by the meddlesomeness of the PAC, Long was eager to restrain it. As he wrote in his diary: ". . . now it remains for the President's Committee to be curbed in its activities so that the laws again can operate in their normal course". Roosevelt, however, expressed his confidence in McDonald. "The President thinks", wrote Eleanor Roosevelt to McDonald, that "you are doing a very remarkable piece of work, and he wants you to continue, and he wants the skeleton committee held together".[78]

During the years 1940 and 1941 the PAC was busy examining

75 See Wyman, *Paper Walls*, p. 147.
76 Minutes of the 41st meeting of the PAC, October 30, 1940 (MP:P); Long, *War Diary*, pp. 134, 144.
77 McDonald to Eleanor Roosevelt, October 10, 1940; McDonald to Felix Frankfurter, October 10, 1940 (MP:P).
78 Long, *War Diary*, p. 131; Eleanor Roosevelt to McDonald, March 2, 1941; Minutes of the 42nd meeting of the PAC, December 19, 1940 (MP:P).

the files of and recommending the grant of emergency visas to 2975 political and intellectual leaders. Out of 2133 persons who received visas, 2000 refugees actually arrived in the United States. Although the credit for the rescue of these persons went to several individuals and organizations, David Wyman rightly argues that pressure from the members of the PAC "played an important role" in their liberation. Bearing in mind the opposition of the State Department, in spite of the small number of individuals that had been saved, the Committee's intervention led to some success.[79]

Another example of considerable pressure to prevent aggravation of administrative regulations concerning refugees, was the PAC's action against the "close relative" clause. In June 1941 Long was "thoroughly convinced that the German and Russian Governments were indulging in the practice of holding as hostages for the performance of services" in America relatives of prospective immigrants who received permission to leave their territories. To guard "the interest of public safety" the State Department issued instructions to American consuls that applications to enter the United States should be denied to any "alien who has close relatives, or who is acquainted with other persons" residing in Occupied Europe.[80] Thus, under the "public safety" cover, the State Department intended to close the gates of America, since almost every visa applicant had close relatives in Europe.

No wonder that McDonald, along with other members of his Committee, was irritated and asked for "an opportunity to explain to him (the President) why we all feel that this unfair practice should not receive his sanction".[81] To countermine the PAC's

---

79 Minutes of the 56th meeting of the PAC, December 1, 1942 (MP:P); see also report from Long to Cordell Hull, January 6, 1941 (FDRL, OF/3186); Wyman, *Paper Walls*, p. 149.

80 Breckinridge Long's memorandum for the President, August 20, 1941 (FDRL, OF/3186).

81 McDonald to Sumner Welles, August 8, 1941; McDonald to F. D. Roosevelt, August 8, 1941 (MP:P).

effort, Long drafted a six-page memorandum for the President, justifying the new regulation. He also discussed the matter with Cordell Hull and Sumner Welles. Hull indeed intervened on behalf of Long, suggesting to the President the "absolute importance" of meeting Long shortly before the interview with the PAC members, "to refresh your memory". When Long met the President on August 27, 1941 he found Roosevelt "thoroughly in accord with our policies and practices".[82]

On September 4, 1941 members of the PAC delegation eventually gained access to the President. They called to cancel or to modify substantially the relative clause, since "it is unnecessary, illogical, ill adapted to the purposes claimed for it, and cruelly burdensome of the refugees effected to it". Among other suggestions they asked for the establishment of a Board of Review that would serve as a court of appeal on cases that the consuls had rejected.[83]

Long, who violently opposed the suggestions, admitted that "I got a little mad and I fear I betrayed it . . . . The exclusion of any person is objectionable to those eminent gentlemen and any system of selection is anathema to them. They would throw me to the wolves in their eagerness to destroy me — and will try in the future as they have in the past to ruin my political status".[84] Long's remarks could be considered as a compliment to the PAC, since they proved the Committee's efforts to block the restrictionist regulations of the State Department. The latter, after consultation with the Justice Department, accepted the alterations suggested by the PAC.[85]

82 Long's memorandum for the President, August 20, 1941; Long to General Watson, August 20, 1941; Cordell Hull to the President, August 25, 1941 (FDRL, OF/3186). See also, Feingold, *Politics of Rescue*, pp. 144—146; Long, *War Diary*, p. 205.
83 McDonald, Statement to the President, September 4, 1941 (MP:P).
84 Long, *War Diary*, p. 216; McDonald to Eleanor Roosevelt, September 5, 1941 (MP:P).
85 Sumner Welles to McDonald, February 17, 1942 (MP:P).

The Committee's intervention led to the improvement of the appeals procedure. Nevertheless, in the long run, Long won his way. By slowing the procedure of screening the applications, as well as by other administrative means, precious months had been wasted. With the entry of the United States into World War II, the transportation obstacle made it very difficult to reach American shores even for those refugees who had already received visas.[86]

While the PAC showed courage and utilized its prestige, Mc-Donald's own attitude needs further examination. On August 8, 1941 the Committee frankly and successfully protested to the President about the new "close relative" regulation and asked for an interview with him. On the same day McDonald apologized to Under Secretary of State, Sumner Welles, for the appeal. He explained that "in order that there may be no misunderstanding, I should like to emphasize that neither George Warren nor I took the initiative in this appeal directed to the President. We both have been deeply troubled by the Visa Division's procedure, but it was our colleagues, who because of their own personal experience with the Administration ... insisted that our Committee could not in good conscience refrain from asking the President" for an interview.[87] One may wonder whether McDonald's longer experience with the Administration's attitude toward refugees did not lead him to object to the meeting with the President. Long's diary confirms that the speakers in the White House meeting on September 4, 1941 were Wise and Rummel and not McDonald, the chairman.[88]

Probably it was only a tactical argument between McDonald and some other members of his Committee, with McDonald considering the issue not sufficiently important to justify a direct

---

86 See Feingold, *Politics of Rescue*, pp. 164—166; Wyman, *Paper Walls*, p. 201; Minutes of the 54th meeting of the PAC, June 18, 1942 (MP:P). See above, p. 83.

87 McDonald to Welles, August 8, 1941 (MP:P).

88 Long, *War Diary*, p. 216.

appeal to the President. It is more difficult, however, to explain McDonald's superlative praise of the heads of the State Department in the middle of a dispute with them. Only a few days before the PAC's protest to Roosevelt, McDonald told Cordell Hull and Sumner Welles that "the American people have come to have such confidence in the soundness of your judgment that in this period of crisis your active leadership gives them complete assurance that our national interests will be fully safeguarded. Never in our history has the Department of State been more efficiently manned and organized than it is today after nearly a decade under your quiet but firm direction".[89] Hull and Welles fully supported Long's activities. One can hardly make any distinction between Long's approach and the Department's negative attitude toward refugees. Therefore, one may wonder how McDonald could reconcile the State Department's restrictionist policy with his appreciation of the creators, or at least supporters, of this line.

In fact, McDonald always showed personal interest in the State Department. In 1933 his name was under consideration for the ambassadorship to Berlin. In 1935 he weighed a suggestion to serve in the Department as Assistant Secretary of State, "if a place were available".[90] Although nothing came of this proposition, McDonald did not give up. In August 1945 he turned to Eddie Cantor, the singer, to help him to establish contact inside the Truman Administration in order to receive the position of Assistant Secretary.[91] This eagerness to maintain personal contact with the heads of the Department led him to send congratulatory letters in cases of nominations, promotions, delivery of a speech or diplomatic moves. One can find warm and sometimes flattering letters

---

89 McDonald to Hull, August 5, 1941; McDonald to Welles, August 6, 1941 (MP:P).

90 McDonald to WTS (William T. Stone), April 24, 26, 1933; "Personal and Confidential", McDonald to Joseph Chamberlain, January 20, 1935 (MP:GC).

91 McDonald to Eddie Cantor, June 15, 18, August 6, 9, 1945 (MP:GC).

to Secretary Hull, Secretary Edward R. Stettinius, Under Secretary
of State, William Phillips and Sumner Welles, Assistant Secretaries,
Adolph A. Berle, George Messersmith and Pierrepont Moffat,
among others.[92] Certainly, there is always the possibility that
through such a personal touch McDonald hoped to gain conces-
sions on the refugee issue. Such a hope, however, never materialized.

This is not to deny McDonald's honesty and devotion to the
refugee cause. He was one of the few Christians who received the
Gottheil Medal as the American "who has done the most for
Jewry".[93] He was rightly referred to by William Rosenwald, the
chairman of the National Refugee Service, as "an outstanding
national leader, as one who has given much time and effort to the
refugee problems".[94] Nevertheless, his inclination to be an insider
weakened his position in negotiating with the Administration. As
he wrote to Sumner Welles concerning his position as radio com-
mentator on world affairs: ". . . unlike some of my colleagues on
the air, I have no desire to try to build up a reputation for omni-
science by constant criticism of those in authority". He regarded
as particularly important his analysis "of the role which our Gov-

---

92   McDonald to William Phillips, March 16, 1933; McDonald to Welles,
      February 15, 1938, October 7, 1941; January 22, May 27, August 17,
      November 9, 1942; September 2, October 25, 1943; McDonald to
      Adolf Berle, August 31, September 24, 1938, February 1, September 4,
      1940, June 2, 1941; McDonald to E. Stettinius, September 27, 1943,
      May 12, October 17, December 1, 1944; McDonald to Messersmith,
      November 29, 1941; McDonald to Cordell Hull, August 5, 14, 1941;
      Moffat to McDonald, June 3, 1940 (MP:GC:P:H).
93   Herbert H. Lehman to Herbert E. Steiner, May 8, 1936 (MP:GC).
94   William Rosenwald to McDonald, June 8, 1939 (The National Refu-
      gee Service papers, folder 111, at YIVO). See also Meyer Schenko-
      lowski's and Michael Tress' cable to McDonald, September 3, 1942:
      "You are the humanitarian individual in this country in whom we
      can place our trust and faith in this dark hour of our people"
      (MP:P).

ernment is playing".[95] The very fact that he stayed as chairman of the PAC from its foundation in 1938 through the war years until President Truman's days indicated his reluctance to declare war and fight out the issue from the other side of the barricade. He preferred to struggle for his ideas from within the establishment.

What could he accomplish by quitting? McDonald clearly remembered his resignation in December 1935 as the League of Nations High Commissioner for Refugees in protest against the racial Nuremberg decrees, as well as in denunciation of the indifference of the member states toward the fate of the refugees. What did he gain by that dramatic act? His *Letter of Resignation* dominated the editorial pages of the press in the democratic countries for several weeks.[96] The world, however, disregarded McDonald's timely warning and no positive action was taken to change the course of German policy.

Thus, he did not consider resignation as a practical step to bring pressure upon the Administration. Besides, why should McDonald be expected to have been more aggressive than his Jewish colleagues? Neither Paul Baerwald, of the JDC, nor even the outspoken leader of the American Jewish Congress, Stephen Wise, threatened to leave the PAC, in spite of its limited achievements. Thinking realistically, McDonald thought it wiser to stay and fight from within. But in this struggle he was not tough enough. He underestimated the reputation he had in governmental circles. Through Eleanor Roosevelt his complaints received attention in the Oval Room.[97] Even in the State Department he was respected,

---

95 McDonald to Welles, September 25, 1942 (MP:P). For McDonald's support of the policy of the State Department in world affairs, see McDonald to the editor of *The New York Times*, November 9, 1942; McDonald to Welles, February 2, 15, 1943 (MP:GC).

96 "Repercussions of McDonald's *Letter of Resignation*", 8 pp. (MP:H). See above, pp. 52—56.

97 See, for example, E. R. (Eleanor Roosevelt) to FDR, September 28 (1940) (FDRL, OF/3186); McDonald to Eleanor Roosevelt, October 10, 24, 1940; September 5, 1941 (MP:P); December 14, 1944 (MP:GC).

as Breckinridge Long — who was not McDonald's friend — admitted: "we had been more generous with the President's Advisory Committee than we had with any of the other groups which have been active in arranging for refugees . . . and that has been the case because he (McDonald) was Chairman of the PAC".[98] The PAC's strong position in the intellectual leaders' cases, as well as in the "close relative" clause showed what could be attained by determination.

The escalation of the war in both Oceans made rescue missions almost impossible. Consequently, the PAC's activities seriously diminished after 1942. With the establishment of the War Refugee Board in January 1944, the very existence of the Committee was in question. In March 1944 George L. Warren and Professor Chamberlain reached the conclusion that "no steps should be taken at present in respect to the Committee. It has been of great value in the past and is likely to become so at any time . . . therefore seems to us to be an instrument which should be kept ready for use when the occasion arises".[99] Since the occasion did not arise and since President Truman was not interested in its existence, the PAC disbanded in the summer of 1945.[100]

Was, then, the President's Advisory Committee a failure? The achievements certainly fell short of the expectations. No fundamental change had been attained in the restrictionist policy of America. Neither the President nor the State Department sought the advice of the distinguished members of the Committee. It served rather as a watchdog to Long's initiatives. McDonald's office was busy screening sterile resettlement projects. It concentrated on preventing new Administrative regulations, but did not always exert enough pressure to attain its goals. When McDonald fought seriously, he had considerable success. Nevertheless, Roose-

98 Long, *War Diary*, p. 134.
99 Chamberlain to McDonald, March 27, 1944 (MP:P).
100 McDonald to President Truman, June 27, 1945; McDonald to Jules E. Kohn, n.d. (*c.* 1945) (MP:P).

velt was elusive and basically supported the line suggested by Long. Therefore, any suggestion that a tougher chairman could have changed the negative attitude of the Administration toward the refugees seems to be mere speculation. One may agree with Paul Baerwald's assessment that "I do not over-estimate the services rendered by the President's Advisory Committee. On the other hand, I certainly feel that ... the Committee has a good many definite accomplishments to its credit".[101]

Thus, the war years created an unfriendly atmosphere toward refugees. In 1933—1934, while the world situation was different and there were no outside obstacles to the coming of immigrants, the public mood was not sympathetic either. The time has come to examine the Christian response in America to the Nazi challenge during the 1930s.

---

101 Paul Baerwald to McDonald, June 5, 1945 (MP:P).

4

THE PROTESTANT RESPONSE AND THE AMERICAN COMMITTEE FOR CHRISTIAN REFUGEES

We have seen the national apathetic mood as well as the Administration's inaction as far as the refugees were concerned. How did the Protestant Churches in America respond to the Nazi persecutions? What was their reaction to their co-religionists' cry for help?

In America, protests against the Nazi treatment of Jews were voiced in 1933 by Protestant leaders and Church organizations. In mass rallies, by means of petitions and from the pulpit, well-known clerics spoke out on behalf of the victims of Nazi persecutions in Germany. Several Church leaders dwelt on the pagan, hence un-Christian, sources of German anti-Semitism. Christian protest against the suppression of German Jewry accordingly constituted, as Uriel Tal has rightly indicated, "an important chapter in the history of Christianity itself".[1]

S. Parkes Cadman, former president of the Federal Council of Churches of Christ in America (FCC), appealed to his Protestant

---

1   Johan M. Snoek, *The Grey Book* (Assen, 1969), p. i.

and Catholic colleagues to officially declare that the Nazi persecutions were "the negation of God".[2] The National Conference of Christians and Jews initiated a campaign to enlist the help of prominent clergymen and college professors to denounce attacks on German Jews. A noted success of the Conference was a petition signed by 1200 clergy of 26 denominations, who were "profoundly disturbed by the plight of our Jewish brethren in Germany". Their Christian conscience constrained them "with sorrow and indignation to voice our protest against the present ruthless persecution of the Jews under Herr Hitler's regime" — thus declared the document prepared by Harry Emerson Fosdick of Riverside Church in New York.[3] The petition received wide press coverage and public attention. *The New York Times* considered that the protest surpassed the problem of German Jewry. "The case is made one of the fundamentals of Christian morality and the human spirit itself". The editorial warned the German rulers that they would commit an error "if they forbid publication of this solemn voice raised in the name of American Christianity".[4]

The Federal Council of Churches was the leading Protestant institution to support the victims of Nazi oppression. As early as March 1933 its Executive Committee adopted a resolution reading: "On Christian grounds we protest against all forms of racial and religious intolerance and express our deep sympathy for its victims . . ., we urge Christians everywhere to reexamine their own racial attitudes and relationships".[5] The FCC asked the State Department to protest against the German policy and even to take international steps to stop the atrocities.[6]

In its efforts to enlist the support of as many Christian groups

---

2   *The New York Times*, March 27, October 31, 1933.
3   *Ibid.*, May 9, 26, 1933.
4   *Ibid.*, Editorial, May 27, 1933.
5   *Ibid.*, March 25, 1933.
6   Samuel McCrea Cavert to Cordell Hull, April 22, 1937 (National Archives, 862.4016/1660); April 11, 1938 (*ibid.*, 840.48/Refugees/139. Hereafter NA).

as possible, the FCC turned to Christians of every denomination to join in protest against Germany's racial policy. The Swiss International Christian Committee was also mobilized. It was asked to issue a statement which would be signed by thousands of ministers in England, the Continent and the United States, and would eventually be personally presented to Hitler. "Imperative Christian Church speak emphatically", read the cable sent to the International Christian Committee.[7] As a symbol of identification, the FCC designated a day in December 1938 as a day of prayer for the three faiths in America, on behalf of the victims of German persecutions.[8]

The aforementioned manifestations of the Christian protest against the oppression of Jews in Germany by no means exhausts the tale of the positive side to the Christian response. However, large segments of the Church kept aloof from these protests. It was Bishop Manning of New York who complained of the "feebleness of the Church. "Why is it that the Christian Church ... does not speak with greater power at this time".[9] His voice was almost a cry in the wilderness.

Particularly characterized by their refusal to speak out against Nazi atrocities were three important denominations: the Southern Baptist Convention, the Lutheran Church Missionary Synod and the American Lutheran Church.[10] The conspiracy of silence, however, was much wider than the Lutheran Church. Many Christians refused to take sides in an issue that they regarded as a German internal affair. Furthermore, even those circles that were far from anti-Semitism, a sentiment that grew considerably during the 1930s, hesitated to believe the reports about German atrocities. Many agreed with Paul Sherer, pastor in the Holy Trinity Lutheran

---

7 *The New York Times*, March 25, 1933; Federal Council, *Bulletin* (Oct. 1938), p. 13; Frank Ritchie to Henry Smith Leiper, August 20, 1936 (AFSC:GF, 1936, C&O).

8 Federal Council, *Bulletin* (Dec. 1938), p. 3.

9 *The New York Times*, March 11, 1933.

10 Snoek, *Grey Book*, pp. 268—269.

Church in New York, who warned against believing in "exaggerated rumors" coming from Germany. He asked for postponement of the verdict until all the facts became available.[11] Even Clarence E. Pickett, executive secretary of the American Friends Service Committee, who was a friend of refugees and sympathetic to the Jewish cause, thought in April 1933 that the oppression of Jews in Germany was "probably slight as compared with the persecutions of minorities in a good many countries that have been going on for a long time in Europe".[12]

The efforts to stir the consciousness of the American Christian community produced meager results. There were Gentiles who complained of Jewish pressure on them to issue anti-German statements. They not only refused to intervene on behalf of German Jewry, but also resented Jewish propaganda in that direction.[13]

So far the Protestant reaction to the persecution of Jews in Germany has been discussed. What was their response to the Nazi suppression of the churches? How far did the American Christian community identify itself with German co-religionists?

The facts were known in the United States. Unlike the veil of secrecy wrapped by the Nazis around the happenings in concentration camps and, later, around the matter of the Final Solution, the decrees responsible for the closing of ecclesiastical institutions and the foundation of the Reich Church were widely publicized by the American press. Voices of protest against the suppression of the Lutheran Church had been heard as early as April 1933. A.B. Moldenka, pastor of St. Peter's Lutheran Church in New York, called upon German co-religionists to oppose "the substitution of German Sagas and folklore for the Biblical Old Testament". The United Lutheran Church in America also protested against the denial of Lutheran autonomy in the Reich. Protestant

---

11   *The New York Times*, March 27, 1933.
12   Clarence E. Pickett to Gilbert and MacMaster, April 3, 1933 (AFSC).
13   Bruce M. Mohler to T. F. Mulholland and Calleros, March 25, 1938 (NCWC, Box 90).

theologians likewise joined in the criticism of Hitler's church policy.[14]

The strongest and most influential opposition was voiced by the FCC. Through official declarations, resolutions, press releases and by dispatching envoys to Germany, the Executive Committee tried to moderate the Nazi attitude toward the churches. Dr. Beaven of the FCC declared that "we can not permanently recognize a church administration in Germany which denies the very fundamentals of the Gospel".[15] During 1933 the leaders of the Council were still seeking a dialogue with Mueller and other Nazi officials. The FCC purposely refrained from public support of the Confessing Church, knowing that this would only serve the cause of its foes. Furthermore, German Protestants explicitly asked the FCC to avoid the severance of relations with the heads of the Reich Church in Berlin. Accordingly, at first the Council's statements were carefully and moderately worded. However, with the arrest of Martin Niemöller and his colleagues and with the violent dispersal of the Pastor's Emergency League, the Council decided to break its silence and to support them publicly. In January 1934 the Executive Committee of the FCC acclaimed "the brave and persistent stand of those German pastors who are struggling to maintain the liberty of the Christian conscience". On another occasion the Council declared that autocratic church rule and the suppression of free dialogue "are incompatible with the true nature of Christian faith". The Council sent a direct letter to the Confessing Church, encouraging its leaders to continue their brave struggle. The time had come to break silence and to state openly that the FCC sympathy and prayers were given to the Confessing Church, the Council's letter declared.[16]

The religious press hardly excelled in its verbal criticism. The

14 *The New York Times*, April 10, 1933; October 24, 1934; December 3, 1933; April 5, 1934. See above, p. 29.
15 *Ibid.*, May 17, 1934.
16 Minutes of the Executive Committee of the FCC, January 26, October 26, 1934 (FCC, Box 19). See above, p. 29.

great majority of the papers was reluctant to treat the subject, avoiding it as far as possible. Notable exceptions were the representatives of the liberal stream, such as the *Christian Century*, *the Churchman* (Episcopal), and *Advance* (Congregational). F.I. Murphy, who investigated the response of the Christian press in America to Nazi Germany, concluded that "the American Christians did not seize this opportunity for moving beyond words to deeds with very great enthusiasm".[17]

Why, it may be asked, did American Christians fail to criticize more emphatically the persecution of their brethren? Their unwillingness to support German Jewry could still be explained by the growing anti-Semitic sentiment in America and by the lack of interest in the fate of a strange minority in a distant country. But why did they fail to extend more help to their own co-religionists, as the Jews did?

There were Christians who "had more fears of offending the Nazi government than their desire to help its victims", bitterly reported K. Vergard of the American Committee for Christian Refugees.[18] Indeed, conservative Catholic and Protestant circles, like the Brooklyn *Tablet* and American Lutherans, gladly accepted Hitler's rise to power. The Lutherans welcomed Ludwig Mueller's nomination as Reich Bishop. They hoped that the new regime would treat Protestants more favorably and Lutherans would gain better positions. The German General Conference of the United Lutheran Church in America congratulated Mueller in September 1933 in the following terms: "With deep sympathy and great joy we have heard ... of the more friendly attitude of the new regime with regard to the Christian religion and its determined struggle against dirt and offal, open immorality...".[19] Interestingly enough,

---

17   F. I. Murphy, "The American Christian Press and Pre-War Hitler's Germany, 1933—1939" (Unpublished Ph.D. dissertation, the University of Florida, 1970), pp. x, 105—106.

18   Report of Robert K. Vergard, in Minutes of the American Committee for Christian Refugees=ACCR, December 7, 1937 (FCC).

19   *The New York Times*, September 28, 1933. See above, pp. 28—29.

on the very same day that *The New York Times* printed the aforesaid letter of support, the same paper published a protest signed by 2000 Protestant bishops and clergymen against Nazi assaults on the Protestant Church in Germany. That dichotomous situation prevailed for years. The editors of *Lutheran*, the organ of the Lutheran Church in America, refused to accept the fact that the attacks on the churches in Germany were being made with Hitler's approval.[20]

There were Christian circles in America which did not regard Hitler as being anti-religious. His attitude toward the Church was explained as attributable to confusion resulting from the struggle between Mueller and Niemöller. Furthermore, the preaching of "Positive Christianity" left upon Americans the impression of Nazi sympathy toward Christianity. Thus, influential American Church leaders refused to believe, even in 1938, that the Protestant Church in Germany was in danger. They regarded the reports coming out of the Reich as exaggerated.[21] Part of the misunderstanding probably derived from Hitler's intention to harness the Church to his regime rather than to ruin it. As Henry Smith Leiper of the FCC put it: "He did not want to destroy the Church; he wanted to prostitute it".[22]

Hitler's assaults on Communism partially explained the tolerant attitude of the American Christians toward him. Declarations about Germany as defender of Christianity and Western Civilization against Russian barbarism were welcomed by American Christians. The Nazi propaganda, which presented the domination over the churches as an essential step in the closing of ranks against Communist threats, softened opposition, particularly in

20 "Lutheran State Churches in Germany Unite", *Lutheran* (June 22, 1933), p. 6; "Incapable Subordinates", *ibid.* (March 21, 1935), p. 14. See also *Presbyterian* (April 21, 1938), p. 5.

21 Ethan T. Colton, "The Fortunes of Religion in Germany", *Christian Advocate* (New York) (October 10, 1935), p. 906.

22 Henry Smith Leiper, "Three Years of Hitlerism", *Christian Evangelist* (Jan. 30, 1936), p. 152.

conservative circles.[23] Even liberals, such as the editors and supporters of *Christian Century*, who unreservedly denounced the
Nazis for their persecution of Christians and Jews, were confused
by the German invasion of Russia in July 1941. Was the fight
against Hitler, on Stalin's part, a Holy War? That question was
a central theme lengthily discussed on the pages of *Christian
Century*, the most influential of the Protestant papers. Oswald
Garrison Villard, editor of the *Nation*, wrote about "Our Moral
Confusion": whom to support, Hitler or Stalin? John Haynes
Holmes, the liberal clergyman, who was known for his sympathy
to the victims of Nazism, refused to accept Winston Churchill's
formula of supporting the devil to beat Hitler. "This is the insane
whirling of war. Lift up the banner and draw the sword, and this
is where we land. Our cause lost, our hope doomed, our integrity
sacrificed and all for nothing", wrote Holmes in an article entitled
"If Russia Wins". The editorial of the *Christian Century* took
the same approach, writing that "Europe saved from Hitler at
the price of Stalin's triumph will seem no triumph at all".[24]

What was the attitude of the American Christian community
in regard to the admission of European refugees from Nazism?
Did they advocate any relaxation of the rigid immigration regulations? While verbal protests against the persecution of Jews and
Christians in Germany related to a suffering minority in a distant
country, the question of admitting more refugees directly concerned Americans in many practical ways. Unlike criticism of the
Nazi terror, which could be expressed through addresses, editorials
and petitions, support of the refugees called for practical deeds.
Along with the appeal to the Administration to relax immigration

---

23 See Samuel Cavert's attitude in *The New York Times*, September 22,
    1933.
24 Editorial, "Is it a Holy War?", *Christian Century*, 58 (October 8,
    1941), pp. 1230—1232; Oswald Garrison Villard, "Our Moral Con-
    fusion", *ibid.*, 58 (July 9, 1941), pp. 881—882; John Haynes Holmes,
    "If Russia Wins", *ibid.* (July 30, 1941), pp. 954—956; Editorial, "Eu-
    ropean Christians Still Fear Russia", *ibid.* (August 13, 1941), p. 995.

regulations, there was a need to secure jobs for the refugees, to find homes for them, to provide relief and to assist in their social and cultural absorption. On this score, therefore, it was necessary to overcome the opposition of large segments of the American people and to provide practical help.

The Federal Council of Churches was again one of the few influential church organizations that came out courageously and openly on behalf of Jewish refugees. When, in the fall of 1933, the League of Nations considered the establishment of the High Commission for Refugees, Samuel McCrea Cavert, the FCC's general secretary, turned to the Secretary of State "to look with favor upon the proposal". He urged the State Department to give it "sympathetic support and cooperate in making it effective". Consistent with this attitude, the FCC welcomed the Administration's initiative for international action on behalf of the refugees. "We rejoice", read the FCC's resolution of April 1938, "in the action of the State Department in appealing for international cooperation to provide a haven of relief here and in other lands for all refugees from Austria".[25]

The growing anti-Semitic sentiment in America was a real challenge to church leaders. Just as in the early years of the Nazi regime the FCC had been the most outspoken critic of German anti-Semitism, so now and for the same reasons this agency challenged the anti-Jewish sentiments in the United States during the late 1930s and the war years. The Executive Committee of the FCC time and again condemned American anti-Semitism. "Recent evidence of anti-Jewish prejudice in our country compels us to

25   "Evian Conference: Editorials", *Congressional Jewish Review*, I (Sep. 1938), pp. 53—54; Editorial, "The Refugees: What to do with them?" *Christian Advocate* (December 16, 1938), p. 1604; Murphy, "American Christian Press", p. 189; A noted exception was the *Christian Evangelist*. See "The Rescue of the Jews" (January 30, 1936), p. 144; "Jewish Exiles and Palestine", *ibid.* (July 28, 1938), pp. 811—812; "The Tormented Minority", *ibid.* (December 8, 1938), p. 1339; "Three Ways to Help the Refugees", *ibid.* (June 22, 1939), p. 651.

speak again a word of solemn warning to the nation. Divisiveness on religious or racial grounds is a portentous menace to American democracy", reads the resolution of the Executive Committee of September 1, 1941. "We condemn anti-Semitism as un-American . . . . Anti-Semitism is an insidious evil which, if allowed to develop, would poison the springs of our national life. Even more strongly we condemn anti-Semitism as un-Christian". The resolution declared its "renewed determination to unite in combating every tendency to anti-Semitism in our country".[26]

The condemnation of American anti-Jewish prejudice was by no means confined to the FCC. In June 1939 the General Synod of the Reformed Church in America adopted a report which proclaimed that "the failure of the Church to recognize the Jews had behind it a record of misunderstanding, intolerance and spiritual malpractice". The United Church of Christ issued a statement in 1940 to the effect that anti-Jewish sentiments were "a covert attack" on Christianity itself. Anti-Semitic propaganda threatened "to destroy the teachings of the Bible", and contradicted St. Paul's teachings, declared the United Church. The Commissioners of the General Assembly of the Presbyterian Church in the U.S.A. joined the voices of protest: "We confess the sins of our country in this respect". The Presbyterians declared that "We could be lacking in sense of common morality and decency if we did not express our strong disapproval".[27]

One may, as did John Snoek, compile a long list of all the resolutions and statements of Protestant leaders against American anti-Jewish prejudice. One may also cite the assertion of the Federal Council's *Bulletin* that "an intolerant attitude toward the Jews is opposed by the great body of American Christians". Never-

---

26   FCC, Minutes of the Meeting of the Committee on Anti-Semitism, June 16, 1939 (FCC, Box 127); *The New York Times*, December 13, 1940; Minutes of the Executive Committee of FCC, September 19, 1941 (FCC, Box 22).

27   *The New York Times*, June 13, 1939; Snoek, *Grey Book*, p. 257; *The New York Times*, May 31, 1939.

theless, the fact was that American anti-Semitism grew significantly during the war years. On December 11, 1942 the Biennial Assembly of the FCC openly acknowledged that "We confess our own ineffectiveness in combating the influence which begets anti-Semitism in our country...". Even Snoek has admitted that three important Protestant denominations refused to condemn anti-Jewish prejudice.[28] What Snoek failed to see, because of his eagerness to prove Protestant support of the Jewish cause, was that a wide gap existed between church leaders and rank and file Christians. While Samuel Cavert, Henry S. Leiper and a few others, who dominated the FCC, were able to initiate strong pro-Jewish resolutions, they had very little backing in local communities. As George Buttrick, president of the FCC, admitted: "The FCC has no authority. It is not a super-church .... It voices convictions, but voice has no coercive power".[29]

In certain Protestant circles, namely, the Home Missions Council (HMC) and other missionary societies, a peculiar approach evolved toward Jewish refugees and American anti-Semitism. It stemmed from the fact that theologically the Church has never given up the hope of converting Jews to Christianity. "With the New Testament in our hands we must conclude that the responsibility (of the church to the Jews) is real and definite and inescapable", read a position paper of the Home Missions Council. To emphasize this point, the document restated that "through all the Christian centuries the obligation of the Church to share its evangel with the Jews has never been questioned". [30]

28   Snoek, *Grey Book*, pp. 82—89, 256—269; Federal Council, *Bulletin*,
     February 1939, cited in Snoek, p. 92; *Bulletin*, January 1943, in
     Snoek, pp. 268—269.
29   George Buttrick to James W. Fifield, November 22, 1940 (FCC,
     Box 11); Murphy, "American Christian Press, p. 188.
30   Home Missions Council (=HMC), "Data Information and Sugges-
     tions for Groups in their Consideration of Topics for Discussion
     in Connection with the Conference on 'The Responsibility of the
     Church to the Jews in the Present World Crisis', to be held on
     December 12, 1941" (FCC, Box 11).

The achievements of the Church in its evangelic mission in America were far from impressive, as John W. Thomas of the Baptist Church admitted : "We have never been particularly successful in converting Jews to Christianity". The world crisis of the late 1930s and 1940s was considered as operating in favor of Christianity. The Jewish situation throughout the world, the refugee problem and the rise of anti-Semitism, created an "unparalleled opportunity" to work for Jewish redemption. "To do nothing for the Jews in a time like this is really to do something grave", maintained an HMC article [31].

To ascertain the best methods of dealing with the situation, the HMC distributed a questionnaire among Protestant denominations in December 1939. Amongst other things, it inquired: "Are you proposing to do anything as a denomination to meet the situation?"; "Should the Council have a policy and a program for the Jews?" Most of the responses supported the idea of continuing and even intensifying evangelic ministration among the Jews through an "intelligent and sympathetic Christian approach". Conrad Hoffmann Jr., of the Board of National Mission of the Presbyterian Church in the U.S.A., was optimistic as to the chances of evangelic success. "In view of the present world situation ... we hope to be able to open up work in St. Paul and Minneapolis . . . . We plan definitely to carry on our good Samaritan ministry to the refugees".[32] Encouraged by the positive response, the HMC established a special Committee of Cooperation on the Christian Approach to the Jews, with John S. Conning as secretary. The latter organized meetings and discussions, sent position papers

---

31 John W. Thomas to Mark A. Dawber, December 29, 1939; HMC, "The Responsibility of the Church to the Jews in the Present World Crisis" (FCC, Box 11).

32 HMC, "The Church and the Jews", December, 1939; Thomas to Dawber, December 29, 1939; Jay S. Stowell to E. D. Kohlstedt, December 29, 1939; J. B. Stocker to Mark Dawber, December 15, 1939; Conrad Hoffmann Jr. to Mark Dawber, December 20, 1939 (FCC, Box 11).

and extensively utilized the pages of the Council's *Press Service* to propagate his ideas in regard to the means of fulfilling the obligation of the Church to the Jews.[33] Friendship and kindness toward Jewish refugees would be the best way, according to Conning, to attract them to the Church.

> When confidence has been established, reserve disappears and as friendship develops the soul of the Jew becomes an open book. Intelligent, disinterested sympathy is the open sesame to the mind and heart of the Jew. A loving heart in time dispels the suspicion of ulterior motives and creates the conviction that not all Christians are antagonistic to Jews.[34]

Several leaders, such as Conrad Hoffmann Jr., saw a natural link between missionary zeal and Christian support for Jewish refugees. Hoffmann, who stressed the need for expansion of evangelical ministry in the United States as well as abroad, was also active in preparing plans for a temporary solution to the refugee problem. Mark Dawber, the HMC's secretary, tried to raise money in the branches for refugee professors, but without results.[35]

Apparently, anti-Jewish prejudice stood in the way of attracting Jews to Christian institutions. Anti-Semitism led Protestant com-

---

33 John S. Conning, "Highways for Christ in the Jewish World", HMC, *Press Service*, 15 (May 14, 1940), pp. 1—4; "The Jews — A Christian Test", *ibid.*, 16, pp. 4—8; "The Soul of the Jew", *ibid.*, 16, (June 27, 1940), pp. 3—7; "Beside the Golden Door: New Hope for Jewish and non-Aryan Refugees", *ibid.*, pp. 7—9.

34 J. S. Conning, "The Soul of the Jew", HMC, *Press Service*, 16 (June 27, 1940), pp. 3—7.

35 See Hoffmann to Dawber, December 20, 1939 (FCC, Box 11); Hoffmann, "Confidential Report Concerning the Conditions of Non-Aryans in Germany with Suggestions for Possible Means of Assistance", September 1, 1935 (AJC, Germany, 1934—1935); Hoffmann, "A Plan for German Refugee Relief", October 15, 1938 (AJC, Refugees); Mark Dawber to Executive Secretaries, April 24, 1940 (FCC, Box 11).

munities to bar their doors to Jewish neighbors. "Particularly disturbing is the overflow of this rising tide of anti-Jewish prejudice into the Christian Church", complained an HMC article. "... There are churches in which this attitude is pronounced, and others in which a latent prejudice makes the people indifferent". A pastor of a community in a big city admitted that he was afraid of inviting Jews to his church because of the hostility of members of his congregation.[36]

Since anti-Semitism led to alienation of the Jews and bred resentment among their Christian neighbors, all of which hampered missionary activity, the Executive Committee of the Home Missions Council resolved on January 7, 1939 to protest against American anti-Semitism. "We recognize with deep concern the rise of anti-Jewish prejudice in America ... we desire to express our determined opposition to all efforts to sow seeds of racial discord in our American life and we earnestly urge every pastor to oppose anti-Semitic propaganda". The resolution indicated that opposition to any form of anti-Semitism was essential, otherwise Christians could not "ask Jews to consider the Christian message". The close connection between the rejection of anti-Jewish prejudice and the Church's evangelic mission was also demonstrated at the annual meeting of the Home Missions Council in November 1940. Along with the appeal to combat anti-Semitism, a resolution was adopted stating: "We desire to record our judgment (that) the Jewish evangelization is a definite responsibility for the missionary boards of the Church and should be considered as an integral part of their program".[37] Thus, Christian denunciation of anti-Semitism and sympathy for Jewish refugees was not merely the outcome of disinterested humanitarianism and Christian charity, but was sometimes motivated by missionary zeal.

36 HMC, "The Responsibility of the Church to the Jews" (FCC, Box 11).
37 Meeting of the Executive Committee on the "Christian Approach to the Jews", January 7, 1939; HMC, Annual Meeting in Atlantic City, November 6, 1940 (FCC, Box 11).

Words were easier than deeds to provide — particularly when the scene of concern was three thousand miles away. What practical steps did Christians actually take up to help their co-religionists? James McDonald wanted action. "I am fed up with Christian protestations of interest, academic expressions of concern and the empty holding out of the hand of fellowship. It is high time that Christian leadership took its obligations seriously", he demanded.[38] Accordingly, in November 1933 he called for a Jewish-Christian drive for "reconstructive purposes", asking the Federal Council of Churches to cooperate with the JDC in an emergency Christmas appeal for German refugees. Henry Smith Leiper of the FCC clearly indicated his emphasis on the appeal's connection with the need of Christian refugees. "If McDonald can furnish convincing specific information regarding number and need of non-Jewish refugees and assure arrangements for administration relief, (FCC) will gladly sponsor appeal in cooperation (with the) JDC".[39] McDonald refused to follow the FCC line and abandoned the whole plan, because "unless the appeal could be made for the support of all refugees alike, it would lose its *raison d'être*". Although one might see the moral point in McDonald's argument, it showed his lack of understanding of the Church's mood with regard to refugees. It did not take long for McDonald to realize his mistake and change his policy. He soon comprehended that an appeal to the Churches would be effective only if confined to the needs of non-Jewish refugees.[40]

The plight of Christian refugees as well as his desire to see the Protestants, Catholics and Jews work in harmony on behalf of the refugees, motivated McDonald in initiating the establishment

38 Cited in Merle Curti, *American Philanthropy Abroad* (New York, 1963), pp. 382—383.
39 Cable, Monsieur Henriod to Henry Smith Leiper, November 24, 1933; Leiper to Henriod, n.d. (*c.* 1933) (MP:GC).
40 McDonald to Esther Ogden, December 3, 1933 (MP:H); High Commission for Refugees, "Meeting Christian Responsibility", July 5, 1934 (MP:H).

of a Christian relief agency. After prior consultation with Samuel McCrea Cavert and H.S. Leiper of the FCC, individuals of the three faiths were invited to attend an informal conference on co-operation with the High Commissioner on January 3, 1934. After general discussion of the problems of the non-Jewish refugees, a sub-committee was appointed, consisting of Cavert, Leiper, Father La Farge, editor of the Jesuits' *America*, and Rabbi Jonah B. Wise of the United Jewish Appeal. This body discussed the functions of the new agency and tried to clarify its basic policy. There was an agreement that the Committee "should be Christian in complexion, although possibly not in name". After further deliberations, Rabbi David De Sola Pool's suggestion was adopted to omit any indication of Jewish cooperation. Thus, the new body was called the American Christian Committee for German Refugees. Although the Initial Informal Consultative Group was non-sectarian, the organization became from the beginning a Christian agency, taking care of Christian refugees.[41]

Robert A. Ashworth, educational secretary of the National Conference of Jews and Christians and the first executive secretary of the ACCR, prepared a Statement of the ACCR's purposes, as follows:

To cooperate in the United States with James G. McDonald,

41 Leiper to McDonald, December 30, 1933; Michael Williams, editor of the Catholic *Commonweal*, represented Father La Farge; Minutes of the Sub-committee appointed by the Informal Conference in co-operation with the McDonald's High Commission on Refugees, Jan-uary 1, 1934; Minutes of the American Committee for Christian Refugees=ACCR, February 26, 1934 (MP:GC). The changes in the name of ACCR shed interesting light on changing conditions and shifting emphases. Here is the history of the Committee's names:
   1934 — The American Committee for Christian German Refugees.
   1936 — The American Christian Committee for German Refugees.
   1939 — The American Committee for Christian Refugees.
   1944 — The American Christian Committee for Refugees.
See *Newscast*, 5 (Sep.–Oct. 1944), 2.

> High Commissioner of the League of Nations for German
> Refugees, in an educational effort to evoke a sense of respon-
> sibility toward the needs of refugees from Germany on the
> part of Protestant and Catholic Christians, and to enlist
> their sympathetic participation in such campaigns for funds
> as may later be projected.

Thus, the initial aim of the new Committee was educational rather
than the provision of relief. Indeed, Ashworth considered his first
task to be "the production of educational literature".[42]

Ashworth soon learned that to print pamphlets and to distribute
them he needed money. So, a financial campaign became the first
priority. In order to receive wide financial support he suggested
the establishment of a national committee, consisting of representatives from different parts of the country. The initial funds
were contributed by the American Jewish Joint Distribution Committee. In conformity with the policy of Jewish agencies to con-
ceal their financial help to Christian organizations so that the
concern of non-Jews with the refugee problem might be demonstrated, the JDC donations reached the ACCR via McDonald and
not directly. Though Jewish help was essential, ACCR leaders preferred to solicit funds from Christian sources, believing that a
Christian committee "should not be financed by the Jews, and
that the sooner we emerge from the present situation the better
it will be".[43]

Committee leaders, who were eager to provide financial help as
soon as possible, decided to collect half a million dollars for distribution among German refugees in Europe. For this purpose
the ACCR, in May 1934, launched an appeal by mail. McDonald
also directed a personal appeal to one hundred wealthy Christian
friends. The results of the two appeals, however, were "exceed-

---

42   Robert A. Ashworth to McDonald, January 31, 1934 (MP:GC).
43   Ashworth to McDonald, March 14, 1934; McDonald to Ashworth,
     June 5, 1934; Ashworth to Olive Sawyer, March 7, 1934 (MP:GC).

ingly disappointing". The returns were $941.[44] McDonald expressed the disappointment of the ACCR's supporters, writing: "It is disheartening that it takes so long to get started".[45] The meager results could not be explained merely by the economic situation, because in 1932, at the peak of the Depression, the FCC denominations had collected $373 million.[46]

The meager results led the ACCR to drop the idea of an independent appeal and to rely on the experience of the United Jewish Appeal. On May 11, 1934 a motion was adopted, with the encouragement of UJA leaders, "to secure Christian cooperation with Jewish campaigns for relief funds". Accordingly, Parkes Cadman, chairman of the ACCR, turned to Felix M. Warburg, national chairman of the UJA, offering nationwide cooperation. Cadman called upon Christian leaders to assist the UJA campaign in securing funds from Christian sources. He promised Warburg "to do all in our power to encourage this in each of the cities in which you work".[47] In spite of an intensive publicity drive, the outcome was disappointing. While the UJA collected $1,800,000, the Christian contribution through the ACCR totaled $8000.[48]

Henry Smith Leiper called the Christian apathy "amazing". Robert Ashworth, too, was disheartened. "I wish that somebody, wiser than I, would interpret to me the indifference of non-Jews in this country to this problem", he complained.[49] The disappointment of ACCR leaders was so deep, and the position of the organization in November 1934 so critical, that its disbandment was con-

44 Minutes of the Executive Committee of the ACCR, March 16, 1934; Ashworth to McDonald, June 29, 1934 (MP:GC:ACCR).
45 McDonald to Ashworth, April 27, 1934 (MP:GC:ACCR).
46 *The New York Times*, September 28, 1933.
47 Minutes of the ACCR, May 11, 1934; Parkes Cadman to Felix Warburg, May 17, 1934 (MP:GC:ACCR).
48 Minutes of the ACCR, November 5, 1934; Ashworth to McDonald, May 28, June 6, 7, 11, 1934 (MP:GC:ACCR).
49 Henry Smith Leiper, "The State of the Church", *Advance* (July 26, 1934), p. 332; Ashworth to Olive Sawyer, February 14, 1935 (MP:GC: ACCR).

sidered. It was decided, however, that "the Committee, in spite of its experience to date, was not justified in dropping its task".[50] Not everyone was so discouraged. JDC leaders, who were eager to enlist Christian cooperation in the refugee issue, found the ACCR's efforts a stimulating factor on local Jewish communities. Even from the financial aspect the Jews gained from the joint campaign. Probably more important was the "spirit of goodwill" that was promoted between Jews and Christians at the local level. In the light of increased anti-Semitism, "this better understanding between local groups may have been of great value", reported Isidor Coons, campaign director of the JDC.[51]

Initially, Catholic leaders took an active part in the foundation of the Committee. McDonald was really "delighted that Catholics and Protestants are working together side by side". Catholic church leaders and editors, like Edward J. Walsh, Henry L. Caravati, John La Farge, Michael Williams, R.A. McGovan, George N. Shuster and Michael F. Doyle, actively participated in the early discussions and some of them were elected to leading posts in the Committee. McDonald's joy, however, was premature, because the cooperation did not last long. The Catholics withdrew from the ACCR, apparently on directives from top echelons. They preferred to work alone. So the American Committee for Christian Refugees became a sectarian agency, operated by Protestant officers who rendered services on behalf of their co-religionists.[52]

The history of the ACCR may be divided into three major periods:
1) 1934—1938 the period of beginning and wrestling with difficulties.
2) 1939—1942 the peak of activities.
3) 1943—1947 the period of governmental help and decline.

50   Minutes of the ACCR Meeting, November 5, 1934 (MP:GC:ACCR).
51   *Ibid.*
52   McDonald to Ashworth, March 2, 1934; Minutes of the ACCR, February 26, 1934; Minutes of the Executive Committee of the ACCR, March 1, 1934; ACCR, *Toward a New Life*, p. 2.

The initial difficulties of the ACCR did not disappear for several years. The obstacles forced the leaders to confess in December 1935 that "we were compelled to make gain slowly, conserving each gain as made until we could reach a position which would make possible a more aggressive effort on a broader front".[53] To provide meaningful service, the Committee found it urgently needed the sum of $ 400,000, but had in its treasury only $ 2004. Only in May 1937, after a study had recommended the preparation of a more realistic budget, did the ACCR decide to drop the $ 400,000 goal. Meanwhile a $ 5000 contribution from a Jewish foundation enabled the continuance of ACCR's operations in 1935. No wonder that the 1935/6 report of the Executive Committee was discouraging.[54]

As a Protestant agency, the ACCR cooperated closely with the Federal Council of Churches of Christ in America, the umbrella organization of most of the Protestant denominations in the country. Influenced by the social gospel movement of the early years of the 20th century, the FCC showed great concern about the social and economic conditions of the immigrants. Theology as well as the idea of social service were the wellspring of the FCC's activities. Accordingly, it was natural that several officials of the FCC, like Samuel McCrea Cavert, its general secretary, and Henry Smith Leiper, its foreign secretary, were among the pillars of the ACCR, following its fortunes for a dozen years. Many of the ACCR's functionaries were representatives of the FCC. Indeed, the ACCR served as the FCC's agent in regard to refugee matters. As Cavert put it: "a primary interest of the FCC

---

53 Report of the executive secretary of the ACCR, September 20 to December 9, 1935 (AFSC:GF, 1935, C&O).

54 *Ibid.*, Minutes of the Executive Committee of the ACCR, March 31, 1936 (FCC, Box 194). See "Statement Regarding the Proposed National Effort for $ 400,000 Under the Auspices of the ACCR" (AFSC: GF, 1936, C&O); "Statement for Financial Appeal through the Newspapers" (*ibid.*); Minutes of the Meeting of the Executive Committee of the ACCR, September 28, 1936 (FCC, Box 102); May 3, 1937 (*ibid.*, Box 194).

and of its constituent bodies is expressed through the ACCR".[55]
Most of the Committee's income came from the Council's denominations. In 1939—1940 the FCC's involvement in refugee matters was so deep and its help to the ACCR so important, as to
prompt Cavert's boast that "the ACCR was created on the initiative of the FCC", in disregard of McDonald's role.[56]

The Council's help to the American Committee was in fact
invaluable. In addition to the former's activities on the publicity
front, it undertook an active role in the resettlement of refugees.
The concentration of refugees in the New York area aroused
strong anti-refugee sentiments there, which alarmed Jewish organizations. In December 1938 Joseph Chamberlain, NCC chairman,
asked Cavert to exert his Council's influence on local Church
leaders to assume responsibility for a refugee family.[57]

After long delays Cavert persuaded Rev. Charles S. Macfarland,
in March 1940, to press the resettlement program "more vigorously" with local Church leaders. The elderly emeritus secretary-
general of the FCC enthusiastically undertook the mission, writing
to Cavert that "nothing gratifies me more than to have a part
in this service". Exploiting his wide contact with Church leaders,
Macfarland tried to enlist their cooperation in stimulating local
communities "to accept a carefully defined responsibility for a
specific refugee family". He toured the country for months persuading, pressing and pleading with pastors to accept refugees.
He issued general appeals, sent thousands of letters to church
leaders and friends, wrote letters to editors and was interviewed
on several radio stations.[58]

---

55   Minutes of the Executive Committee of the ACCR, March 23, 1934,
     November 22, 1935 (FCC, Box 19, 11); Cavert to Richard Hertz,
     December 6, 1939 (FCC, Box 105).
56   Cavert to George Buttrick, January 24, 1940 (FCC, Box 11).
57   Chamberlain to Cavert, December 22, 1938 (FCC, Box 103); Cavert's
     memorandum on "Relation of Church Agencies to German Refugee
     Problem", March 15, 1939 (FCC, Box 105).
58   Cavert to E. Hersey, March 25, 1940 (FCC, Box 11); Charles S.
     Macfarland to Cavert, April 16, 1940 (FCC, Box 96); Macfarland,

Of great help to the FCC in the resettlement program was the Women's Cooperation Commission, with Dr. Mary E. Wolley as chairman and Anne E. Caldwell as secretary. This group of women, with members and volunteers in forty cities, established local advisory committees, supplied furnished rooms and secured jobs for refugees. Those women provided the personal touch and individual care that the national committees were unable to give. In April 1941 the ACCR praised their "splendid coopera- tion", describing the women's work as "the backbone of our hospitality".[59] Besides the help of the Women's Cooperation Com- mission, Macfarland also enjoyed a measure of cooperation from different Church bodies, like the YWCA and YMCA branches, and from the Episcopal, Lutheran, Baptist and Congregational Churches.[60]

In spite of the constant refusal of different Churches to admit refugees into their communities,[61] and in spite of natural obstacles, the program did bear some fruit. During the first ten months of 1940, 286 refugees were resettled. This momentum, however, slowed in 1941. In short, the ACCR, with the active help of the FCC and several denominations, resettled about 300 refugees during the whole period of its operation.[62]

"Resettlement of the Refugees for Parish Committees", n.d. (FCC, Box 11); Report of the Federal Council Refugee Service, October 11, 1940 (FCC, Box 96).

59 Mimeographed report of the ACCR, January 1—May 1, 1940 (FCC, Box 11); Katherine H. Barbour to Mrs. H. S. Coffin, October 17, 1940, April 22, 1941; Anne E. Caldwell to Mrs. Henry Conland, May 1, 1940 (FCC, Box 150).

60 Minutes of the Meeting of the ACCR and the YMCA, May 8, 1940 (FCC, Box 11).

61 Cavert to E. Hersey, March 8, 1940 (FCC, Box 11); Minutes of the Meeting of the FCC Committee on Anti-Semitism, March 20, 1940 (FCC, Box 127).

62 Minutes of the Resettlement Advisory Committee of the ACCR, November 25, 1940 (FCC, Box 150); Statistical Report of the ACCR for October, 1940; ACCR, Service for January — through June 1941 (Moss papers, Box 143, FCC).

Even though the results were far from satisfactory,[63] there were some positive consequences of the resettlement plan. The Christian groups not only found a haven for a certain number of refugees, but also expanded the circle of people who were laboring on behalf of refugees. Furthermore, meaningful contacts were made with local and national Church leaders.

This link between the agency and the Church was an important factor in the ACCR's activities. Leland Rex Robinson, the president of the Committee, emphasizing the Churches' responsibility toward his organization, declared in April 1942 that "the ACCR was created by the Churches and is the instrument of the Churches. Its life and future rest with the Churches".[64] Indeed, the ACCR tried time and again through conferences and appeals to enlist the pastors' cooperation for both moral and financial support of the refugees. However, all these arrangements and projects failed to bring adequate results. Notwithstanding five years of activity, the ACCR was unable to penetrate Church circles effectively. On January 18, 1939 it requested the FCC "to suggest a method by which the cooperation of Church federations and local Church associations could be best secured".[65] After some deliberations the Committee on Foreign Relief Appeals in the Churches was formed in November 1939. The new body had three main functions: to provide information in regard to the nature and direction of foreign relief, to coordinate existing appeals and to plan united action in the future and, finally, to allocate the funds. Dr. John R. Mott of the FCC was nominated as chairman and Leslie B. Moss, of the International Missions Council, became its executive secretary and the moving spirit of the Committee. The contributions were allocated among eight religious agencies. The ACCR and the AFSC

63 The NRS in 1940 alone resettled 5113 Jewish refugees, Lyman C. White, *300,000 New Americans*, p. 397.

64 Robinson to Leslie B. Moss, April 29, 1942 (Moss papers, Box 143, FCC).

65 Minutes of the Executive Committee of the ACCR, January 20, 1939 (FCC, Box 21).

were not the main beneficiaries, each receiving only one-sixth of their budget.[66]

In addition to the problem of coordination among the agencies, the Committee on Foreign Relief Appeals in the Churches confronted the more difficult task of opening Christian hearts and purses. J.R. Mott complained in September 1942 that "the Church is still slow to support the undertaking in any genuinely Christian measure". Leslie Moss rhetorically asked: "Do Christians Really Care?". To deepen the involvement in the refugee matter, a literary campaign was launched in 1942.[67]

The funds allocated by the Foreign Relief Appeals, although helpful, constituted only a small portion of the agencies' budget. Thus, an organization that had been formed by the FCC and was maintained by Church interests was unable to collect more than one-sixth of its budget from these sources.[68]

66 Minutes of the Executive Committee of the FCC, June 7, 1939, October 6, 1939 (FCC, Box 21); Roswell P. Barnes to Otto A. Piper, August 13, 1940 (FCC, Box 11); Confidential Minutes of the Advisory Committee of the Committee on Foreign Relief Appeals in the Churches, April 18, 1941 (Moss papers, Box 143, FCC). Although these eight agencies were the major beneficiaries, twenty-two relief organizations were eventually associated with the Committee on Foreign Relief Appeals in the Churches. See Committee on Foreign Appeals, Annual Report of the FCC, October 23, 1942 (Moss papers, Box 143, FCC).

67 Leslie B. Moss to the Representative of Denominational Committees on Relief, September 9, 1940; "Notes from a Conference on Relief, called by the Committee on Foreign Relief Appeals in the Churches, October 3–4, 1940, p. 15 (Moss papers, Box 144, FCC); LRR (Leland Rex Robinson), "Note of Agreement Reached on Distribution of Overseas Refugee Work", August 25, 1942; Summary Report of the Consultation on the Relief Work of the Churches", September 10–11, 1942 (AFSC:GC, 1942, C&O); L. B. Moss, "Do Christians Really Care?" December, 1943 (3 pp. ms.) (Moss papers, Box 143, FCC).

68 *Newcast*, 1 (March 1941), 5; 4 (Feb.—March 1943), 1; Report of the ACCR to Committee on Foreign Relief Appeals in the Churches, May 1 — October 31, 1940, November 16, 1940 (Moss papers, Box 143, FCC). See below, pp. 122—123.

In spite of the stated reservations, the Committee on Foreign Relief Appeals in the Churches served Christian agencies as an important instrument for the collection of money from Protestant churches. It was the first centralized effort to achieve a considerable success in mobilizing the Protestant denominations on behalf of refugees. With the reorganization of this body in 1943, it expanded its work for the refugees. With the increase of the Churches' part in the ACCR's budget (for 1944, $140,000 was the amount of the denominations' contribution), closer association with the Church Committee for Overseas Relief and Reconstruction (CCORR) was needed. For that purpose even the name of the agency was changed, in 1944, from "American Committee for Christian Refugees" to "American Christian Committee for Refugees", "to emphasize the fact that this is a committee with close relationships with the churches of America and acts as their agent in caring for refugees".[69]

ACCR's close ties with the Churches continued even after CCORR ceased its support. After World War II the Committee was still led by FCC officers and the "spirit of cooperation with church bodies is as constant as from the beginning", reported *Newscast* in 1945. One may conclude that in spite of enjoying only partial support of the Churches in its operations, the ACCR may be characterized as having acted as an arm of the Church for the purpose of refugee relief administration.[70]

Having examined the ACCR's relationship with the Protestant Churches in general and with the Federal Council of Churches in particular, we shall now pass to the second stage of the Com-

---

69   Minutes of the Meeting of the Executive Committee of the ACCR, July 6, 1943; Minutes of the Board of Directors of the ACCR, October 19, 1943 (FCC, Box 3); *Newscast*, 4 (Feb.—March 1943), 3; Memorandum by the ACCR, October 2, 1944 (FDRL, the papers of the War Refugee Board, Box 1).
70   *Newscast*, 4 (Nov.—Dec. 1945), 4; ACCR, "The Church and the Refugee" (NRS papers, folder 1316, YIVO).

mittee's activities in 1939—1942. The *Anschluss* and the Nazi occupation of Central and Western Europe multiplied the problems and sufferings of the refugees. Thousands who had fled from Germany to its neighboring countries now looked for new temporary havens, thus adding to the pressure of immigrants. The German authorities were interested in getting rid of their non-Aryan population, and as late as March 1940 the Nazis still sought their emigration. "They are even continuously pressing on the Jewish and Christian relief organizations to increase the number of those that they can help to leave", reported A. Freudenberg of the World Council of Churches from Geneva.[71]

The rise in the number of refugees led the ACCR to a significant expansion of its activities. In 1940 the agency offered services to 9047 individuals, an increase of 81% over the number helped in 1939. Learning from the experience of the National Refugee Service, the ACCR divided its operations into several departments. In 1940, the busiest year of the agency, it provided services through a number of departments. The Migration Department carried on correspondence in America and abroad with refugees of twenty nationalities. It received frantic appeals from separated families. The Casework Department helped refugees to plan their lives. In a single month, October 1940, the department handled 2148 cases. The Resettlement Department, which explored and organized resettlement possibilities, was particularly active in 1940. Its workers made field trips, interviewing refugees as well as community leaders. One of the most useful services of the ACCR was provided through its Vocational Department, namely, in retraining and job location. In 1940, 678 people received advice and vocational guidance; 256 individuals gained employment through the department and 127 refugees were retrained.[72]

---

71 "Report on Germany", by A. Freudenberg, March, 1940 (FCC, Box 11).
72 ACCR, "Report of the Executive Director"; ACCR, *Our Story for 1940* (1940), pp. 1 ,7; Mimeographed Report of the ACCR, January

To make the service more efficient and in order to carry the activities into the communities, the Committee established local committees in a dozen cities all over the country. However, only three branches actually operated: The New England Division in Cambridge, Mass., the Mid-West Division in Chicago, and the Los Angeles branch on the West Coast. These offices were poorly managed. Sometimes the whole branch was operated by a single part-time employee. In May 1940 the most successful branch, that of New England, still reported grave difficulties. "We are where the Jewish people were in 1935", complained Katherine W. Sellers. In 1941, with the ACCR's growing financial troubles, the Chicago office was closed and the New England branch's operations were drastically reduced. Thus, except for 1940, the ACCR failed to activate local offices and operated almost solely from its New York headquarters.[73]

The increase of services was made possible by a proportional growth in the Committee's income. The budget for 1940 was the biggest since the agency's foundation, amounting to $226,214, an 11% increase over the previous year.[74] As to the sources of the Committee's income, the most obvious one, the Churches, contributed only 15.7% of the budget. "It is amazing how small a proportion of the total work of this Committee has been provided by

1 — May 1, 1940 (FCC, Box 11); "Statistical Report of the ACCR for the Month of October, 1940" (Moss papers, Box 143, FCC). See below Table II.

73   "Local Committees at Work", *Newscast*, 4 (April—May 1943), 3, 5; ACCR, *Our Story for 1940*, pp. 10 — 11; Katherine Sellers to Mrs. Coffin, May 12, 1940 (FCC, Box 11); *Newscast*, 1 (April 1941), 1—2.

74   Between September 1935 and June 1940 the total income was $521,014, of which the operating expenses amounted to $169,672. This high rate of overheads, one-third of the income, indicated incompetent management of the ACCR. ACCR, "Condensed Statement of Operations, September 1935 — June 1940", in Karl J. Wiener to the ACCR, August 1, 1940, Exhibit B (NRS papers, 1319, YIVO); ACCR, Statement of Operations, January 1 — December 31, 1940, Exhibit B (Moss papers, Box 142, FCC).

the Churches", commented Leslie B. Moss, who was in charge of the Church appeal.[75] Among the methods used to raise money were specific appeals to schools, general mail appeals, art auctions and banquets, but with poor results. Thus, in May 1940 the Committee found itself in a desperate situation. Efforts to stimulate the interest and support of well-to-do Americans "did not prove very successful", as the executive director admitted. Some help came from the American Federation of Labor, which contributed $30,000 in 1940 and called on its members to support the ACCR.[76]

The United Jewish Appeal (UJA) came to the rescue of the ACCR at this critical moment, donating the sum of $125,000 to the Protestant Churches, "as an acknowledgment on our part of the sympathy and support of the leaders of the Protestant Churches for all victims of religious and racial persecution".[77] George A. Buttrick, president of the FCC, considered the contribution "a clear token of goodwill". Samuel Cavert was equally enthusiastic: "In my entire experience in connection with the FCC for a period of two decades, nothing has happened which has moved me more deeply than your action". He saw the UJA donation as "the high point in the spirit of cooperative understanding and goodwill". The gift came at a time when "we would have just been on the rocks or we would have had to cut down a large part of our work", remarked James M. Speers, the Committee's president.[78]

75 ACCR, *Our Story for 1940*, p. 17; L. B. Moss to Denominational Committee Chairmen, December 31, 1940 (Moss papers, Box 143, FCC).

76 John Caccio to Cavert and E. G. Wilson, November 29, 1940 (FCC, Box 11); ACCR, *Our Story for 1940*, pp. 2, 4, 17; Minutes of the ACCR Meeting, May 3, 1940 (FCC, Box 11); *Newscast*, 1 (April 1941, 1.

77 Abba Hillel Silver and Jonah B. Wise to George A. Buttrick, December 26, 1939 (FCC, Box 142).

78 Buttrick to Silver and Wise, December 28, 1939; Cavert to Wise, January 19, 1940 (FCC, Box 142); James M. Speers to G. S. Bilheimer, May 4, 1940 (FCC, Box 11).

It soon became evident that even that large sum was not enough to save the Committee from serious difficulties. While in 1940 there was less income than in 1939, the expenses were much higher. In October the Board of Directors decided to cut the staff's salary by 10—15% and $ 2000 off the monthly expenses. On October 28 the treasurer reported that "the entire resources of the Committee had been either spent or balanced by unpaid bills and unmet obligations".[79] Despite desperate appeals sent to private and church foundations, the situation continued to deteriorate. In November it was described as "a continuing state of extreme urgency". Once again the JDC came to the American Committee's help. An emergency request for a $ 10,000 loan was made to the JDC "with the understanding that it will be repaid as soon as possible, but with no guarantee". The Jewish organization immediately responded, approving a loan of $ 5000.[80]

The financial difficulties were, however, only symptomatic of other problems that the Committee faced. Intrigues and personal quarrels caused frequent changes in the personnel. Unlike the stability of the staff of the Catholic Committee for Refugees, the ACCR witnessed a parade of individuals who influenced the agency at one time or another. Among them there were Robert A. Ashworth, Frank Ritchie, William Z. Fuller, K. Brent Woodruff, Evelyn W. Hersey, Parkes Cadman and L. Rex Robinson. Even friendly circles saw fit to criticize the Committee's inefficiency. Bishop Welch, chairman of the Methodist Committee for Overseas Relief, complained that clients whom he had referred to the agency did not receive proper treatment. Furthermore, the ACCR's high overhead expenses made its presentation to his own Committee and to other groups "more difficult".[81] The Quakers

---

79   Minutes of the Board of Directors of the ACCR, October 9, 1940;
      Minutes of the ACCR, October 28, 1940 (FCC, Box 11).
80   Minutes of the Board of Directors of the ACCR, November 12, 26,
      1940 (FCC, Box 11).
81   Bishop Herbert Welch to Henry Israel, December 19, 1940 (FCC,
      Box 11).

were more critical. The Refugee Committee of the AFSC decided on February 19, 1939 to have "a frank conference" with key members of the ACCR, in order to discuss "any reorganization or change of personnel that may be necessary". The Quakers wondered whether the constituency of the American Committee could be converted "from a paper organization into a reality".[82] The same diagnosis was made by K. Brunt Woodruff, the incoming executive director, who confided to Cavert that "we are faced with more problems than just the financial one I have mentioned; they concern policy, function and organization".[83]

In the light of that criticism a Committee on Organization was established in November 1940, which promptly recommended drastic action in several areas, as follows: reduction of the staff by dismissals, the curtailment of branches, strengthening cooperation with other relief agencies, the reduction of the Service Division's operations and the transfer of the care of certain cases to other organizations.[84] With the adoption of the report of the Board of Directors, the staff of the Committee was reduced by 36% and the annual budget by 42%. The Chicago branch was closed and a month later the Cambridge office's operations were substantially reduced.[85]

The reduction of the Committee's staff and budget inevitably curtailed its services, such as resettlement, at a time when there was a growing cry for help. About 8000 refugees, among them 3000 non-Jews, were waiting in Lisbon for transportation. In un-Occupied France many refugees were interned. Even in the United States, there were 300 refugees with temporary visas, waiting for

---

82   Minutes of the Refugee Committee, AFSC, February 19, 1939 (AFSC, MF).

83   K. Brent Woodruff to Cavert, September 10, 1940 (FCC, Box 11).

84   Report of the Committee on Organization of the ACCR, November 26, 1940; Minutes of the Board of Directors of the ACCR, November 12, 26, 1940 (FCC, Box 11).

85   ACCR, *Our Story for 1940*, pp. 1, 9; Audit for January 1 — June 30, 1941 (Moss papers, FCC, Box 143); K. B. Woodruff to L. B. Moss, May 7, 1941 (Moss papers, Box 145, FCC). See above, p. 122.

help to emigrate to Cuba or Canada. It was indeed a real challenge for the ACCR to overcome its difficulties and to provide the maximum help. The record of 1941 justified expectations.[86]

We have seen how the ACCR struggled with internal and financial difficulties during the crucial period for immigration, between May 1940 and May 1941. The entry of the United States into the war, as we have seen, aroused strong anti-alien feelings. In certain places, for instance in New York, the anti-refugee prejudice led to the dismissal of newcomers and a semi-boycott of refugee enterprises. In December 1941 Mayor La Guardia, of New York, made a call in the name of the Justice Department "to prevent hysteria" and "unlawful treatment" of refugees. The refugees were also charged with shirking military service.[87]

The care of a certain Burgess family illustrates the situation. Burgess was an author who left Germany in 1939 and settled in a small community in the United States, where he opened a souvenir shop. The items for sale were made by members of his family. Because of the anti-German atmosphere he was forced to close his shop. Through the help of the ACCR he was given a job in another community, but was again dismissed. After pressure from the local committee of the ACCR, an inquiry was made into the circumstances of his dismissal, which cleared him of the charge of disloyalty to America.[88]

This hostile atmosphere created hardships for many refugees, who only in the last resort turned to the ACCR for help. First they tried to find their own way, accepting any job offered. The impediments of language and skill, intensified by the prevailing xenophobia, forced them to seek welfare aid, advice and vocational guidance. The Committee now faced "the second generation problems". In spite of falling immigration, the agency was flooded with

86 "Facts and Figures from 1941 Annual Report of ACCR", *Newscast*, 2 (Feb. 1942), 3. See below, Table III.
87 *Newscast*, 4 (Feb.—March 1943), 4; (April—May 1943), 2; 2 (Jan. 1942), 1—3; (May 1942), 3. See above, pp. 82—83.
88 *Ibid.*, 5 (May—June 1944), 2.

calls for help. In the first half of 1942 it distributed 82.5% more relief than during the same period in 1941. There was also a 52% increase in the candidates for vocational guidance.[89] The financial situation was also affected by the shift of attention to the war problems. The budget for 1942 was 11% smaller than that for the previous year. In April 1942 the energetic new president, L. R. Robinson, made an urgent appeal to the churches not to allow his agency "to wither away and perish because of the pressure of other events".[90]

To face the problems of the war situation, the Committee made an effort to transfer part of its burden and responsibility to local communities and other relief agencies.[91] Thus, lack of funds, inefficiency, and the desire to share the expertise of others led to the call for closer cooperation with relief agencies. As regards the policy and practical attitude of the ACCR in the matter of sharing responsibility and functions with other organizations, it may be said that the American Committee, unlike the Catholic Committee for Refugees, cooperated wholeheartedly from the outset with Jewish, Quaker and other agencies. From its foundation the ACCR became an affiliated agency of the National Coordinating Committee and its successor, the National Refugee Service, which were the biggest and best organized refugee organizations in the country, providing a wide spectrum of services for refugees.[92] The Ameri-

89 Ibid., 4 (Feb.—March 1943), 1; 2 (March 1942), 1; K. B. Woodruff, "Statement before the Committee on Foreign Relief Appeals in the Churches", June 15, 1942 (Moss papers, Box 143, FCC).

90 ACCR, "A Statement for the National Committee, Supporting Groups and Cooperating Agencies", April 1, 1943 (NRS papers, folder 1316, YIVO); L. R. Robinson to L. B. Moss, April 29, 1942 (Moss papers, Box 143, FCC).

91 ACCR, "Excerpt from the Report of the Survey Committee, with additional comments by K. B. Woodruff", May 29, 1942 (Moss papers, Box 143, FCC).

92 Although the NCC and the NRS were basically Jewish organizations, they never refused help for needy non-Jewish refugees. Minutes, Meeting of the ACCR, June 11, 1936 (FCC, Box 102). See below, pp. 286—301.

can Committee shared offices with the NCC, which saved money
and increased efficiency. When the ACCR suffered financial difficulties, in 1940—1941, it not only referred its clients to the services
of the NRS, but received thousands of dollars from the Hebrew
Loan Society as well.[93] Unlike its close cooperation with Jewish
organizations, there were no practical relations between ACCR and
the Catholic Committee for Refugees. Mutual dislike and suspicion
between the two Christian faiths prevented their effective cooperation.[94]

Because of its limited resources, the ACCR encouraged Protestant denominations to establish national refugee committees. These
efforts enjoyed very limited success. The Lutherans were a case in
point. The National Lutheran Council assumed responsibility for
its co-religionists by founding the Lutheran Refugee Service, with
C.E. Krumbholz as director. In 1939—1940 the Service secured
jobs for 447 refugees, referred 768 persons to pastors "for spiritual care", provided two scholarships and transferred the names
of 1376 needy refugees to local churches. It also printed three
pamphlets propagating the refugee cause. Considering the fact
that in 1939—1940 Lutherans constituted approximately 58% of
the Protestant refugees, it would seem that the performance record
of the Lutheran Refugee Service was rather poor. The strong
anti-Semitic feelings in Lutheran circles probably accounted, in
part at least, for a resentment against even non-Jewish refugees.[95]

93   Karl J. Wiener to the ACCR, August 1, 1940, Exhibit 1 (NRS papers,
     folder 1319, YIVO); William Haber to Evelyn Hersey, September 20,
     1939; Cavert to Haber, July 19, 1940 (FCC, Box 11); RRT, Informal
     Conference of Representatives of Agencies in the Refugee Field,
     June 24, 1943 (Chamberlain papers, p. 2851, YIVO).

94   Minutes of the Executive Committee of the FCC, May 18, 1943
     (FCC, Box 23); "Resolution Adopted by the Executive Committee of
     the FCC", January 26, 1940 (FCC, Box 11); Roosevelt to Buttrick,
     March 14, 1940 (FDRL, PF, 1628).

95   Lutheran Refugee Service, "Refugees Are People Like Us", n.d.;
     "Who Says I Am an Enemy Alien?" n.d.; "What About Refugees",
     n.d. (NRS papers, 1318, YIVO).

The Episcopal Church also established a Committee for European Refugees, which was formed in 1938 and began to operate
toward the end of 1939, under the chairmanship of Bishop Paul
Jones, with Almon R. Pepper as executive secretary. the Episcopal Committee undertook the tasks of education and propaganda
among church members, and cooperation with other agencies,
particularly with the ACCR and AFSC. Between December 1, 1939
and October 1, 1940 the Episcopal Committee secured 45 affidavits,
provided 40 refugees with transportation expenses of $375 each,
granted 8 scholarships, put 26 students into its church summer
camps and provided weekend hospitality for 300 individuals. Although the Committee was not engaged in fund raising campaigns,
it did collect the sum of $6855 during that period. As to resettle-
ment, the Episcopal Committee guided local church members in
ways of helping newcomers. The project of activating local parish
refugee committees bore some fruit. In 1940 the Episcopal Committee helped in the resettlement of refugees in Pittsburg, Utica,
Los Angeles, Seattle, Houston, Flint, Louisville, Cincinnati and
Portsmouth.[96] In May 1940 Anne E. Caldwell, secretary of the
Women's Cooperation Commission, who was involved in the resettlement program, praised the Episcopal Committee for "doing
the best piece of refugee work being done by any of the denominations". The ACCR was of the same opinion.[97] There is unfortunately no further record of the Episcopal Committee's activities.

Understanding and cooperation marked the relationship between

96 "Activity Report of the Episcopal Committee for European Refugees,
    December 1, 1939—October 1, 1940" (FCC, Box 150). The Episcopal
    Committee for German Refugees, n.d., pp. 5—6; *The Emigrés Among
    Us*, n.d., pp. 3, 5—6; The Episcopal Committee, *Resettlement, A
    Program for Parish Communities*, n.d. (NRS papers, 1318, YIVO);
    Activity Report of the Episcopal Committee, 1940 (FCC, Box 150).
97 Anne E. Caldwell to Lester M. Stearns, May 20, 1940; "The Epis-
    copal Church has been most successful not only in placing refugees,
    but in setting up a central committee" (FCC, Box 150); Report of
    the ACCR, January 1 — May 1, 1940 (FCC, Box 11).

the American Friends Service Committee and the ACCR. Friction
and competition were not entirely absent, however. Relations between the ACCR and its sister agencies were more problematic
than those with Jewish organizations, because these Christian agencies drew on the same financial resources, appealed to the same
Protestant communities and tried to help the same category of
refugees. Accordingly, complaints of confusion and overlapping,
and repeated cries for a better division of functions were heard.
When the two agencies, as members of the Committee on Foreign
Relief Appeals to the Churches, turned to the denominations for
funds, a "clear-cut understanding" was the order of the day. As
L.R. Robinson of ACCR stated to Read C. Cary of AFSC: "... it
behoves us to work out a mutually satisfactory plan giving assurance of efficiency and complete agreement".[98] Accordingly, the
ACCR was entrusted with primary responsibility for work with
individual refugees in the United States and for immigration services handled from America, whilst the AFSC's principal function
was to be overseas relief work.[99]

There was, in fact, nothing new in this division of functions. Ever
since 1935 the AFSC had served as the ACCR's representative in
the distribution of funds in European and Latin American countries. Moreover, when the American Committee expanded its
activities from the domestic to the foreign scene, the Quakers were
not happy. "I am still convinced", maintained one Quaker to another, "the only orderly settlement is for the Christian Committee

98 In 1943 James Vail replaced Pickett, *Newscast*, 4 (Nov.—Dec. 1943), 2;
     ACCR, Service Department Report, December 1939—January 1940
     (NRS papers, 1319, YIVO); "The American Committee for Christian
     Refugees", by Kathleen Hanstein, March 6, 1941 (AFSC: GF, 1941);
     L. R. Robinson to Reed C. Cary, August 18, 1942 (AFSC: GF, 1942,
     C&O).
99 "Note of agreement reached on distribution of overseas refugee
     work as regards functions and funds, by the ACCR, AFSC and the
     Central Bureau for Relief of the Evangelical Churches of Europe,
     at a meeting on August 25, 1942, at the Town Hall Club" (AFSC:
     GF, 1942, C&O).

to retire from the field of foreign relief and develop the domestic field".[100] In spite of the above mentioned division of functions, ACCR funds were distributed by Unitarians in Spain and North Africa, much to the annoyance of the Quakers.[101] Such friction should not, however, be overstressed, for it never led to any severance of relations and, in fact, clarifications and compromises enabled a good atmosphere to prevail. One may conclude that the attitude of the ACCR toward other refugee organizations was positive and cooperative, which proved to be helpful to the relief agencies as well as to the refugees.

The war situation, the gradually increasing concern of the Administration with relief work, along with a marked decline in the number of appeals by immigrants to the committees, caused the operations and functioning of the ACCR to change drastically during the third stage of its existence, from 1943—1945. In 1943, a year which saw a 50% decrease in new cases, a new and powerful source came to the ACCR's aid, namely, the National War Fund (NWF), which had been formed by a Presidential order on December 15, 1942.[102] From August 1943 onwards the ACCR, like other relief agencies, no longer had serious financial problems. The NWF provided the lion's share of the Committee's budget, covering four-fifths of the total expenses in 1945. Thus, in 1944, the first full year of NWF's support, this body contributed $334,001 (and the CCORR $99,196). So, the target of raising $400,000, set in 1934, was realized only a decade later — and then only due to the generosity of the Roosevelt Administration.[103]

100 Report of the executive secretary of the ACCR for September 20—December 9, 1935, pp. 3—4; John Rich to James Vail, September 2, 1942. Rich added, "This is a *must* item". (AFSC: GF, 1935, 1942, C&O).

101 Rich to Pickett, December 11, 1942 (AFSC: GF, 1942, C&O).

102 Harold J. Seymour, *Design for Giving*, pp. 5—7, 71, 87; *Newscast*, 4 (April—May 1943), 2.

103 The Church Committee for Overseas Relief and Reconstruction contributed $99,196 in 1944. *Newscast*, 5 (Jan.—Feb. 1944), 4; 6 (Jan.—Feb. 1945), 2; ACCR, *Toward a New Life*, p. 4.

The termination of hostilities did not put an end to refugees and relief needs. Thousands of starving displaced persons were stranded on the European highways. Realizing the appalling need of these miserable victims of the war, the ACCR became "increasingly eager to take a more active part in the solution of those global problems".[104] This shift of emphasis from the U.S. to the European scene was made when the volume of work in America markedly declined. A foreign program was developed, based on concrete reconstruction projects, which would be conducted by ACCR personnel. The Committee planned to focus attention on vocational guidance, hoping to ease the employment demands in Europe. Another problem, closely related to the first one, vexed the members of the Committee: "whether or not the ACCR should continue as a church affiliated agency". A Committee on Relations with the Churches was nominated to investigate the issue, which recommended that "the newly formed World Council Service Commission should undertake the church related work supported by the ACCR". Upon the adoption of that recommendation, the ACCR became, on June 1, 1945, a secular agency.[105]

Though the major shift of interest to Europe greatly diminished the Committee's activities at home, it continued to take care of Protestant refugees when this was necessary. Among the services provided in America between 1945—1947 there were the corporate affidavits, which as late as February 1947 enabled 437 displaced persons to reach American shores. Noteworthy was the Committee's protest against a bill before Congress to cut immigration by 50% during the ten-year period commencing 1945. The Committee recorded "a strong conviction that no steps of this kind should be taken". Open opposition to anti-immigration legislation, which was accompanied by a request to testify at the hearings, was a marked change in the Protestant attitude from the earlier refusal

---

104   *Newscast*, 6 (May—June 1945), 1—2; 5 (March—April 1944), 4; 6
        (Nov.—Dec. 1945), 2.
105   *Ibid.*, 6 (May—June 1945), 1—2.

to voice criticism on that matter during the Nazi era. Despite such domestic activities it is clear that after 1945 the ACCR concentrated on overseas operations. The official bulletin, *Newscast*, reflected that situation, concentrating on reports from the European theater and almost disregarding the American scene. It seems proper, therefore, to examine in some detail the ACCR's foreign activities.[106]

One of the basic factors in the establishment of the ACCR in 1934 was the desire to alleviate the distress of Christian refugees in Europe, by providing means for immediate relief and for resettlement projects. It took two years until the Committee was able to send its first contribution abroad. Through local and international refugee committees the ACCR systematically began to transfer funds to Holland, Switzerland, France, Austria, Spain and Portugal. In 1940 the ACCR considerably expanded the allocation of funds to European refugees through the Friends, the Unitarians, the JDC, the YWCA and the World Council of Churches.[107]

Altogether, between 1934—1945 the ACCR expended on relief work outside the United States the sum of $ 353,054, which constituted 42% of the total relief expenses.[108] After the war attention was fully devoted to liberated Europe. In September 1945 the Paris office was opened. Four staff members who had joined the UNRRA now returned to the Committee and operated from the Paris office. The Committee planned to expand its activities all over Europe, intending to establish branches in Switzerland and in Germany. The services were aimed at supplementing the mass aid rendered by UNRRA, with individual care and a "personal touch".

106 Annual Meeting, Board of Directors of the ACCR, January 28, 1946; Meeting of the Board of Directors of the ACCR, February 19, 1947 (Chamberlain papers, pp. 2884, 2926, YIVO); L. R. Robinson to John Lesinsky, February 26, 1946 (Chamberlain papers, p. 2886, YIVO).
107 Frank Ritchie, Interim Report of the ACCR, January 2, 1936 (AFSC: GF, 1936); Minutes of the Executive Committee of the ACCR, May 3, November 1, 1937 (FCC, Box 194); Evelyn W. Hersey to Mary Rogers, March 15, 1940 (AFSC: GF, 1940; FR: RS).
108 ACCR, *Toward a New Life*.

Evidently the operations were drastically reduced in 1946. The
ambitious plan of covering Europe with a network of offices never
materialized. Up to October 15, 1946, 600 refugees turned to the
headquarters for help, of whom 407 were secured affidavits.[109] In
September 1946, with the termination of the NWF's support, financial difficulties reminiscent of the ACCR's early days reappeared.
Because of the National War Fund's aid, the ACCR had broken
its ties with the church committees. Meanwhile a Church World
Service (CWS) had been developed, which filled the vacuum left
in Church circles by the American Committee. Now the Committee
was entirely stripped of its sources of income. The last issue of
Newscast, dated March–April 1947, urgently pleaded for financial
help. The Rev. Dr. Harry Emerson Fosdick appealed to his co-
religionists "to overcome the stubborn misunderstanding of millions
of American Protestants, who suppose that the problem of 'Dispossessed Persons' in Europe is exclusively Jewish". The responsibility for these Christian victims of Nazism "rests squarely upon
us", wrote Fosdick.[110] In 1947 he still found need to sound his
plea of 1934—1935 for Christian support. He repeated almost
verbatim his criticism of Christian apathy. It seems to have been
one of the major failures of the ACCR, that after thirteen years
of activity in Protestant circles, there was no basic change in the
response of the Christian community to the refugee issue.

Due to its desperate position the Committee had to turn to the
denominations for help, in spite of its promise not to do so. In an
agreement with the Church World Service, it was decided to divide
the sphere of activities so that the CWS would work with the
Churches and the ACCR would appeal to the secular community.
A.L. Warnshuis, vice-president of the former, complained of the
ACCR's intrusion and wrote to L.R. Robinson as follows: "speaking quite frankly to you it seems to me that all of the circumstances

109 *Ibid.*, p. 36; *Newscast*, 6 (Nov.—Dec. 1945), 2.
110 Minutes, Meeting of the Board of Directors of the ACCR, November
     20, 1946 (Chamberlain papers, p. 2901, YIVO); *Newscast*, 8 (March—
     April 1947), 1.

as they exist today, and all of the logic of this whole problem, combine to emphasize the urgency of our taking immediate steps to unite these two bodies related to the Protestant work for displaced persons. Just as the Roman Catholics and the Jews have one agency through which they can work, so the Protestant churches ought to have one agency".[111]

The Board of Directors of the ACCR responded positively to the CWS call for a merger and decided on April 16, 1947 "to lodge immediately in one organization all activities" of the two bodies. The new agency would be built on the existing foundations, with insistence on its "autonomous, but definitely church-related" character.[112] This desire for autonomous status wrecked the negotiations, because the CWS was prepared only "to enlarge and reorganize" its Committee on Displaced Persons, without giving up any control of the organization. Since the ACCR preferred liquidation to such a merger, the Board of Directors decided on May 8, 1947 "to proceed to liquidate the ACCR as a corporate entity at the earliest feasible time".[113]

Thus, the American Committee for Christian Refugees was liquidated in July 1947, when its 61 staff members were dismissed. In all, from the time the war ended, the Committee brought 800 persons to the United States and placed them in 65 communities.[114]

111   A. L. Warnshuis to L. R. Robinson, February 27, 1947 (Chamberlain papers, pp. 2954—2955, YIVO).
112   Minutes of the meeting of the Board of Directors of the ACCR, April 16, 1947 (Chamberlain papers, p. 2956, YIVO).
113   Minutes of the Emergency Meeting of the Board of Directors of the ACCR, May 5, 1947 — Annex — "Statement Presented to Temporary Committee in Explanation of Differences in View of Preventing Agreement", by L. R. Robinson (Chamberlain papers, pp. 2975—2977, YIVO); Minutes, Emergency Meeting of the Board of Directors of the ACCR, May 8, 1947 (Chamberlain papers, pp. 2970—2972, YIVO).
114   Minutes of the meeting of the Board of Directors of the ACCR, June 18, 1947 (Chamberlain papers, pp. 2980—2982, YIVO); Minutes of the first meeting of the Temporary Committee, April 27, 1947 (*ibid.*, p. 2965).

These figures show that after 1945 there was no real justification for the existence of the Committee. When the generous support of the National War Fund was abruptly stopped, that fact became evident to the leaders of the Committee as well.

We have reviewed the activities of the ACCR during the 13 years of its existence. To 18,000 individuals of 42 countries it gave advice, granted affidavits, secured jobs, settled newcomers in communities, offered vocational training and sent funds abroad to help Christian refugees there.[115] The moral support given to the refugees was sometimes as important as the practical and financial aid. As one beneficiary, an Italian scholar, wrote to the Committee: "it seems to me that I would belittle the best part of your work if I had not told you that your advice and liberal understanding had a great deal of influence in securing my good start and also directing me towards a sound acquisition of the American spirit".[116] Indeed, in spite of its shortcomings, the ACCR emerged as the American nation's greatest Christian relief agency, which dedicated its services to a stream of refugees who were generally left to their own devices. If it failed to achieve more, it was more the fault of the American Christian community at large.

115   See below, Table IV: ACCR, *Toward a New Life*, pp. 5—6.
116   *Ibid.*, p. 23.

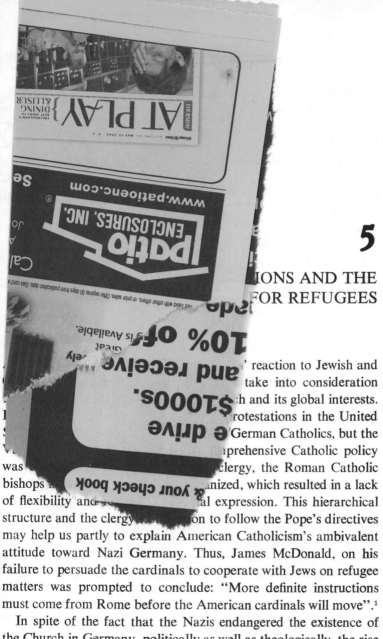

5

IONS AND THE
FOR REFUGEES

' reaction to Jewish and
take into consideration
h and its global interests.
rotestations in the United
German Catholics, but the
prehensive Catholic policy
clergy, the Roman Catholic
bishops ... nized, which resulted in a lack
of flexibility and ... al expression. This hierarchical
structure and the clergy ... on to follow the Pope's directives
may help us partly to explain American Catholicism's ambivalent
attitude toward Nazi Germany. Thus, James McDonald, on his
failure to persuade the cardinals to cooperate with Jews on refugee
matters was prompted to conclude: "More definite instructions
must come from Rome before the American cardinals will move".[1]

In spite of the fact that the Nazis endangered the existence of
the Church in Germany, politically as well as theologically, the rise

1 James McDonald to Norman Bentwich, January 11, 1935 (MP:H).

of Hitler was hailed by conservative Catholic circles in America. *Tablet*, for example, the organ of the Brooklyn diocese, called for establishing relations with Germany, from which, it was claimed, both sides would benefit. Even after the political power of the Catholics had been crushed and many priests arrested, many American Catholics were still reluctant to acknowledge such facts, dismissing them as "horror stories".[2] The editors of the influential Catholic weekly, *Commonweal*, complained that after four years of Catholic suppression in Germany there was "a prevalent lack of Catholic interest in the whole Nazi situation".[3]

One of the explanations given for the apathy displayed by American Catholics to the fate of their co-religionists was the fact of Hitler's sophisticated and relatively bloodless assault on the Catholics in Germany, which left no impression of fear or urgency on the American people. A headline of *America*, the organ of the Jesuits, proclaimed in 1938: "The Nazi Persecutors Break No Bones, Shed No Blood". "This bloodless warfare", remarked a Catholic visitor in Germany, "is shrouded in silence". George N. Shuster of *Commonweal*, one of the most outspoken anti-Nazi Catholics in America, exposed Nazi anti-Catholic aims as early as June 1934, but failed to shake his readers' apathy.[4] A pretext for the silence of the American Catholics was the fear that criticism might worsen the position of the Church in Germany. This fear was strengthened by a direct appeal from the German hierarchy to limit the accusations of the American Catholics against Nazi Germany.[5]

2 *Tablet* (July 22, 1933), p. 7.

3 "Anent the Olympics," *Commonweal* (July 17, 1936), p. 296.

4 *America* (October 15, 1938), p. 30; Marieli G. Benziger, "The Nazi Dictators Steal Faith from Germans", *America* (March 26, 1938), pp. 580—581; George N. Shuster, "Catholics in Germany", *Commonweal* (June 29, 1934), p. 234.

5 "Notations from the Sub-committee of the Most Rev. Archbishop Rummel, Archbishop Stritch and Bishop Noll: From the Oral Conference of the Most Rev. Archbishop Rummel with the Represen-

There were certainly voices of Catholic protest from the very beginning from such leaders as Governor Al Smith, George Shuster and Michael Williams, editors of the liberal *Commonweal*, and John LaFarge, editor of *America*. However, these were isolated efforts, not involving the rank and file Catholics. "There is no general knowledge of that persecution, no general understanding, no general determination to help the victims", lamented Williams in 1937.[6] Only Pius XI's encyclical, of March 1937, persuaded the Catholic hierarchy to direct attention to the German scene. Thereafter, in 1938, the "News Service" of the National Catholic Welfare Conference and the annual reports of the Catholic Committee for Refugees began to publish detailed reports of the opposition of Catholics in Germany.[7]

The muted Catholic response to the situation in Germany stood in marked contrast to the outcry against the persecution of Catholics in Mexico and Spain. With the change of the government in Mexico in 1934, the power of the Catholic clergy was curtailed, religious schools were closed and priests attacked. The legislature of the State of Aguascalientes expelled most of its priests, closed the churches and a school was attacked. In response, the American Catholic bishops issued a strong protest against the "anti-Christian tyranny", and called on Americans "to do everything in their power by word and by act" to fight this regime. Bishop John F. Noll of Fort Wayne, Indiana, urged President Roosevelt to support

tative of German Bishops, Father Groesser", n.d. (*c*. November 1936) (NCWC archives, the papers of the Catholic Committee for Refugees, Box 6. Hereafter, CC papers NCWC archives).

6   Michael Williams, "Blood and Tears", *Commonweal* (July 2, 1937), p. 258.

7   *Report of the Committee for Catholic Refugees from Germany*, from October 1, 1937 to March 31, 1938, p. 2; CC, *Report*, January 1, 1937—September 30, 1938, pp. 2—4; *Fourth Annual Report*, January 1, 1937—September 30, 1939, pp. 5—8; NCWC, "News Service", July 9, August 29, 1938 (NCWC papers, Box 80, 82); Editorial, "Roman Catholic Bishops Define the Crisis of Christianity", *Christian Century*, 58 (December 3, 1941), p. 1493.

the rights of people "to religious liberty in belief and practice". Such a declaration, Bishop Noll believed, "would be a help to oppressed people throughout the world, especially in Russia, Mexico and Germany".[8] Although Noll mentioned religious oppression in Germany along with Russia and Mexico, the American bishops refused to join with Jewish and Protestant delegations in demanding of the State Department that it issue an official protest against Germany. Under Secretary of State William Phillips, noting the absence of Catholics from the joint delegation of July 26, 1935, observed to the President that "it may well be that they prefer to act through the Pope".[9]

James McDonald tried to persuade Jewish and Protestant leaders to cooperate with Catholics in issuing a joint protest against the situation in Mexico. "Is this not an occasion when Protestants and Catholics should stand together against tendencies which would undermine them both", asked McDonald. He urged Samuel Cavert of the FCC to enlist his agency's support for that cause. He also appealed to Felix M. Warburg and James N. Rosenberg of the JDC, explaining the "usefulness" of Jewish help in the Mexico case, which he felt might lead to a more favorable Catholic approach to the refugee issue. To Cardinal Hayes of New York he suggested "extremely interesting possibilities of effective cooperation".[10] The Protestants, however, were reluctant to support the Catholics. The Executive Committee of the Federal Council of Churches decided that "in the absence of sufficient authentic and unbiased information, we do not undertake at

8   *The New York Times*, November 1, 17, 1934; Bishop John F. Noll to President Roosevelt, May 13, 1935 (FDRL, Personal Presidential Files, Box 2); For other Catholic appeals in regard to Mexico see McIntyre to Roosevelt, May 27, 1935 (FDRL, OF, 28).

9   William Philips to Roosevelt, July 29, 1935, in Edgar B. Nixon (ed.), *Franklin D. Roosevelt and Foreign Affairs* (Cambridge, Mass., 1969), Vol. III, p. 591.

10 McDonald to Cavert, January 28, 1935; McDonald to Felix Warburg, January 25, 1935; McDonald to James Rosenberg, January 29, 1935; McDonald to Cardinal Hayes, January 29, 1935 (MP:GC).

this time to pass judgment on various aspects of the controversy between the Mexican Government and the Church". Accordingly, the FCC considered as "unwarranted" American intervention in Mexico's internal affairs.[11]

With the accession of the Republican regime in Spain, the Cortes brought the Church under governmental control and gradually restricted its influence. The position of the Church deteriorated during the Civil War, when Catholic priests were murdered. The failure of Protestants and Jews to side with American Catholics in their protest caused bitter feelings. An analogy between the persecution of Jews in Germany and the suppression of Catholics in Spain was only natural. The editor of *Sign*, the journal of the Passionist Fathers, complained that "when the windows of Jewish shops in Berlin were broken by the Nazis, our 'liberals' screamed their protests, held mass meetings... calling on the civilized world to act. When Spanish Catholics were murdered by the tens of thousands in cold blood, for no other reason than they were Catholics, our 'liberals' were silent".[12]

One may, however, view the situation from a different angle. When in March 1934 the High Commissioner for Refugees appealed to Michael J. Curley, Archbishop of Baltimore, to identify himself with the victims of Nazi persecutions, Jews as well as Christians, the Archbishop refused to take sides, writing: "I am not passing (judgment) upon the German situation, since it is rather difficult for any man to form a judgment three thousand miles away from the scene".[13] Yet, when the issue was Spain rather than Germany, American Catholics were quite capable of passing judgment on the situation.

11 Minutes of the Executive Committee of the FCC, March 1, April 26, 1935 (FCC, Box 19); see also Cavert to McDonald, February 8, 1935 (MP:CC).

12 Editorial, "Catholics in Spain", *The New York Times*, May 19, 1933; see Letters to the Editor, *ibid.*, May 23, 1933; *Sign*, 22 (April 1943), p. 543.

13 Michael J. Curley to McDonald, March 5, 1934 (MP:GC).

Such criticism of the Catholic establishment should nevertheless be voiced with reservation, since a comparison of the situation in Mexico, Russia or Spain to that in Germany would not be entirely accurate. One has to bear in mind that American Catholics had been protesting against the persecution of the Church in Mexico since the mid-1920s, and they could hardly have considered this open and bloody oppression in the same light as the Nazi policy toward the Christian Church. The difference between the American Catholic attitude toward the Communists and that toward the Nazis could to some extent also be explained on the basis that the former had a record of anti-Christian policy dating back to at least 1917, while the latter had been in power for only a few years. Thus, religious and political attitudes, rather than geographical distance, determined the reaction of the heads of both Churches.

If the Catholic press and the American hierarchy were reluctant to campaign for the sake of their own co-religionists in Germany, one should not be surprised to learn of their silence when the fate of European Jews was at stake. Most of the American Catholic press initially disregarded the rise of German anti-Semitism and the legal and physical harassment of Jews. Only after the publication of the encyclical *Mit Brennender Sorge*, on March 14, 1937, in which Pius XI denounced racial and religious intolerance in Germany, did the American Catholic press direct its attention to the German scene. Catholic organizations began to publish detailed reports about the oppression of German Catholics. D. Cardinal Dougherty, Archbishop of Philadelphia, appealed to President Roosevelt on behalf of the persecuted Jews, writing: "I beg you to please use the influence of your high office to safeguard their rights as far as it may be in your power".[14] On October 1, 1938 the American bishops attempted to launch a campaign

14   NCWC, "News Service", July 9, 1938 (NCWC papers, Box 80); D. Cardinal Dougherty to President Roosevelt, October 26, 1938 (FDRL, OF, 3186).

against anti-Semitism, because it was "un-Godly, uncharitable and un-Christian and against the natural and divine law".[15]

The denunciation of anti-Semitism was aimed not only against Germany, but directed internally as well. Manifestations of Catholic anti-Semitism were not a new phenomenon in the United States, but during the second half of the 1930s it gained a wide following and open support. The most influential anti-Semitic leader in America was the Catholic priest, Charles E. Coughlin of Royal Oak, Michigan. In his Sunday radio broadcasts he blamed the international Jewish-Communist forces for the Depression and un-employment in America. His anti-Semitic propaganda, which some-times followed Joseph Goebbels's speeches verbatim, reached millions of listeners, most of whom supported his views. Through his weekly organ, *Social Justice*, which had a circulation estimated at between 185,000 and 350,000, he further propagated his anti-Semitic approach. The Brooklyn *Tablet*, an avowed anti-Semitic organ, enthusiastically approved Coughlin's opinions and regularly printed the priest's radio speeches. As a result, the *Tablet*'s circulation increased considerably.[16]

Coughlin's oral and written diatribes served to galvanize anti-Semitic feelings in Catholic circles. Encouraged by the priest, Christian Front Organizations were established in several cities in America to fight the Popular Front of the Left, the Jews and the refugees. Irish Catholics of the lower middle class, who with the Depression had lost their economic security and with it their political status, turned to militant activities in the streets of Baltimore, New York and Philadelphia. Provoking street brawls, shout-ing anti-Jewish slogans and urging the public to buy only from Christian shops, the Christian Front movement represented the

15 NCWC, "News Service", October 7, 1938, p. 7 (NCWC papers, Box 80).

16 Wyman, *Paper Walls*, pp. 17—18; Charles J. Tull, *Father Coughlin and the New Deal* (Syracuse, 1965); *Tablet*, 31 (February 4, 1939), p. 1; 30 (December 3, 1938), p. 11; (December 10, 1938), p. 13; 31 (March 11, 1939), p. 1.

reactionary elements among American Catholics during the years 1938—1940.[17]

Catholic criticism of Father Coughlin, the Christian Front, or *Tablet* was sparse and uninfluential. Most journals either supported Coughlin or preferred silence. Protests by the *Catholic Labor Leader*, *Catholic Worker*, and *Commonweal* were exceptions rather than the rule. When the editors of *Commonweal* decided in December 1938, after considerable hesitation, to attack Coughlin's anti-Semitism, a heated debate was waged on the pages of that paper — with not a few siding with the priest. George N. Shuster bitterly complained in 1940 that those Catholic journalists and intellectuals who dared to support the victims of Nazism and to oppose Coughlin's broadcasts had been attacked by the reactionary forces. "There is no parallel in all our history for the rabid abuse they brought down on themselves", lamented Shuster.[18] A number of Church leaders and laymen, among them George Cardinal Mundelein of Chicago, John A. Ryan, director of NCWC and Cardinal O'Connell of Boston, publicly denounced the priest of Royal Oak. However, the significance of Coughlin's influence lay not only in his popularity and the wide support he had gained, but also in the failure of the Catholic Church, especially his own bishop, to silence him officially. The bishops' reluctance to attack him openly gave the impression that his opinions were in accordance with the official line.[19]

17 Edward McCarthy, "The Christian Front Movement in New York City, 1938—1940" (Unpublished Master's Thesis, Columbia University, 1965), pp. 1, 187; T. Irwin, "Inside the Christian Front", *Forum*, 103 (March 1940), pp. 102—107.

18 "Father Coughlin and the Jews", *Commonweal* (December 9, 1938), p. 169; (December 16, 1938), pp. 213—214; (December 30, 1938), pp. 268—270; (January 26, 1940), p. 293; *Time* (November 14, 1938), p. 37. See also the *Nation*'s call to investigate the promoters of anti-Semitism, *Nation*, 150 (January 6, 1940), p. 3; George N. Shuster, "The Conflict Among Catholics", *American Scholar*, 10 (Winter, 1940—1941), p. 11.

19 Wyman, *Paper Walls*, p. 19.

There were undoubtedly prominent Catholic Church leaders and institutions that unequivocally voiced their protest against Hitler's racial and anti-Semitic policy. Until 1937, however, these voices were sporadic and the outcome of individual initiative. After the Papal pronouncement such protest became the official line of the American Catholic hierarchy. Nevertheless, a certain gap existed between Church leaders and rank and file Catholics. As far as the refugee issue was concerned, this gap represents a notable exception in Catholic communal life. Anti-alien and anti-Semitic feelings were so strong that even Vatican directives were not complied with in local communities.

Apathy and even hostility characterized the Catholic attitude toward refugees. These sentiments were partly attributable to the Depression. With 13 million people out of work in 1933, there was no room for newcomers. "Hospitality to refugees doubtless has its place", editorialized the Jesuit *America*, "but at present we cannot take care of our own unemployment. Incidents of American citizens losing their jobs to find them filled promptly by refugees are of sufficient frequency to cause alarm".[20] Father Joseph D. Ostermann, a Catholic official in New York, was "completely disgusted" with the refusal of the Central Verein "to do anything that will involve any work or expense" in favor of the refugees. Catholic individuals and organizations failed not only to provide practical help, but even sympathy and support for Catholic refugees. In March 1936 *Commonweal* complained that "there is no organized Catholic assistance". Even liberal elements saw fit to discourage massive immigration into the country. *Commonweal* printed an article called "No Room at the Inn", in which the victims of Nazism were seen as a burden. Archbishop Rummel of New Orleans, chairman of the Catholic Committee for Refugees, also sought to discourage the coming of refugees from Germany because of a "general

---

20 Editorial, "Hospitality of the United States", *America* (September 10, 1938), p. 531.

unwillingness to take responsibility for unknown persons". Louis Kenedy, president of the National Council of Catholic Men, reported in October 1938 that the opposition to the admission of refugees into the country had reached "alarming proportions" among Catholics. Prominent Church leaders, as well as laymen, glibly believed rumors that "refugees are pouring into this country daily in complete violation of the immigration laws".[21]

Another reason for Catholic indifference to the refugees was the impression that the problem was basically a Jewish one, since most of the refugees were Jews. Catholic leaders refused to believe the repeated reports of Catholic journalists who had visited the Reich about the existence of thousands of non-Jewish refugees who were in need of immediate help. Even a person as familiar with the refugee problem as Bruce M. Mohler, director of the Bureau of Immigration of the NCWC, refused to believe in May 1934 in the possibility of Catholic refugees coming to America. T.F. Mulholland of the New York Port Authority and Mohler's right hand in the Bureau, believed a rumor that 96% of the dentists in New York were Jews. Mohler protested against the publicity about Christian refugees. "It sounds to me like the usual Jewish trick to get Catholics aroused to the point where we will protest and thus in the end help the cause of the Jews, both in Germany and here", he wrote in May 1934.[22]

The anti-refugee attitude found expression in strong opposition to any relaxation of the immigration laws. A suggestion to modify the quota system was rejected by the Catholics. When, in March 1938, Secretary Hull proposed a plan for international action on behalf of refugees from political, religious and racial persecution, the officials of the National Catholic Welfare Con-

---

21   "No Room at the Inn", *Commonweal* (November 18, 1938), p. 86; Joseph F. Rummel to William Berning (Bishop of Osnabrück), June 27, 1937 (CC papers, Box 6, NCWC archives); Memorandum, Beth to Wallach, October 7, 1938 (AJC, Refugees, 1938—1944).

22   Bruce Mohler to Mulholland, May 14, 25, 1934 (NCWC, Box 82).

ference reacted hostilely. "It is interesting how tne State Department shows itself as having a different philosophy from many of our legislators, who have more than once in the last few years denied that America was any longer a haven of refuge", wrote Mulholland.[23] The NCWC was opposed not only to the quota increases, for which Congressional approval was required, but also to modification of the process of selection that was being practiced by American consuls abroad.[24] While some of the leaders of the Catholic establishment, such as Archbishop Joseph Rummel and Cardinal Mundelein of Chicago, supported with some reservations a more lenient administrative approach toward immigration regulations, the major part of the religious press, as well as rank and file Catholics, remained hostile to such a policy.[25]

23 See "Digest of Opinion on Increasing Quotas; Compiled from Letters received by Rabbi Louis D. Gross", May 1938 (AJC, Immigration, 1939); Mohler, "Memo for Record", March 31, 1938; Mulholland to Mohler, March 26, 1938 (NCWC, Box 82).

24 Mohler to Ready, January 17, 1939 (NCWC, Box 82).

25 The Catholic disregard of, and even hostile attitude toward, the refugee problem during the 1930s stood in marked contrast to the concern about the same subject which was displayed after World War II had ended. During the postwar years most of the refugees admitted to the United States were Christians, of whom Catholics constituted more than half. Thus, only when in reality the problem of the refugees was one of Christian concern, did they show sustained interest in the issue. Now the American Catholic press accused Jewish organizations of focusing public attention only on Jewish refugees. Whereas during the 1930s Catholics had opposed any change in the immigration laws now, after the war, they called for an opening of the gates of America to the Catholic immigrants. Their call for unrestricted immigration was prompted by the fact that many Catholic displaced persons were unwilling to go back to their countries of origin which had since been overtaken by Communist regimes. *Catholic World*, 163 (Aug. 1946), pp. 390—392; Boston *Pilot* (May 6, 1947), 5; *New World* (July 11, 1947), 1; *Catholic Action*, 29 (Sep. 1947); *America*, 76 (Oct. 19, 1946), 65 ff.; (Dec. 1, 1946), pp. 236—238; *Sign*, 25 (Jan. 1946), pp. 12—14; (Feb. 1946), pp. 27—30; *Com-*

In January 1936 there were 9000 German Catholic refugees and more than 20,000 Catholic Spanish refugees in need of immediate help. The Bureau of Immigration of the National Catholic Welfare Conference received a constant flow of information about the gravity of the situation, as well as appeals for help. Everything confirmed the view of Father Joseph D. Ostermann that "the refugee problem was becoming acute". Protestants, such as James McDonald and the American Committee for Christian Refugees, increased their pressure on Catholic leaders in America to activate the Catholic hierarchy on behalf of Christian refugees.[26] Criticism of the "obvious lack of Catholic solidarity", and "of the lack of organized Catholic refugee work all over the world", came also from Catholic circles in Holland. The *Katholiek Comité voor Vluchteling* called for realization of the "urgency of a *general Catholic solution* of the misery of Catholic refugees".[27]

In spite of pressures from different directions, the American Catholic bishops still refused to act without an explicit appeal from the German hierarchy. Since a direct appeal from the latter was certain to be considered an insult by the Nazi authorities and an invitation to foreign elements to intervene in internal German affairs, the German bishops were reluctant to seek the sympathy of the Catholic world. Unofficially, however, they did appeal for the Pope's help, but the Vatican refused to respond, believing that such a move would aggravate the persecutions and

monweal, 44 (Sep. 1946), pp. 498—502. See also Esther Feldblum, "On the Eve of a Jewish State", *American Jewish Historical Quarterly*, 64 (Dec. 1974), pp. 99—103.

26 Bruce M. Mohler, "Re-Assistance to Catholic German Refugees", April 17, 1938; see also Groesser to Mohler, June 6, 1934; Mohler, "Memorandum for Record", April 16, 1936 (NCWC, Box 82); Report of the Executive Secretary of the ACCR, June 1—September 15, 1936; Minutes of the Meeting of the ACCR, June 11, 1936 (FCC, Box 102).

27 *Katholiek Comité voor Vluchteling* to Joseph Rummel, March 1, 1937 (NCWC, Box 82).

do the Church more harm than good. During a certain period this dilemma stifled efforts on the part of outside Catholics to help their German co-religionists.[28]

Eventually, on August 31, 1936, Adolf Cardinal Bertram, Archbishop of Breslau and President of the Conference of the German Bishops, appealed for help to the American cardinals. Until the summer of 1936 German Catholics had taken care of their refugees. But the "unsurmountable (*sic*) difficulties" brought the German bishops to the conclusion that "to our great regret . . . we cannot fulfil our charitable obligations by ourselves". Consequently, they took the liberty "to apply to the wonderful sense of charity" of the American Church. Fully aware of the economic difficulties in America and in spite of the restrictionist policy of the Administration, the bishops decided to put "the most urgent request to kindly consider, if and how a small Catholic movement for assistance could be formed for those parties intending to emigrate to the U.S.A.".[29]

The explicit German appeal finally moved the American Catholic hierarchy to action. On November 18, 1936 the Episcopate in Washington approved, in principle, the need for relief work. It also decided to nominate a sub-committee, consisting of three bishops, whose task was "to discuss and decide the necessary particulars about handling of the relief work". Apparently, the Episcopate did not consider the situation to be desperate, since it only required the sub-committee to submit its recommendations by the end of April 1937.[30]

Eager to gain American approval, Cardinal Bertram sent Dr. Rev. Max Groesser, secretary general of the St. Raphael's Society,

---

28 Minutes of the Executive Committee of the ACCR, September 28, 1936 (FCC, Box 102); George Shuster, "Catholics in Nazi Germany", *Commonweal* (Jan. 26, 1934).

29 Adolf Cardinal Bertram to William Cardinal O'Connell, September 10, 1936 (NCWC, Box 82).

30 "Notations for the Sub-committee", n.d. (CC papers, Box 6, NCWC archives).

the central Catholic relief organization in Germany, to the United
States, as his authorized representative. Groesser's task was to
pave the way for understanding and cooperation between the St.
Raphael's Society and the new American refugee Committee. He
prepared a list of preconditions for the establishment of the
Catholic Committee for Refugees.[31] Among the stipulations was
the demand that the Committee be comprised solely of clergymen
without any political affiliation, and that no German should serve
on it, in order to avoid possible difficulties in dealing with German
authorities. While non-Aryans and mixed Catholics were the main
object of the relief work, Groesser accepted the Committee's proposal to help also German Catholics persecuted for religious and
political reasons. He made it clear, however, that assistance should
only be given to refugees whose papers were in order and who
had been cleared by the St. Raphael's Society. He insisted that
"No unworthy or adventurous people may take undue advantage

31 During its lifetime the official name of the Committee was changed
    several times. At the beginning it was called The Catholic Episcopal
    Committee for German Refugees. Later its name was changed to
    The Committee for Catholic German Refugees. In August 1940 it
    became the Catholic Committee for Refugees. For convenience, it
    will here be referred to consistently as The Catholic Committee, or
    CC, disregarding its other names. Mohler to Mulholland, August 6,
    1940 (NCWC, Box 80). While the Catholic Committee for Refugees
    represented the Catholic establishment in America, there were several
    short-lived Catholic bodies based on national origin which operated
    independently in the interests of their countrymen. The Polish Refu-
    gee Committee, based in Detroit, and the group formed in New York
    by the Austrian Archduke, Prince Otto, are noteworthy. In contrast
    to the former, which received financial support from the Catholic
    Committee, the latter had no contact with official Catholic relief or-
    ganizations. Because of their short-lived and small scope of activities,
    they do not deserve separate treatment. See *Fifth Annual Report of
    the Catholic Committee*, October 1, 1940—September 30, 1941, p. 20;
    Sixth Annual Report..., p. 17; *Seventh Annual Report...*, p. 14;
    Eighth Annual Report..., p. 17; *Ninth Annual Report...*, p. 14;
    Foreign Relations of the United States, 1940, Vol. II, pp. 232–233;
    "Catholic Refugees in Lisbon", n.d. (NCWC, Box 84).

of the means of the relief work", having in mind Communists, Socialists, political leaders and criminals.[32]

Seeking to minimize the seriousness of the situation, Groesser termed the general estimate of the number of non-Aryan Catholic refugees "too high". According to his figures there would be 100–120 urgent cases annually and 400–500 less urgent cases. This meant that, at the utmost, 2500 individuals would need relief in the coming three years. Total expenses for that period were estimated at $ 181,000.[33] More meaningful was Groesser's effort to prevent, or at least to moderate, American criticism of the Nazi treatment of German Catholics. He demanded "to limit or to omit altogether" press propaganda. He threatened that if his conditions were not accepted he would "leave it entirely to the most Rev. German bishops, if they deem it possible to cooperate with the generous American relief work".[34]

Groesser's stipulations and tough attitude were hardly welcomed by the Americans. Joseph D. Ostermann, executive director of the Catholic Committee, complained to Archbishop Rummel that "though Dr. Groesser emphasizes that he wants to cooperate wholeheartedly with us, I feel decidedly that there is great danger of his gaining too much control over our work here by shaping it by subtle suggestions . . .". He was exasperated by Groesser's desire to minimize the gravity of the situation. Ostermann was particularly disturbed by the declaration that "Catholics can with good conscience become members of the Nazi Party". He concluded his complaint with the hope that German relief organizations "could not and should not be the only channels through which we should work".[35] Archbishop Rummel was in full accord with Ostermann's

32 "Notations" (CC papers, Box 6, NCWC).
33 *Ibid.*, J. D. Ostermann to J. F. Rummel, March 28, 1937 (CC papers, Box 6, NCWC).
34 "Notations" (CC papers, Box 6, NCWC); Groesser to George Timpe, October 29, 1936 (NCWC, Box 82).
35 Joseph D. Ostermann to Joseph F. Rummel, March 28 ,1937 (CC papers, Box 6, NCWC).

attitude, and on April 13, 1937 he clarified to Groesser the American position as follows:

> In all this it is well to bear in mind that our Committee must be free to judge and outline its own policies according to our knowledge of American conditions. We will welcome the cooperation of St. Raphael's Society, but it must recognize our judgment on individual issues. A clear understanding of this relationship will smooth the way for satisfactory mutual cooperation.[36]

With this declaration of independence, the Catholic Committee started to function as a relief agency. Its sphere of activities was circumscribed by three main objectives: to provide German Catholic refugees with material, spiritual and professional help; to raise funds for immediate relief and for resettlement; and finally, to launch an educational campaign in order to enlist the moral and financial support of the Catholic community in America. Although the decision to establish the Committee had been taken on November 1936, by April 1937 some crucial issues still remained unresolved, such as the method to be used for fund raising and the extent of the relief to be given. Father Ostermann, director of the Leo House in New York, was appointed as executive director of the CC and began to function in January 1937. But the staff of the Committee had "yet much to do before we can take over the responsibilities involved in this work of charity", confessed in April 1937 Archbishop Rummel, chairman of the CC.[37]

A suspicious attitude toward people who volunteered to help refugees, as well as toward the victims themselves, was typical of

---

36   Rummel to Max J. Groesser, April 13, 1937 (CC papers, Box 6, NCWC).

37   "Organization and Rules of Procedure", n.d. (NCWC, Box 80); Rummel to Amleto G. Cicognani, April 16, 1937; "Directions for the Cooperation Between the German St. Raphael's Society and the Catholic Episcopal Committee for German Refugees", n.d. (CC papers, Box 6, NCWC).

Catholics. Instead of immediately beginning the organization work, the heads of the Committee wasted valuable time and energy over the question of whether to employ a Reverend H.A. Reinhold. The latter, a German priest, was active in the Catholic Seamen's Mission at Hamburg. The Nazis accused him of having made "indiscreet remarks" to the seamen. Instead of waiting for instructions from his bishop, he fled to England and later came to America. In spite of warm recommendations from the Netherlands Catholic Committee, where Reinhold had done a good job among refugees, Rummel decided that "we do not deem it advisable to associate (him) directly with our work". The subject was considered so important by the Committee's chairman that he sent two detailed reports to the Apostolic Delegate at Washington on the results of the investigation of Reinhold's activities.[38]

There were clearly-defined criteria for dealing with refugees. Entitled to the Committee's assistance, according to the decision of the Episcopate of November 18, 1936, were *bona fide* non-Aryan refugees who had to leave Germany because of racial discrimination. Help was to be provided also to Aryans who fled for conscientious reasons and to political refugees persecuted on account of their activities in the Catholic Center Party. It was expressly stated that no help should be given to any individual unless he could produce "satisfactory references" from reliable Catholics. "This measure is absolutely necessary", read a memorandum which served as the basis of the Committee's work, "in order to protect the organization against deception, imposition and

---

38 *Katholiek Comité voor Vluchteling* to Rummel, March 1, 1937 (NCWC, Box 82); Nunzio Olandese Comitato pei rifugiati Catholici to Internonciature Apostolique, Foreign Affairs, March 18, 1937 (CC papers, Box 6, NCWC); Minutes, Meeting of the Executive Committee of the ACCR, September 28, 1936; Report of the executive secretary of the ACCR, June 1—September 15, 1936 (FCC, Box 102); Rummel to Amleto Cicognani, April 16, May 17, 1937 (CC papers, Box 6, NCWC).

imposture".[39] The Committee refused to handle refugees who were unable to produce their baptismal certificates. This was a serious obstacle because under war conditions refugees were often unable to obtain the necessary documents. This procedure clearly differed from that followed by Protestant and Jewish relief agencies, who readily accepted the client's declaration concerning his past and religion.[40]

A great concern for the refugees' religious life was also unique to the Catholic Committee for Refugees. Its first purpose was "to safeguard the faith" of the newcomer. A special sub-committee was formed to take care of the religious and social absorption of the refugees. Cardinal Pacelli, in a circular to the bishops, demanded that when the establishment of a separate settlement for Catholic refugees be considered, "care should be taken that churches and schools are provided to safeguard their spiritual welfare and to protect their customs and traditions".[41] The concern for a satisfactory atmosphere was so important that it was used as a strong argument in favor of the establishment of the Committee in the United States. For if Catholic immigrants did not have a separate agency of their own, there was the danger that they would turn to the Communists. The Dutch Committee pressured Americans to institute such an agency by explicitly arguing that on account of Catholic apathy, Catholic refugees, "driven by their desperate plight, are forced to turn to *Socialist and Communist organizations*". The Dutch Catholics lamented that "some strong anti-Catholic powers of evil seem to be holding back our own Catholic people from helping those devoted children of the Church who are now languishing in exile".[42]

39   "Organization and Rules of Procedure", n.d. (NCWC, Box 80).
40   Author's interview with Harry D. Biele, April 19, 1974.
41   Bruce Mohler to Charles D. Gorman, October 4, 1935 (NCWC, Box 23); "Organization and Rules of Procedure"; E. Cardinal Pacelli to the Bishops, January 9, 1939, no. 77/79 (NCWC, Box 80).
42   *Katholiek Comité voor Vluchteling* to Rummel, March 1, 1937 (NCWC, Box 82).

Fear of Protestant proselytism came only second to fear of Communism in Catholic circles. Bruce Mohler, director of the NCWC's Bureau of Immigration, considered the activities of certain Protestant relief organizations to be aimed at the conversion of Catholic immigrants. Thus it was considered that evangelistic groups, such as the Home and Foreign Missions Councils as well as the YWCA, would "frankly proselytize", while others indirectly, and perhaps unconsciously, would weaken the religious faith of Catholic refugees.[43] Since refugees were vulnerable and "practically every immigrant problem, and surely every social work, had a religious angle", the need for a separate relief agency was the order of the day.[44] Hence, theological rather than humanitarian arguments were the persuasive factor in the Catholic propaganda accompanying fund raising campaigns on behalf of refugees. In contrast, the main concern of non-Catholic relief agencies was the economic and social welfare of their beneficiaries, in almost complete disregard of their spiritual needs.

The Catholic Committee for Refugees also differed from other refugee organizations in the type of help it provided. While the former gave only small-scale aid to overcome initial and immediate difficulties, the latter tried to resettle refugees all over the country. "We are not directly involved or interested in any refugee resettlement project", it was stated in the Committee's Annual *Report*.[45] As a result, Catholics failed to offer any long-term and far-reaching resolution of the refugee problem. It follows that the expenses of the CC were much lower than those of other relief agencies.

The Catholic Committee had not only a hard birth but also a difficult childhood. Financial as well as administrative obstacles hampered the development of the Committee in its formative years. The original plan had been to collect $ 181,000 over a period of three years. Most of the funds were supposed to come from the

43   Mohler to Gorman, October 4, 1935 (NCWC, Box 23).
44   SW (Sara Weadick) to Mohler, June 20, 1936 (NCWC, Box 82).
45   *Fourth Annual Report of the Catholic Committee for Refugees, October 1, 1939 — September 30, 1940*, p. 10.

dioceses, where every bishop was personally responsible for a certain quota. During the first nine months only $ 7840 was raised, with $ 6900 having been contributed by the chairman and the treasurer of the Committee. Its first fiscal year report indicated that 526 cases received urgent care; 26 affidavits were granted; 36 jobs were secured and 11 persons were brought to the country. The total expenses were $ 5378.[46]

With the annexation of Austria in March 1938, the problem of Catholic refugees became more acute. Approximately a quarter of a million non-Aryan Catholics and persons of mixed marriages were in danger of persecution and exile. By February 1939, 35,000 Catholics from the Reich had already turned for help to the Committee. To meet the situation, Archbishop Rummel appealed personally to the American bishops asking them to assist at least ten refugees by providing affidavits for them.[47] Most of the responses were polite but firm rejections. Little wonder that Rummel bitterly complained about the difficulty of placing priests and sisters in local parishes.[48] In January 1939 Cardinal Pacelli endeavored "to enlist the active interest" of bishops all over the world in the fate of the Catholic refugees. He suggested practical steps, such as the establishment of local refugee committees under the direct guidance and "active assistance" of the bishops. Each committee would not only take care of the absorption of a number of poor refugees, but also cooperate with national relief societies, in order

---

46 Rummel's circular to the American Bishops, June 30, 1937 (CC papers, Box 6, NCWC); *Report of The Committee for Catholic Refugees, covering the first fiscal year, January 1, 1937 — September 30, 1937*, table V (CC papers, Box 7, NCWC).

47 Joseph Rummel to John T. McNicholas, May 10, 1938 (CC papers, Box 6, NCWC); *Report of the Committee for Catholic Refugees, covering the period January 1, 1937 — September 30, 1938*, pp. 6—7; NCWC, "News Service", October 17, 1938 (NCWC, Box 80).

48 Floyd L. Begin (Secretary to Bishop of Cleveland) to Rummel, June 4, 1938; Bishop of Nashville to Rummel, May 21, 1938; Rummel to Christopher N. Byrne (Bishop of Texas), September 22, 1938 (CC papers, Box 6, NCWC).

to ease the conditions of the refugees' admission into the country. He wanted the bishops also to protect the immigrants and to see to it that they would "find hospitality and sympathetic reception". Pacelli expressed his confidence that the bishops "will favor such an important work for those distressed people".[49] The appeal met with little positive response from the American hierarchy, as Ostermann's complaint to Rummel attested. To increase the pressure, it was decided to publish Pacelli's circular — despite the fact that it was designated "not for publication". The official "News Service" of the National Catholic Welfare Conference printed the full text, emphasizing its practical suggestions.[50] Although Archbishop Rummel reported to the Vatican "that the wishes of the Holy See are practically being carried out", no local refugee committees had been formed, nor had Church leaders made any serious effort to absorb refugees in their neighborhoods. As far as refugees were concerned, especially those of Jewish ancestry, there was a gap between the Papal directives and their implementation.[51]

The unresponsive attitude of the Catholic community was reflected in the Committee's financial position. "At the present we are very sorely in need of funds at our headquarters", complained Rummel to McDonald. Obviously, Rummel preferred a general fund raising campaign conducted by all relief organizations to a separate Catholic campaign. However, Roosevelt's refusal to support the project led to its abandonment. The Catholic Committee had no choice but to handle its own fund raising problems.[52]

---

49 Cardinal Pacelli to Amleto G. Cicognani, December 30, 1938, no. 5075/38; Pacelli to Rummel, June 7, 1938, no. 169268 (CC papers, Box 6, NCWC); Pacelli's circular to the Bishops, January 9, 1939, no. 77/79 (NCWC, Box 80).

50 Joseph Ostermann to Joseph Rummel, March 15, 1939 (CC papers, Box 6, NCWC); NCWC, "News Service", March 13, 1939, p. 3 (NCWC, Box 80).

51 Chancellor to Amleto Cicognani, February 1, 1939 (CC papers, Box 6, NCWC).

52 Rummel to McDonald, December 29, 1938 (MP:P); SW to Mohler, November 5, 1938 (NCWC, Box 80); Rummel to Cicognani, Novem-

Gradually the Committee's financial position improved. From an income of $ 40,778 during 1937—1938, it leaped in 1938—1939 to $ 244,708. Overheads amounted to 42% of the total expenditure, which was indicative of an ineffective administration. Remarkable too was the large surplus in the budget, since more than 50% of the budget was not utilized.[53] This phenomenon recurred in later years. The period 1939—1940 was the peak in immigration and in the agency's activities. The pressure of the increased number of refugees was so high that the Committee saw fit to reduce its relief by 20%. Despite the increased demand for financial assistance, a quarter of the budget remained unutilized.[54]

In contrast, other refugee agencies spent all their available funds. Thus, for example, in September 1939 the Committee only utilized three-quarters of its budget. Yet, in the "Instructions to Refugees" which was issued by the executive director of the CC, it was stated that, concerning refugees abroad "all we can do is to put our full confidence in God and pray". The members of the National Refugee Service had reason to wonder about the effectiveness of such Catholic relief "activity".[55]

The fact that a considerable amount of money remained unutilized was a reflection of the disrespect shown by the Committee's staff toward their supplicants. The criticism of Dr. Anna Selig, a Catholic who tried to help Catholic intellectuals and was eager to improve the Committee's image, expressed the disappointment and despair of many:

ber 16, 1938, January 19, 1939 (CC papers, Box 6, NCWC); NCWC, "News Service", February 20 ,1939 (NCWC, Box 80).

53   Rummel to John McNicholas, May 10, 1938 (CC papers, Box 6, NCWC); *Report of the Committee for Catholic Refugees, January 1, 1937 — September 30, 1939*, pp. 10—18.

54   *Fourth Annual Report of the Committee for Catholic Refugees, October 1, 1939 — September 30, 1940*, table vii (CC papers, Box 7, NCWC).

55   Joseph D. Ostermann, "Instructions to Refugees", September 1939; Hanna Ziegler to William Haber, September 21, 1939 (NRS papers, file 57, YIVO).

I feel so ashamed over and over again that the Catholic refugee work in New York causes such rising criticism and
among refugees, internationally speaking, unanimous indignation. I cannot grasp why American Catholics permit this
situation to continue and waste their money on such appalling methods of 'relief', the effect of which seems to be
equally repulsive to the refugees as destructive to the Catholic cause as well as to the faith and sympathy for America.
It is such a pity that all this effort is wasted spiritually and
socially speaking. It is needless to say that reports of all Non-
Catholic organizations are confirming the impressions of the
refugees by their own experience.[56]

Bruce Mohler admitted that he had received letters of complaints
about lack of courtesy of the Catholic Committee's staff, the inability to meet and talk with the executive director, an extremely
suspicious attitude toward refugees, the failure to reply to letters
and to give correct information. The attitude of Dr. Stephanie Herz,
an important figure on the staff, was a particular source of criticism. "His Excellency told us that Dr. Herz was largely to blame",
was how Mohler recorded his conversation with Archbishop Rummel, "and we both agreed that she was extremely suspicious, quite
clumsy in handling such cases and that she never succeeded in con-
cealing her suspicion from the persons involved". In spite of
repeated complaints, Miss Herz was not replaced.[57]
Lack of cooperation as well as rivalry characterized the relationship between the Catholic Committee for Refugees, which
operated from New York City, and the Bureau of Immigration of
the National Catholic Welfare Conference, the Washington-based
organization. The division of functions had not been defined clearly

---

56 Extract from Anna Selig's letter; SW (Sara Weadick) to Mohler,
    June 5, 1941; Extract from memorandum received from Mulholland
    in the case of Dr. Anna Selig, June 5, 1941 (NCWC, Box 80).
57 Mohler's "Memorandum for Record", September 10, 1941; Mohler
    to Mulholland, March 27, 1937 (NCWC, Box 80).

enough and the parties did not care to follow the decisions made in that matter. Due to its close ties with governmental departments and because of its familiarity with immigration regulations, the Bureau of Immigration was responsible for the preparation of visa applications and affidavits. The Catholic Committee, on the other hand, was expected to handle relief work, to secure employment and to provide free board. The former was scheduled to handle those refugees who were still in Europe, and the latter to care for those who had already reached America. The Bureau preferred to deal with the clergy, leaving the cases of laymen to the Committee. Such decisions were difficult to implement. Even after operating for three years many still appealed to the Bureau for help, which had to refer them to the CC. The heads of the Bureau did not regard the Committee as a sister agency, complaining about "invasion" of its sphere of influence. Although a confidential memorandum of the Bureau indicated that "it was not intended that there should be duplication of effort", overlapping and inefficiency were quite regular.[58]

If this was the relationship between two Catholic relief agencies, it is not surprising that distrust marked the attitude toward Protestant and Jewish organizations. Cooperation, for the heads of the NCWC, meant exposure of Catholic secrets to outsiders. Bruce Mohler was reluctant to open his Bureau's files to other relief agencies and opposed joining a central clearing system aimed at avoiding duplication. The National Coordinating Committee's invitation to the CC, in April 1937, to cooperate with other refugee agencies, was interpreted by Catholics as a Jewish plan to dominate the field. As T.F. Mulholland, the Bureau's representative in New York, wrote to his chief, Bruce Mohler:

---

58   T. F. Mulholland to Bruce Mohler, March 31, October 14, 1937 (NCWC, Box 82); Mohler to J. D. Ostermann, September 19, 1938 (NCWC, Box 80); March 29, 1939 (NCWC, Box 82); Mohler to Mulholland, December 12, 1938, October 12, 1937, March 25, 1937; Mulholland to Mohler, March 18, 1937 (NCWC, Box 80, 82).

> You will thus see that the Jewish direction of the whole scheme is particularly absolute — it has all the machinery for its own ramifications and cooperations, local and national: it gives office room to the NCC as well as to the ACCR, it now calls through the latter Committee a meeting with the Catholic Episcopal Committee ... to see apparently that the latter fall in line with procedure already adopted.... I merely point out that they want to have their finger ready to plunge into any aspect of the German refugee question.[59]

This hostile attitude toward the NCC had gradually changed. "Undoubtedly the Catholic Episcopal Committee will get much assistance from the NCC and the others", observed Mulholland, adding: "a good working agreement in the various cases can be worked out if insistence on who should get the credit is put into the background".[60]

The distrust was not confined to the heads of the Bureau of Immigration, but infected high-ranking Catholic officials as well. Monsignor Michael J. Ready, chairman of the National Catholic Welfare Conference, questioned the honesty of Clarence E. Pickett, executive secretary of the American Friends Service Committee, who was a devoted friend of both Jewish and Christian refugees. Ready accused Pickett of using the refugees and relief means in Europe, where the Quakers were active, in order to promote the latter's influence. He was also convinced that the conference of relief agencies at Princeton, which Pickett had helped to organize, had "the benefit of ballooning his prestige and influence nationally".[61]

Against this background of distrust toward other agencies and

---

59 Mulholland to Mohler, April 6, 1937 (NCWC, Box 82).
60 Mulholland to Mohler, April 9, 14, 1937; Mohler to Mulholland, April 12, 1937 (NCWC, Box 82).
61 Bruce Mohler, "Summarization of Correspondence", February 25, 1941 (NCWC, Box 82); Mohler to Mulholland, December 11, 1941 (NCWC, Box 81). See below, pp. 256—258.

the inefficiency of the CC, it comes as no surprise that the Catholic representatives were excluded from many inter-agency meetings. T.F. Mulholland, the Bureau's representative, complained that the NCWC was not considered an "inside" organization and therefore was "being brought in after cut-and-dried schemes have been agreed to".The Bureau's representative was invited mainly when it was necessary "to make a big show of the extent of interest".[62] Certainly, other bodies did not overlook the Catholics. Protestant, Quaker and Jewish agencies invited the CC to their meetings. The Jews, in particular, were eager to gain Catholic sympathy in order to fight anti-alien and anti-Semitic sentiments.[63]

Catholic refugees were regularly referred to the CC by other organizations and the National Refugee Service helped the Committee with service and advice. William Rosenwald, co-chairman of the NCC, was particularly satisfied with the performance of the Catholic Committee. In September 1938 he reported thus to Paul Baerwald, chairman of the Joint Distribution Committee:

> Up to present time, our experience has been that any Catholic cases referred to them have been handled well. They give relief, and take care of change of status cases and immigration cases without having to call upon us for any financial aid. They do, however, call upon us often for advice and guidance. We work together very well.[64]

Not everybody shared Rosenwald's evaluation. In NRS and ACCR circles, workers were wondering about the ignorance of the CC's staff concerning refugee matters. In 1938—1939, after three years of constant relief work, CC members were still not

62   Mulholland to Mohler, February 8, 1941 (NCWC, Box 87).
63   American Jewish Committee, "Analysis of the Present Situation", 11 pp. ms., December 3, 1935 (AJC, German Jews); William Haber to Joseph D. Ostermann, July 11, 1939 (NRS papers, 57, YIVO); Mohler to Mulholland, August 5, 1940 (NCWC, Box 87).
64   William Rosenwald to Paul Baerwald, September 21, 1938 (NCC papers, 15, YIVO).

familiar with the exact speciality of every agency and did not know to whom to refer a particular case. The Catholic body's confusion and lack of expertise irritated the workers of other agencies.[65] When the CC was invited, along with the ACCR, to move its offices to the NCC building, which was the headquarters of the refugee organizations, it refused because Catholic leaders preferred to operate alone. Thus, an offer to utilize the facilities and advice of other agencies, which would have served to improve the Committee's operations, was turned down.[66]

These reservations notwithstanding, the Catholic Committee gradually became one of the country's major relief agencies, along with the NCC, ACCR and AFSC. It developed working relations with other organizations and its staff overcame, though not entirely, the difficulties of its formative years. The Committee's achievements up to September 1939 were noteworthy.[67]

The outbreak of hostilities in Europe sharply increased the pressure on the CC. Therefore, in 1940 relief was reduced by 20%.[68] Although in 1941 the number of refugees who turned to the Committee decreased by 50% due to the war situation, it was still far from able to solve the problems of its clients.[69] As the war dragged on, the Catholic Committee's activities markedly declined. In 1943—1944 only 69 new cases were handled and 33 refugees were offered employment. Paradoxically, at that time,

65 J. D. Ostermann to W .K. Thomas, May 23, 1938 (HIAS–HICEM papers, xxxiii; Carl Schurz Foundation, 28, YIVO); William Haber to Stephanie Herz, October 4, 1939 (NRS papers, 57, YIVO).

66 Mohler to Mulholland, February 13, 1941 (NCWC, Box 87).

67 Report of the Committee for Catholic Refugees, January 1, 1937 — September 30, 1939, pp. 8—18, table iii.

68 Fourth Annual Report of the Committee for Catholic Refugees, October 1, 1939 — September 30, 1940, pp. 3—4, table vii (typed report, in CC papers, Box 7, NCWC).

69 Fifth Annual Report of the Catholic Committee for Refugees, October 1, 1940 — September 30, 1941, pp. 3—5, 7—9, 16—17; Memorandum by Mohler; "Subject: Meeting in New York — Refugees", n.d. (NCWC, Box 84).

as the scope of the services declined, the Committee's budget meaningfully increased due to the National War Fund having taken over the financial responsibility of the relief agencies. From August 1943, the NWF was the main source of the CC's income.[70]

Although the original purpose of the Catholic Committee was to help the refugee's admission into the United States, from the beginning it also helped Catholic Committees in Holland, Germany, Italy, Switzerland and England. In 1939—1940, the Committee's busiest year, $18,367 were sent abroad. In consequence of the occupation of Western Europe in 1940, American Catholic help to European Committees ceased entirely.[71]

Since relief work in Europe, though badly needed, provided no final solution to the refugee problem, resettlement projects, particularly in Latin American countries, were considered by the Intergovernmental Committee and the President's Advisory Committee on Political Refugees. Efforts were made by the latter to interest the American Catholic hierarchy in refugee settlements in Cuba, the Dominican Republic and Brazil. George Warren of the PAC met several times with notable Catholics, like Basil Harris, Louis Kenedy, Michael J. Ready, J.D. Ostermann and Father Duffy, "to discuss the organization of Catholic auspices for approaches to Governments interested in Catholic refugees".[72] This endeavor was important in light of the permission given by Getulio Vargas, President of Brazil, for the settlement of 3000 non-Aryan Catholic German refugees in his country. The project was under the direct supervision of the Vatican. Indeed, the Brazilian Government put 3000 visas at the disposal of the Brazilian delegate to the Holy See. A special representative, Father A. Turowski of the Pious Society of Missions, was sent to Lisbon to facilitate the passage of converted Jews to Brazil. The instructions, as well as the funds, came

70 *Eighth Annual Report...*, p. 25; *Ninth Annual Report...*, p. 26.
71 *Fourth Annual Report...*, *October 1, 1939 — September 30, 1940*, pp. 6—8.
72 George L. Warren to Myron C. Taylor and George Rublee, December 15, 23, 1938; January 3, 1939 (MP:P).

from Rome. The project failed, however, because of a serious lack of funds — a $700 bond was required for every immigrant — and the unfitness of German Catholics for agricultural work.[73]

Several Catholic resettlement programs in Latin America were supported by the Vatican, but the American Catholic Committee gave no financial help to these ventures, as was explicitly stated in the *Annual Report* for 1940: "... chiefly because of the limited resources at our disposal and the need of rather elaborate organization, we are not directly involved or interested in any refugee resettlement project".[74] The interest of the CC was mainly focused on European committees. However, it kept in touch with programs in Ecuador, the Philippines and the Dominican Republic. When the JDC established a Settlement Corporation for the Dominican Republic the CC played its part, contributing $5000.[75]

Diplomatic intervention by Vatican officials in America on behalf of victims of Nazi persecutions became more frequent as the atrocities of the Germans became known. Particularly helpful was the Apostolic Delegate at Washington, Amleto G. Cicognani. With the establishment of the War Refugee Board in January 1944, a concerted effort came to be made by the American Administration to save as many Jews as the situation enabled. John W. Pehle, the energetic executive director of the WRB, was convinced that a message to the Pope through the Apostolic Delegate "would produce results more quickly than if it were sent directly through the American delegate at the Vatican".[76] Especially so since Cicognani had

73 See "Catholic Refugees in Lisbon", n.d. (*c.* 1944) (NCWC, Box 84); *The New York Times*, June 25, 1939; *Annual Report of the Committee for Catholic Refugees, January 1, 1937 — September 30, 1939*, p. 24; Translation of a letter from Dr. Menningen to Timpe, October 8 (1940) (NCWC, Box [W] 29).

74 *Fourth Annual Report of the Committee for Catholic Refugees, October 1, 1939 — September 30, 1940*, p. 10.

75 *Ibid.* See also Joseph D. Ostermann to the NRS, July 20, 1939 (NRS papers, 57, YIVO). See above, p. 81.

76 Pehle to Edward R. Stettinius, June 12, 1944 (WRB papers, Box 2, FDRL).

personally given the United States Government "repeated indications of the concern with which (he) viewed the persecution of Jews".[77] Edward R. Stettinius, Under Secretary of State, turned to Cicognani to use his good offices with the Vatican and secure the latter's pressure on German satellite countries, such as Hungary and Rumania, to alleviate the suffering of the victims of discrimination. The prompt answer of the Apostolic Delegate indicated his positive attitude. He assured that the "Holy See will do everything in its power to obtain for these unfortunates a treatment similar to that accorded to civilian internees".[78]

Archbishop Francis Spellman of New York also joined Catholic protests against the enforcement of discriminatory laws in Hungary, where Jews were being herded into ghettos after their property and homes had been systematically looted. On June 30, 1944 Archbishop Spellman issued a statement to the Hungarian people, saying that "It is incredible that a people with such profound Christian faith ... would join in a hymn of hatred and willingly submit to the blood lust and brigandage of tyranny". He authorized Secretary of State Hull to broadcast the appeal to Eastern Europe. While Spellman's voice was almost unheard until 1944, too late for real help, one may detect the favorable approach of Cicognani already in 1942. The efforts of the Apostolic Delegate at Washington were noteworthy, despite the meager results. He did not serve as a mere courier, but transmitted American requests to the Vatican in refugee matters "with sympathetic recommendations", as Archbishop Rummel observed.[79]

In spite of the fact that the CC was recognized by private and governmental agencies as the clearing house for, and prime source of, information concerning Catholic refugees in America, its very existence was constantly in question. The problem "whether it is

77 Edward Stettinius to Amleto Cicognani, June 24, 1944 (WRB papers, Box 2, FDRL).
78 Cicognani to Stettinius, June 26, 1944; Pehle to Cicognani, April 3, 1944; Cicognani to Pehle, April 4, 1944 (WRB papers, Box 2, FDRL).
79 Rummel to George Warren, August 28, 1942 (MP:P).

desirable to continue the operation of the Catholic Committee for Refugees" was discussed almost annually. The conviction that the refugee crisis would not pass while the war lasted, and that after the cessation of hostilities it would assume even larger proportions, led to the recommendation that "this work of charity be permitted to go on".[80]

With the advance of the Allied forces on the European and African fronts, new categories of displaced persons came to need relief. From political, racial and religious refugees, the attention now shifted to prisoners of war and seamen. Due to the growing need for a Catholic welfare agency abroad (since most of the local committees had ceased to operate under German occupation) along with the increased budget provided by the National War Fund, the Bishops' Committee of the NCWC founded a special organization called the War Relief Services (WRS) in the summer of 1943 to carry out the overseas relief work. The WRS became the supervisor and coordinator of Catholic relief activities, serving as the single address for the NWF and transferring part of the funds to the Catholic Committee. While the latter continued to take care of those refugees who had already arrived in the United States, the War Relief Services assumed responsibility for displaced persons abroad. Under the executive directorship of Monsignor Patrick A. O'Boyle, the Services initiated projects for Polish refugees in Palestine, Egypt, Iran and India and sent relief workers to establish centers or to help in existing refugee camps in Spain, Portugal and Colonia Santa Rosa in Mexico.[81] During 1944—1945 the WRS had special programs in Malta, where relief was given by American volunteers, and in England — where evacuated children were aided.

---

80 *Eighth Annual Report . . .*, p. 14; *Sixth Annual Report . . .*, p. 25; *Fifth Annual Report . . .*, p. 3; *Fourth Annual Report . . .*, pp. 15—16.

81 *Seventh Annual Report . . ., October 1, 1942 — September 30, 1943*, pp. 13, 24. Accordingly, The NCWC appeared on the cover of the *Annual Reports*, beginning the Eighth; See Patrick A. O'Boyle's circular from February 17, 1944 (WRB papers, Box 6, FDRL).

It also assisted prisoners of war and merchant seamen, and sent money to help orphans and refugees in China. Agents of the Service went to organize relief work in Lisbon, Madrid, Cairo and Santa Rosa. Funds were transferred to Catholic Committees in Switzerland and the Balkans. Altogether, the approved budget of the WRS for the fiscal year October 1, 1944 — September 30, 1945 totaled $ 1,245,900.[82]

Dr. Henry Amiel's activities in Lisbon well illustrated the kind of relief work done by the WRS' agents. The Lisbon office of the War Relief Services began to operate in April 1944. While the JDC, AFSC and the USC had been working on behalf of refugees in Lisbon since 1940, Catholics — who comprised 10% of the refugees — were said to "sit around Lisbon for months, going from consulate to consulate with no organization to clear the path for them".[83] Indeed, the JDC office provided relief without checking the beneficiary's religion and, up to the time of Amiel's arrival in April 1944, 80 Catholic families were supported by the existing agencies. Moreover, Catholic Poles were taken care of by a local Polish Committee, which assisted any Pole, regardless of his religion. Interestingly, the only contact between American Polish Catholics and their brethren in Lisbon was made through the representative of the Unitarians, and not through Catholics. Amiel tried to organize the relief work and to systematize the operations, but the chaotic situation — with contradictory verbal *ad hoc* agreements reached — made his task a difficult one. He was in fact unable to change the involved channels through which the funds were funneled.[84]

82 The Budget Office, The National War Fund, October 31, 1944; War Relief Services, NCWC. See also WRS, NCWC, Description of Projects in Proposed Budget, for Period from October 1, 1944 to September 30, 1945. Out of the proposed budget of $ 2,718,920, the National War Fund approved less than one half, $ 1,245,900 (WRB papers, Box 7, FDRL).

83 "Catholic Refugees in Lisbon", n.d. (*c.* 1944) (NCWC, Box 84).

84 Amiel to O'Boyle, July 22, May 6, 1944 (WRB papers, Box 16, FDRL).

In Lisbon, as in America, the spiritual welfare of the refugees was very important to the Catholics. While the large agencies were busy providing relief for the maintenance of refugees and offered counsel to facilitate their migration, Amiel was instructed to establish social centers and to provide educational and religious help. The fostering of the refugees' morals was as important as their economic welfare.[85]

The operations of the War Relief Services in Lisbon in 1944 serve as a good example of what could be attained by determination, goodwill, cooperation with other agencies as well as financial backing. Between November 1943 — July 1944, the Lisbon office received from the United States approximately $58,000.[86]

During 1944—1945 the War Relief Services employed 51 paid workers in various areas of the world, including Malta, England, Italy, Spain, Portugal, the Balkans, the Middle East, China, Mexico and the United States.[87] With the liberation of Europe from Nazi occupation, the WRS extended its activities, cooperating with UNRRA on the one hand, and with local church committees which had been reestablished on the other hand. Altogether, it operated in 41 countries, providing relief and rehabilitation programs for the victims of the war. Utilizing the channels of the Church, the Services operated at low cost. It was able to act swiftly, sometimes being the first agency to reach the scene of need. Harold J. Seymour, director of the National War Fund, highly praised the work of the Services, writing: "The scope of its program was so vast and the nature of its services so varied as to make a brief summarization impossible. The agency was everywhere, with aid of all kinds, and set an enviable record for com-

---

85 *Ibid.*

86 War Relief Services, NCWC, "Statement of Operations, December 31, 1944"; Amiel to O'Boyle, July 22, August 18, 1944 (WRB papers, Box 16, FDRL).

87 War Relief Services, NCWC, "Summary Analysis of Amounts Requested in Budget Projects", October 1, 1944 — September 30, 1945 (WRB papers, Box 16, FDRL).

petence and economy". The Services' income during its four years
of operation totaled $ 10,893,507.[88] Compared with Catholic activi-
ties on behalf of refugees in the United States, this was a creditable
achievement. It was the record of the War Relief Services that lent
justification to John W. Pehle's public testimony about "the generous assistance which the Catholic Church has rendered in
rescuing and protecting refugees".[89]

During the first decade of the Catholic Committee's operations,
1936—1946, it provided 3776 affidavits, gave relief to 1226 persons,
secured employment for 1052 refugees and rendered immigration
services to 6967 individuals. Its total income during that decade
was $ 812,463.[90] The Catholic Committee for Refugees also ex-
panded its activities after World War II, mainly among those who
refused to return to their countries where the Communists had
assumed power. Under President Truman's directive of December
22, 1945, the Committee became responsible for the relief work
with all displaced persons, including minors. With the inception of
the Displaced Persons Act of 1948, the CC turned over 7381 of its
cases to the National Catholic Resettlement Council, continuing to
handle the cases of priests, scholars and orphans. After 1950 there
were more than 500 Catholic displaced priests in Europe waiting
to immigrate to the United States. Professors were even more difficult to place than priests, because of unwillingness in academic
circles to absorb foreign scholars. Probably one of the most successful areas of the CC's activities was its children's program. Until
1962 the sub-committee for refugee children helped to find homes
for 5313 minors.[91]

88   Harold J. Seymour, *Design for Giving: The Story of the National
     War Fund Inc.*, 1943—1947 (New York: Harper and Brothers, 1947),
     pp. 88, 71.
89   Pehle to Cicognani, October 16, 1944 (WRB papers, Box 2, FDRL).
90   See below, Tables VII—VIII; *Tenth Annual Report of the Catholic
     Committee for Refugees, October 1, 1945 — September 30, 1946:
     "Summary: 1936—1946"*, pp. 34—35.
91   See, 8 pp. undated ms. reporting on the activities of the CC. See
     also NCWC, "News Service", December 8, 15, 29, 1947 (NCWC).

In conclusion, the American Catholic community's benevolence toward Catholic refugees did not match the response and charity of Jews and Protestants toward the fate of their brethren. A favorable change occurred in 1943—1944, at a time when prosperity supplanted the earlier Depression and unemployment. Unfortunately, very few refugees were able to reach American shores during that period. Even then, the lion's share of the expenses was covered from governmental sources. The War Relief Services, which was a highly-regarded agency, received its funds from the National War Fund and treated mainly victims of the war, rather than refugees from Nazism.

6

THE QUAKERS AND THE
AMERICANIZATION OF REFUGEES

The services rendered to refugees by the American Friends Service Committee (AFSC) differed markedly, in aim as well as scope, from those offered either by the American Committee for Christian Refugees or by the Catholic Committee for Refugees. While the ACCR took care of Protestants and the CC assumed responsibility for Catholic refugees, the AFSC, as a Quaker organization, worked on a non-sectarian basis. Its aim was not to duplicate, but rather to supplement the services rendered by the principal sectarian agencies.[1] The AFSC was established in 1917 in order to offer food, clothing and comfort to people in distress, especially German children. Up to 1924 the Quakers, with the financial support of American philanthropists, were instrumental in feeding up to 1,200,000 children a day in Germany.[2] As an agency of the Society of Friends, the Committee was an instrument through which

1   AFSC, Refugee Section September 1941. (The archives of the American Friends Service Committee, Philadelphia: General Files = GF, Refugee Section = RS, 1941).
2   See the Foreword of Rufus M. Jones and Clarence E. Pickett in AFSC's *Refugee Facts* (1939), p. 3.

Quakers were able to "carry into action their deepest religious convictions and insights". They felt "an inner necessity to minister humbly to the suffering of their fellows", because "there is in every human being something of the Divine", as was indicated in a policy statement. In addition, by providing opportunities for service the Committee could give practical expression to its "desire to meet urgent needs".[3] Throughout its history the Committee undertook projects in countries of acute distress, trying "to promote mutual understanding, to relieve human suffering and to give witness by example to a way of life that releases the forces of friendliness, tolerance and simplicity", to name but a few of its purposes.[4] Even after the conclusion of the feeding project in Germany, the AFSC's staff remained in Europe to coordinate relief work. American and British Friends maintained Centers in Berlin, Vienna, Paris, Geneva, and, until 1931, in Warsaw and Moscow as well. In 1927, when there were no urgent calls for help and the AFSC did not want to undertake permanent relief work, there was some talk of disbanding the Committee. Eventually, it was decided to keep a skeleton staff in reserve for an emergency situation.[5]

The Nazi ascent to power and the suppression of non-Aryans in Germany provided an opportunity to respond again "to the cry of human suffering". As a matter of fact, the Quakers were in a position that enabled them to intervene more efficiently on behalf of the persecuted than almost any other agency. Through their existing centers they could easily expand the type and scope of the services. Furthermore, as a result of their earlier operations in Germany, they had gained experience in mass feeding

---

3 Draft of a Foreign Service Policy, November 20, 1944 (AFSC: Foreign Service = FS: 1944: Policy).

4 "A Proposed World Quaker Service", February 11, 1944 (AFSC: FS: 1944: Planning).

5 Minutes Sub-committee of Foreign Service Executive Committee on Report of Study of Refugee Division, April 14, 1942 (AFSC: Minutes File = MF).

and firsthand knowledge of Germany and her people. They had won the Germans' appreciation and were known for their impartiality, devotion and political non-involvement. In most cases even the Nazis treated them respectfully. Quaker non-partisanship and dedication to human need, irrespective of race, creed or nationality, opened before them doors which neither governmental nor religious officials were allowed to enter.[6]

During the first year of Hitler's regime, the scope of the AFSC's activities on behalf of refugees was surprisingly small. Though in 1933, for example, it contributed $20,000 to Quaker centers in Berlin, Paris, Vienna and Geneva, only part of that sum was intended for refugees.[7] Paul Baerwald, chairman of the American Jewish Joint Distribution Committee, who was eager to enlist the Quakers' help for the refugee cause, turned in May 1933 to the AFSC, inquiring as to its readiness to undertake relief work in Germany. The Friends' response was cautious and conditional. Any expansion of activities necessitated further funds. Therefore, the Committee asked the JDC for $5000 for 1933 and $10,000 for 1934.[8]

Every JDC board member favored cooperation with the Friends. Cyrus Adler, president of the American Jewish Committee, believed that "they are rendering a very distinct service and can be of service where other groups would fail". Joseph C. Hyman, executive secretary of the JDC, and Felix M. Warburg were also "quite sympathetic".[9] There were, however, some key members, such as David M. Bressler and Paul Baerwald, who thought that

6 AFSC, *Refugee Facts*, p. 3; Report of the Quaker Commission to the Third Reich, July 1, 1939 (JDC archives, AFSC).
7 A Statement of AFSC to the JDC, October, 1933 (JDC archives, AFSC).
8 *Ibid.*, AFSC; Minutes of the Meeting of the Foreign Service Section, May 25, 1933 (AFSC: MF); Pickett to Hyman, October 31, 1933 (JDC archives, AFSC).
9 Cyrus Adler to the JDC, November 7, 1933; Joseph Hyman, Memorandum to the Board of JDC, November 2, 1933 (JDC archives, AFSC).

the AFSC "should not rely exclusively upon JDC to make up its deficit", recommending that half of the sum be granted. Accordingly, the JDC voted to contribute for 1933 the sum of $2500.[10] A second allotment of $2500 was granted in April 1934 out of the JDC's "very genuine desire to continue to cooperate with you", as Hyman wrote to Pickett.[11]

Indeed, in the long run, this sum of $5000 proved to be one of the best "investments" that the JDC made. Thus began a period of productive and trustworthy cooperation. As a matter of fact, it was the continuation rather than the commencement of collaboration between the two agencies. Already during World War I, the Friends and the JDC had worked together in the German mass feeding project. They had very much in common. Both were humanitarian organizations, devoted to service on a non-sectarian basis. Although the JDC funds came from Jewish sources, they were distributed to the needy, regardless of race or religion. As Pickett wrote to James N. Rosenberg, vice-chairman of the JDC: "We are already deeply indebted, as Christians, for the way in which Jews have helped us to carry on our work, but it is because of the common purpose to serve the needs of humanity that many of us share that we venture to offer this opportunity of cooperation".[12]

Cooperation was the keynote to a smooth relationship. The Friends frequently reported to the JDC on the refugee problem. Jewish leaders appreciated these reports highly. Coming from an impartial non-Jewish source, they were regarded as the best objective information on what was really going on in Germany.[13] The close and warm relationship between the two bodies found dis-

10 David M. Bressler to Joseph Hyman, November 3, 1933; Evelyn M. Morrissey to Pickett, November 29, 1933 (JDC archives, AFSC).
11 Hyman to Pickett, April 12, 1934 (AFSC: GF, 1934, Committees and Organizations = C & O).
12 Clarence Pickett to James N. Rosenberg, April 1, 1935 (JDC archives, AFSC).
13 Hyman to Robert Ashworth, June 18, 1934; Rosenberg to JDC, November 13, 1933 (JDC archives, AFSC).

tinct expression in JDC participation in Quaker projects. In early 1934 the JDC office in Paris supported the Entr'aid — a Quaker relief project in the French capital — with a monthly contribution of $ 330, which amount was later substantially increased. While the Jewish Committee provided financial support as well as staff members and local workers, the Friends' own contribution to that partnership was no less valuable. As Joseph Hyman indicated to James Rosenberg: "I have no doubt that they render a type of service that no other organization is in a position to do".[14]

Encouraged by the JDC support, Clarence E. Pickett, the energetic executive secretary, went, in April 1934, on a fact-finding mission to the European Quaker centers to expand relief activities. However, the AFSC was not free of difficulties, even in maintaining the level of its annual budget. Thus, in 1933 the Committee allocated $ 20,000 for overseas relief, whereas in 1934 the sum dropped to $ 17,000. An appeal to 3000 non-Friends brought meager results.[15]

Not only non-Friends but also committed Quakers showed apathy toward the fate of refugees. James McDonald tried to enlist the AFSC's support for the Paris Entr'aid, pleading, politely at first and later more directly, but apparently in vain. "Mr. McDonald has not succeeded in getting much from the American Quakers", reported his secretary in July 1934.[16] Norman Bentwich, the British Jewish leader and chief assistant of the High Commissioner, toured the United States in 1935, campaigning for Christian support of non-Jewish refugees. He came out frustrated from a meeting with a Quaker group in Philadelphia, who were "disappointingly passive". "Even with the Friends, the springs of charity

14   Hyman to Rosenberg, April 11, 1935; Pickett to Hyman, December 6, 1934 (JDC archives, AFSC).
15   Minutes of a Meeting of the Foreign Service Section, AFSC, December 11, 1933 (AFSC:MF); Grace E. Rhodes to James McDonald, April 10, 1934 (MP:GC:AFSC).
16   Olive Sawyer to André Wurfbain, July 17, 1934 (MP:H); McDonald to Hugh W. Moore, March 18, 1934 (MF:GC:AFSC).

seem to have dried up in this dry land", he lamented to Mc-
Donald.[17] "I must say that I was bitterly disappointed with the
reception. I could not believe that there was such indifference to
the human work which the Friends are doing in Europe for these
victims of religious and racial persecution", he wrote to Pickett.
"I do feel so strongly that American Friends cannot stand aloof".[18]
McDonald, after his own experience at Philadelphia, was not surprised. "I am not very optimistic about the Quakers here", he
observed.[19] Up to August 1935, no funds had been collected by the
AFSC for the Paris Entr'aid. Thus, contrary to the general con-
ception, the American Friends were reluctant to assume responsibility for Christian refugees. During the period 1933—1938 there
was little to distinguish the American Quakers from the Christian
community at large as regards their apathy toward the victims of
Nazi oppression.

Unlike their American counterparts, the European Friends were
very active during that period. The French Quakers maintained
the Paris Entr'aid, feeding about 1200 children daily. In addition
to the JDC support, the British Society of Friends also assisted
the project with a monthly payment of £100. In Ohman, Holland,
a Dutch Friend opened an agricultural school for adult refugees
and a school for refugee children, most of them Jewish. In Vienna,
the Quakers distributed food, through the generous help of a
Socialist fund, to 4800 workers. Likewise in Berlin, Geneva, Oslo
and Stockholm, the Friends were busy providing relief. Norman
Bentwich rightly singled out the Society of Friends as one of the
few exceptions to Christian indifference. They "have worked
devotedly and untiringly to help the refugees from Germany without distinction of race, creed or community".[20]

17 Norman Bentwich to McDonald, May 7, 1935 (MP:GC).
18 Bentwich to Pickett, May 14, 1935 (AFSC: GF, 1935, C&O).
19 McDonald to Bentwich, June 21, 1935 (MP:GC).
20 Bentwich to McDonald, August 5, 1934; February 20, 1935; April
    9, 16, 1936 (MP:GC); "Aryan and Non-Aryan Refugees from Ger-
    many", 1935 (MP:GC).

Quaker help to Jewish refugees in Europe was indeed a remarkable phenomenon. In some cases Jewish refugees preferred to turn for help to the Friends than to their co-religionists. A number of German Quakers were arrested and sent to concentration camps because of their help to Jewish neighbors. In Havana, Cuba, Jewish refugees received shelter and vocational training in a Quaker hostel.[21]

Friends offered services to Jews in the United States as well. "I do want us to help the Jewish friends in any way we can", insisted Pickett.[22] Hertha Kraus, who was in charge of the casework in the AFSC, expressed time and again her wish to provide vocational and professional counseling to Jewish refugees. Eventually, in February 1939, the Refugee Committee of the AFSC decided to offer its services to Jews, "providing the load was not too heavy".[23] Although Bentwich correctly stated that the Quakers did not favor one group or religion above the other, the latter, because of the particular situation, did concentrate their efforts on non-Aryan Christians. This was the case mainly because Jewish relief agencies were already providing services in European countries, whereas Christian agencies at that time lacked efficient refugee committees.

When in 1934 the High Commission for Refugees considered plans for overseas settlement of non-Aryan Christian refugees, it naturally turned to the London Friends, asking them to assume responsibility for administering the project. G.B. Jeffrey, chairman of the German Emergency Committee of the British Society of Friends, frankly rejected the proposition. This was because the peculiar contribution of the Quakers came from their "intimate personal contact" with individuals in trying to understand their problems. The big agencies, on the other hand, were better equipped

21 Clarence E. Pickett, *For More Than Bread* (Boston, 1953), pp. 141, 120, 126, 130, 138; AFSC, Minutes of the Refugee Committee, October 27, November 17, 1939 (AFSC: MF); Chase L. Conover to John Rich, n.d. (AFSC:GF, 1941, FS:R).
22 Pickett to H. Wood, March 31, 1938 (AFSC:GF, 1938, FS).
23 Minutes, Refugee Committee, AFSC, February 3, 1939 (AFSC:MF).

to tackle the large-scale settlement projects, and the Quakers were neither able nor interested to compete with them.[24] Thus, even the British Friends, who earned much praise, were reluctant to take the lead when it came to more ambitious plans, despite the fact that the financial burden would not rest on their shoulders.

The events in 1938 and especially the riots of *Kristallnacht*, on November 10, 1938, roused the American Quakers to action. Up to that time the care of refugees was almost a one-man effort, that of Hertha Kraus. An associate professor of social economy at Bryn Mawr College, she personally rendered services to 150 refugees of all denominations in Germany, Latin America and the United States. Herself a German immigrant, she had been associated with the Committee while still in Germany during World War I. Her firsthand knowledge of the immigrant mentality and the problems confronting immigrants in America singled her out as the Quakers' expert on refugee matters. She helped to establish the Refugee Committee and later served as its Consultant. She initiated and supervised some of the Committee's unique projects, such as the hostels and American Seminars.[25]

With the growing refugee cry for help, institutionalization of the relief services in the United States became the order of the day. The Foreign Service Section, which was chiefly responsible for overseas operations, was interested in forming a separate committee that would deal with those refugees who were already in the country. In October 1938 a Foreign Service Section memorandum called for the strengthening of refugee services in the United States through the establishment of a Refugee Committee with an office of its own. Listed among that body's aims were coordination of the Services' different divisions on refugee matters, the provision of affidavits, vocational guidance and jobs, and fighting anti-Semi-

---

24 Bentwich to G. B. Jeffrey, August 22, 1934; Jeffrey to Bentwich, August 2, 1934 (MP:GC).
25 See Hertha Kraus' memorandum for CEP (Clarence E. Pickett), n.d. (c. 1938) (AFSC:GF, 1938, FS:RS).

tism by means of an educational campaign. The memorandum ended with the warning that the AFSC "should recognize the urgency of the need and not shirk the inevitable consequences of its work in Europe".[26]

In a series of meetings the members of the new Committee discussed organizational problems as well as the type and scope of services to be provided. So in December 1938 the Quakers confronted the same issues that other refugee agencies had faced earlier. Thus, the institutionalized help of the Quakers for refugees in America made a belated appearance, years after several other sectarian agencies had first entered the field. The fact that other relief organizations had already been operating was naturally an advantage for the Quakers. It enabled them to define independently their function and areas of activity, and to refer unwanted cases to other appropriate agencies. Since the AFSC was neither a fund raising body, nor a relief organization proper, it limited its services to certain fields, generally services not provided through other committees. The Quakers were eager "to get beyond relief into the more far-reaching openings for reconstruction and rehabilitation", to use the words of Clarence Pickett.[27] It was impossible for a Committee with limited financial resources to offer actual relief on any practical scale. "Orientation and hospitality" were the catchwords of the Friends in supplementing the services of other agencies. It gave thought to social and intellectual absorption, and to the psychological crisis that enforced immigrants had to undergo. One of the chief purposes of the Refugee Committee was to prepare newcomers to become not only American citizens, but also an integral part of the American society and its culture.[28]

---

26 "To the American Friends Service Committee", October 1938, signed by Margaret E. Jones, Albert Martin, Anne H. Martin, Elizabeth B. Yarnall and D. Robert Yarnall (AFSC:GF, 1938, FS).

27 Pickett, *For More Than Bread*, p. 202.

28 *Ibid.*, p. 142; Kathleen H. Hanstein to Carolyn Zelany, January 25, 1946 (NRS papers, 1315, YIVO).

Volunteer staff was characteristic of the Quaker help for refugees. A considerable part of the services, both in offices and in the field, was rendered by volunteers, both Friends and sympathizers. In August 1940, for example, 25 volunteers contributed 1250 hours of work to the Refugee Committee. That ensured lower overhead expenses than burdened other committees. While 27% of the ACCR's budget for 1940 was expended on administration and promotion, the AFSC in that year spent only 9.5% of its budget for that purpose.[29]

From the outset it was decided to limit the case load to the handling capacity of the staff; to refrain from publicity and the attraction of refugees to the Committee. The intake policy was carefully examined. Hertha Kraus' opinion was accepted that the agency should undertake "only those (cases) for whom we, as Friends, felt a peculiar responsibility".[30] Indeed, the Committee dealt only with Friends or those recommended by them. This policy met with reservations even on the part of Committee members. James Vail thought that "any refugee coming in should be judged on the merits of the case", rather than because a Quaker recommended him. In spite of such criticism, the original line prevailed.[31]

If, to become eligible for help, refugees had to be referred by Friends, to be accepted as a worker obviously such a recommenda-

29 Minutes of the Refugee Committee, AFSC, September 26, 1940 (AFSC:MF); Confidential Study concerning the Cost of Raising Relief Funds of the Foreign Relief Appeals in the Churches, June 1941 (Moss papers, 145, FCC archives). In 1941, however, the Refugee Committee of AFSC disbursed for administration of its Philadelphia and New York offices 27.5% of its budget. See AFSC, Refugee Section, Financial Statement, December 31, 1941 (AFSC:GF, 1941, RS).

30 Report of Hertha Kraus, AFSC Counselor for Refugees, n.d. (AFSC: GF, 1938, FS:RS); Minutes, Refugee Committee, AFSC, February 3, 1939 (AFSC:MF).

31 Minutes, Sub-committee of Foreign Section, Executive Committee on Report of Study of Refugee Division, April 14, 1942 (AFSC:MF).

tion was necessary. Although not every staff member had to be a Quaker, he was supposed to share the AFSC's basic ideology and motivation. When the candidacy of Mary M. Rogers was considered for the post of executive secretary of the Refugee Committee, her status as a Friend was mentioned in the discussion. In certain inner-circle meetings it was understood that for an important or delicate job only a Friend could be trusted and selected.[32] Such an attitude was only natural, and prevailed also with other agencies. Just as the NRS was interested in caring for Jewish refugees, the ACCR for Protestants and the CC for Catholics, so the AFSC rendered its services mainly on behalf of Friends or their relatives. However, if the AFSC's avowed policy was to support German refugees "without distinction of race, creed or community", one may question the validity of such an approach. Still, that reservation was aimed only at services offered on an individual case basis. The group projects were open to the members of the three religions, without discrimination.[33]

Several orientation and training programs were offered, which may be considered the Quakers' unique contribution to the absorption of refugees. Hostels were one of the means used to help newcomers adjust themselves to the American scene. Commencing from the summer of 1939 the Sky Island hostel in West Park, New York, opened its gates to 35—40 refugee guests at a time. For a period of 3–4 weeks courses were given, in an informal way, in American history, U.S. politics, geography of the country, music and driving. Cooperative life with the American staff, along with personal tutoring in English, greatly improved the newcomers' ability to speak English. The volunteer staff aimed at closing the

---

32 Draft of Foreign Service policy, November 20, 1944 (AFSC:GF, 1944, Policy); Minutes, Refugee Committee, AFSC, December 8, 1938 (AFSC:MF); Lyn Whelden to Margaret Frawley, November, 1943 (AFSC:FS, 1944, Planning).

33 Report of the Refugee Division of AFSC, taken from Arthur Dunham's study, n.d. (AFSC:GF, 1942, FS:R).

linguistic gap, as well as giving a realistic understanding of the American way of life.[34]

The success of the Sky Island project led to the establishment of another two hostels, in Scattergood, near West Branch, Iowa, and in Quaker Hill, Richmond, Indiana. The places were carefully selected in friendly communities, with a view to the settlement there of most of the refugee visitors. While Sky Island was a summer hostel, where people came for a 3–4 week vacation, in Scattergood refugees stayed for four months and sometimes more. Here newcomers were not only helped to orient themselves but also provided with a temporary haven, especially for those who needed that stage of adjustment before taking their place as self-supporting Americans. This hostel began to operate in April 1939, accommodating 35 people at a time. During its first year 22 guests were secured jobs.[35] The hostel idea won support among refugee organizations like the NRS and ACCR, that referred their clients to the hostels, covering their expenses.[36]

Because of the refugees' eagerness to stay in the New York area there was some difficulty in persuading them to go to a hostel in Iowa or Indiana. W.Z. Fuller of the ACCR was required "to use more pressure in getting people out there".[37] This was the case in 1939—1940, when unemployment was high and a wave of refugees poured into the country, whereas in 1942—1943, when the gates of the country were almost closed and war effort brought prosperity, the Mid-West hostels were unable to attract guests. The "Quaker

34 "Summary of two memoranda in re-projects of the AFSC", 1939 (JDC archives, AFSC); John F. Rich, "Americanization Through Quaker Hostels", 5 pp. ms. n.d. (NRS papers, 1315, YIVO). The article was prepared for publication in 1939 for *Social Work Today*; John Rich to William Haber, October 24, 1939 (NRS, 10, YIVO).

35 AFSC, Refugee Division, Report, January 1 — May 31, 1942 (NRS papers, 1315, YIVO).

36 Joseph Hyman to Henry Ittleson, July 24, 1939 (JDC archives, AFSC); AFSC, Minutes, Refugee Section, Executive Committee, January 15, 24, 1940 (AFSC:MF).

37 Fuller to Pickett, November 28, 1939 (AFSC:GF, 1939).

Hill", in Richmond, Indiana, which had operated as a refugee center from July 1940, terminated its emergency work for newcomers in September 1941, "due to immigration restrictions". During its fifteen months of operation 55 refugees were given an opportunity to adjust to the American way of life.[38] Scattergood hostel also encountered difficulties. In 1942 only 14 refugees were resident there, leaving the place half empty. To adjust themselves to the changing situation, the hostels transformed their function in 1942—1943. Being committed to serve the most needy, the Friends began to help Japanese Americans, opening to them the gates of Scattergood and teaching them agriculture.[39] Though the Sky Island hostel continued to serve European refugees, it too changed its function. Instead of the guidance of newcomers in orientation and adjustment, which were the aims during 1939—1940, the focus of activity shifted to the elderly, who were mainly interested in resting for a week or two.[40]

Another somewhat similar Quaker project was the Cooperative College Workshop. The Refugee Division, with its small budget, concentrated its services on a selected group of refugees, teachers and college professors. To overcome their painful process of adjustment to the American educational system, Hertha Kraus initiated the College Work Shop in Haverford, Pennsylvania as an educational center. From 1940 a selected group of 20—25 teachers were given intensive instruction in orientation courses in English, American history, American education, U.S. government and social sciences. They also made observation trips to educational institutions. By means of social contacts made with the Haverford community

---

38 "Quaker Hill: A Friends Service Center", January 1, 1942 (AFSC: GF, 1942, FS:R).
39 Minutes of the Advisory Committee, Refugee Division, December 16, 1942, February 5, 1943 (AFSC:MF).
40 AFSC, "The Powell House Crier", August 1944, September 1944 (HIAS–HICEM papers, VII:61, YIVO); Report of the Refugee Division, AFSC, June—August, 1942 (NRS papers, 1315, YIVO).

they had a firsthand opportunity to become familiar with the American way of life.[41]

The financial burden fell chiefly on the shoulders of the National Refugee Service, which directed its suitable clientele to the Workshop. After two and a half years of operation the NRS's supervisor, Dr. Samber, proposed the Workshop's transfer to a new locale. He also urged a stricter selection of candidates as well as cutting the expenses by a reduction of staff. It seems that the NRS report had some influence on the Refugee Division's decision to close the Workshop in May 1942.[42]

The American Seminar for Refugee Scholars, Teachers and Artists was a parallel project to the Cooperative College Workshop, with almost the same aims and very similar methods. It also had the same initiator and organizer, namely, Hertha Kraus. The American Seminar was a summer school, planned "to provide an opportunity for newcomers with specialized training to accelerate adjustment to American community life, to get a better understanding of American democracy and history, with emphasis upon principles and methods of education".[43] It also offered intensive courses in oral and written English. While the College Workshop was a one-term program for adjustment, including sitting in and actual teaching, the Seminar was a summer session, with heavy emphasis on social activities and entertainment. The former was scheduled to secure jobs for the clients in the vicinity, but the latter had no direct placement purpose.

The first American Seminar was held in the summer of 1940 in Wolfeboro, New Hampshire. The volunteer staff of American in-

41   Minutes, Refugee Committee, AFSC, September 26, 1940 (AFSC: MF); AFSC, Haverford Cooperative College Workshop, 1941 (AFSC: GF, 1941, RS).
42   Jim Abrahamson to Pickett, January 2, 1942 (AFSC:GF, 1941, C&O); AFSC, Refugee Division, "Report", January 1 — May 31, 1942 (NRS papers, 1315, YIVO).
43   AFSC, "American Seminar for Refugee Scholars, Teachers and Artists, Summer 1942 (AFSC:GF, 1942, FS:R).

structors and tutors contributed to the success of the experiment. In the first year 40 refugees and 25 Americans lived on the campus, studied, read and shared outdoor recreations for two months. The experiment was so successful that in the following year the number of participants doubled. Because of the numerous candidates referred to the Seminar by relief agencies, it was divided into two centers.[44] It is hard to evaluate the Seminar's usefulness, particularly its immediate results. As a concentrated program of vocational counseling and intensive preparation at low cost, it did teach newcomers about the American people and their culture. Probably equally important was the psychological effect, which was vividly described by an American participant as follows:

> They began to join in the easy give and take of daily life in America. Shyness was gradually forgotten, depression came less often; faces grew livelier, laughter more spontaneous. But most important of all, the consciousness of being a 'refugee', a victim of past circumstances, was offset by the possibility of becoming a contributor to the future.[45]

The problem of the placement of teachers, scholars and students gradually gained the attention of the Refugee Committee. Lack of understanding as to how to handle the problem was responsible for meager results. Not only were there few openings and many candidates, but the manner in which agencies and individuals flooded universities irritated college executives. A study, prepared by the educational counselor, recommended that the Refugee Committee should act as the clearinghouse for well-qualified and successful teachers, but should also have another

---

44 Claudia Gardiner, "An Experiment in Cooperative Scholarship", (AFSC:GF, 1940, RS); *Newscast*, 2 (June 1942), 2; AFSC, "The American Seminar", 1942.

45 C. Gardiner, "An Experiment in Cooperative Scholarship", (AFCS: GF, 1940, RS).

list of candidates who need a period of readjustment before being ripe for appointments.[46]

Adopting part of the recommendations, the Refugee Committee of the AFSC offered a variety of services during 1940—1942 for scholars, teachers and students, such as securing teaching positions, scholarships, internships, hospitality, training opportunities and counseling. In 1941, 375 teachers and students were placed by the Committee.[47] In evaluating the achievements of the AFSC with regard to the placement of refugee scholars, one has to bear in mind the tremendous difficulties that it confronted. By means of the orientation projects and due to the Friends' good contacts in the academic world, as well as their reputation for providing reliable information about their clients, they offered an important service and performed quite successfully. Between 1939—1945 the AFSC found positions for 200 scholars in colleges and research institutions, as well as the many openings found for high school teachers and fellowships for students. During that same period the Emergency Committee in Aid of Displaced Foreign Scholars, with the financial backing of several trusts and relief agencies, placed a total of 330 refugee scholars.[48] This comparison indicates that the Quakers, despite the smaller number of people helped by them and considering their circumstances, may be credited for that achievement.

One of the means employed by the Quakers for the Americanization of refugees was the organization of social and cultural activities. The provision of hospitality to 20—25 newcomers in Friends' homes was one of the missions of the Philadelphia

46 "Excerpts from Informal Report of Field Study made to the Refugee Section of AFSC, May 28, 1940 by Ruth V. Pope, Educational Counselor; AFSC, Minutes, Refugee Committee, May 26, 1939 (AFSC: MF).

47 AFSC, Minutes, Refugee Section, October 24, 1940 (AFSC:MF); Services for Refugee Scholars, Teachers and Students; AFSC, Foreign Service, Annual Report, 1941 (AFSC:GF, 1941, FS).

48 Davie, *Refugees in America*, p. 110. See below, pp. 310—318.

Quakers. In addition, refugees and Friends were invited to the monthly parties in the Meeting House, which attracted up to 150 participants. By meeting to listen together to a lecture or concert, followed by small talk, refugees had a rare opportunity to meet friendly Americans. The same approach, although on a larger and more institutionalized scale, was followed at Powell House in New York City. The Committee's hospitality center was opened in September 1943 to offer language courses, lectures, parties, trips, and a variety of cultural and social activities. English and Quakerism proved to be the most popular study courses. Altogether the Powell House entertained more than a thousand monthly refugee visitors.[49]

In Catholic circles such operations were criticized, the Friends being accused of aiming their activities at the conversion of refugees to Quakerism. In fact, not only Catholics but also Orthodox Jews complained of Quaker efforts at conversion.[50]

To carry out even such small-scale projects, the Refugee Committee of the AFSC badly needed the practical support of large relief agencies as regards information, counsel and especially funds. Its cooperation with the American Jewish Joint Distribution Committee during the years 1933—1934 has already been discussed. The lively correspondence between them reveals a close relationship during the entire Nazi period, covering a wide spectrum of subjects.[51] A minor friction between the JDC and the AFSC occurred in 1939 when the latter made an appeal in Iowa to cover the expenses of its hostels — including the one in

---

49   AFSC, "Bulletin on Refugees Abroad and at Home", no. 18, March 27, 1944 (NRS papers, 1315, YIVO); *Ibid.*, AFSC, *The Powell House Crier*, September, November 1944 (HIAS–HICEM papers, VII:61, YIVO).

50   Bruce M. Mohler to Charles D. Gorman, October 4, 1935 (National Catholic Welfare Conference papers, Box 23); Mohler, "Summarization of Correspondence", February 25, 1941 (NCWC, Box 82). The author's conversation with Prof. Hyman, August 3, 1978.

51   See, for example, Hyman to Pickett, November 23, 1936 (JDC archives, AFSC).

Havana — which the JDC had agreed to maintain. "It is not clear to me", complained Joseph Hyman to Henry Ittleson of the United Jewish Appeal, "why our Quaker friends make us a proposition, which of course we were very happy to accept . . . and thereafter they go out to try and get special gifts for these hostels, frequently from important Jews". The appeals certainly hurt the UJA's campaign and "aroused a great deal of comments and misunderstanding".[52] Eventually, Pickett gave instructions to stop the appeal, abandoning the idea of competing with the UJA, which really contradicted the basic purposes of the AFSC.[53]

Another Jewish organization that was interested in enlisting the Quakers' help was the American Jewish Committee. Unlike the JDC, the AJC was not a relief agency and did not provide actual help for refugees. It focused attention on the growing anti-Semitism in America and the ways of combating it. In 1939 an educational campaign was launched to correct misconceptions concerning the number of refugees coming into the country. Jewish leaders were particularly anxious to highlight Christian activities on behalf of refugees. They accordingly turned to Pickett to publish the Quakers' record of operations in that field. He was reluctant to do so, fearing that such publication might do harm to the Friends' activities in Europe. However, the Board of the AFSC agreed to issue a pamphlet which would give exact information about the refugee problem, and correct serious misunderstanding. Pickett demanded that "the manuscript ought to be very carefully read and checked by someone here, so that we could speak with final assurance when questions of fact are raised".[54] Accordingly, the AJC prepared, printed and distributed a quarter of a million copies

52 Hyman to Ittleson, July 24, 1939; P. Mendes to Robert Hertram, April 27, 1939 (JDC archives, AFSC).
53 Hyman to Pickett, May 4, 1939; Hyman to Ittleson, July 24, 1939 (JDC archives, AFSC).
54 Memorandum: FNT (Frank N. Trager) to SW, December 29, 1938 (AJC, Refugees, 1938—1944); Pickett to Trager, April 5, 1939 (AFSC: GF, 1940, C&O).

of "Refugee Facts", which appeared under the imprint of the AFSC. The pamphlet received wide publicity, including coverage in 100 newspapers, and Pickett was interviewed on the radio which gave him an opportunity to propagate the cause of Christian refugees.[55]

The Protestant Churches were one of the sources of the Committee's income. The contribution of the Committee on Foreign Relief Appeals in the Churches to the Quakers totaled 14% of the AFSC's budget in 1940.[56] Several suggestions were entertained as to how to increase the Churches' support in order to meet the growing demand for relief, particularly in France, but without positive results.[57]

We have so far discussed the Refugee Committee's characteristics, its unique projects and its cooperation with other agencies. We may now turn to the actual operations of the Committee, to its problems and achievements throughout the war years. Duplication marked its activities from the outset. That small body had three offices. In addition, the Foreign Service Section of the AFSC was also involved in refugee affairs. Several precautions were taken to avoid, or reduce, overlapping, such as the decision to keep a record of every case handled by one of the other offices. However, eighteen months after its foundation, the Committee was still wrestling with the problem.[58]

55 Pickett, *For More Than Bread*, p. 148; H. W. Levy to Trager, September, 1939 (AJC, Refugees).
56 Lillian Trangott to Leslie B. Moss, November 21, 1940 (Moss papers, 143, FCC); John F. Rich to Moss, July 13, 1942; (AFSC:GF, 1942, C&O). Ten days later Rich reported only the sum of $ 75,000. See Rich to Moss, July 23, 1942 (Moss papers, 143, FCC).
57 Rich to Moss, October 6, 1942 (Moss papers, 143, FCC); Minutes of the Executive Committee of NRS, November 18, 1941 (Chamberlain papers, p. 1999, YIVO).
58 AFSC, Minutes, Refugee Committee, December 8, 1938; Minutes, Refugee Section, Executive Committee, September 17, 1940; Annual Report of the Refugee Section, 1939 (AFSC:MF).

The Refugee Committee's low scale of operations was revealed in the report covering its first year of activity. Out of an income of one million dollars in 1940, the AFSC disbursed on account of the Refugee Committee for relief work in the United States only 15% of the former's budget. Apart from the hostels, the Committee secured jobs for 63 teachers, placed 54 students and provided 137 affidavits. Out of 3737 appeals for help, the staff handled 1245 cases, "a figure we are not proud of, for it shows we are spreading ourselves too thin and taxing our present staff severely", reported Mary M. Rogers, the executive secretary.[59] During 1940—1941 the activities expanded, particularly the hospitality program. Quaker centers in San Francisco, Seattle, Washington D.C., Hartford, Ann Arbor and Cambridge, took care of refugee children in summer camps and invited newcomers to American homes.[60]

With the entry of the United States into the war, which was followed by a drastic reduction in immigration and the appearance of the Fifth Column scare, the Friends, like other refugee agencies, were confronted with the need to adapt their services to the changing conditions. The age level of newcomers was much higher now, averaging about 50 and frequently as high as 70 and even 80. Vocational training became almost impossible for these old people. Their continuing physical and emotional strain took its toll and curtailed their ability to function adequately. They therefore needed more personal attention and a different kind of treatment. In 1942 difficulties were encountered with some of the services of the Refugee Committee, such as the hostels and the College Workshop. The active cases had dropped from 2454 in December 1941 to 632 in May 1942.[61]

The situation became so grave that the very existence of the

59 AFSC, Annual Report of the Refugee Section, 1939; Pickett, *For More Than Bread*, pp. 168—169; AFSC, Refugee Section, Financial Statement, 1941 (AFSC:GF, 1941, RS).
60 Report of the Refugee Committee, 1941 (AFSC:GF, 1941, RS).
61 Annual Report of the New York Office, 1941 (February 9, 1942) (AFSC:GF, 1941, FS:R): "Present and Recent Services and Projects of Refugee Section, AFSC, as agreed upon at staff meeting of Refugee

Refugee Committee was put into question. Arthur Dunham, an American Quaker, was asked to prepare a study of the Committee's effectiveness and to make recommendations as to its future. In a thorough report, submitted on March 3, 1942, Dunham categorically stated that "The R.D. (Refugee Division) should continue its services. It should not look toward any complete liquidation of its program now, or in the immediate future. As far as one can see, at present, there will probably be a need for the R.D. until the end of the war and probably for several years thereafter". As a result of the drastic reduction of migration services, the report recommended a staff reorganization, a cut in the budget, the transfer of cases to other agencies, and the establishment of an Advisory Committee. The orientation and retraining programs, as well as the placement of a limited number of professional refugees, should continue, since these services were effective, successful and one of the "unique contributions" of the Committee.[62]

The Dunham Report and the adoption of its recommendations created frustration and demoralization among the Division's staff. In February 1943 the situation was so unclear that there was the feeling that everything should start from the beginning, in disregard of the activities of the previous years. Mary Rogers appealed "to think through the whole situation". Unable to accept the changes, she resigned her top job as executive secretary in protest. Although the Division continued its services, the reduction of its budget, the changes in personnel and the frustration of the staff, hampered the effectiveness of its work.[63]

Section, December 30, 1941", revised on January 5, 1942 (AFSC:MF); AFSC, Refugee Division, Foreign Section Service, Report, January 1 — May 31, 1942 (NRS papers, 1315, YIVO).

62 Report of the Refugee Division of AFSC, taken from Arthur Dunham's Study, n.d., pp. 1, 8—9; see below, Table IX: "Brief Summary of Major Recommendations from Report of Study of Refugee Division", May 1942 (AFSC:GF, 1942, FS:R).

63 Minutes, Advisory Committee of the Refugee Division, February 23, 1943 (AFSC:MF); AFSC, Annual Report, 1943 (NRS papers, 1315, YIVO).

With the spread of the war, new avenues of activity were found by the Quakers. Although German refugees were unable to reach American shores, the war also inflicted hardships upon other groups, such as enemy aliens. Thus, Japanese on the West Coast were interned with no one to take care of their families. Accordingly, attention was paid by the Friends to the needs of the internees' families. The vicissitudes of the war led the Friends to undertake a program on behalf of German prisoners of war and internees. Since German Friends had operated in Germany on behalf of British and American POWs, the American Quakers were determined "to offer our German Quakers whatever strength to their program that may accrue through our rendering similar service in this country", observed the executive secretary.[64] Therefore the AFSC offered services in the internment camp at Seagoville, which included entertainment and an educational program to cater for the intellectual needs of the internees. Since the Young Men's Christian Association specialized in services to POWs, one should not overstress the Quakers' help on behalf of enemy aliens. It was, as Clarence Pickett put it, more of the dimension "of token participation than of a major role".[65]

Thus, the Quakers' activities on behalf of refugees in America were unique, concentrating as they did on orientation and Americanization. The hostels, the American seminars and the College Workshop were only pilot projects on a small scale, which signaled to the big relief agencies the way that refugees should be treated. Yet these programs had independent momentum. Though the Friends initiated and implemented them, a considerable part of the funds and most of the beneficiaries came from other agencies, including Jewish ones. The American Friends were only belatedly roused to action on behalf of refugees, in 1938—1939. Their suc-

---

64 AFSC, Report of the Refugee Committee, 1941 (AFSC:GF, 1941, RS). Mary M. Rogers to Evelyn Hersey, August 12, 1943 (AFSC:GF, 1943, RS, Internees).
65 Pickett to Marc Peter, March 24, 1943 (AFSC:GF, 1943, C&O). See below, pp. 282—284.

cess in educational programs was questionable. Although their representatives participated in almost every refugee conference, voicing their protest against immigration policy, against anti-alien, and anti-Semitic prejudices, it seems that they were unable to change the hostile atmosphere. Even more significant was the Committee's failure to rouse the Quakers to favorable action in regard to that subject. Clarence Pickett, Hertha Kraus, along with several dozens of Friends, enthusiastically and wholeheartedly labored on behalf of the victims of oppression. But the rank and file members of the Quaker communities contributed neither financially nor by absorbing refugee families. As James Vail, an active Quaker on behalf of refugees, bitterly complained as late as 1943: "We cannot have people in desperate need in Europe, finding one Friend who cares what happens to them, and then coming to this country to find no Friends who care". Therefore, it seems that as far as the activities on behalf of refugees in the United States were concerned, the Quakers probably received more credit than they deserved.[66]

In regard to AFSC's operations abroad, however, the picture was quite different. The whole organization was "foreign minded", concentrating on help of the needy overseas. Ever since its foundation, the American Friends had been operating in Europe. It was only natural, then, that the Foreign Service Section, with its experienced staff, proved to be more effective and more influential in the AFSC's circles than the Refugee Division, which was responsible only for operations in the United States. In Europe, Friends of different nationalities had already been working on behalf of refugees. Thus, by their living example they served as a catalyst in activating and deepening the involvement of the American Quakers in refugee affairs.

---

66   AFSC, Minutes, Advisory Committee, Refugee Division, February 23, 1943 (AFSC:MF); AFSC was on the *Nation*'s Honor Roll for 1939 "for its unostentatious non-political and enormously effective work of bringing physical relief to the innocent victims of war and aggression". *The Nation*, 150 (January 6, 1940), 6.

Anti-Nazi propaganda was carefully avoided by the Quakers. If they intended working in Germany or in Nazi-occupied territories, they had to maintain an impartial stance. Indeed, objectivity was their most valuable asset. As a Quaker commission to the Reich expressed it:

> ...we have kept entirely free from party lines or party spirit. We have not used any propaganda, or aimed to make converts to our own views. We have simply, quietly, and in a friendly spirit endeavored to make life possible for those who were suffering. We do not ask who is to blame for the trouble which may exist, or what has produced the sad situation. Our task is to support and save life and to suffer with those who are suffering... we do not come to judge or to criticize or to push ourselves in.[67]

Due to their reputation for neutrality, the American Friends were flooded with requests for help from different countries. "There seemed to be a feeling", complained Clarence Pickett, "that ... we ought to be able to go anywhere and do anything. Unfortunately such was not the case".[68]

Pierrepont Moffat, of the State Department, recognized that the Quakers were "apparently in a position to play an active part" in respect to the refugee problem. His only warning to them was not to work independently, but to coordinate their activities with existing agencies. Moffat's anxiety was superfluous, because the AFSC's staff was in fact praised for close cooperation with other organizations.[69]

Jewish agencies especially, among them the JDC and HICEM,

---

67 "What is the Quaker Motive?", memorandum by Rufus Jones, Robert Yarnall and George Watton, July 1939 (GJCA papers, 151, YIVO).
68 Pickett, *For More Than Bread*, p. 169.
69 Pierrepont Moffat to Myron C. Taylor, April 8, 1939 (NA, 840,48 Refugees/1553).

benefited from Quaker intervention when their own members were
unable to act. In November 1940 Morris C. Troper and Dr. Joseph
Schwartz, of the JDC European office, turned to the AFSC to send
its representative to Lisbon, because only a non-Jew could nego-
tiate with the Portuguese government.[70] When the relationship
between the JDC and the American consul in Lisbon deteriorated
in May 1941, the American Friends once again came to the help
of the Jewish Agency. Due to the friendly relationship the problem
of the issue of visas was satisfactorily solved. In 1942 Josiah
Marvel, the AFSC's man in Paris, succeeded in persuading the
German Commandant in Paris not to close the JDC canteen. These
are only a few examples of the value to Jewish bodies of AFSC
services as a Gentile, non-partisan organization.[71]

In their relations with official authorities, abroad as well as at
home, Jewish bodies welcomed Gentile mediation on behalf of
refugees. The AFSC enjoyed a particularly good relationship with
the Roosevelt Administration. So much so, that in 1938 President
Roosevelt, seeking to capitalize on the Friends' reputation in
Germany, considered the possibility of nominating Clarence Pickett
as U.S. Ambassador to Berlin.[72] The American consuls in Europe
were severely criticized by the Quakers for their arbitrary interpretation of the regulations, which seriously limited the prospects
of refugees finding a haven in the United States. Still, the Friends
were more interested in establishing good relations with the consuls
than in attacking them. In Berlin, Vienna, Prague and Lisbon, the
Quakers collaborated closely with American immigration authorities. In 1939, when Pickett learned of a shortage of clerks at the

70   AFSC, Minutes, Refugee Section, Executive Committee, November
     13, 1940 (AFSC:MF).
71   *Ibid.*, Schauffler to Staff, March 12, 1941, April 1941; Letter no. 76
     from Philip Conard, October 4, 1941 (AFSC:GF, 1941, RS); Memo-
     randum: Margaret Frawley to Pickett, March 30, 1942 (AFSC:GF,
     1942, C&O).
72   Pickett, *For More Than Bread*, p. 167.

American Consulates in Vienna, Berlin and Prague, he offered to recruit German-speaking Friends, whose salaries would be covered by private contributions. Avra Warren, chief of the Visa Division, welcomed the offer but George Messersmith, Assistant Secretary of State, turned it down because of the Department's need of its approval by Congress.[73]

After *Kristallnacht*, Paul Baerwald of the JDC asked the AFSC to send a Commission to Germany to ascertain the exact situation of the Jews. The Quakers promptly gave their favorable response and turned to German authorities for permission. The Nazis guaranteed the two appointed commissioners "freedom to circulate freely and to investigate the need and meet it", as regards both Jews and non-Aryan Christians. In order not to travel with empty hands, the Quaker delegation requested from the JDC $500,000 for relief distribution in Germany. The American Jewish Joint Distribution Committee, being "most anxious" to help, approved the sum of $100,000. Following the JDC policy, Baerwald asked that "the source of such contribution should perhaps not be mentioned or publicized".[74] Secrecy was important concerning not only the financial source but also the departure of the Commission itself. However, the *Philadelphia Record* broke the news of the mission and its aims, which the Friends considered to be "the worst crime in newspaper history".[75] But the publication evidently brought no harm. After a meeting with Heydrich, head of the Gestapo, the

---

73 See for example the criticism on the consuls' behavior in Oslo and Stockholm, Harvey and Julianna Perry to Pickett, June 23, 1939 (AFSC:GF, 1939); Pickett, *For More Than Bread*, pp. 140—141; Pickett to James G. Vail, February 4, 1939 (AFSC:GF, 1939); AFSC, Minutes of Refugee Committee, April 28, 1939 (AFSC:MF).

74 Pickett to Hyman, January 4, 1939; Rufus M. Jones and Clarence E. Pickett to Paul Baerwald, January 20, 1939; Baerwald to Pickett, January 25, 1939; Memorandum by Herbert Katzki, February 9, 1939 (JDC archives, AFSC).

75 *Time*, December 19, 1938; Hyman to Pickett, January 3, 1939; Pickett to Hyman, January 4, 1939 (AFSC:GF, 1939).

commissioners reported that German officials had been "unfailing in their courtesy and friendly interest". They visited refugees, concentration camps, Quaker centers and refugee relief agencies in the Reich and its neighboring countries.[76]

The commissioners' visit had some direct results. The Nazis were made aware of the Friends' concern about the persecutions. The Jewish organizations were encouraged by the impression that the delegation left in Germany.[77] It spent the JDC funds very cautiously. The remaining sum of $ 40,000 was distributed for the relief of internees in France, mainly for children.[78]

Indeed, the care and feeding of helpless children was one of the issues that had occupied the Quakers ever since the Committee's foundation. Friends of different nationalities operated in Europe to rescue refugee children. Between November 1938 and August 1939 the Society of Friends in Vienna handled 1978 cases of children, 882 of whom it helped to emigrate to England, Scotland, Belgium, Holland and Sweden.[79] Since the mission of bringing children to the United States was organized under the responsibility of the New York-based "German Jewish Children's Aid", the AFSC cooperated and shared functions with it. The selection and examination of the youth was made by the Quakers in Vienna or Prague, and their transportation, reception at the piers and placement in private homes were under GJCA auspices. In spite of goodwill and a desire to cooperate, duplication and misunderstanding were almost inevitable, particularly when the operations

76 Report of Quaker Commissioners to the Third Reich, July 1, 1939 (JDC archives, AFSC).
77 Recommendations of Delegation to Germany of the AFSC, January 2; January 10, 1939 (AFSC:GF, 1939, C&O).
78 Summary of Financial Reports of American Friends Commissioners to September 1, 1939 (JDC archives, AFSC); Minutes, Combined Meeting of Foreign Service Section and Refugee Committee, November 22, 1940 (AFSC:MF).
79 Society of Friends, Vienna, October 16, 1939 (the papers of German Jewish Children's Aid, 151, YIVO).

took place in a number of countries, thousands of miles away from the headquarters.[80]

The Quakers' commitment to the rescue of refugee children and to their reception into the United States was clearly demonstrated by their role in the Non-sectarian Committee for German Refugee Children and its successive bodies. Pickett was the moving spirit and acting director of the Non-sectarian Committee, and later served as president of the Non-sectarian Foundation. Furthermore, in several plans made for the rescue of children, the Quakers were assigned a major role, such as contact with governmental authorities, both in the United States and abroad, and the selection of children and their escort to America. The Friends' efforts in that direction were praiseworthy, despite the limited success of these programs.[81]

When the horrors of war reached Great Britain in June 1940, a movement to save English children by bringing them over to America quickly sprang into existence. First to act were the American Friends, who offered to place the children of British Quakers in American homes. At the end of June the AFSC opened an office in New York to channel the matter, which was soon "almost inundated with a great number of communications and offers of assistance". The AFSC took care only of Quaker children, since the U.S. Committee for the Care of European Children assumed responsibility for the evacuation of British children. Eventually, fewer than fifty children arrived through the Quakers. Much ado about almost nothing.[82]

More serious was the plight of the refugees in France. As the

---

80   See Mary Rogers to Lotte Marcuse, February 15, 1940; Marcuse to Greenleigh, February 20, 1940 (GJCA, 151, YIVO).

81   For the aims and achievements of these committees, see below, pp. 321—323. See "Proposed Plan for German Refugee Children", n.d. (GJCA, 151, YIVO).

82   AFSC "Report on the Placement and Care of the British Quaker Children", October 28, 1940 (GJCA, 151, YIVO). On the evacuation of British children, see below, pp. 324—325.

biggest democratic country neighboring Nazi Germany, France became reluctant host to thousands of political and racial refugees from Nazism. In 1939, 400,000 victims of the Spanish Civil War added to the gravity of the situation in southern France. Un-Occupied France became the major scene of the AFSC's operations. The Quakers, however, were confronted with the British refusal to lift the naval blockade of Occupied and Vichy France, because of the risk that the food, medicine and clothing might fall into German hands. The Roosevelt Administration "understood the British position so well that little pressure was brought to bear to change it", complained Pickett later.[83] Contrary to the traditional behind-the-scenes activities, in December 1940 the AFSC publicly criticized the British refusal to lift the blockade. "We can assert categorically", read the AFSC's statement issued on December 11, "that there is no danger of seizure of our supplies by military authorities or interference with our administration". Moreover, nobody would gain any military advantage from such a humanitarian service.[84]

Although the Quakers' efforts to feed European children were "largely a story of frustration", as Pickett put it, they nevertheless succeeded, with the help of pressure from the White House and the American Red Cross, in sending two ships in 1941 with supplies for French and Spanish children. Trunks of food and clothes that arrived at Bordeaux in May 1941 were deteriorating in warehouses. Only a special permit enabled their distribution. In spite of such obstacles, the AFSC maintained a feeding program in France in 1941, helping some 50,000 children daily during a period of twenty weeks.[85] Collaborating with the Unitarian Service Committee, the JDC and HICEM in an effort to alleviate the desperate

83 Pickett, *For More Than Bread*, pp. 171, 172, 174.
84 Statement issued by the AFSC, December 11, 1940 (Moss papers, 143, FCC).
85 Pickett, *For More Than Bread*, pp. 181—182, 179; F. Van den Arend (Acting Assistant Chief, Special Division, State Department) to AFSC, May 27, 1941 (AFSC:GF, 1941, FS:R).

situation of internees in France, the American Friends provided in 1941 food for 84,000 children and vitamins for 100,000 children.[86]

The relations with the American Red Cross (ARC) were markedly different from those with other agencies. At first politeness characterized the approach. Strife, however, appeared when the ARC, which dominated the governmental relief work, refused AFSC participation in that service. President Roosevelt relied on the former, stating on March 12, 1940 that "the spear-head of our relief policy is the American Red Cross", which "is the first to enter the field" in case of emergency.[87] Referring to Pickett's request to distribute food in France, the President indicated that "such relief would be coordinated through the American Red Cross". He suggested that the ARC "would allot to the American Friends a portion of supplies for distribution by them".[88] Strain between the two organizations was almost inevitable, since both were engaged in the same type of activity and both had worldwide reputations as humanitarian and impartial agencies. However, the supremacy of the Red Cross in the field of international relief lent the Quakers an inferior status, which they were reluctant to accept. Furthermore, it seems that the core of the problem was their different approach to the refugee issue. While the Red Cross constantly maintained a 100% objectivity, the Quakers were on occasion ready to depart, even if only temporarily, from a strict impartiality. Their efforts to continue mass feeding in France, in spite of the fact that part of the food had been confiscated by the Germans, was only one example of their readiness to prefer refugee interests

---

86   Statistics in regard to the supplies transferred to France could be misleading because a considerable number of coupons and part of the wheat supplies reached the hands of German agents. Robert Dexter to Pickett, April 2, 1942 (AFSC:GF, 1942, C&O). For disagreement with the Unitarians, see below, p. 220.

87   Statement by the President, March 12, 1940 (FDRL, OF/3186).

88   F.D. Roosevelt to Clarence Pickett, August 16, 1940 (AFSC:GF, 1940, Individuals).

above legalities. While the ARC feared losing its reputation for impartiality, the Quakers tried to exploit their credit in favor of action on behalf of refugees.

The strain in their relationship reached its peak in 1942 with the ARC's refusal to collaborate with the Quakers in relief distribution in France. "Our best strategy", it was stated in an inter-office memorandum of the Friends, "may lie in approaches to influential members of the ARC, who may be able to convince the Chairman that we may share in the work that is being done".[89] Accordingly, Pickett met on July 10, 1942 with Richard Allen of the ARC asking, for the sake of the improvement of relations, "to be frank about the difficulties in the way". Allen considered the Quakers' policy of employing non-American staff for the distribution of relief to be the greatest obstacle, since his agency was committed — to the American people, as well as to the French authorities — to entire American handling of the relief. In spite of that criticism, Allen was ready to continue cooperation in France. Thus, "the groundwork is laid . . . for clarifying some of these misunderstandings", as Pickett noted with relief.[90] Apparently his joy was premature, because still at the end of September 1942 it was attested by a Quaker that the relations "have not always been the most cordial and we are trying very hard to live this down".[91]

Rivalry came to light again in October 1944, when a Quaker delegation visited the ARC headquarters to propose that the Quakers move personnel and supplies into France under Red Cross auspices. The proposal was immediately rejected on the ground that the army instructions recognized the ARC as the single agency in charge of the relief. Misunderstanding and rivalry not-

---

89 Memorandum: James G. Vail to C.R. Cary, September 4, 1942 (AFSC:GF, 1942, C&O); see also L.B. Moss to Miller, February 26, 1942 (Moss papers, 143, FCC).

90 Pickett's office memorandum of the conference with Richard Allen, July 10, 1942 (AFSC:GF, 1942, C&O).

91 Excerpts of letter from Lindsley Noble, September 30, 1942 (AFSC: GF, 1942, C&O).

withstanding, the two organizations managed to maintain some kind of *modus vivendi* during the war years.[92]

The deportation of Jewish refugees from southern France in August 1942 prompted the American friends of refugees into action. The U.S. Committee for the Care of European Children undertook the initial project of rescuing 1000 children, and AFSC, OSE and the French Quakers were in charge of selecting and escorting the youth. The performance of the American Quakers in regard to the children's emigration was not satisfactory. The complicated operations, spread over several countries and carried out under pressure of time, brought criticism from the AFSC's staff in Marseilles. The office "was forced to fall somewhat short of its expected functions". Not only was the selection process unsatisfactory, but the escorts were also not fully qualified for their task. Some questions were raised by the Quakers as to the wisdom of expending large sums of money and great efforts on the emigration of a comparatively small number of children. Would it not be more desirable to spend those funds for relief of more children in France, they wondered.[93] The AFSC and the U.S. Committee had made strenuous efforts to evacuate children from France even before the deportations of Jews in August 1942. During the eighteen months preceding that date, 309 children were evacuated from France in five transports. The Friends were responsible for the selection of the children and the U.S. Committee provided the funds for transportation and was in charge of their placement in American homes. Even that small achievement necessitated a great deal of work. It took eight months of struggle to overcome the bureaucratic red tape holding up the evacuation of one group of fifty children.

The entrance of the United States into the war and the growing

---

92 Lois Jessup to Margaret Frawley, October 13, 1944 (AFSC, 1944, FS:C&O).

93 Part of a ms. begins with "ch. 7: Emigration of Children", n.d. (AFSC:GF, 1942, FS:R).

German intervention in un-Occupied France necessitated the reorganization of the American agencies' operations. American
Friends left Germany and Austria, leaving the Berlin and Viennese
Centers to the German Friends. In Marseilles the AFSC's staff
remained and continued to offer services, jeopardizing their freedom and even their lives. Eight AFSC personnel were arrested and
were sent by the Germans to a prisoner camp in Baden Baden.
Soon after the arrests, in November 1942, the relief work in France
was transferred to the French Quakers — Le Secours Français —
who operated under a French license. With a staff of 23 men the
French Quakers worked in Marseilles, Montauban, Toulouse and
Perpignan. Only with the advance of the Allied Forces and the
liberation of France and Belgium in 1944, were the American
Quakers able to renew their activities, once more distributing vitamins, food and blankets.[94]

Simultaneously with the AFSC's operations in France, there developed a growing need for relief work in Italy and Portugal. The
American Quakers were asked to open centers in Rome and
Lisbon to take care of refugees, particularly Christians. The Rome
office was a short-lived venture. It operated between October 1940
and July 1941 and provided financial help to 314 persons and
rendered assistance to the emigration of 62 refugees.[95] The Lisbon
office, due to the importance of that neutral port, was more active.
From May 1941 the Quakers maintained a favorable relationship
with the American consulate, as well as with other refugee agencies. The AFSC personnel visited internment camps and provided
help for stateless persons.[96]

94 AFSC, Report of The Refugee Committee, 1941 (AFSC:GF, 1941,
    RS); Pickett, For More Than Bread, pp. 183, 189—190; Seton Porter
    (Le Secours Français) to the State Department, December 1942 (AFSC:
    GF, 1942).
95 Mary Rogers to Evelyn Hersey, March 5, 1940 (AFSC:GF, 1940, FS);
    H. and M. McClelland to Pickett, August 4, 1941 (GJCA, 151, YIVO).
96 Letter no. 76 from Philip Conard, October 4, 1941 (AFSC:GF, 1941,
    RS). In spite of the decreased volume of work, the American Friends

The Spanish Civil War and Franco's rise to power brought suffering to thousands of Republicans. Most of them fled to France and looked for final settlement in Latin America. In Spain itself children and adults were badly in need of food and medical supplies. In November 1938 Clarence Pickett turned to the State Department with a proposal to establish a small committee "to engage in the effort to afford greater relief and on a strictly impartial basis". Since that humanitarian proposal was in accord with American tradition, the Department of State approved the formation of such a committee. With the cooperation of the International Red Cross, the AFSC distributed food, clothing and medicine to Spanish refugee children in Spain, as well as in southern France.[97] The occupation of France brought new categories of refugees to Spain, such as victims of Nazi persecution, Allied and French soldiers, who were desperately trying to make their way, via Spain, to Portuguese seaports. Since Spanish transit visas were difficult to obtain, many risked illegal crossing of the border. Most of them were arrested and imprisoned in concentration camps. The American and British embassies obviously made strenuous efforts to have their countrymen released from the camps and evacuated to North Africa. They also labored on behalf of the French refugees, whose potential military power was of importance. Between November 1942 and July 1944, 25,000 refugees were evacuated from Spain to the Fedhala camp in North Africa. Most of these refugees were Allied and French soldiers, while 4500 of them belonged to other categories, including stateless persons, many of them Jewish. Approximately 1400 stateless refugees had been evacuated up to July 1944, but 1000 of them still remained in Spain.[98]

spent in 1944 $ 40,000 for refugees in Portugal. AFSC, Foreign Section Budget, January 1, 1944 — January 1, 1945 (AFSC:FS, 1944, Finance).

97   R. Walton Moore to Clarence Pickett, November 4, 1938 (NA, 852.48/278A).

98   Niles W. Bond's "Memorandum on Refugee Relief Activities of

The lion's share of the relief work and the efforts made for the release of stateless persons from camps was undertaken by private relief agencies. To coordinate the relief work in Madrid and render it effective, the Representation in Spain of American Relief Organizations (RSARO) was established at the beginning of 1943 at the initiative of Carlton J.H. Hayes, the American Ambassador. It consisted of the AFSC, the JDC, the Unitarian Service Committee and the War Relief Services of the NCWC. The new office, headed by David Blickenstaff of the AFSC, received not only constant support of the American Embassy, but was also officially recognized by the Spanish Government. The police accepted Blickenstaff's guarantee concerning documents of a stateless refugee and provided him with "safe conduct" in his travels in Spain. Thus, the RSARO served stateless persons "in much the same way that the diplomatic representation care for their own nationals".[99]

The Quakers enjoyed great prestige in Madrid due to Blickenstaff's energetic leadership. He won the confidence of Ambassador Hayes, who was very enthusiastic about his competent work.[100] This put him in the powerful position of being virtually the consul of stateless refugees. While many praised his sincerity and devotion, others had some reservations. Even R.M. Brandin, a friend on the consular staff, regarded him as "a little more idealistic than practical and a little more of a Quaker than an American. He tends

American Embassy in Madrid . . ." July 7, 1944; "Relief of Refugees in Spain", July 19, 1944; (Carlton J.H. Hayes papers, Box 1, at the Butler Library, Columbia University). For detailed discussion of the Spanish Government's approach to the refugees, as well as the American and British rescue efforts, see Haim Avni, *Contemporary Spain and the Jewish People* (Jerusalem, 1975), pp. 107—148 (Hebrew).

99   Minutes, Foreign Service Section, AFSC, January 13, 1945 (AFSC: MF); Bond, "Memorandum on Refugee Relief Activities of American Embassy in Madrid" (Hayes papers, Box 1).

100   Carlton Hayes to Secretary of State, March 1, 1944 (FDRL, WRB, Box 7); Confidential notes on Lois Jessup's talk with Mrs. Carlton J.H. Hayes in New York on April 28, 1944 (AFSC: FS, 1944, Washington Trips).

to withhold a good deal of information".[101] The JDC exerted upon him heavy pressure to help as many Jews emigrate to the United States as possible. While he wanted to help stateless persons leave Spain, he was opposed to the idea that America should be the only haven for them. The JDC, which operated mainly from Barcelona, was reluctant to submit to Blickenstaff's supervision. The controversy over policy, as well as over practical matters, became so heated that Blickenstaff asked for the removal of two JDC men from Spain.[102] The Madrid office, nevertheless, operated effectively. Centralization permitted a controlled division of functions among the various agencies. Each offered different kinds of services, or served different types of refugees. The agencies shared not only information but the cost of maintaining the RSARO as well. Every agency was free to expend on relief as much as it was able. In 1944 the AFSC's expenditures in Spain totaled $ 124,354. It also handled clothing for other agencies and administered money transfers. In that year the two Friends who headed the Madrid office handled almost half a million dollars of relief on behalf of other agencies.[103]

The War Refugee Board was so impressed with the successful cooperation that it recommended a similar consolidation of non-Jewish refugee committees in Lisbon.[104] At least partial credit for that achievement went to Blickenstaff and his associates, who devotedly and skillfully handled relief work in Spain.

The extension of AFSC services to French North Africa was a natural continuation of their activities in Portugal and Spain. The

101 R.M. Brandin's memorandum, June 28, 1943 (Hayes papers, Box 6).
102 *Ibid.* See about the complaints concerning Blickenstaff that John Pehle and Pickett received from different circles. Pehle, "memorandum for the files", July 20, 1944 (FDRL, WRB, Box 24).
103 Relief and Administrative Expenditures of Madrid Office, January 27, 1944 (AFSC:GF, 1944, FS:C&O); AFSC, Foreign Service Budget for Year January 1, 1944 — January 1, 1945 (AFSC:FS, 1944: Finance).
104 Minutes, Joint Foreign Service Executive Committee, AFSC, December 4 ,1944 (AFSC:MF).

Spanish authorities agreed to the release of internees on condition of their immediate departure from the country. And, indeed, the prisoners' release was followed by their prompt evacuation. In this way thousands of refugees reached Fedhala camp, near Casablanca. The German conquest of un-Occupied France on the one hand, and the occupation of North Africa by Anglo-American divisions on the other, brought about a concentration of thousands of refugees in North African camps, where food and medical supplies, as well as sanitary conditions, were quite poor.[105]

Since September 1942, still under Vichy rule, the AFSC had begun to provide services for internees in North African camps. The expenses of these activities amounted to $78,000 in 1944.[106] The Quaker team also contributed to the liquidation of the camps in Morocco and Algiers. Their help was particularly appreciated when they arranged matters which Jewish organizations were unable to do.[107]

Also badly in need of help were those refugees who had succeeded in crossing the Atlantic, but had remained stranded in Cuba. Since the Cuban Government prohibited them from working, thousands of refugees were waiting impatiently for funds and visas to continue their search for a permanent home. In 1939 there were about 4000 refugees idling in Cuba and living on welfare, most of them Jewish. Hertha Kraus of the AFSC located a farm of 30 acres near Havana, which she suggested turning into a trade and farm school for young refugees aged 16—25 years. In May 1939 she proposed a cooperative project to the JDC. The AFSC

---

105 David Blickenstaff to Carlton Hayes, July 23, 1943 (Hayes papers, Box 6); Blickenstaff's memorandum, "Evacuation of Stateless Refugees to North Africa", December 27, 1944 (*ibid.*, Box 1).

106 Ilja Dijour to James Bernstein, July 23, 1942; Marjorie P. Schauffler to Ilja Dijour, October 4, 1943 (HIAS–HICEM papers, vii: 59, 61, YIVO); AFSC: Foreign Service Budget, January 1, 1944—January 1, 1945 (AFSC:FS, 1944, Finance).

107 J. Oattinger to Ilja Dijour, July 5, 1943; Dijour to James Andrew, September 14, 1943 (HIAS–HICEM papers, vii:60, YIVO).

would be responsible for the maintenance of the hostel, for the overheads of the training school and would employ the American staff. The JDC, on the other hand, would cover the maintenance and tuition costs of the refugees. The Cuban cooperation, which lasted for some years, was fruitful.[108]

We have endeavored in this chapter to outline the AFSC's overseas operation in various parts of the world. In the course of a decade the scope of its services was meaningfully expanded, from an expenditure of $ 17,000 in 1934, to $ 1,911,300 in 1944.[109] Although the needs were always greater than the available funds, generally speaking the Quakers enjoyed a better financial situation than did other relief agencies, like the ACCR. In 1940, for example, the income was near to one million dollars and in 1944 it more than doubled, reaching the sum of $ 2,106,512.[110]

As early as June 1943, as the tide of the war turned in favor of the Allied Powers and even before final victory was clearly in sight, the AFSC's staff initiated preliminary discussions in regard to postwar relief work. The Committee wanted to continue its services along the lines followed by it for several years, such as mass feeding for children, Quaker hostels and joint projects with other agencies. However, suggestions were made to explore new patterns and directions of activity, such as community centers — an extension of the neighborhood centers, volunteer corps and leadership training.[111]

108 Memorandum from the AFSC to the JDC, May 4, 1939 (JDC archives, AFSC); A. Jaretzki to C. R. Cary, May 22, 1939 (AFSC, 1939, C&O); AFSC, "A Friendly Service for Refugees", n.d. (NRS papers, Box 1315, YIVO).

109 AFSC, *Annual Report, 1943* (NRS papers, 1315, YIVO); AFSC, Foreign Service Budget, January 1, 1944 — January 1, 1945 (AFSC:FS, 1944, Finance). See below, Tables X—XI.

110 AFSC, Minutes, Refugee Section, Executive Committee, May 22, 1940 (AFSC:MF); AFSC, Statement of Available Cash, Relief Division, November 30, 1944 (AFSC: FS, 1944).

111 AFSC, "Planning for Foreign Relief", June 25, 1943; Minutes of a meeting of the Foreign Service Staff, June 15, 1943 (AFSC:GF, 1944).

An interesting plan taken into consideration, which was suggested by a group of Friends interned in Baden Baden, called for a World Quaker Service. Having lived together for a long period, the internees of different nationalities evolved a proposition to extend "Quaker service to deal with human needs which are not now being met adequately". The plan, which was intended "to provoke constructive criticism", called on Quakers and others to "unite on a modest scale in a fellowship above political or racial barriers, without the hindrances that attach to an organization identified with a single nationality". The World Quaker Service, it was proposed, should be a non-profit corporation, with a central committee that would direct the agency and shape its policy. The personnel, who "should be provided with a thorough understanding of Quaker beliefs and social service", should act on a voluntary basis, though personal and family obligations should be met. The advantages of such a plan were visible to the authors. It would unite Quakers around the world into one big family, who would grasp world problems more easily. It would strengthen the neutral status of the Friends, avoiding the "nationalistic stigma". They would not be subject to political pressures of different countries. However, the proposition also outlined its possible drawbacks, such as the difficulty of finding financial supporters, the danger of growing inefficiency, the complexity of coordination with national services, and the unreality of the idea of maintaining a genuine cosmopolitan policy.[112]

As the months elapsed with the discussions bearing no positive results, a certain uneasiness made itself felt among the AFSC's staff. Without a clear-cut policy and well-prepared plans "we shall find ourselves making quick and ill-concerned decisions", warned a participant at a meeting of the Joint Foreign Service Executive Committee in January 1944.[113] In the course of the twenty months'

---

112   "A Proposed World Quaker Service", February 11, 1944 (AFSC: FS, 1944, Planning).
113   Minutes, Joint Foreign Service Executive Committee, AFSC, January 17, 1944 (AFSC:MF).

deliberations the Committee's aims, means and areas of service were reexamined. While the Baden Baden plan of a World Quaker Service was rejected as such, certain parts of it, relating to the selection of the area of services and the methods of carrying them out, were adopted. It was decided that the Friends' special responsibilities were "for the pioneering and experimental tasks which are unpopular, inconspicuous, or misunderstood". A more practical aspect was the desire which was expressed to render services only when a qualified relief organization was uninterested or unable to act. The program recommended that the agency work in close contact with community members and organize its activities through community centers. As to the termination of the agency's services, two grounds were suggested: either when some other responsible agency would extend its services, or when the need for such should become permanent rather than temporary.[114]

The new policy prompted practical decisions in regard to its implementation in the field work, such as whether to withdraw from the Madrid office, from individual migration work in Italy, Portugal and Spain, and whether to discontinue the money transfer service. Also, an answer had to be found to the question whether to give preference in future relief work to Axis countries.[115]

One of the factors the AFSC had to take into consideration with the expansion of the operations was the attitude of the local Friends. When aid to Sweden was being organized, the delegation to Stockholm carefully planned its action to avoid the impression that Americans were independently deciding the fate of the Swedish Friends. The latter hoped that such a mission would be "a Friend to Friend visit". That considerate approach marked the relations with other Continental Quakers as well. It was decided that consultation with the Quakers concerned was imperative before the

---

114 AFSC, "Draft of a Foreign Service Policy", November 20, 1944 (AFSC:FS, 1944, Policy); "Suggested Revision of Foreign Service Policy", January 12, 1945 (AFSC:FS, 1944, Planning).

115 *Ibid.*

planning of operations reached the stage of implementation.[116]

The Committee's expressed policy was to prefer "work with individuals in a personal relationship", and to avoid competition with public agencies. As pacifists, the Friends decided to refrain from working under the direction of army authorities.[117] That policy was tested when the question of cooperation with governmental agencies, such as the War Refugee Board and the United Nations Relief and Rehabilitation Association, was under consideration. The WRB respected the AFSC's neutral position and did not intervene in its operations. Although the Board encouraged the escape of refugees from Nazi-occupied territories, it "expressed its unwillingness to have our name associated" with underground work on the Continent, as the Joint Foreign Service Executive Committee reported. The Quakers cooperated fully with the Board. In spite of relatively limited contacts between the two agencies, mutual appreciation marked their relationship. Pickett expressed this attitude to Florence Hodel of the WRB in June 1945 as follows: "The Board has shown vigor, concern and vitality in its efforts to get something done in a tragic human situation. It has been a matter of immense satisfaction to us to have the opportunity of working as we have with the Board".[118]

Quite different was the Friends' attitude toward UNRRA. Like other private agencies, the Quakers feared losing their identity in a huge relief organization. "It would not be acceptable ... to go in merely to take orders and without freedom of action to shape the pattern of relief", protested the American Council of Voluntary

---

116 Lyn Whelden to Margaret Frawley, "Discussions of Foreign Service Staff with Roger Wilson", November, 1943 (AFSC:FS, 1944, Planning).

117 AFSC, "Draft of a Foreign Service Policy", November 20, 1944 (AFSC:FS, 1944, Policy).

118 Minutes, Joint Foreign Service Executive Committee, AFSC, February 24, 1944 (AFSC:MF); Pickett to Florence Hodel, June 12, 1945 (FDRL, WRB, Box 1).

Agencies.[119] Apart from loss of identity, Pickett was apprehensive that the Quaker idea of fellowship to oppressed people might lose ground in mixed teams with UNRRA, which would be some kind of betrayal of confidence. While UNRRA was solely concerned with physical relief, the AFSC had a "special duty toward spiritual reconstruction", argued the executive secretary.[120] After some hesitation, the American Friends decided to cooperate with UNRRA. A representative was dispatched to the latter's directorate and 8—9 Quakers joined the UNRRA personnel in Europe. Pickett later termed the relationship as "most cordial", and even defended the agency against its critics. In spite of repeated complaints of inefficiency, he regarded the international service to be as competent "as could reasonably be expected".[121] Not everyone in the AFSC shared that view. In Spain, for example, UNRRA exerted economic pressure on refugees to gain their consent to be evacuated to Casablanca. The Quakers, along with HICEM, opposed this compulsory policy, calling for a solution without moving the refugees further away from the Continent. After one year's experience, the Friends found their early fears had been justified. In retrospect they questioned the desirability of collaboration because of their inability to contribute, as Quakers, to the cause.[122]

After World War II the American Friends continued to provide aid to the most needy. While during the Hitler era Jews and non-Aryan Christians were the main victims of persecution, after 1945 the Quakers focused their attention on helping the German and Japanese peoples.[123] Since 1948 they have been working, among others, in Arab refugee camps.

119 Minutes, Foreign Service Executive Committee, AFSC, January 17, 1944 (AFSC:MF).
120 Minutes, AFSC's Foreign Service Section, April 27, 1944 (AFSC: MF).
121 Pickett, *For More Than Bread*, p. 191.
122 Dijour to L.K. Cleveland, February 13, 1945; Cleveland to Dijour, February 15, 1945 (HIAS–HICEM papers, vii:63, YIVO). Minutes, Foreign Service Section, AFSC, May 5, 1945 (AFSC:MF).
123 Pickett, *For More Than Bread*, p. 193.

In the AFSC's activities on behalf of refugees from Nazism there were "small successes and enormous disappointments", as Pickett summed up his Committee's record. A great part of its efforts was devoted to the presentation of the refugee issue to the Roosevelt Administration, as well as to the American public. Probably no other group was more suitable for this task than the Quakers. However, in spite of their great prestige and reputation for impartiality, the AFSC "did not have much success", as Pickett admitted.[124] It was not their fault, but rather that of the American people. The Quakers demonstrated what could be done with a small personnel and limited resources, but with devotion and faith, to help the oppressed. The American Friends Service Committee, along with the British Quakers, surely deserved the Nobel Peace Prize it received in 1947 for efforts made and services rendered on behalf of the victims of Nazism.

---

124   *Ibid.*, p. 154.

7

AMERICAN CHRISTIAN RELIEF
ACTIVITY ABROAD

THE UNITARIAN SERVICE COMMITTEE

Several relief organizations, such as the American Committee for Christian Refugees and the Catholic Committee for Refugees, operated almost solely in the United States. For overseas relief work they relied on other bodies, using them as agents. There were bodies, like the American Friends Service Committee and the International Migration Service, that did not concentrate solely on America but expanded their activities on behalf of refugees to several countries abroad. As we have seen, the Quakers, for example, operated in Europe, North Africa and the Far East in addition to their projects maintained in the United States. A third category included bodies such as the Unitarian Service Committee (USC) and the International Rescue and Relief Committee (IRRC), which operated solely abroad in disregard of the home front.[1] In this chapter we shall discuss the latter type of relief Committees.

---

1 The USC projects in America were dedicated to minorities and other groups rather than to refugees. See below, p. 231.

The Unitarians' independent and active response to the refugees' cry for help came rather slowly. Only in 1940, when the Germans overran Western Europe, did they rise to action by establishing a Service Committee. Earlier, however, there had been sporadic displays of interest in oppressed people under Nazi occupation, and back in October 1938 the first Unitarian relief workers joined an AFSC commission to Prague, to investigate the possibilities of rendering assistance to the victims of persecution. In collaboration with the Quakers, the Unitarian representatives helped in obtaining the release of 1500 Czechs from Hungarian prisons.[2]

With the increasing misery in Occupied Europe, it became evident to the Unitarians that they could no longer refrain from helping these victims of the war. The foundation of a Service Committee in May 1940, with William Emerson as chairman and Robert C. Dexter as executive secretary, was a natural outgrowth of the Commission to Czechoslovakia, which had begun a year earlier. The purpose of the Service Committee was "to translate into terms of humanitarian service the Unitarian traditions of brotherly love and devotion to freedom and justice".[3] Indeed, this was the realization of more than a century-long Unitarian preaching. Since the beginning of the 19th century, the liberal-minded Unitarians had been rebelling against the conservative flank of the Congregational Church. The former emphasized the rights of private conscience over Scriptural and ecclesiastical authority and stressed the inherent capabilities of man. The outcome of that rupture was the establishment of the American Unitarian Association in 1826, with Massachusetts as its stronghold. It was only natural, then, that by carrying out the ideas of justice, tolerance and goodwill, it put into

---

2 Unitarian Service Committee, *Reporting for Service*, n.d. (*c.* 1945), p. 2. For a detailed discussion of the USC's activities, see the unpublished doctoral dissertation of James Ford Lewis, "The Unitarian Service Committee" (University of California, 1952), which I was unable to reach.

3 "The Unitarian Service Committee, 1939—1944" (mimeographed, 8 pp. ms.), p. 1.

practice the belief in the ability of man to build a better world. Along with propagating that idea, the Service Committee endeavored "to strengthen the forces of democracy by making every effort to aid those victims of totalitarianism and war".[4]

One of the characteristics of the USC was its patriotic stance. While the AFSC, the American Red Cross and the International Migration Service tried not to take sides, working under the neutral cover, the Unitarians did not hesitate to indicate their support of the Allied war efforts. "The Unitarian Service Committee has never been a neutral committee. It has always been committed to the victory of the United Nations", stressed William Emerson, the Committee's chairman, to Breckinridge Long. Indeed, in un-Occupied France the Unitarians operated as Americans, gathering a geat deal of valuable information for U.S. officials. This approach led to a clash with the Quakers and the American Red Cross.[5]

Another characteristic was the Unitarians' religious motivation. It was not surprising that some of the personnel were ministers. The Service Committee stemmed "from Christian traditions", as was declared in its annual report. This was also testified to by the seal on its letterhead, which showed a chalice resembling a cross. Yet, from the very beginning it offered services "to all races and creeds and nationalities".[6] Jewish refugees in Lisbon received transportation fees and other services from the USC; it tried to rescue Jewish children from France, and provided medical aid to Jewish children and infants in Marseilles and Switzerland. A friendly cooperation with the JDC, HICEM and OSE also proved the non-sectarian attitude of the USC. On several occasions the Unitarians provided services of a kind that Jews were not in a position to offer. In Vichy France, in Franco Spain, in

---

4 USC, *Reporting for Service*, p. 3.
5 William Emersoon to Breckinridge Long, November 4, 1942 (NA, 851.48/736); Robert Dexter to Clarence E. Pickett, April 2, 1942 (AFSC:GF, 1942, C&O).
6 USC, *Reporting for Service*, p. 3.

neutral Portugal and in Poland after its liberation, a gentile minister was very helpful. Still, as a result of the division of work among the relief agencies, the USC, sometimes with Jewish encouragement, devoted its major efforts to helping Christian refugees, such as the non-Aryan Germans, the Spanish Loyalists and the Basque children.[7]

The new Committee established its offices at the headquarters of the American Unitarian Association in Boston. Since most of the relief agencies were in New York, the USC eventually in 1942 also had to open a branch in that city, though directives came from the Boston center. The USC's activities gradually gained momentum. Medical units and social workers were sent to France. New centers were established in Paris, Marseilles and later in Lisbon and Geneva. Even a monthly bulletin was published under the title *Standing By*.

Between 1940 and 1942 the Committee devoted its energy to children in un-Occupied France. The feeding project for infants was one of its first activities in 1940. Milk and baby food were distributed for sick Basque babies in the Pyrenees and for French children in Marseilles. Since the Red Cross and the Quakers took care of refugee feeding, the Unitarians decided to concentrate on medical aid. From 1941, the Service Committee was the single relief agency to provide medical and sanitary aid in southern France. Its personnel frequently visited internment camps, distributing medical and sanitary supplies, as well as contributing to the establishment of medical laboratories in the camps. In Toulouse a hospital was operated under Unitarian supervision. Likewise in Marseilles a dental clinic, a dispensary with X-rays and a pharmacy offered to refugees free surgery, therapy and dental services.[8] The

7   Henry Muller to Ilja Dijour, February 3, 1944; Charles R. Joy to Dijour, November 2, 1942; Emerson to Dijour, September 30, 1944; (HIAS–HICEM papers = HH) first series, roll VII, folder 56, YIVO); Charles Joy to Noel Field, January 10, 1945 (FDRL, WRB, Box 20).
8   Lowrie, *The Hunted Children*, p. 40; USC, "The Second Mile", May 1941—May 1942 (AFSC:GF, 1942, C&O).

clinic was operated in collaboration with OSE (*Oeuvre de Secours aux Enfants*), a Jewish children's relief agency. The medical services expanded from aid to 495 persons in July 1941 to 2560 refugees aided in March 1942. Soon Unitarians were synonymous with medical aid. Even the International Red Cross recognized the USC as its sole agent in southern France for the distribution of medical supplies.[9]

Combating hunger was another target of the Service Committee. Successful efforts were made to cure the effects of extreme malnutrition. Children already afflicted with consumption were traced. Through international sources the Committee received donations of large quantities of vitamins A and D, as well as calcium, for distribution among children in un-Occupied France. Dietetic kitchens were opened in the camps, providing special food for sick people. The orthopedic and dental work for 3000 interned children led to the foundation of kindergartens and primary schools. In camp Rivesaltes, the central children's internment camp in France, 400 children played in USC-run kindergartens. In Marseilles, too, a school was opened for refugee children who were waiting for emigration. Thus, educational services on a limited scale became part of the USC's activities.[10] Still another dimension of the Unitarians' assistance given to refugees was casework. Social workers served as consultants providing guidance to individuals, also helping them to prepare for their immigration. By means of JDC financial support, a variety of services were provided by Unitarians in Lyons. For these operations, between May 1941 and May 1942, the Committee expended the sum of $ 30,000, which constituted more than 40% of its annual budget. In addition, it served as an agent for other committees and distributed supplies and offered relief to the value of more than $ 50,000.[11]

9 USC, "Saving the Future in Europe", n.d. (*c.* 1942).
10 *Ibid.*; Excerpts from a report made by the USC, August 7, 1942 (AFSC:GF, 1942, C&O); Donald Lowrie, *The Hunted Children* (New York, 1963), p. 128; USC, "Second Mile", p. 3.
11 USC, "Saving the Future in Europe"; "Second Mile".

In spite of good relations with the American Friends Service Committee, the latter's mass feeding program met strong Unitarian opposition on account of the fact that a considerable part of the supplies fell into the hands of German agents.[12] Pickett was afraid that the feeding project would be stopped by the American and British authorities. He therefore turned to Dexter with a request that the USC join the AFSC in asserting that "food supplies entrusted to American relief agencies for distributing in unoccupied France without exception have reached the persons for whom they were intended", and "in no way tampered by the French or German agents". In case of the Unitarians' refusal, "the public would gain the impression that two Christian bodies, both presuming to be helping the victims of war, are in complete disagreement", warned Pickett.[13] That argument did not move the USC. Thus, there was "a decided difference of opinion" between the two agencies, as Dexter indicated.[14]

Apparently the AFSC's policy led to an attempt to restrict even the USC's operations in southern France. The State Department recommended that "any American relief operations in France be conducted through the American Red Cross...". The same opinion was expressed by Joseph E. Davies, chairman of the War Relief Control Board. Davies, however, did not blame the international situation but "the friction and duplication among American relief organizations overseas".[15] William Emerson of the USC rejected the State Department's proposal. He pressed Breckinridge Long for "a prompt decision" and for "a clarification of our position in relation to the Government and the war effort".[16] In the end it was not the State Department, but the war developments that put a stop to the USC's activities in France. On November 8, 1942

12   Dexter to Pickett, April 2, 1942 (AFSC:GF, 1942, C&O). See above, pp. 200—201.
13   Pickett to Dexter, March 30, 1942 (AFSC:GF, 1942, C&O).
14   Dexter to Pickett, April 2, 1942 (AFSC:GF, 1942, C&O).
15   Emerson to B. Long, November 4, 1942 (NA, 851.48/736 PC/TL).
16   Ibid.

Allied forces landed in North Africa, which resulted in a rupture of American diplomatic relations with the Vichy Government and, a few days later, the Germans effected the total occupation of France. In view of these developments, Long observed that "the question of American relief operations in France would now seem to be closed".[17]

With the termination of relief work in France, the importance of Portugal as a relief center increased. Due to Lisbon's position as virtually the single gateway to freedom, the establishment of a USC European office at that strategic place was natural. In April 1940 Dr. Robert C. Dexter, the USC's executive director, founded the Lisbon center, which soon became the Committee's European headquarters. The office was chiefly concerned with problems of emigration, transportation and relief of French, Polish and Spanish Christian refugees. Among the refugees served by the Unitarians was a large number of political leaders, including former cabinet members and at least one former prime minister. The Committee also offered services to refugee intellectuals, authors, editors, physicians, Church and labor leaders.[18] As a liaison between American and European agencies on the one hand, and refugees on the other, the Service Committee expanded its activities, amongst other things, to delivering parcels to camp internees in France via Lisbon. As a result, the Committee administered more funds than were allocated under its own budget. Between May 1941 and May 1942, the USC in Portugal distributed for relief and transportation the sum of $60,000, thrice the sum which came from Unitarian sources.[19]

Although the number of refugees decreased after 1941, a greater effort per family was needed for the rescue of refugees. Despite local and international obstacles, the Unitarians became one of the major relief agencies in Portugal, along with the JDC, HICEM,

---

17 Long to Emerson, November 20, 1942 (NA, 851.48/736).
18 USC, "Second Mile"; ACCR, *Newscast*, 4 (Sep.–Oct. 1943), 4.
19 USC, "Second Mile".

and AFSC. In 1940—1941 the Committee allocated $20,000 for
relief in Lisbon and in 1944—1945 the sum was more than
tripled.[20] So reliable were the USC's services that when the British
authorities wanted to establish another resident force near Lisbon,
they turned to the Unitarians "to accept financial responsibility
and general supervision" of that program. The British Embassy
preferred the Unitarians, because they had "less red tape and more
energy than the others", as Elizabeth Dexter, who was in charge
of the Lisbon office, proudly claimed. "I feel it quite a compliment
to have the British Embassy ask our aid in this way", she added.[21]
Sir Herbert Emerson, High Commissioner for Refugees, also had
a high regard for the USC's relief work. He singled it out, along
with JDC and AFSC, as illustrating "that the light of humanitarian
assistance, though dim, is not utterly quenched".[22]

The evacuation of Spanish Loyalists and their resettlement in
Latin American countries was one of the tasks of the Lisbon office.
In December 1942 a contract was offered to the Service Committee, which the Ecuador government had already signed, concerning
the settlement of 5000 non-Communist refugee families, preferably Spanish Loyalists. An office was established in Ecuador to
facilitate the project. The USC turned for financial help to Herbert
H. Lehman, director of Foreign Relief and Rehabilitation Operations. HICEM was also approached, particularly in regard to fees
for the transportation of Jewish refugees from Portugal to Ecuador. Since the response was meager, an agreement was made with
the International Rescue and Relief Committee, whereby the latter
would be responsible for transportation funds and the USC would

20   *Ibid.*; USC, *Reporting for Service*, p. 7.
21   Elizabeth Dexter's urgent memorandum on conversation with repre-
     sentative of the British Embassy, March 10, 1944 (the archives of
     the International Social Service, New York).
22   League of Nations, *Report Submitted by Sir Herbert Emerson, High
     Commissioner for Refugees* (C. 19, M.19, XII Geneva, August 1943,
     p. 7).

take care of all other expenses of the program.[23] Apparently this undertaking was too onerous for the USC. Only small groups of 15—50 Spanish refugees were transported with its help to Ecuador.[24] Later, additional Latin American countries, like Chile, Venezuela and the Dominican Republic, were included in the settlement program. However, the Unitarian part in these projects was nominal. In 1944—1945, out of a total budget of $ 456,833, the Committee allocated only $ 4150 for Ecuador and the Dominican Republic.[25]

Robert Dexter tried to extend Unitarian activities on behalf of refugees to Spain. Until August 1943 the Committee was unable to devote its energy to Spain, mainly because of a lack of funds. However, promptly after the National War Fund had begun its generous support, Dexter turned to Ambassador Carlton J. H. Hayes offering his agency's help.[26] Almost a year elapsed without any positive reaction from Madrid. Eventually, the USC became a member of the Representation in Spain of American Relief Organizations, covering 12% of its expenses. The USC also offered services in Spain, independently of Blickenstaff's organization. Nevertheless, the USC's Spanish episode, like the Ecuador project, was not a Unitarian success. While in 1944—1945 the Committee's

23 Charles R. Joy to Herbert H. Lehman, December 9, 1942 (NA, 840.50/1045); Joy to Maze, October 29, 1943; Dijour to Joy, November 12, 1943; Joy to Dijour, November 2, 1943 (HH, 1, VII:55, YIVO). For a detailed discussion of the International Rescue and Relief Committee, see below, pp. 238—244.

24 Dijour to Joy, November 12, 1943; Alexis O. Hay to Ann S. Pettrick, May 3, 1945 (HH, 1, VII:57, YIVO); see also H.E. Muller to Maze, October 2, 6, 1942; Dijour to Joy, November 8, 1943 (HH, 1, VII:55, YIVO).

25 USC, *Reporting for Service*, p. 7. Another source gave different data, though without meaningfully changing the situation, RRT, Summary of Approved Budget, Long-Term Projects for year ending September 30, 1945 . . ., October 31, 1944 (FDRL, WRB, Box 7).

26 Robert C. Dexter to Carlton J. H. Hayes, September 11, 1943 (Hayes papers, Box 6).

relief allocation for France was $ 116,333, and for Portugal $ 61,000, the figure for Spain was only $ 13,500. Good Unitarian intentions and readiness to act were cooled by the American authorities in Madrid.[27]

The Unitarians made up for their belated start on relief work overseas by their eagerness to act and by their alertness to new fields of operation. On December 9, 1942, only a month after the Allied landing in North Africa, while the fighting was still going on, Charles Joy, acting director of USC, offered Herbert H. Lehman the Committee's assistance in relief work among North African internees. He called for a quick decision concerning the preparation of large-scale programs in connection with 60,000 North African refugees. He proposed the dispatch of a Unitarian, on behalf of the private relief agencies, to visit North Africa, in order to discuss with UNRRA representatives the role that private agencies might be able to play in relief work. Lehman, however, rejected the suggestion and declined at that stage to discuss the private agencies' part in the rehabilitation program. "It may be some time before a policy, even of a temporary character, can be formulated", he answered. To start with, the army and governmental agencies would carry on the relief work.[28]

In June 1944 a similar request was made by the Service Committee to permit a survey trip to the Near East. Recognizing the importance of the Near East for the postwar refugee migration planning, the USC was eager to send its representative on a survey trip to the area in order to determine "what work, if any, within our means might now be undertaken", and where to erect the headquarters. The USC had envisaged that need and included in the budget of 1944—1945 the sum of $ 36,000 for UNRRA staff in the Balkans and $ 30,000 for services in the Near East. However, unlike the North African proposal, where the Committee offered to cover the expenses of the trip here it not only requested from the appropriate governmental agencies an allocation of funds

27   USC, *Reporting for Service*, p. 7.

for the survey, but also wanted to utilize it for inspection of other Unitarian projects that had nothing to do with refugees and immigration. The Unitarian representatives intended to call on Dr. Albert Schweitzer's Mission in French Equatorial Africa, and to visit Cairo, Jerusalem and Syria, where the Hibbert Houses, supported by the Committee, offered recreation to Allied soldiers. Once again the USC's suggestion was turned down.[29]

Unitarian activities in Switzerland began toward the end of 1942, after Noel H. Field, the director of the Marseilles center, had fled to Geneva. The Geneva office gradually became the springboard for later programs in liberated Europe. Meanwhile, for a period of two years, efforts were devoted to helping refugees who had reached that neutral country. In 1943 a Vacation Home was opened which offered rest to refugees. Field was instrumental in helping to smuggle refugees across the Swiss borders from Nazi-occupied territories. "Underground or any other methods may be used", read the War Refugee Board's directive. He was asked "to speed up the process in Switzerland".[30] In cooperation with other agencies, a training course was established which prepared refugee social workers for relief work. In November 1944 this course was given to a selected group of Poles, who planned to return to their country as relief workers. Medical aid, which was almost the symbol of the USC in certain parts of Europe, was also offered in Switzerland. Medico-social emergency units were organized by the Geneva office. It encouraged Polish refugee physicians to take the initiative in establishing a network of "hygiene posts", each comprised of a doctor, a nurse, a laboratory assistant,

28 Joy to Lehman, December 9, 1942; Lehman to Joy, December 16, 1942 (NA, 840.50/1045).

29 Seth T. Gano's memorandum to the Passport Division of the State Department; President's War Relief Control Board, War Refugee Board and American Council of Voluntary Agencies for Foreign Service, June 21, 1944 (FDRL, WRB, Box 25).

30 Joy and Dexter to Noel Field, March 9, 1944 (FDRL, WRB, Box 20).

a secretary and a welfare worker. Each team was to be equipped with X-ray facilities as well as medical supplies.[31]

Communications between Geneva and Boston were not easy in spite of Swiss neutrality. Since it was surrounded by Axis countries, instructions were sent by cable through several American authorities via Lisbon and Washington. Inevitably the Committee suffered from misunderstandings, which necessitated further clarifications and delays in the transmission of directives. These and other obstacles nothwithstanding, the Unitarian operations in Switzerland reached a volume of $ 70,000 in 1944—1945.[32]

A change in Unitarian policy concerning relief aid occurred in August 1944, with the provision of medical services to the Resistance movement in France. Field's request for financial support for that purpose was opposed at the Boston headquarters, where it was argued that such a move was "not within the scope of the Committee" and would be dangerous because the Germans could easily trace the source of the funds for those medical supplies. The Unitarians were reluctant to support such a controversial movement, since helping the French Maquis was a political act rather than a humanitarian operation. But Field fiercely fought for his proposal. Assistance to the Resistance movement meant offering aid to the refugees too, since the former was "the only reliable element that can save refugees", he argued. Without providing aid to the Maquis nobody could expect that refugees would be helped by them. Furthermore, there were many victims of persecution among these freedom fighters. "I hope that this is not the last word", wrote Field to Dexter.[33] The representative of the War Refugee Board in Lisbon concurred with Field's position. From Lisbon Elizabeth Dexter also seconded Field's plea "with all possible solemnity.... Once these doors are closed they can never be reopened and more valuable lives will be lost". She considered the proposition "the most important obligation and opportunity before

31   Field to Joy, November 10, 1944 (FDRL, WRB, Box 20).
32   USC, *Reporting for Service*, p. 7.
33   Field to Dexter, August 11, 1944 (FDRL, WRB, Box 20).

the Committee". In the end Field won his way.[34] Thus, the Unitarians became pioneers in what is now the commonplace phenomenon of religious charities actively aiding "resistance movements".

Field's real success and the heyday of Unitarian relief work arrived with the liberation of France. On September 9, 1944, even before the final liberation, when fighting was still going on, Field made a survey trip to southern France escorted by the Maquis. He was the first American relief worker to reach the scene, and the result was that the USC became the first agency to offer help to the refugees in that area. The Committee was eager to resume its operations in France after an interruption of almost two years. Field, who was promoted to the position of USC Director for Western Europe, was a capable organizer, finding unconventional solutions to difficult problems. In the Maurienne Valley, in Savoy, he established a relief office at Chambéry, in the only usable room of a bombed building. With the help of the International Red Cross and the local French authorities, milk, sugar and medical supplies were brought and distributed. In nearby Mondane a canteen was opened.[35]

In Paris, too, a Unitarian office was opened, which soon established a warehouse and workrooms to handle the clothing which had been arriving from the United States at the rate of 9000 pounds per month. Another project for the help of refugees carried on in the United States was known as "American Youth to help European Youth". School supplies, sewing materials, tools and garden equipment were donated by schoolchildren to children in liberated Europe.[36]

The rapid expansion of services in 1944 necessitated a reorganization of the entire European network. A new director was nominated to the Lisbon center and new workers were added to the

---

34 Elizabeth Dexter to Raymond Bragg, August 11, 1944 (FDRL, WRB, Box 20); USC, *Standing By*, February 1945 (HH, 1:VII:66, YIVO).
35 USC, *Reporting for Service*, p. 12.
36 *Ibid.*, pp. 10, 14; USC, *Standing By*, November 1944; February 1945 (HH, 1:VII:66, YIVO).

personnel. The Service Committee was especially careful not to employ Communists or anyone with a dubious past. Thorough investigations were made before new workers were employed, close scrutiny being given to nationality, political activities and even the personal life of candidates.[37]

The expanded relief work in France posed a severe problem for the Committee. Was it justified to differentiate between refugees from Nazism from other countries and needy Frenchmen who had also suffered from the German occupation and from the war? "I soon realized (that) a program limited to foreign refugees was both impracticable and unwise", argued Field. To prefer foreigners "would weaken ... unity, create feeling against the refugees themselves". Approving that line, the Committee decided to change its policy and to include non-refugee Frenchmen among its beneficiaries. However, the distribution of relief to French patriots from grants of the National War Fund was forbidden. To overcome the legal problem, only specially earmarked contributions were allocated for French civilians, as was done through the American Relief for France.[38]

Basque children who had been helped by the Service Committee in 1940 gained renewed attention after liberation. A children's colony was established at Côte Basque with the approval of the French Government. Boys and girls, victims of the war, especially those suffering from malnutrition, were given curative treatment over a period of several months. Up to September 1945, the sum of $ 23,000 was expended on essential help given to many children in the Côte Basque Home. The same type of rehabilitation home was planned for other refugee youth, including French children. It is not clear whether these plans ever materialized.[39] Aid to the Spanish Loyalists in France was also renewed. Contact was made

---

37 Charles Joy to Noel Field, December 7, 1944; Field to USC, January 24, 1945 (FDRL, WRB, Box 20).

38 Field's cable quoted in USC, *Reporting for Service*, p. 12.

39 Joy to Field, January 10, 1945; Field to USC, January 24, 1945 (FDRL, WRB, Box 20); USC, *Reporting for Service*, pp. 7, 14.

with the Spanish Refugee Committee that had been established in
Toulouse under the chairmanship of Manuel Azcarate. The Unitarians' interest in that body, which was supposed to serve in an
advisory capacity, was mainly financial. It was thought that it
would enable the USC to collect large sums in the United States
for the Spanish refugees. However, because of the Toulouse Committee's Communist leadership and its partisan character, the USC
demanded personal changes in this Committee before effective
cooperation would be possible.[40]

In 1944 the Marseilles Clinic, which had continued to operate
under the Nazi occupation, was returned to the joint management
of the USC and OSE. While the latter was responsible for the
children's department, the former took care of the adults. In addition, a thorough study was conducted by the French personnel
with regard to the rehabilitation of starving people, which was published in a medical journal.[41] The Unitarian relief activity in France
after September 1944 proved the Committee's ability to exploit
new possibilities, particularly when funds were available. The increase in the number of unscheduled projects found its expression
in the difference between the approved budget and the actual expenditure. Thus, for projects in France $ 30,000 was allocated for
the period October 1944 — September 1945, whereas actual expenditure amounted to $ 116,333.[42]

The Unitarians' experience in medical aid, particularly in devas-
tated areas, was also made available in Italy. With the collapse
of the partisan movement in the Ossola Valley in the winter of
1944, 12,000 refugees, of whom 3000 were children, found themselves badly in need of relief. Noel Field asked the USC's headquarters to encourage and support the Italo-American organizations' appeal for funds. "Outside assistance is very definitely

---

40 Joy to Field, January 10, February 8, 1945; Field to USC, January
    27, 1945 (FDRL, WRB, Box 20).
41 USC, *Standing By*, March 1945; "USC, 1939—1944", p. 4.
42 NWF, RRT, Summary of Approved Budget October 31, 1944
    (FDRL, WRB, Box 7); USC, *Reporting for Service*, p. 7.

needed", he cabled home. The USC was instrumental in transmitting and distributing funds for these helpless Italians.[43] An
important contribution was the medical mission organized and
sent to Italy. The team of fifteen physicians, nurses and technicians
that arrived in Italy in April 1945 concentrated particularly on
caring for people suffering from extreme malnutrition. Utilizing the
findings of the above mentioned French study, the Unitarians became experts in that pressing field. The medical mission worked
under UNRRA auspices, which described the former — with some
exaggeration — as "the most significant proposal for the relief of
suffering in Europe yet made to us by a private relief agency".[44]

The determination of the Service Committee to reach the scene
first and to expand its aid to new areas also found expression with
regard to the dispatch of relief missions to Poland, Hungary and
Czechoslovakia. Eager to inaugurate a relief program in Poland,
Charles R. Joy, now the executive director, instructed Field on
December 7, 1944 to dispatch a delegate to investigate relief possibilities there. Funds would be available on condition that relief be
distributed only by USC personnel and to all people who needed
help, without discrimination. After a month had elapsed, Joy
began to press Field, cabling as follows: "Please push to utmost
delegation to Poland. It might open enormous possibilities to us.
Do not hesitate show your characteristic initiative in getting committee established soonest by sending personnel (to) Czechoslovakia or Hungary".[45] In February 1945 Joy was impatient at the
fact that the delegation still had no definite timetable. "Please urge
immediate decision departure", he directed Field. Speedy entry
into Poland, Hungary and Czechoslovakia "will attract money and
tardy entry will defeat our hope of procuring money", Joy's cable
continued, disclosing one of the motives behind Joy's interest in
the delegation. "Please push vigorously the importance and ur-

43 Field to Joy, December 6, 1944 (FDRL, WRB, Box 20).
44 Quoted in USC, *Reporting for Service*, p. 4.
45 Joy to Field, December 7, 1944; January 10, 1945 (FDRL, WRB,
    Box 20).

gency of this enterprise", he closed the cable to Europe.[46] Although
the delegation to Poland eventually included other elements besides
the USC, the latter's initiative and its role were emphasized by the
press.[47]

While the USC devoted its energy mainly to refugees in its
foreign service, in the United States it developed several programs
with different aims. Since none of the Home Service projects were
meant to take care of refugees, they were financed through a
separate budget of the United Unitarian Appeal and by means of
earmarked contributions from societies and individuals. The Home
Service Committee, which was made up of several subdivisions,
worked mainly with local Church leaders. Naturally, most of the
projects were concerned with the effects of the war, like recreation
programs for war-workers, social centers for soldiers, religious
services for Unitarians in the armed forces and work camps to
help out the labor shortage on the home front. A special program,
differing markedly from the usual services provided by other relief
agencies, was the People's Institute of Applied Religion in Detroit.
Under the direction of Rev. Claude Williams, the Institute assisted
hundreds of preachers to develop a "more liberal interpretation
for their Biblical texts". The participants in the course, who were
recognized leaders in their communities, were offered lectures on
tolerance, justice and economic fair play. Through the promotion
of such liberal conceptions the Institute intended to combat growing Fascist influence in the country. The Unitarian projects in the
United States were of much smaller dimensions, both as regards
the efforts made and funds invested, than those undertaken by the
Service Committee for refugee work abroad.[48]

46 Charles R. Joy to Noel Field, February 8, 1945 (FDRL, WRB,
    Box 20).
47 Field to Joy, March 22, 1945 (FDRL, WRB, Box 20).
48 While the USC expended the sum of $ 456,833 in 1944—1945 for
    overseas operations, the budget of the Home Service Committee,
    as well as other projects in the United States, totaled only $ 28,000.
    "USC, 1939—1944", pp. 5—8; USC, *Reporting for Service*, pp. 7—
    18.

Thus, the USC, which entered the relief field only in 1940, soon became a major refugee agency abroad. Its dedicated staff avoided duplication by selecting special assignments, such as providing medical and hygienic aid and fighting malnutrition. By mainly helping Christian refugees, though not withholding aid from Jews, the Unitarians were true to their beliefs and preaching. The initial financial difficulties were overcome thanks to the National War Fund, which covered the entire budget of all services carried on by the USC outside the country. The Committee's policy of energetic pursuit of new openings led to a meaningful expansion of activities. It expended in 1944—1945 more than twice its original approved budget and its personnel increased threefold during that year. The Unitarian Service Committee, with a staff of more than one hundred men and women and with an annual budget of more than half a million dollars, represented living proof of what could be accomplished by goodwill, determination and governmental support.[49]

THE INTERNATIONAL RESCUE AND RELIEF COMMITTEE

Another American agency that operated exclusively abroad was the Emergency Rescue Committee (ERC), which was established in July 1940 as a result of the Nazi advances in Europe. Numerous intellectuals in the United States were particularly shocked by the French agreement to surrender German refugees in accordance with the Nazi demand. Unlike the denominational welfare bodies of the Quakers, the Unitarians and the Catholics, which were in existence before Hitler's accession to power, the Emergency Rescue Committee was founded and supported by a variety of individuals, whose common purpose was to save democratic leaders whose lives were directly endangered because of their active opposition

---

49   *Ibid.*, pp. 7—10; NWF, Summary of Approved Budget, October 31, 1944.

to Nazism. The formation of the ERC was inspired by intellectual emigrés like Thomas Mann, Alfred Baar (Karl B. Frank) and Paul Hagen. Among the American sponsors were the news analysts Elmer Davis and Raymond Gram Swing, and academic leaders, such as Robert Hutchins, Alvin Johnson and William A. Neilson.[50]

The Committee, led by Frank Kingdon, president of the University of Newark, chose Varian Fry as its agent to go to France with a single assignment, "to bring the political and intellectual refugees out of France before the Gestapo and the Ovra and the Seguridad got them". Fry, although experienced neither in refugee work nor in underground activities, accepted the mission "out of deep political conviction", as he stated. Along with other members of the ERC he believed in democratic solidarity. He also had sentimental reasons for wanting to save men of the arts, whom he greatly admired. Another feature of his activities was his sympathetic attitude to exiled German and Austrian Socialist leaders. He left the United States for a month and stayed in France for more than a year.[51]

Fry opened an office in Marseilles, which became the base of his rescue operations. At first the Committee was able to offer help to everyone who turned to it, thanks to the Quakers' readiness to provide food for all those cases that the ERC was unable to handle. However, when in the fall of 1940 the AFSC drastically

50 See Laura Fermi, *Illustrious Immigrants: The Intellectual Migration from Europe, 1930—1941* (Chicago: The University of Chicago Press, 1968), pp. 85—86. The ERC was not a coordinating committee as Henry Feingold has stated. See Feingold, *Politics of Rescue*, p. 138. The Emergency Rescue Committee and the International Relief Association were in fact genuinely non-sectarian organizations. Although their leaders were Christians, their relief work had been conducted on a purely non-sectarian basis. We prefer to discuss their activities separately rather than in Chapter 9 because the latter focuses mainly on agencies the nature of whose "non-sectarianism" was somewhat dubious.

51 Varian Fry, *Surrender on Demand* (New York: Random House, 1945), pp. x—xi.

cut down its relief work, the ERC was forced to limit its help to political and intellectual leaders. For a while Fry hoped that through the financial support of either the AFSC or the JDC his Committee would be able to resume full-scale activity. "I continue to hold to the notion that it is *essential* for us to mix the intellectuals and politicals with the ordinaries", he argued. This was important in order to cut down the risk of Gestapo and police searches, since to focus attention only on leaders watched by German agents would have placed his activities under constant surveillance.[52] However, Fry's wish was not fulfilled and so the ERC restricted its activities to anti-Nazi leaders. That aim was defined in an ERC pamphlet: "Our mission is to aid those who have proven at the price of exile ... that they stand for freedom against tyranny".[53]

In July 1940 the Roosevelt Administration agreed, under heavy pressure, to issue emergency visas beyond the quota system for political leaders and intellectuals who were in imminent danger. The President's Advisory Committee on Political Refugees became responsible for the screening and recommendation of persons who were eligible for these special visas.[54] Thus, Fry's arrival in France coincided with a significant relaxation of the American visa policy for a certain category of refugees. Though it became easier to gain entry to the United States, there was still the problem of liberating the inmates of French prisons or internment camps. This became one of the major tasks of the ERC. Indeed, "rescue by any means" was the Committee's catchword. It operated by legal as well as illegal means — in the latter it collaborated closely with anti-Nazi resistance movements in Europe.[55]

52 Excerpt from letter of Varian Fry, September 19, 1940 (AFSC: GF, 1940, C&O).
53 IRRC, "Two Years Against the Gestapo", n.d. (HH, 1:VII:53, YIVO).
54 See above, pp. 85—87.
55 Report of the International Rescue and Relief Committee, n.d. (HH, 1:VII:66, YIVO).

This activity distinguished the ERC from any other refugee agency. Rather than concentrating on the distribution of food or offering medical or spiritual aid, the Committee was actually engaged in helping refugees to escape from prison, to hide from the police and to sneak across the border to neutral countries. It provided forged papers, money, transportation, harbor and other means for the refugees' escape. The case of Lion Feuchtwanger, the German-Jewish author, demonstrated the ERC's methods. With the use of a car he was "kidnapped" from a line of marching prisoners near his camp in France and reached Marseilles disguised as an old woman. With forged papers he crossed the Spanish border on foot. The rescue operation was a joint effort of the ERC, the visa consul in Marseilles, Hiram Bingham Jr. and the Unitarian Service Committee, whose man escorted the author through Portugal to the United States.[56] Among those rescued, sometimes out of the hands of the Gestapo, were Marc Chagall, the Jewish painter, and his family; Nicholai Chiaramonte, the Italian writer who fought for Loyalist Spain; Marcel Duchamp, the French painter; Hans Habe, the Hungarian journalist and writer; Konrad Heiden, anti-Nazi biographer of Hitler; Jacques Lipchitz, the French sculptor; the novelist Heinrich Mann, Thomas Mann's brother; André Masson, the French painter; Jaine Miravittles, the Spanish minister of public education; Franz Werfel, the Czech poet and novelist; and Josef Wittlin, the Polish poet.[57]

The French police knew about the ERC's activities, but sometimes purposely disregarded them. The Marseilles police chief in charge of foreigners, M. Barelet, who sympathized with the refugees, conveyed to Varian Fry the names of foreigners whom the Gestapo wanted to imprison. He promised to hold off the arrest so that the Committee could arrange hiding for them. It was dangerous, however, to rely on French cooperation, since most of the French officials did not regard collaboration with Germans as a

56   Donald Lowrie, *The Hunted Children*, pp. 177—178.
57   IRRC, "Two Years Against The Gestapo".

national dishonor. Some deluded themselves that by helping the Nazis they could improve their country's situation.[58] As the time passed, the Vichy authorities surrendered to the German demand and turned in refugee leaders. Sometimes arrests were made at the last minute, while the refugees were waiting for a boat in Marseilles. Not every rescue operation was successful. On several occasions the Laval police arrested not only the refugees, but members of the ERC as well. On June 9, 1942 the Committee's office in Marseilles was raided and the personnel imprisoned on the charge that they had incited "seditious elements" and shown "an interest in political refugees". In response to French public protest the staff members were released. "We plead guilty to that charge", it was noted in a circular of the IRRC. Despite the harassment and imprisonments suffered over a period of two years, of which that of June 9 was only the latest, "we will carry on until the last hunted anti-Nazi is evacuated to safety", declared the Committee.[59]

Opposition to the ERC's unconventional rescue methods was also voiced in the United States. Richard F. Allen, European delegate of the American Red Cross, was "very much disturbed that Fry's actions would bring discredit on all Americans in un-Occupied France". He complained about Fry to the American Consul in Marseilles and to the Chargé d'Affaires in Vichy. He accused Fry of misrepresenting his mission. Allen was particularly worried about a rumor concerning alleged Red Cross cooperation with the ERC. "You may deny as positively as possible any rumors that any of the American Red Cross Personnel were identified with Fry's activities in any way", wrote Allen to Ernest J. Swift, vice-chairman of the ARC.[60]

The State Department and American officials in un-Occupied

---

58 Excerpt from letter of Varian Fry, September 19, 1940 (AFSC:GF, 1940, C&O).
59 Frank Kingdon to Dear Friend, June 12, 1942 (AFSC:GF, 1942, C&O); IRRC, "Two Years Against the Gestapo".
60 Richard F. Allen to Ernest J. Swift, October 24, 1940 (AFSC:GF, 1940, C&O).

France were even more embarrassed by Fry's operations. In fact, the consuls were annoyed to the extent that they refused to provide help for ERC clients. They also asked Fry, and later even demanded of him, to leave France immediately — which he flatly refused to do. Alvin Johnson, of the New School of Social Research and a supporter of the Committee, complained to Adolf A. Berle, Assistant Secretary of State, about the attitude of the American consuls toward Fry, declaring that "He is ... getting less than he has a right to expect in the way of support, or aid, or even tolerance" from American officials in Vichy France. Johnson asked Berle "to encourage our foreign service men to give Mr. Fry the aid due an American citizen representing a broad American interest".[61] "Varian Fry has got to get home as soon as he can", responded Berle angrily. He had already demanded of Frank Kingdon, ERC chairman, to bring Fry home. The State Department believed that not only were his chances of accomplishing anything "completely finished", but that he was also in danger of arrest.[62] Fry left France only after he was forced to do so by the Vichy Government. He was an outstanding example of what could be achieved through the determination and courage of even a single individual. For thirteen months he had received the constant help of the *Centre Americain de Secours* and other organs of the Resistance movement, and without the assistance and cooperation of the USC, AFSC, and other refugee agencies he could not have succeeded as he did. When he left France, against his will, a great deal of rescue work still remained to be done. His French associates remained in the country and continued to operate, sometimes under the nose of the Gestapo.[63]

Unlike other refugee organizations, which were eager to publish their activities in great detail, for security reasons the ERC was

61   Alvin Johnson to Adolf A. Berle, July 7, 1941 (NA, 851.48/459).
62   Berle to Johnson, July 8, 1941 (NA, 851.48/459).
63   Fry, *Surrender on Demand*, pp. xii, 189—190, 226. On Fry's activities in France, see also his *Assignment: Rescue* (New York: Four Winds Press, 1968); Fermi, *Illustrious Immigrants*, pp. 87—89.

compelled to maintain a discreet silence. To protect underground agents ERC reports were rare and deliberately vague.[64] An almost inevitable outcome of the secret operations was a measure of duplication of work being done by other agencies. Thus the AFSC and the ERC made separate efforts for two years to obtain a visa for a political refugee. Only when each succeeded in securing the visa, did they discover the fact of their duplicated efforts.[65] Nevertheless, the record of the ERC was impressive. During the nineteen months of its existence (July 1940 — January 1942), it saved nearly 1500 prominent political and intellectual leaders, many of them Jewish. Of its expenditure of $341,807 the lion's share went to rescue and relief activities, with only 5% going on administration and general expenses. The markedly low overheads was another characteristic of the ERC activities.[66]

The International Relief Association (IRA), like the Emergency Rescue Committee, was inspired by European intellectuals, themselves former refugees, who knew the situation on the Continent. The Association, which was founded by Albert Einstein, Kaethe Kollwitz, Graf G. von Argo, Edward Fuchs, Helen Stoecker and H. E. Vogt, passed through several stages. In May 1936 it was reinforced by a merger with the Emergency Committee in Aid of Political Refugees from Nazism. With the merger Charles A. Beard, the historian, replaced Oswald Garrison Villard of *The Nation*, as chairman.[67] In July 1940 the Association was reorganized, attracting well-known liberal intellectuals, like Freda Kirchwey, John Dewey, George S. Counts, John Haynes Holmes, Reinhold Niebuhr, John Dos Passos, Dorothy Thompson and William Allen White. In spite of the impressive list of names on the letterhead, the Association encountered constant difficulties in covering the cost of its operations. This small relief agency, operating in Marseilles, Lisbon and Casablanca, offered relief and payment of

64   See IRRC's "Report for 1944".
65   Lowrie, *The Hunted Children*, p. 174.
66   IRRC, "Two Years Against the Gestapo".
67   Francis Henson to James McDonald, April 9, 1936 (MP:GC:ACCR).

the costs of transporting anti-Nazi leaders to the United States and Latin American countries. Since 75% of its beneficiaries were Jewish, the Association turned to HICEM for financial support. "The IRA is not an organization that receives contributions amounting to millions of dollars from the Jewish community as do the large Jewish organizations", stated Freda Kirchwey, the treasurer. HICEM, however, did not even bother to reply, but some help did come from the JDC to cover transportation expenses of IRA clients.[68]

The IRA, run by intellectuals who had good intentions but little time and experience, was poorly managed. A lack of energetic staff and field workers seriously hampered its effectiveness. The Association's income between July 1940 and January 1942 amounted to $76,954, less than a quarter of the ERC's budget. The IRA offered aid to the same category of refugees as did the ERC, namely political anti-Nazi leaders. While the latter agency acted to rescue them from camps and smuggle them to neutral countries, the IRA assisted these refugees to reach American shores. A merger between two refugee agencies that complemented each other's work was only natural, and in February 1942 the Emergency Rescue Committee and the International Relief Association were indeed so merged into a body called The International Rescue and Relief Committee (IRRC). Frank Kingdon, director of the ERC, was nominated as chairman and Sheba Strunsky as executive secretary. The new Committee continued to fulfill the two functions of its predecessors, rescue and relief. However, since the ERC was the wealthier, the bigger and the more energetic of the two, it clearly dominated the IRRC, both in the determination of policy and in the actual management.[69]

68 Freda Kirchwey to James Bernstein, December 18, 1941 (HH, 1: VII:52, YIVO); Sheba Strunsky to Isaac Asofsky, February 16, 1942 (HH, 1: VII:53, YIVO). The JDC donated $2254; G. R. to International Relief Association, November 24, 1941 (HH, 1:VII:52, YIVO).
69 IRRC, "Two Years Against the Gestapo".

The payment of accumulated debts to HIAS-HICEM was one of the matters the IRRC had to decide upon. With the merger, the new committee undertook the debts of its predecessors to HICEM, totaling $ 23,915. The IRRC's refusal to pay strained the relationship between the two bodies.[70] To end the long dispute Frank Kingdon, the new chairman, offered in April 1943 to pay $ 5000 in settlement of the debt. Although at first HIAS considered the amount "too small", eventually it reluctantly agreed. So came to an end a year and a half of dispute, which soured the otherwise good and warm relations between HICEM and the IRRC.[71]

The expansion of the Committee's operations was made possible by the support of the National War Fund. Commencing from the summer of 1943, the IRRC's expenses were entirely covered by that governmental agency. These funds were spent almost entirely on rescue and relief work with overheads reduced to the minimum. In 1944, for example, only 6% of the budget was allocated for administration, a much lower percentage than for the ACCR or the USC.[72]

The IRRC's activities in Turkey clearly demonstrated the methods employed to achieve its aim — "to rescue democratic men and women in Axis-dominated countries, whose lives were endangered by their active opposition".[73] Leon Dennenberg was sent as the IRRC's agent to Turkey. Possessing the resourcefulness and skill to operate in unconventional ways, he reached Istanbul on

70 James Bernstein to Sheba Strunsky, April 24, 1942; Strunsky to Asofsky, February 16, 1942; Dijour to IRRC, August 4, 1942; Bernstein to IRRC, December 23, 1942 (HH, 1:VII:53, YIVO).

71 Sheba Strunsky to Ilja Dijour, April 9, 1943; Dijour to Strunsky, April 23, 1943; Strunsky to Dijour, July 23, 1943 (HH, 1:VII:54, YIVO).

72 The National War Fund's support totaled $ 390,000 in 1944 and $ 450,000 in 1945; "IRRC in 1944" (FDRL, WRB, Box 9); WRF, RRT: Summary of Approved Budget, October 31, 1944 (FDRL, WRB, Box 7).

73 "Relief and Reconstruction Excerpts", II, p. 6 (HH, 1 : VII : 66, YIVO).

June 8, 1944 and reestablished his former contacts with the Hungarian, Rumanian, Bulgarian and Yugoslav underground movements. Turkey was selected as the basis of operations because of its neutral status and the relatively easy access from there to the Balkan states. From refugees who had reached Turkey he gleaned information about non-Jewish intellectuals and political leaders in German-occupied countries who were in imminent danger. After several weeks' preparation, Dennenberg submitted to the War Refugee Board representative in Ankara a list of anti-Nazi leaders whose rescue was essential. He also compiled a list of 200 Hungarians to be rescued, some of them non-Jewish, and presented it to the Jewish Agency for Palestine, which subsequently provided them with Palestinian immigration certificates. Dennenberg was also instrumental in evacuating 60 Polish refugees stranded in Rumania. He sent agents to several countries to arrange illegal border crossings by refugees. Money and food packages were sent to leaders in prison, in the hope that a display of foreign interest in their fate would ease their conditions.[74]

With the rupture of diplomatic relations between Turkey and Germany in August 1944, access to Axis-controlled countries was denied. Not only was the possibility of saving opposition leaders from these countries drastically reduced, but immediate action was needed to prevent the deportation to Germany of German and Austrian anti-Nazi leaders who had found refuge in Turkey. At the request of Gestapo agents, a number of such refugees were located and forcibly deported by the chief of police of Istanbul. Dennenberg submitted a list of 70 refugees in danger of such deportation to the WRB and himself warned the refugees, most of whom were ignorant of their fate. He also successfully intervened on their behalf with the British and American consuls. After Turkish investigation it became evident that the deportations were illegal, and had been carried out by pro-Nazi police officers without

74 John Pehle to Sheba Strunsky, October 19, 1944 (FDRL, WRB, Box 9).

governmental authorization. Though the deportations to Germany were stopped, it was not the end of the suffering of the refugees, because of a Turkish order to intern all German subjects in Central Anatolia.[75]

In order to carry out rescue operations, Dennenberg established a sub-committee of the IRRC in Istanbul on August 17, 1944. Composed of exiled refugee intellectuals, the immediate tasks of the Committee, which was headed by Alexander Rustow, a German professor, were to combat deportations to Germany, to distribute relief in Turkey and to provide help, including moral support, to internees. It was intended that the agency should later expand its activities to the Balkan and Central European countries. For that purpose the sub-committee was composed of one Czech, one Austrian, one Yugoslav, two Hungarians and two Germans, each of whom was familiar with the language and ways of the country to which he was assigned. At first there was little activity, since the members of the Committee were unable to communicate with underground leaders in Axis-controlled countries, and were forbidden to visit the internees in Anatolia. Gradually, with the liberation of Bulgaria and Greece, contacts were made with these countries and the establishment of sub-committees there was considered.[76]

This, then, was the IRRC's pattern of operation as demonstrated by Leon Dennenberg: setting up of a base in a neutral country; aggressive and daring actions; contact with underground movements in neighboring countries; cooperation with local and international agencies, and the enlistment of foreign nationals as part of the local personnel. Although no more than the sum of $ 6000 was expended in Turkey in 1944, the lives of several hundred refugees were saved there during that year.

75   Ibid.
76   Ira A. Hirshman to John Pehle, September 1, 1944; Ph. Schwartz
     to Frank Kingdon, November 27, 1944; Alexander Rustow's Report
     of the Istanbul Sub-committee of the IRRC, n.d. (FDRL, WRB,
     Box 9).

In contrast to Turkey, where the IRRC's agent stayed for seven months only, Switzerland, thanks to its neutrality and proximity to France and Italy, served as the Committee's center in Europe throughout the German occupation. Through its Zurich office the IRRC maintained close contacts with French resistance movements and smuggled refugees across the Franco-Swiss border. Help was also provided for those French people who managed to reach Switzerland. In special cases of illness, efforts were made to release the persons concerned from Swiss internment camps. Altogether in 1944 a sum of more than $ 30,000 was spent on these operations.[77]

In addition to the rescue and evacuation of refugees, the IRRC also engaged in Sweden, Mexico and Italy in providing relief to particular groups of anti-Fascist leaders who suffered because of their past record. Particular provision was made for Spanish Loyalists in France, described in a Committee memorandum as "the most neglected of all refugee groups".[78]

With the liberation of Europe the IRRC was confronted with new problems and targets. Now, the Committee faced "an overwhelming task of rehabilitation and repatriation".[79] For these purposes other agencies, particularly governmental ones such as UNRRA, were more suited. Nevertheless, the IRRC actively participated in the postwar rehabilitation programs. Renamed in 1951 as the International Rescue Committee, it still operates as a major refugee-aid agency in America. Thus, it was a remarkable venture of brave and daring rescue operations, conducted by a devoted

---

77 "The International Rescue and Relief Committee in 1944" (FDRL, WRB, Box 9).

78 Report of the Rescue and Relief Committee's Contributions Disbursed by Stockholm Stads Committee for Stateless Persons, April 1945; "IRRC in 1944" (FDRL, WRB, Box 9); IRRC, Memorandum on the Situation of Spanish-Republican Refugees in France, February 10, 1944; R. B. Parke to Miss Hodel, March 24, 1944; Pehle to Kingdon, July 19, 1944 (FDRL, WRB, Box 37).

79 "The International Rescue and Relief Committee in 1944".

group of American Christians determined to save by all means and methods people whose lives were endangered on account of their active anti-Nazi opposition. In spite of the great secrecy of the Committee's operations, enough information is available to appreciate the methods, merits and achievements of the International Rescue and Relief Committee.

8

THE MULTIPLICITY OF
RELIEF ORGANIZATIONS

One of the signs of the American public's increasing interest in
the fate of refugees, as World War II developed, was the growing
number of relief committees which sprang up in the United States.
In the fall of 1939 there were 208 organizations collecting money
on behalf of European refugees. With the continuance of the war
the foreign war relief agencies mushroomed, reaching the number
of 700 by October 1941, of which 331 agencies were officially
registered with the State Department.[1] The multiplicity of relief
organizations was a mixed blessing for the refugee cause. They
"stole" public attention from the major agencies, which had the
experience and knowledge in the fund raising field. Some of the
committees were ephemeral, backed by little more than an address
and a letterhead, bearing a long list of famous sponsors. Quite

---

1 George L. Warren to Joseph Chamberlain, December 22, 1939
   (Chamberlain papers, p. 578, YIVO); "Summary of Interim Report
   of President Roosevelt's Special Committee to Investigate War Relief
   Agencies", chairman Joseph E. Davies, October 22, 1941 (Moss
   papers, FCC, Box 145).

frequently a part-time secretary was in charge of the whole body. The income of private relief agencies for overseas relief — not necessarily for refugees from Nazism — amounted in September 1939 to $ 90,000,000. In 1940 that sum dropped to $ 65,000,000. However, 90% of the total was raised by fifty agencies.[2]

Only part of the funds actually reached their destination. Inefficiency and duplication marked the operation of most of the agencies. Consequently, the expenses for administration were particularly high. Even key organizations, such as the National Coordinating Committee and the American Committee for Christian Refugees, suffered from maladministration.[3] Since there was no proper supervision of the relief committees, chaos ruled in that field. Thus, for instance, the Committee of Mercy took advantage of the situation and collected money without proper authorization. This Committee, which had been active during World War I, revived its operations under the initiative of a Miss E. A. Nash, who served as its secretary. Some of the people listed on the original letterhead, which was reprinted without modification, had died and others were no longer functioning on the Committee. Under investigation she was unable to specify the details of a "Jewish Alliance" in France, for whom her Committee had purported to collect money. Joseph D. Ostermann of the Catholic Committee demanded time and again that action be taken against this organization, "to prevent possible fraud". He accused the Committee of Mercy of being a "self-authorized movement" which raised funds "without really rendering proper assistance".[4] The story of the Committee of Mercy, however, was an exception to

2   "Summary of Interim Report...".
3   Joseph Hyman to Cecilia Razovsky, July 10, 1936 (NCC papers, JDC archives); Minutes, Refugee Committee of AFSC, February 19, 1939 (AFSC:MF).
4   Louis Berg to Cecilia Razovsky, June 19, 1939; Joseph Ostermann to William Haber, September 21, 1939; Ostermann to Razovsky, April 13, June 14, 1939 (NRS papers, folder 57, YIVO).

the general rule. On the whole, the personnel of the relief agencies were devoted, sincere and highly motivated people.

Most of the relief agencies fell into one of four categories: professional bodies organized to deal with specific problems, mainly on a non-sectarian basis; organizations based on national origin; religious groups and Church committees; and, finally, community services.

The forced mass migration of intellectuals, artists and skilled workers during the 1930s greatly intensified the usual difficulties experienced with the integration of immigrants in their new country, in particular when they reached America in the midst of the country's most serious economic depression. The placement, vocational training and case-treatment of certain categories of newcomers with unique problems, necessitated the establishment of professional committees. Refugee lawyers were a case in point. Since the American legal system and practice differed substantially from the Continental (including the German) system, most of the 1800—2000 German refugee lawyers were unable to practice law in America without retraining. To help talented young refugee lawyers, the American Committee for the Guidance of Professional Personnel was founded in 1938. It helped some of them to complete their studies in law schools, retrained them and found positions for them. However, the great majority of refugee lawyers changed their profession. A survey of 311 lawyers revealed that only 19 of them continued to practice law. The others became, amongst other things, bookkeepers, accountants and businessmen. Another Lawyers' Committee, that of the Non-Sectarian Anti-Nazi League, was founded in 1938. But because of its inexperience and ignorance of the refugee situation in America, it failed to provide any real services or solution to the peculiarly difficult problems of that group of refugees.[5] Likewise, committees were founded for social workers, psychologists, physicians, dentists, musicians, scholars

5 Davie, *Refugees in America*, pp. 111—112, 287—288, 299; Razovsky to Chamberlain, September 11, 1938 (NCC papers, 6, YIVO).

and children, most of which operated on a non-sectarian basis.[6]

While the professional committees tried to comprehend and overcome the peculiar problems faced by their protégés in America, the agencies concerned with the interests of their countrymen were mainly interested in the political and economic situation of their people, disregarding almost entirely detailed casework. After the outbreak of the war, there were in America refugee agencies pertaining to almost every occupied country, such as the Polish Relief Committee, the Spanish, Finnish, Austrian, Yugoslav and Czechoslovakian Relief Committees, among many others. These committees collected money and sent it to their countrymen. In addition to providing financial help, they were eager to attract public attention to the fate of the population under occupation. Charles Rozmarek, president of the Polish National Alliance, lodged a protest with President Roosevelt against the German massacre of 150,000 Poles in 1944 in Warsaw.[7] Likewise, the Spanish Refugee Relief Committee camplained about Franco's treatment of Loyalists. The Spanish Committee also worked for the immigration of Republicans to Mexico but, lacking funds and leadership, its achievements were small.[8] Lack of funds, which reflected the public apathy, was one of the major weaknesses of the agencies in this category. Most of them, with rare exceptions — like the Polish Relief Committee — were unable to provide help or render any services in the United States.

Local and national Church bodies also enlisted their followers to help refugees. Some of them encouraged the settlement and

---

6 Committee for Displaced Foreign Social Workers (NCC papers, folder 33, YIVO); Confidential Memorandum to Members of American Psychological Association on Displaced Foreign Psychologists, by B. S. Burks, n.d. (*ibid.*, folder 35); Lawrence S. Kubie to Cecilia Razovsky, April 21, 1938 (*ibid.*, folder 5). For a detailed discussion of the "non-sectarian" committees, see below, Chapter 9.

7 See Rozmarek to F. D. Roosevelt, August 30, 1944 (FDRL, OF/3186).

8 Herman F. Reissig (Spanish Refugee Relief Campaign) to Harold L. Ickes, July 29, 1940 (FDRL, OF/3186).

placement of newcomers. Others collected funds for their co-religionists in Europe. The Central Bureau for Relief of the Evangelical Churches, for example, sent $ 28,750 to France during the first nine months of 1940.[9]

The "Good Neighbor Committee on the Emigré and the Community" differed somewhat from other relief agencies in its aims. The leaders of the Committee were preoccupied with the problem of "how to fit the refugee into American life". In 1938 Dr. John Lovejoy Elliott, of Hudson Guild and the Society for Ethical Culture, established the Committee in New York, composed of a small group of relief and religious leaders of the three faiths. After twelve months of organizing, during which the Committee enjoyed other agencies' help in pooling information and experience, a conference was held in May 1939 with the participation of 300 individuals and representatives of major refugee agencies. It was decided to expand the organization in New York, hoping that it would stimulate kindred committees in other places. The emphasis would be "on community acceptance of refugees". However, the Committee failed to stir the interest of the communities. After holding several monthly meetings, the Good Neighbor Committee became defunct following the death of its founder, John L. Elliott.[10]

The problem of educating Christian neighbors of refugees in urban and rural societies to overcome anti-alien prejudices occupied other groups as well. Several programs were suggested, some of them with detailed plans, but few of them materialized. The very recurrence of such propositions from time to time indicated the failure of earlier efforts in this direction.[11]

---

9   A. H. Froendt to L. B. Moss, October 3, 1940 (Moss papers, FCC, Box 143).
10 Paul Kellogg, "Team Play for Refugees", *Survey Midmonthly*, June 1939; Final Report, Committee on Refugees, National Board, YWCA, February 1, 1946, p. 36 (YWCA archives, roll 99; Immigration, Refugees).
11 See, for example, Unidentified, "Statement of Purpose", n.d. (AFSC, 1938, FS:RS).

Another organization, which was neither a relief agency nor included the rescue of refugees among its aims, but which became interested, however, in refugee problems, was The Women's International League for Peace and Freedom (WIL). In order to take care of the German WIL members, who had suffered from the suppression of religious and political freedom, WIL established a Refugee Committee in America. It was particularly active in combating the restrictionist American immigration laws. Dorothy Detzer, executive secretary of WIL's American branch, dejectedly admitted her failure to change not only the immigration laws and regulations, but even the arbitrary decisions of the American consuls: "Only once during those years was I able to override a decision made by one of the consulates", she recalled. This was the case only after she visited Avra M. Warren, chief of the Visa Division and George S. Messersmith, Assistant Secretary of State, and after discussing the matter with Cordell Hull and Eleanor Roosevelt.[12]

Thus, toward the end of the 1930s and mainly during the war, there was some increase of interest in the refugee problem among certain sectors of the population. Most of the hundreds of relief committees that gave expression to that inclination were, however, short-lived and ill-managed by enthusiastic but inexperienced persons. They had neither the ability nor the public support to carry out their programs. The very nature of these bodies made overlapping inevitable. In 1934 there were five committees to take care of foreign physicians, and the situation was much the same with foreign social workers.[13]

Competition and rivalry between key relief agencies also led to friction and duplication. Probably there was no more heated dis-

---

12 Dorothy Detzer, *Appointment on the Hill* (New York: Holt and Co., 1948), pp. 227, 220—234.
13 Memorandum by Cecilia Razovsky: "Refugee Physicians in the United States", July 1934; Razovsky to Chamberlain, July 6, 1934 Chamberlain papers, pp. 2762, 2765—2766, YIVO); Maurice J. Karpf to Razovsky, January 11, 1939 (NCC papers, folder 33, YIVO).

pute than among Zionist and non-Zionist groups of the Jewish organizations.[14] Other disputes between Jewish relief agencies were not ideologically motivated but centered rather on matters of prestige or independence. Thus, HIAS, which had been offering services to Jewish immigrants since 1881, refused to accept domination by the National Coordinating Committee and its successor, the National Refugee Service. For long years the controversy between the two agencies lingered on. In Lisbon, Casablanca and Havana, among other places, the HIAS disregarded the activities of other committees, operating according to its own program. When, in 1939, Isaac Asofsky of the HIAS opened an office in Havana, Adolph H. Kates, a social worker in Cuba, complained that "this can only lead to overlapping of efforts as well as unnecessary duplication and waste of expenses .... The fact remains that the HIAS so far have done nothing of a constructive nature, and on the contrary, have at times interfered needlessly with the execution of plans...".[15] Despite various compromises, agreements and division of spheres of activity, the HIAS refused to cooperate fully with the central relief agencies.[16] This rivalry continued through the war years. As late as February 1945 it refused to utilize the NRS central index, a fact considered by Lotte Marcuse of the European Jewish Children's Aid to be "the source of much duplication and argument".[17]

To be sure, the record of HIAS-HICEM was impressive. In 1940—1941 it helped the immigration of 25,000 refugees, including Christian leaders, from Western Europe, North Africa and the Far East, contributing more than a million dollars for that purpose.

14 Bentwich to McDonald, March 26, 1936 (MP:GC).
15 Adolph H. Kates to Morris Waldman, December 23, 1939 (NRS papers, folder 11, YIVO).
16 Isaac L. Asofsky to William Haber, August 13, 1940 (Chamberlain papers, p. 4295, YIVO).
17 Lotte Marcuse to Gertrude M. Dubinsky, February 5, 1945 (GJCA papers, folder 244, YIVO); Marjorie P. Schauffler to Isaac Asofsky, August 1, 1944 (HIAS–HICEM papers, first series, VII:61, YIVO).

These accomplishments notwithstanding, the HIAS' independent policy was not always helpful to the refugee cause.[18]

Nor was rivalry absent among Christian groups. "The number of various relief and refugee agencies has developed keen competition for available charitable contributions", reported the American Committee for Christian Refugees.[19] The relationship between the latter and the American Friends Service Committee was a case in point. The misunderstandings and disagreements between them, including the question of the division of responsibilities, has been discussed elsewhere.[20]

If there was rivalry among subdivisions of the same religious denomination, it is understandable that agencies of different faiths were sometimes at loggerheads. Both the German Jewish Children's Aid and the non-sectarian U.S. Committee for the Care of European Children operated on behalf of the same category of refugee children. The former, which had been active for several years, was reluctant to give up its independent status and it took years until the controversy ended. Meanwhile, duplication reduced the efficiency of this important relief work.[21]

Merger would have been a natural solution to the problem of duplication. However, committee leaders were reluctant to give up their independence and power basis. Only in circumstances of extreme pressure, such as financial deficit, lack of leadership or public interest, and change in the political situation abroad, which

---

18   In the United States too, HIAS was very active. Its staff welcomed 1500 immigrant boats at the piers, provided 84,000 night shelters, transferred more than two million dollars for the benefit of relatives in Europe, filled out 20,000 citizenship applications and handled 641,655 appeals for advice. Mark Wischnitzer, *Visas to Freedom: The History of HIAS* (Cleveland: World Publishing Co., 1956), pp. 172—175.

19   Report of the ACCR to the Committee on Foreign Relief Appeals in the Churches, May 1—October 31, 1940 (Moss papers, Box 143, FCC).

20   See above, pp. 130—131.

21   On the GJCA–U.S. Committee relations see below, pp. 326—327.

brought into question the committee's continued existence, was there willingness to combine resources. The story of the Emergency Committee in Aid of Political Refugees from Nazism demonstrated that situation. The Emergency Committee was established in May 1935 in response to Norman Bentwich's appeal for the care of political refugees who were suffering in exile. Prominent figures joined the agency, like Freda Kirchwey, Margaret I. Lamont, Frank Bohn, William G. Schram, Leland R. Robinson, Lucille Milner, and Francis A. Henson. Henson, the executive secretary, soon learned that the sponsors were always ready to sign a protest or add their names to the letterhead, but that this was not enough to run a committee. His first obstacle was to find a chairman for the organization. More serious, however, were his financial difficulties. Although the Committee was founded in May, the drive for funds began only in December 1935. The outcome was disappointing. Up to January 1936, only $ 2312 were collected. The Committee soon showed a deficit.[22]

Facing reality, in December 1935 the ECPR began discussions toward merger with the ACCR. Frank Bohn, National Campaign Chairman of the Executive Committee, proposed this step "because of our increasingly strong conviction that a unified campaign for funds for refugees is necessary". While his aim was "the unification of all committees, including the JDC", as the first step he suggested a merger with the ACCR. Bohn further argued that the "understandable confusion in the public mind in regard to the functions of these two ... committees", created the need for union. However, the proposed merger did not materialize, probably because of the opposition of the AFSC to attacks on the Nazis.[23]

Since the Emergency Committee failed to attract public interest

22 Frank Bohn (National Campaign Chairman of the Committee in Aid of Political Refugees from Nazism) to S. Parkes Cadman, January 2, 1936 (FCC, Box 102).
23 *Ibid.*, Francis A. Henson to James McDonald, December 31, 1935 (MP:GC:ACCR); Clarence E. Pickett to Frank Ritchie, January 9, 1936 (AFSC:GF, 1936, C&O).

and financial support, and was unable to function independently, it proposed a merger with the International Relief Association. As Francis Henson, the executive secretary, reported to James Mc-Donald: "Our Committee has not succeeded in raising as much money as it should have raised from non-Jewish and non-radical Americans.... I feel that our work has not been very successful and that such a merger is very desirable".[24] Dr. Otto Nathan, in his plan for the merger, admitted the lack of need for the continued operation of his Committee: "The Committee feels that the tasks for which it originally came into being are still important, but may not need any longer the attention of a special committee, and may be handled now by the existing relief organizations". The merger became effective on May 15, 1936, whereupon the Emergency Committee in Aid of Political Refugees from Nazism disappeared from the relief scene.[25]

By the same token, cooperation and consultations among refugee agencies sometimes helped to avoid duplication and increase efficiency. Conferences called on a non-sectarian basis discussed the major problems of the refugees and decided upon policy and plans for future action, such as the desired policy in regard to immigration regulations, interfaith appeals on behalf of refugees, long-range strategy to forestall immigration, and practical problems of absorption.[26] Of a more permanent character were the meetings of the Refugee Consultative Council, which was established in 1939 by the National Refugee Service to serve as an "effective liaison" between the Christian and Jewish relief agencies. Although several problems were solved and some questions were

24 Henson to McDonald, April 9, 1936 (MP:GC:ACCR).
25 "Merger Between the Emergency Committee in Aid of Political Refu-gees from Nazism and the International Relief Association. Plan Proposed by Dr. Otto Nathan", n.d. (MP:GC); Henson to McDonald, April 9, 1936 (MP:GC:ACCR). Further mergers of IRA are discussed above, pp. 238—239.
26 "Joint Conference on Immigration Legislation", May 2, 1933 (AJC, Immigration, 1933); Minutes of 29th Meeting of the President's Advisory Committee on Political Refugees, October 23, 1939 (MP:P).

clarified through the Council, real and lasting coordination was unattainable. One issue will illustrate the situation. The NRS was anxious to prevent contacts between individual refugee agencies and government officials. In order to present a unified approach it wished to serve as mediator between the refugees and the State Department. However, agency leaders refused to comply because of a desire to protect their own status and prestige.[27]

A natural answer to the existence of so many refugee organizations was the formation of a coordinating committee to oversee their activities. As early as 1933 several Jewish coordinating committees were established, such as the Council of Nine and the Joint Clearing Bureau.[28] The foundation of the National Coordinating Committee in March 1934 was a real effort to centralize the activities on behalf of refugees, both Jewish and Gentile. The NCC, however, gradually departed from its envisaged function, and began to provide relief itself. Nevertheless, through its central card index system, its affiliated agencies and consultations, the Committee retained some of its coordinating functions.[29]

With the increase in scope of the refugee work and the corresponding multiplication of relief agencies, appeals for coordination were made from time to time. Rufus M. Jones, chairman of the AFSC, called in November 1938 for the creation of a "centralized refugee service".[30] While the President's Advisory Committee on Political Refugees (PAC) was not exactly the realization of Jones' plan, it did serve as an intermediary between the State Department and the relief agencies between the years 1938—1945.[31]

27　Harry Greenstein, *Reorganization Study of National Coordinating Committee and its Affiliated Agencies* (May 1939), p. 29 (NCC papers, JDC); Meeting of Refugee Consultative Council, July 8, 1942 (AFSC:GF, 1942, C&O).

28　Cecilia Razovsky-Davidson, "Suggested Set-Up for American or Emergency Joint Bureau for German Refugees", January 3, 1934 (MP:H).

29　The NCC and the NRS are discussed in detail below, pp. 286—301.

30　Rufus M. Jones to Frank Aydelotte, November 3, 1938 (AFSC:GF, 1938, FS).　　　31　See above, pp. 76—95.

The numerous Church federations and local Church committees were also in need of supervision and coordination. The Committee on Foreign Relief Appeals in the Churches, which was formed in November 1939, aimed at providing information in regard to foreign relief needs, at coordinating existing appeals, centralizing plans and activities among the Churches, and at allocating the funds collected from the Churches. During the war years it served relief committees such as the AFSC, ACCR, YWCA and the Central Bureau for Relief of Evangelical Churches with a considerable measure of success.[32]

Efforts were made to unite Christian action on behalf of refugees at the international level as well. In October 1935 Walter Kotschnig, of the High Commission for Refugees, persuaded representatives of large Protestant international organizations, such as the World Alliance of Churches, the Ecumenical Council and the Inter-Church Aid, to set up a central Church agency in Geneva to help refugees. The Central Christian Office was supposed to unite efforts, to build joint committees, to initiate appeals and mainly "to serve as a clearing center" for relief and resettlement projects.[33] The plan did not materialize until February 1939, when the Ecumenical Committee for Refugees was established by the World Council of Churches. Dr. Adolf Keller of the World Council, who was the living spirit of the Committee, strove to "coordinate the activities of Christian refugee committees in the different countries" and to further emigration. Although the Ecumenical Committee for Refugees failed to play a central role, it nevertheless cooperated with several Protestant agencies in Europe, particularly in France, spending the sum of 189,330 Swiss Francs between February 1939 and December 1941.[34]

The Princeton Conference also sought to "mobilize leadership

32   See above, pp. 118—120.
33   Walter Kotschnig to James McDonald, October 7, 1935 (MP:H).
34   "Church Refugee Work in War Time", 22 pp. report of the Ecumenical Committee for Refugees, World Council of Churches, January 1942 (Moss papers, Box 145, FCC).

and cooperation on a very broad basis". Roy Veatch, a YMCA staff member, supported by Eleanor Roosevelt, Clarence Pickett, Martha B. Taft and Frank Aydelotte, invited prominent leaders of refugee agencies to a conference (February 28 — March 1, 1941), to discuss the major refugee problems. After careful examination of the needs and objectives, the conference proceeded to consider the ways and means of attaining these goals. One of the controversial plans suggested was the "amalgamation, or very close coordination, of all refugee programs — resulting in a single or united direction and control in the fields of publicity and education, fund raising, planning and actual assistance to refugees". Alternatively, it proposed the establishment of a new organization, "assuming the responsibility for a national presentation of all refugee problems", preferably in cooperation with the major refugee agencies, but even without their help.[35]

No definite action was taken at the Princeton Conference, except the decision to appoint a Continuation Committee, which would study the problem raised and prepare a report for the next session.[36] During the following months the Council on Refugee Aid, as the new committee was called, held a series of meetings. Roy Veatch's project raised strong opposition. The National Refugee Service was particularly suspicious. When in April 1941 the Council announced its establishment "as a coordinating committee in the entire refugee field", members of the NRS were infuriated. They agreed to cooperate with the Council only after they had received further assurances that the Council on Refugee Aid "was not to become a super-body or to attempt any type of activity either in fund raising or functional work which might affect or

35   See the invitation to Joseph F. Rummel, February 7, 1941 (NCWC, Box 82); "Alternative Lines of Action", 5 pp. memorandum for the Princeton Conference, February 28—March 1, 1941 (AFSC:GF, 1941, FS:R).
36   Roy Veatch's "Report of the Princeton Conference on Refugee Problems and Needs", February 28—March 1, 1941 (NCWC, Box 82).

embarrass the work of the existing agencies".[37] The National Catholic Welfare Conference also strongly opposed Veatch's venture, regarding him as an "energetic and persistent young man", who developed "a rather elaborate paper organization".[38] According to Bruce Mohler of the NCWC, many participants in the discussions "attended the meetings merely because they felt they could not refuse to go". With the passage of time many of the Council's associates withdrew their support, including Cecilia Razovsky of the NRS, leading to the eventual collapse of the project for a roof-agency for refugees.[39]

Disappointed with the failure, Clarence E. Pickett turned in June 1942 to the NRS, with a request that "consideration be given to the possibility of consolidating into one agency the work being done on behalf of refugees in the United States by various organizations". A small sub-committee was appointed to consider "the feasibility of integrating the service activities of the ACCR and AFSC, the Catholic Committee and NRS".[40] The discussions led to no positive results because "the Protestant Committees are anxious first to coordinate their own activities before submitting a proposal for consolidation with NRS". Indeed, the AFSC, ACCR and USC decided, as the first phase of a coordinated plan, to unify their budget.[41] However, once more enthusiastic proposals were watered down by so-called practical considerations and neither Pickett's suggestion, nor the more limited plan to coordinate the

37 Quoted in the Minutes of the Executive Committee of the NRS, August 12, 1941 (Chamberlain papers, pp. 1975—1976, YIVO).
38 Bruce M. Mohler to Joseph F. Rummel, August 18, 1941 (NCWC, Box 81); SW (Sara Weadick) to Bruce Mohler, Meeting on Extending and Coordinating Aid for Refugees, January 2, 1941 (*ibid.*, Box 87).
39 Mohler to Ready, July 17, 1941 (NCWC, Box 81).
40 Minutes, Executive Committee of the NRS, June 18, 1942 (Chamberlain papers, p. 2026, YIVO).
41 Minutes, Executive Committee of the NRS, July 16, 1942 (Chamberlain papers, p. 2028, YIVO); Minutes of a Meeting of Representatives of Several Relief Agencies, July 29, 1942 (Moss papers, Box 143, FCC).

budget of three Protestant relief agencies, were implemented or even given serious consideration.

As an alternative to consolidation, the NRS' Executive Committee issued a call to other relief organizations to form a "conference of refugee agencies to explore from time to time matters of general policy and procedures common to all of them".[42] Thus, a consultative body was suggested, which would in fact be a duplicate of the Refugee Consultative Council, established by the NRS in 1939. In 1942, then, the situation was not much better than it had been in 1934, with leaders of committees which had been in operation for some years being reluctant to give up their basis of power and influence, even for the good of the refugees they wished to serve. Only pressing circumstances, usually financial, could induce the agencies to some kind of cooperation. At the request of the National War Fund, which was interested in reducing the number of its subsidized agencies, the Refugee Relief Trustees was established in January 1943, consisting of the American Committee for Christian Refugees, the Unitarian Service Committee and the International Rescue and Relief Committee. The agencies divided their spheres of responsibility, functionally as well as geographically, though they retained their sectional autonomy. In the light of the Bermuda Conference's failure to suggest any practical plan for the solution of the refugee problem, the RRT initiated another relief conference, in May 1943, with a view to formulating a unified policy toward the refugee cause. The Catholics refused to participate, while others came without much enthusiasm.[43] The scheduled two-day conference terminated after a few hours' discussion. The JDC report clearly summarized the situation: "... although there were many interesting reports rendered and valuable suggestions offered, the conference did not bring forth any practical results".[44]

42 Minutes, Executive Committee of the NRS, July 16, 1942 (Chamberlain papers, p. 2028, YIVO).
43 T.F. Mulholland to Bruce Mohler, May 24, 1943 (NCWC, Box 84).
44 Notes on the Informal Conference of Representatives of Agencies

Outside pressure, such as the establishment of the United Nations Relief and Rehabilitation Administration, pushed private agencies to found a council through which they would be able to form a united policy in negotiating and cooperating with UNRRA. The American Council of Voluntary Agencies for Foreign Service (ACVAFS) was established in September 1943 in the shadow of the threat posed to the continuation of small relief committees by that huge, well-financed international agency called UNRRA. The AFSC, for example, was eager to exploit the collective approach of the Council as a point of strength in dealing with UNRRA.[45] The ACVAFS represented the member agencies in matters of common interest in Washington. The Council effectively functioned through committees and sub-committees.[46] The American Council of Voluntary Agencies, under the chairmanship of Joseph P. Chamberlain, was the realization of the original plan of the National Coordinating Committee dating back to 1934. Practically, this was the maximum attainable in the area of cooperation at that time. Thus, after ten years of effort, the striving for coordination among American relief agencies gained only partial fulfillment.

THE INTERNATIONAL MIGRATION SERVICE

We have so far in this chapter concentrated attention on comparatively minor and sometimes short-lived refugee committees, all of which combined to create a picture of confusion and over-

in the Refugee Field Arranged by the Refugee Relief Trustees Inc., June 24, 1943 (JDC; Refugees, General). For the Bermuda Conference, see Feingold, *Politics of Rescue*, Chapter 7.

45   Minutes, Joint Foreign Service Executive Committee of the AFSC, January 17, 1944 (AFSC:MF).

46   See, for example, William O'Dwyer (of the WRB) to the American Council of Voluntary Agencies, May 5, 1945 (International Migration Service papers (= IMS) file 5, at the office of International Social Service = ISS, New York City).

lapping in the field of relief work in the United States. There were, however, other agencies with long-standing reputations, such as the International Migration Service and the Young Women's Christian Association, that also offered services to refugees. Although important, these were not major agencies in the category of the ACCR and the AFSC and will therefore not be discussed in the same detail as the latter. In the following pages we shall seek to outline the contribution of these Christian organizations to the refugee problem in America.

Shortly before the outbreak of World War I an urgent need was felt among American YWCA circles for a welfare agency at an international level, but the war postponed the realization of the idea. When peace came and many countries adopted restrictive immigration regulations while large numbers of refugees were languishing in European ports awaiting visas to their country of destination, the need intensified for an organization that would give technical advice on immigration and visa regulations and be able to operate simultaneously in several countries. The establishment of the International Migration Service (IMS) in London in 1924 came in answer to that need. The basic principle of the Service's activities was to make every possible effort to unite separated families. It aimed "to render service through cooperative effort to individuals whose problems have arisen as a consequence of migration and the solution of which involves action in more than one country".[47] The Service concentrated on providing technical and legal advice, and guiding immigrants through the complicated visa forms and immigration regulations. Cordial relations with governmental authorities enabled the IMS staff to overcome bureaucratic red tape. The Service's reputation as a non-sectarian, non-political and non-partisan agency, carried some weight in its dealings with officials in different countries.

Since considerable emphasis was placed on employing only ex-

47   IMS, "Memorandum on Work and Finances for Calendar Year 1934" (IMS, folder 2, ISS).

perienced social workers, training courses were provided for new staff members. Like the Bureau of Immigration of the National Catholic Welfare Conference, the IMS was not a relief-dispensing agency. Since it was never its policy to promote migration, the IMS never provided actual financial help and, indeed, refrained from distributing relief or covering transportation costs. This approach was justified by the argument that the IMS specialization lay in giving highly skilled technical and professional advice, whereas financial assistance could be obtained through many other local and national agencies. Accordingly, the IMS' collaboration with public and private relief organizations characterized its activity.[48] The approach of backing up local committees made fund raising a difficult task for the IMS, because the people were "relief minded", as George L. Warren, the international director, complained. So the IMS refrained from special campaign methods, relying on grants from individuals and foundations. No wonder that the annual budget never exceeded $ 80,000.[49]

The international nature of the IMS structure was a feature of its activities. The general headquarters was housed in Geneva, but branches were soon established in New York, Paris, Marseilles, Berlin, Athens, Prague and Warsaw. When the situation so demanded, associated correspondents were nominated in Canada, Italy, Norway, Denmark, Rumania, Hungary, Yugoslavia and Finland. The budgets and the various programs of the branches were submitted to the international Executive Committee for approval and remained under its supervision. Because the United States was the source of the major part of the Service's budget, the office of the international director, held by George L. Warren, was in New York and not at the Geneva headquarters. During World War II the financial share of the American branch meaningfully increased, and it covered, among other things, the expenditure of the Geneva

48 M. Schauffler to Mary Rogers, April 26, 1942 (AFSC:GF, 1942, FS:R).

49 George Warren to William F. Fuerst, March 9, 1934; IMS, "Memorandum on Work...1934" (IMS, folder 2, ISS).

headquarters.[50] Thus, the branches' good relations with government officials on the one hand, and with local relief committees on the other, along with frequent communication among themselves, made the IMS with its 130 staff members a useful social service agency. As a Service source proudly claimed: "This facility of a trained personnel in working together between countries on the common problems of displaced persons is the special contribution of the IMS for the immediate and long-term future".[51]

By virtue of the help extended by the IMS to Russian and Armenian refugees during the 1920s, it had gained intimate and valuable experience with victims of political and religious persecution, which was certainly helpful when the problem of German refugees arose. It was natural that IMS workers were invited to serve on different committees aiming to bring about constructive changes in immigration procedures. Professor Joseph P. Chamberlain, vice-chairman of IMS American branch, was nominated by President Roosevelt as the U.S. representative on the Governing Body of the High Commission for Refugees. The IMS also became a member of the High Commission's Advisory Council and of its Bureau of Information. Three members of the American branch were designated by the Secretary of Labor to the Committee on Ellis Island, to suggest changes in methods and procedures of the immigration laws. Likewise, George L. Warren was appointed by the President to represent the United States on the League of Nations Committee on Assistance to Aliens. These nominations were, indeed, "a signal recognition of the contribution the IMS can make to solving the problem of the German refugee", as was indicated by the Service's annual report.[52]

In addition to its efforts to alleviate undue legal hardships facing

---

50 Marjorie Schauffler to Mary Rogers, April 26, 1942 (AFSC:GF, 1942, FS:R); "Project of the IMS", May 1944 (IMS, folder 7, ISS).
51 "Project of the International Migration Service", May 1944 (IMS, folder 7, ISS).
52 IMS, "Memorandum on Work ... 1934" (IMS, folder 2, ISS).

prospective immigrants, the American branch of the IMS also engaged in rendering individual assistance to refugees. Between July 1933 and June 1934, 2681 cases were handled, involving 14,745 people who received some kind of assistance, mainly technical advice. The search for relatives, a service also undertaken by the IMS, required correspondence with 60 countries and collaboration with 900 public and private welfare agencies in America. While in 1934 German refugees constituted only a small part of the caseload (100 active cases), their weight gradually increased in the following years. The total income of the IMS for July 1933 — June 1934 was $ 68,546, of which the American branch collected $ 39,449. While in 1934—1935 the volume of work increased, the income of the American branch dropped meaningfully.[53]

Collaboration with other refugee agencies was an inseparable part of the IMS activities. Professor Joseph P. Chamberlain and George L. Warren actively participated in the foundation and management of the National Coordinating Committee, the former becoming its chairman and the latter a member of the Executive Committee. Indeed, in 1935 the IMS was singled out by Cecilia Razovsky of the NCC as "the only non-Jewish body which cooperates effectively" with her Committee.[54] In addition, IMS personnel provided services, mainly legal and technical advice, to the ACCR, the National Students Federation, Sigma Delta Fraternity, Hospites and HIAS, among others.[55] With the establishment of the President's Advisory Committee on Political Refugees (PAC) in 1938, Warren became its executive secretary. In this capacity he participated at the Evian Conference and was instrumental in the foundation of the Intergovernmental Committee in London. Through

---

53 IMS, "Statement of Receipts and Expenditures for the Entire Service", Fiscal Year, July 1, 1933—June 30, 1934; July 1, 1934—June 30, 1935 (IMS, folder 3, ISS).

54 Norman Bentwich to James McDonald, April 12, 1935 (MP:GC).

55 Minutes, Meeting of the Board of Directors of ACCR and IMS, February 24, 1943 (FCC, Box 3); *Newscast*, 4 (Feb.—March 1943), 4.

the war years he was actively involved in and helped to shape the PAC's policy and activities.[56]

Such collaboration extended also to Jewish organizations, and indeed the IMS gave assistance to Jewish refugees too, as part of its policy. Although it had been established under YWCA initiative and was composed of Christian personnel, the IMS operated on a non-sectarian basis. Many of its beneficiaries were Jewish. The American branch, for instance, provided services for more than 35 local and national Jewish welfare Committees during 1940—1941.[57]

The IMS was helpful in preventing the return of two refugee ships to Europe. In November 1941, when the Brazilian Government denied the validity of visas issued by its consuls to the passengers aboard the S.S. *Cabo de Hornos* and refused to permit the landing, the American Jewish Joint Distribution Committee asked Patrick Malin, former director of the IMS' American branch, to go to Trinidad and Curaçao, to facilitate the disembarkation of the refugees. Likewise, in the case of the S.S. *St. Thome* the IMS rendered a particular service to the JDC. In April 1942 the Cuban authorities held up for ten days the admission of this boat, carrying refugees to Havana. George Warren took an active role in the organization of the protests and appeals, which eventually led to the disembarkation of the refugees.[58]

As an international organization, the IMS was particularly close to similar agencies, such as the International Red Cross and the International Students Service (ISS). The latter, a Geneva-based agency, was established in 1920 with the aim of "providing a meeting ground where students from many nations could discuss their

---

56 Warren to Fuerst, May 11, 1939, May 13, 1940 (IMS, folder 3, ISS). See above, pp. 76—95.

57 IMS, American Branch, "Some of the Jewish Organizations Served", Fiscal Year 1940—1941; "Memorandum on the Work of the Preceding Year, May 1942" (IMS, folder 3, ISS).

58 IMS, "Memorandum on the Work of the Preceding Year, May 1942" (IMS, folder 3, ISS).

common problems". After 1933 it offered aid to German refugee students to continue their studies. The American office of the ISS helped about 700 students between 1933—1943. Jewish and Christian agencies, such as B'nai B'rith, Hillel, the NRS, ACCR and the Refugee Scholar Fund, provided the financial support. Up to 1939 the ISS collected $ 54,000 and financed 130 scholarships at 100 colleges, to a total value of $ 143,000.[59] The IMS American branch offered its services to the ISS and the Phi Sigma Delta Fraternity (which arranged scholarships and board at American universities), assisted the students with documents, affidavits and advice in dealings with American consuls in Europe.[60]

World War II materially changed the activities of the IMS branches in Europe as well as in the United States. The Berlin office was closed in 1937, and in 1939—1940 the offices in Prague, Warsaw, and Athens also ceased to function. On the other hand, the operations in Switzerland, France and the United States greatly expanded. While the war and the resulting communications difficulties reduced the number of appeals for help, nevertheless, every case now consumed more time and more energy.[61] In 1940 the American branch was active in securing visas for refugees who wanted to resettle in the Dominican Republic and in persuading their American relatives to deposit the necessary funds for their admission. In spite of the war, these and other arrangements enabled a small group of immigrants to reach that country via New York.[62]

Cooperation with the projects of the U.S. Committee for the

59 Davie, *Refugees in America*, pp. 114—115; Robert G. Spivack to William Rosenwald, May 31, 1939 (NRS papers, folder 146, YIVO).
60 Thus, in 1938 the New York office extended services to 3982 families, while in 1940 the figures dropped to 2253. IMS, "Memorandum on Work and Finances for Calendar Year 1935" (IMS, folder 3, ISS).
61 See Warren to Fuerst, May 11, 1939, May 15, 1941 (IMS, folder 3, ISS).
62 IMS, "Memorandum Prepared by the American Branch, May 1941" (IMS, folder 3, ISS).

Care of European Children was another aspect of IMS enterprise. Starting in 1939, the IMS collaborated with the AFSC in planning the selection of refugee children in Europe in accordance with the proposed Wagner Act. The IMS undertook the training of the personnel for that mission. When the U.S. Committee for the Care of European Children replaced the Non-sectarian Committee, five IMS members were seconded to the former, which planned the procedure by which governmental consent to use corporate affidavits would be secured.[63]

The Swiss branch director, Leni Calin, became the secretary of the Coordinating Committee of Refugee Agencies in that country. Due to her good connections with the Swiss authorities, she functioned effectively as liaison between the Government and the private agencies. The IMS Swiss personnel also helped the International Red Cross to set up a bureau which handled requests for the location of missing relatives. In September 1939 a large flow of inquiries came in for the location of uprooted families in Poland. The bureau, under the direction of the IMS associate director in Geneva, employed 75 volunteers to cable short messages to Poland and to American relatives. The location of their relatives was a great undertaking for which the IMS became responsible.[64]

The IMS offices in France, probably more than the other branches, rendered services for other relief organizations during the war. The Paris office, at the request of the French Government, acted as liaison between the authorities and the refugee agencies. After the Franco-German armistice in June 1940, it was the only agency in Occupied France that continued to operate legally on behalf of aliens. Some of the staff were arrested and tortured by the Germans for their assistance to refugees. Other committees either ceased to function or had to move to the un-Occupied zone. The Paris branch dealt with complicated cases referred by the International Red Cross, helping the former to obtain the neces-

63 *Ibid.*, Warren to Fuerst, May 11, 1938. See below, pp. 321—326.
64 Warren to Fuerst, May 13, 1940; "Memorandum on the Work of the Preceding Year, May 1942" (IMS, folder 3, ISS).

sary documents and visas, and presenting their cases to the American consul. The Marseilles office was particularly helpful in regard to emigration of refugee children and intellectual and labor leaders who had been interned. The new offices, which were established in Lyons in 1940 and in Casablanca and Algiers in 1941—1942, extended their services beyond the regular provision of legal and technical advice. The IMS staff actively helped to administer relief to camp internees and their families. Good relations with the Vichy Government as well as with American consulates were important factors in the IMS success.[65]

IMS officeholders contributed of their experience and expertise to the newly-established agencies. George Warren, international director, was lent as a part-time consultant for the development of UNRRA's program for displaced persons. Warren's services were also sought by the State Department, which asked him to function as a liaison officer with the War Refugee Board. Likewise, the chairman of the American branch, Joseph P. Chamberlain, took the lead in organizing and directing the American Council of Voluntary Agencies for Foreign Service. Other IMS personnel also actively participated in the work of several committees of the American Council. An IMS leader was appointed chairman of a team that worked out the program for a Central Location Index.[66]

With a modification in the strict censorship regulations by U.S. authorities, the possibilities of operating in Europe were further widened. The case-load of the American branch increased. Services were provided for cases emanating from 31 neutral and Allied countries. Although there were requests relating to people living under Nazi occupation for whom almost nothing could be done, the groundwork of documentation was at least being laid.

65 IMS, "Memorandum on Work for Year 1944—1945"; Warren to Fuerst, May 13, 1940; IMS, "Memorandum Prepared by the American Branch, May 1941"; "Memorandum on the Work of the Preceding Year, May 1942" (IMS, folder 3, ISS).
66 IMS, "Memorandum on Work for Year 1943—1944" (IMS, folder 3, ISS). See above, p. 260.

One of the new assignments of the American branch in the last year of the war was to help out the Swiss branch with emigration of the refugee children. Since the autumn of 1942 approximately 12,000 refugee children, mainly from France, had reached Switzerland. The IMS Geneva office put itself at the disposal of an agency called the Swiss Assistance to Emigrant Children. Among other activities, children were freed from internment camps, clothed and put into three foster homes.[67] After the liberation of western France, some agencies hastily started their repatriation. Children were taken from internment camps and foster homes and hurriedly returned to France, only to find their homes destroyed and their parents missing. To prevent an emotional shock of this kind and the need to return children to internment camps, the IMS was asked by Swiss and French authorities to first investigate the situation of the children's families and to effect their repatriation only after certain conditions had been met. Exit permits for France would be granted only with the recommendation of the IMS Swiss branch (*Aide aux Emigrés*). The latter became responsible for those children whose parents were dead or missing. More than 280 cases were referred to the American branch for location of their relatives, and to find out how far the latter could be helpful.[68]

Most of these children had been admitted to Switzerland during the war as "guests" only, and on condition that the United States would guarantee their permanent settlement after the war. The pledge was made by the U.S. Committee in Care of European Children, backed by the assurance of the European Jewish Children's Aid and the NRS to take care of the children after their arrival in America. Although the Jewish agencies paid transportation fees, met the children at the piers and placed them in private homes, the IMS also contributed by planning the procedure of

---

67 Swiss Branch of the IMS, Annual Report, July 1, 1943—June 30, 1944 (IMS, folder 1, ISS).
68 *Ibid.*, IMS, "Memorandum on Work for Year 1944—1945" (IMS, folder 3, ISS); Ruth Larned to Lotte Marcuse, November 15, 1944 (GJCA papers, folder 143, YIVO).

their handling and particularly by advising on the methods of completing applications to secure corporate affidavits.[69] IMS cooperation with German Jewish Children's Aid with regard to children in Switzerland, Prague and Vienna dated back to 1939, when data concerning Jewish children, including visa treatment, was referred by the IMS to the GJCA. Likewise, there were cases of Christian children who had been sent to the IMS office. Despite much goodwill, the complicated procedures and multiplicity of agencies created much confusion, as was testified to by Lotte Marcuse, secretary of GJCA, in December 1939: "I regret exceedingly that there was any misunderstanding, but so many offices are involved that perhaps it was inevitable".[70]

The preparation of a registration form and the demonstration of its importance was another joint project between the American and the Swiss branches of the IMS. When postwar planning was under consideration in 1943, it became increasingly evident to the IMS leadership that a considerable proportion of the refugees would not be able to return to their homes. What was to be done with displaced persons for whom repatriation was impossible? Resettlement and special aid programs were suggested as at least a partial solution. It was crucial for any long-range planning to know as early as possible the scope and directions of the aid needed. To meet that problem, the IMS devised a form which called for information concerning personal particulars of the refugee, his relatives, his vocational training, education and professional experience. The material gathered would be of great value in planning his resumption of normal life. Furthermore, the early gathering of data could be utilized in the locating of scattered family members, in reducing confusion when repatriation later took place under the great pressure of the postwar situation and, finally, in "demonstrating that planning can be more constructively

---

69   Lotte Marcuse to Gertrude M. Dubinsky, February 5, 1945 (GJCA papers, folder 244, YIVO).
70   Lotte Marcuse to Hanna Steiner, December 27, 1939 (GJCA papers, folder 243, YIVO).

conceived and effectively carried out if based on adequate information". The IMS suggested that this program be carried out on a
limited scale among different types of refugee camps in Switzerland, Egypt and Mexico.[71] Official bodies, like the Intergovernmental Committee, expressed interest in the undertaking, contributing £ 1000 toward the expenses of the project.[72]

In Switzerland the demonstration project, which in 1943 was
already under way, "was accepted with enthusiasm" by private
and public organizations, it was noted in the IMS annual report.
Indeed, the trial enquiry among 366 refugees was so useful that
the Central Office for the Assistance to Refugees and its branch
agencies decided to expand the survey to all refugees in Switzerland. The IMS was entrusted with the program. During 1943—
1944 more than 10,000 questionnaires were distributed among
refugees.[73]

In contrast, the planned Middle East survey met with difficulties
because of a lack of adequate personnel. Instead, the IMS suggested
that the study be conducted in the newly-constructed camp in
Oswego, New York. The study, carried out by Frank L. Auerbach,
former IMS Canadian staff member, in Fort Ontario, Oswego,
in 1944—1945, was termed "the special project" of IMS in that
year. The report was praised by the Intergovernmental Committee as "a valuable demonstration of a method and a helpful contribution to a study of the problem".[74]

With the liberation of Europe the IMS reopened its branches

71 "Project of the International Migration Service", May 1944 (IMS,
    folder 7, ISS); IMS, "Memorandum on Work for Year 1943—1944"
    (*ibid.*, folder 3).
72 Unsigned and undated cable beginning with the words "Please inform
    Chamberlain and Larned" (IMS, folder 7, ISS).
73 Swiss Branch of the IMS, Annual Report, July 1, 1943—June 30,
    1944 (IMS, folder 1, ISS).
74 IMS, "Memorandum on Work for Year 1944—1945" (IMS, folder 3,
    ISS); Frank L. Auerbach to Miss Larned, October 29, 1944; see
    Oswego Project: Refugee Case Study Report, 1944—1945 (IMS,
    folder 5, ISS).

in Athens, Prague, Berlin and Warsaw. Its services were expanded, with corresponding offices established in additional countries. The International Migration Service, with its small personnel and very limited resources, proved what could be done for refugees by a carefully planned strategy. The advantages of the Service, such as its international character, its highly trained staff, its non-sectarian and non-political approach, which granted it access to the governmental authorities, contributed to its success. Nevertheless, it should be remembered that the actual help of the Service to the rescue of refugees focused mainly on technical and legal advice on immigration regulations, and on the location of relatives. This service was only a small, yet not unimportant, part of the wide spectrum of aid given to the victims of persecution.

YOUNG WOMEN'S CHRISTIAN ASSOCIATION (YWCA)

Another international Christian organization that had been operating long before Hitler's rise to power was the Young Women's Christian Association (YWCA), which had been founded in 1871. The Council of the World's YWCA, based in Geneva, directed the movement's activities among young women and girls in 65 countries. Unlike the International Migration Service, which became active on behalf of German refugees already in 1933, it was only in September 1938 that the Council became increasingly aware of the acute suffering of victims of political and racial persecution. In its conference of September 1938, the Council of the World's YWCA gave "serious consideration" to the tragic situation of refugees, particularly non-Aryan Christians. The YWCA considered its specific task as being "to stir the conscience of Christians in this matter", read one of the resolutions. Following its decisions. Ruth W. Woodsmall, general secretary of the World's YWCA, urged the national associations in October 1938 "to give special attention to the problem of the non-Aryan Christian refugees, working with other Christian organizations in an effort to meet their needs, and to facilitate their integration into the Christian fellowship of the receiving countries". The council also called for a struggle against anti-Semitism and the encouragement of governmental cooperation with the Intergovernmental Committee. The national associations received detailed recommendations in regard to the area of activities concerning the refugee issue.[75]

The American National Board of the YWCA, at its convention in Columbus, Ohio, on April 27, 1938, expressed its commendation to President Roosevelt for his initiative in convening the Evian Conference for Political Refugees. Another resolution read that "we also feel responsibility for helping to create public opinion... which will prevent the growth of intolerance, injustice and discrimination in our country on account of religious belief, especially the growth of anti-Semitism".[76] Thus, the American branch voiced its protest even before the call came from the World's YWCA. After *Kristallnacht*, the National Board of the YWCA cabled President Roosevelt "to join in constructive efforts to ameliorate the suffering of the victims". The persecutions in Germany were regarded as a "crime against humanity itself".[77] In response to the World's YWCA appeal, the American National Board decided on November 21, 1938 on a series of steps to be taken, among others: to distribute accurate information in regard to immigration and the quota system; to promote tolerance and understanding toward refugees; and to cooperate with Christian and Jewish agencies. To carry out those aims, a Committee on Refugees was

---

75 Ruth F. Woodsmall, "Refugee Problem: To the National Associations from the World's Council of the YWCA", *Woman's Press* (YWCA) (December 1938), p. 561; Ruth Woodsmall to General Secretary, September 30, 1938 (YWCA, roll 99).

76 YWCA, "Resolutions Adopted at Columbus Convention", n.d. (*c.* 1938) (YWCA, roll 99).

77 YWCA, National Board, "Call to Action", n.d. (Chamberlain papers, p. 1135, YIVO).

formed, with Dr. Emily Hickman as chairman and Mabel B. Ellis
as secretary.[78]

"The Committee on Refugees was always a sort of step-child at
the National Board", complained Mabel Ellis, the secretary, who
knew the facts at firsthand. "It was born at a moment when rigid
economy and 'program planning' were the watchwords at 600
Lexington Avenue (YWCA's headquarters in New York City),
and for the first two years of its life had constantly to fight for its
very right to exist. Had it not been for the volunteers, who formed
the majority of the Committee membership, the Committee could
never have survived", concluded Ellis.[79] Indeed, the maintenance
of the Committee was regarded by the National Board as a burden,
financially as well as politically. It was impossible to implement
fundamental decisions on account of a lack of funds. The Committee was manned by staff members of several divisions of the
YWCA. Although it received a mandate to work "as long as the
need of such urgency lasts", most members were reluctant to
devote time and energy to the refugee cause. There was a contra-
diction between the aim of the Committee and the tasks allotted
to the secretary. The National Board pledged to "undertake
responsibility for assisting in the aid of refugees". Mabel Ellis,
however, was only asked to coordinate relations with other agencies and to run an information center. For the purpose of more
direct aid, the Committee on Refugees pressed for a widening of
its duties. Eventually, on April 5, 1939, the National Board decided
"to assume definite responsibility for assistance to individual
refugees". However, that step was taken "with the distinct understanding that any help given was not to be considered a charge
against the budget of the National Board", as Ellis pointed out.[80]

78   "Action Taken by the National Board of YWCA", n.d. (YWCA,
     roll 99).
79   Mabel B. Ellis, "Final Report", Committee on Refugees, The National
     Board of YWCA, February 1, 1946, p. 85 (YWCA, roll 99). Here-
     after, "Final Report".
80   Ibid., pp. 4—6.

It was in such an unfavorable atmosphere that the Committee on Refugees had to operate. In adherence to its aim of supplementing rather than competing with other relief agencies, five areas of activity were selected: work with individual refugees; provision of information, advisory services and influencing of public opinion; contacts with private and governmental organizations; work with camp internees; and visiting the Emergency Refugee Shelter.[81]

The National Board's hesitations in undertaking the care of individual refugees were partly the outcome of its "failure to comprehend just how dangerous the situation really was", claimed the secretary in her report in 1946. Even its decision to assume responsibility in that field was confined to YWCA members in foreign countries. Thus, in 1939, 68 people were given information and some aid. In 1941, the busiest year, 122 cases were handled involving 190 individuals who received some kind of service. After Pearl Harbor the work with individuals virtually ceased. Altogether, 118 service cases were handled. Most of the refugees were YWCA board members in Holland, Belgium, Czechoslovakia, China and Japan. On account of the Committee's inexperience, "many carefully laid plans went wrong in these hectic days", admitted the secretary. However, part of the blame for the meager results must be assigned to the National Board, which refused to permit any approach to YWCA members for the purpose of obtaining affidavits. Only three refugee families received affidavits through the Committee. When eventually the Board approved a more lenient approach, "it was too late to accomplish much".[82] Among the services provided for refugees through the local associations were placement in summer camps as consultants, teachers and physicians, a distribution of clothing to a number of refugees;

81 Excerpts from a memorandum prepared for Mrs. Grace L. Elliott by M.B. Ellis, n.d. (YWCA, roll 99); *Report of the National Board for the Biennium, 1938—1940*, part II of the Report of the National Board of the YWCA to 16th National Convention, p. 31 (YWCA Library, NYC).

82 "Final Report", pp. 6—7, 16.

English courses, hospitality, tea parties, boarding in YWCA's dormitories, and location of relatives. Although the Committee on Refugees did not administer relief, it distributed the sum of $4670 by way of grants, scholarships and gifts between 1941 and 1945.[83]

Statistics concerning the cases handled and services provided for individual refugees cannot, however, serve as a criterion for evaluation of the Committee on Refugees' record, since its major efforts were directed toward different aims. To utilize the YWCA's numerous local associations, other relief agencies recommended that it concentrate on the shaping of public opinion as the best way to contribute to the refugee cause. "Throughout the seven-year period", stated the Committee's "Final Report", "the chief emphasis in the work for refugees was laid upon activities in the field of public opinion, rather than upon services to individual refugees for whom other resources were available".[84] Indeed, the most significant work was done in the field of publicity. An effort was made to keep the YWCA constituency, as well as the general Christian public, well informed and ready to fight misconceptions concerning the refugee issue. The Committee circulated facts about the number of refugees being admitted to the country and called YWCA members "to do all we can, personally, to prevent the dangers of an increasing public sentiment against Jews and refugees in general".[85] In its appeal for toleration and understanding toward aliens, the Committee on Refugees turned to local YWCA associations as well as to organizations like the American Association for University Women, the General Federation of Women's Clubs, and the National Federation of Business and Professional Women. These were asked to discuss with their members ways of stimulating more active cooperation with existing refugee commit-

---

83 *Ibid.*, pp. 12—16; Memorandum on "Volunteer Service", prepared by M.B. Ellis, n.d. (YWCA, roll 99).
84 "Final Report", p. 2.
85 National Board, YWCA, "A Few Basic Facts on the Refugee Problem in the United States", January 1939 (YWCA, roll 99).

tees.[86] The YWCA joined other agencies in refuting the misconception that all of the immigrants were Jews, although it propagated chiefly the cause of Christian refugees, calling for their support financially as well as morally.[87]

Particular efforts were made to fight anti-Semitic sentiments in the United States. As a Christian organization, the YWCA was in a better position than the AJC to protest against the growth of that evil in the country. At the National Convention in Columbus, Ohio, on April 28, 1938, a resolution was adopted, calling on local associations to report on every anti-Semitic publication that appeared in the neighborhood. Detailed instructions were sent by the Committee as to how to handle the problem. It was suggested that anti-Semitism be discussed at closed meetings with Jewish women invited to such gatherings. "Work quietly in close cooperation" with local Jewish committees, advised the YWCA directive.[88] For better understanding of the Jews and for the development of a better relationship with them, a reading list of basic books on Jews was recommended.[89]

Part of the public opinion campaign was to stress the loyalty of the newcomer to America. "The entire refugee community is on the side of democracy, eager to strengthen it", it was noted in an article in *Woman's Press*, the YWCA's monthly organ.[90] The

86 Committee on Refugees, National Board, YWCA, "Recent Developments", March 5, 1940 (YWCA, roll 99).

87 National Board, YWCA, "A Few Basic Facts", January, 1939; World's YWCA, "An Appeal for Help for the Refugees", February 1, 1939 (YWCA, roll 99).

88 *Refugees*, Bulletin of the National Board of YWCA, Committee on Refugees (January 9, 1939), p. 1 (NCC papers, folder 17, YIVO); "Final Report", pp. 46—48; Emily M. Hickman's Foreword to *Refugees*, p. 1 (YWCA, roll 99).

89 YWCA, "Brief Reading List", *Refugees*, January 1939 (YWCA, roll 99).

90 Hertha Kraus, "The Plight of Refugees in a Preoccupied World", *Woman's Press* (July—Aug. 1940), p. 323; Ellis, "Alien Registration Plans", *Woman's Press* (Sep. 1940), p. 379.

YWCA Committee was eager to prove the refugees' contribution to the war effort. It pointed out that many of them served in the army, and that some of them had even been awarded the Order of the Purple Heart; that the scientists' contribution was particularly important in the development of secret weapons; and that women also worked for the military industry. The Committee defended refugee physicians against "the most insidious and unfair criticism" of evading enlistment and of stealing the practice of those doctors who went to the army.[91] Various methods were used to fight these sentiments in the country. *Woman's Press* was mobilized. Reports, short stories, impressions of visits to a refugee home, and summaries of discussions on the refugee problem were printed in the pages of the *Press*.[92] The Committee also published booklets, which were circulated among women's organizations. Probably the most effective publications were the pamphlets called *Meet the Refugees* (September 1940) and *Refugees in War Time* (February 1943), both of which were prepared, printed and distributed in 30,000 copies by the American Jewish Committee, which also saw to

---

91   YWCA, *Refugees in Wartime* (Feb. 1943), pp. 11—13 (NRS papers, folder 1317, YIVO).

92   "Refugee Problem", *Woman's Press* (Dec. 1938), p. 561; Mabel Ellis, "The Refugee Problem and the War", *ibid.* (Nov. 1939), pp. 452, 486; "Alien Registration Plans", *ibid.* (Sep. 1940), p. 379; "Children in Flight from War", *ibid.* (Sep. 1940), p. 391; "Women's Organizations and the Woman Refugee", *ibid.* (Jan. 1942), pp. 20—21; Rhoda E. McCulloch, "The Dispossessed", *Woman's Press* (Jan. 1939), pp. 14—16; Mary E. Hurblutt, "The World Crisis and New Americans", *ibid.* (Feb. 1939), pp. 58—60; Hertha Kraus, "The Plight of Refugees in a Preoccupied World", *ibid.* (July—Aug. 1940), pp. 321—323; Alice M. Kimball, "Uprooted Children", *ibid.* (Aug. 1941), pp. 175—179; A. Walldton, "Christmas Eve in a Refugee Camp", *ibid.* (Dec. 1941), pp. 495—496; Clara S. Roe, "Some Go Abroad", *ibid.* (Jan. 1942), p. 13; "And War Victims", *ibid.* (April 1943); K.T.B. Perlman, "Refugees: Hazards or Opportunities?", *ibid.* (Feb. 1942), pp. 65—66; C.O.C. — (A German Refugee), "Germans in America Today", *ibid.* (Oct. 1942), pp. 410—411.

attracting wide public attention to their appearance.[93] In addition to printed matter, recourse was also frequently had to the spoken word. Lectures and discussions on the refugee issue were held at the Association's gatherings, clubs, at church meetings, and tea parties in private homes.[94]

Cooperation with local and national agencies was high on the agenda of the Committee on Refugees. Particularly helpful were the local branches of the National Council of Jewish Women, with whom the YWCA members found a common language. Regional conferences were held at which projects of mutual interest were discussed.[95] In San Francisco cooperation was established with a B'nai B'rith group, "for the purpose of reducing discrimination against Jews in employment". Collaboration with the AJC was not confined to combating anti-Semitic prejudice. The AJC showed interest in inter-cultural education in public schools. It was considered "most helpful" to those who worked with young girls. The two committees had much in common, both concentrating as they did on influencing public opinion, and leaving the physical care of refugees to other agencies.[96]

The YWCA's efforts to stir Christian conscience on behalf of Christian refugees led it to cooperate with other Christian relief organizations. On account of its experience in community associations, the YWCA was asked to help organize local resettlement committees. It also opened its Christmas bazaars to refugee art. The international center, as well as those of the associations, sponsored the sale of handicrafts made by German refugee women.[97]

---

93   "Final Report", pp. 27—28, 29, 33.
94   YWCA, *Report of the National Board for the Biennium, 1938—1940*, part II, p. 32.
95   Committee on Refugees, National Board, YWCA, "Recent Developments", March 5, 1940 (FCC, Box 11).
96   "Final Report", pp. 44, 42.
97   *Newscast*, 1 (Nov. 1941), 4.

How successful, it may be asked, was the public opinion campaign? Mabel Ellis boasted that "the fact that a large Jewish agency considered our approach so effective that it was willing to finance a pamphlet for us, indicates the value of the name of the YWCA".[98] That was not necessarily so. The basic policy of the AJC was to use every available Christian source to defend refugees and combat anti-Semitism. While the AJC's praise did not prove much as regards the effectiveness of the YWCA's activities, there were indications that its pamphlets helped to correct some misconceptions about refugees in certain YWCA circles, as was demonstrated in a survey.[99] Beyond the confined YWCA group, however, the Committee on Refugees was no more successful than other agencies in changing public opinion as the prevalence of anti-alien sentiments clearly witnessed.

The National Board's unsympathetic approach to refugees was demonstrated again in June 1939, when it voted "to drop work for refugees". However, on account of the growing waves of refugees being admitted into the country at that time, it was persuaded to allow the continuance of the Committee, on condition that for financial support "only Jewish sources be approached". That was the case when the YWCA's income for 1939 was $448,073.[100] On November 27, 1940 the Program Planning Committee once again recommended "the termination of full-time professional service for the Committee as of January 1, 1941". Only after repeated protests did the YWCA drop the proposal, but again with the stipulation that the Committee's expenses be covered by other groups.[101] This policy was described in the secretary's report as "a source of constant embarrassment to the

---

98 "Final Report", p. 26.
99 Mabel Ellis, "Before and After Taking", *Woman's Press* (June 1941), p. 279.
100 "Final Report", p. 83; National Board, YWCA, *Statement of Income and Expenditure, Year Ended December 31, 1939* (YWCA Library).
101 "Final Report", p. 84.

Committee",[102] since it was compelled to rely on Jewish help. The American Jewish Committee covered half of the administrative expenses for the years 1939 and 1940. Only from January 1941 was the Committee "no longer under the humiliating necessity of appealing to a Jewish agency for help in financing the refugee work of the largest Christian organization for women in the United States", it was bitterly remarked in the Committee's Final Report.[103] The World Emergency Fund of the YWCA, which collected money in America for overseas relief, began in January 1941 to participate in the Committee's budget.[104]

With the U.S. entry into the war and the YWCA's termination of work on behalf of individual refugees, the latter turned its attention to the fate of German, Italian and Japanese women interned in American camps. Also acute was the situation of Japanese evacuees on the West Coast of the United States. In 1942 the Community Division started to provide some kind of help to these women.[105] Likewise, girls and women in the Emergency Shelter in Oswego, New York, were given limited assistance by the YWCA. Thus, knitting wool and handicraft materials were supplied. Local groups visited the camp and organized the youth, and Christmas was jointly celebrated in 1944, with gifts distributed.[106]

Apart from the activities of the Committee on Refugees in the United States, the YWCA's World Emergency Fund also provided help in Europe in camps, established hostels for girl-workers, offered rooms for refugee women and housing for homeless families. It opened youth clubs, canteens and recreation centers,

102   *Ibid.*, p. 7.
103   *Ibid.*, p. 92.
104   Report of the Secretary, Committee on Refugees, YWCA, November—December 1940 (YWCA, roll 99); see the Annual "Statement of Income and Expenditure of the National Board, YWCA", for the years 1938—1945 (YWCA Library).
105   "Final Report", p. 2; excerpts from a memorandum prepared for Grace L. Elliott by M.B. Ellis, n.d. (YWCA, roll 99).
106   Excerpts from a memorandum . . ., p. 4; Mabel Ellis, "Guests for the Duration", *Woman's Press* (Nov. 1944), pp. 487—488

and offered vocational projects to train city girls for agricultural work. The Geneva-based Fund operated in Hungary, Rumania, France, England, Holland, Belgium, China, Egypt and Finland. While in 1940 the total income was $64,171, in 1944, with the support of the National War Fund, the budget of the YWCA's Emergency Fund leaped to $458,129.[107]

We may sum up the operations of the Committee on Refugees between November 16, 1938 and September 1, 1945 thus: it was a small body, struggling for years for its very right to exist. Its twofold struggle, with the National Board on the one hand, and with local associations on the other, clearly reflected the national mood in the country with regard to the refugee issue. Unlike the Federal Council of Churches, or the Quakers, which took the lead in the matter, the YWCA headquarters in America failed to give material backing in that direction. It is not surprising therefore that under such circumstances the accomplishment of the Committee on Refugees was correspondingly poor.

YOUNG MEN'S CHRISTIAN ASSOCIATION (YMCA)

The YWCA's twin organization, the Young Men's Christian Association (YMCA), was even less concerned with refugees than the former. The YMCA, which had been active since 1844 on behalf of Christian youth, had neither a special committee on refugees, nor undertook any intensified activities on their behalf.

The disinterest in working for refugees probably resulted from its preoccupation with helping Prisoners of War. During the war years the agency's major efforts were concentrated on working on behalf of Allied POWs in Axis internment camps. Personnel of the Prisoners' Aid Committee visited camps in an effort to

---

107 Clara S. Roe, "Some Go Abroad", *Woman's Press* (Jan. 1942), p. 13; National Board, YWCA, Statement of Income and Expenditure for the years 1940, 1941, 1944.

meet the recreational, intellectual and spiritual needs of the prisoners. Classes were opened at different levels. Textbooks, educational supplies, libraries, games, educational films and musical instruments were also provided. Chaplains offered religious services. The total income between October 1, 1939 and September 30, 1945 was $ 12,642,622.[108]

In addition to Allied prisoners of war and a next-of-kin service in America, YMCA personnel also visited German, Italian and Japanese POWs. For every dollar spent on an Axis prisoner, twenty dollars were expended on an American soldier. Civilian internees in the United States, such as Japanese and German aliens, also enjoyed the benefits of YMCA services.[109]

A remarkable exception to the YMCA's disregard of refugees occurred in France. The French YMCA, with the help of the World's Alliance, operated from 1939 onwards among the victims of the war. With the constant cooperation of CIMADE, a joint relief agency of French Protestant youth organizations, mixed teams organized social and religious activities among the youth in southwestern France. The Vichy Government permitted YMCA personnel to distribute clothes and food.[110] The American YMCA was also involved in rescuing refugees. Donald A. Lowrie and his wife, who were working in Paris as the YMCA's representa-

---

108   J.E. Manley, "Administration and Relationships of War Prisoners Aid of the YMCA in the United States During World War II" (typescript, c. 1947), pp. 22—23, 74—75, 106 (YMCA's Historical Library, New York City); André Vulliet, *The YMCA and Prisoners of War During World War II: Preliminary Report* (New York: International Committee of YMCA, 1946), p. 79; C. Howard Hopkins, *History of YMCA in North America* (New York: Associated Press, 1951), pp. 713—714.

109   Report made by Conrad Hoffmann Jr. at War Prisoners' Aid Committee Meeting, January 22, 1943 (YMCA archives, X676.6, New York City).

110   D.A. Davis to John E. Manley, November 2, 1939, "Confidential Report on the Work of the French YMCA on Behalf of the Victims of War", May 1941 (Moss papers, Box 144, FCC).

tives, decided to stay in France after the German occupation in spite of pressure from the American consul to return home. Lowrie became one of the leading persons in organizing relief activities in southern France. He initiated and participated in the establishment of the Coordinating Committee for Refugee Work in Internment Camps, better known as the Nimes Committee. The Committee coordinated the activities of 25 national and international relief agencies. Lowrie became its chairman and established his headquarters at the YMCA center in Marseilles. The full collaboration between Protestants, Catholics and Jews was one of the accomplishments of the Committee which, due to Vichy recognition, was the single patron of thousands of defenseless refugees.[111] YMCA staff members visited internment camps, such as Gurs, bringing games, musical instruments, books, altars and prayer books. With the occupation of France in November 1942, the Committee was disbanded. Several of its workers were arrested and Lowrie escaped to Switzerland. That was a remarkable chapter in the story of the rescue of refugees, for which part of the credit must go to the YMCA.[112]

Thus, the YMCA lived out its policy of helping people in need by concentrating on aid to the POWs. Indeed, many prisoners expressed their personal gratitude for the recreational and spiritual services they had received, which lifted their morale in the camps.[113] One may wonder, however, whether, simultaneously with that program, more could not have been done to help refugees. The well-established, century-old Christian Association, with its 98 branches in the United States and with an annual budget of millions of dollars, could hardly explain its failure to devote some effort during the war, at least on behalf of young Christian refugees.

---

111   Donald A. Lowrie, *The Hunted Children* (New York: Norton and Co., 1963), pp. 14—15, 82—95.
112   *Ibid.*, pp. 63—64, 190, 206—207, 230.
113   Hopkins, *History of YMCA*, pp. 713—714.

9

"NON-SECTARIAN" REFUGEE ORGANIZATIONS

In addition to Jewish and Christian agencies, about a dozen "non-sectarian" organizations devoted to solving the refugee problem functioned in the United States in the 1930s.[1] What services did the non-sectarian organizations provide which the refugees were unable to receive from the existing agencies? Jewish organizations made great efforts to co-opt well-known Christian personalities onto the refugee committees in order to make the

1 Among "non-sectarian" organizations the following should be noted: American Committee for the Relief of Victimized German Children; American Council of Voluntary Agencies for Foreign Service; Emergency Committee in Aid of Displaced Foreign Physicians; Emergency Committee in Aid of Displaced German Scholars; National Committee for Resettlement of Foreign Physicians; National Coordinating Committee for Aid to Refugees and Emigrants Coming from Germany; National Refugee Service; Non-Sectarian Committee for German Refugee Children; Non-Sectarian Foundation for Refugee Children; Placement Committee for German and Austrian Musicians; President's Advisory Committee on Political Refugees; Self-help of Emigrés from Central Europe; and the United States Committee for the Care of European Children.

American public aware of Christian interest in this problem. Moreover, the opinion was widely held that appeals from Christians had a better chance of being successful. Thus, the creation of "non-sectarian" committees was designed to ensure the greatest possible public support. The establishment of "non-sectarian" committees also stemmed from the need to care for professional groups with specific problems. Physicians, scientists, musicians, psychologists, lawyers and children required special care which only professional committees could provide.

In deciding whether a given organization was "non-sectarian", the following points should be considered: what was the source of the funds from which the administrative expenses and the welfare activities were financed? To what extent was the committee dependent on its source of funds? Who did the actual work? Who made the decisions and executed them (as opposed to those whose names merely graced the letterheads)? Members of which religions were entitled to receive help from the "non-sectarian" committee?

COORDINATING COMMITTEES:
THE NATIONAL COORDINATING COMMITTEE (NCC)

In an effort to prevent duplication, the Jewish organizations established coordinating committees such as the "Council of Nine" and the Joint Clearing Bureau, which were made up of representatives of the American Jewish Committee, the American Jewish Congress and the B'nai B'rith.[2] It became clear, however, that these bodies did not solve the problem and that there was still a need for a strong central committee. Since there was much duplication of effort and certain agencies were ignorant of the basic procedures for obtaining entry visas, officials of the State Department as well

2   Cecilia Razovsky-Davidson, "Suggested Set-Up for American or Emergency Joint Bureau for German Refugees", January 3, 1934 (MP : H).

as of the Department of Labor were "very anxious for some central coordinating committee to be formed through which authoritative communications could be had on matters pertaining to the German refugees". James McDonald, the High Commissioner for Refugees, was also interested in having a central address in the United States to which he could turn when the need arose. McDonald's initiative in inviting the various organizations to a joint meeting, his high position and political connections did in fact aid those who desired to create a national coordinating committee.[3]

Twenty-six individuals representing sixteen Jewish, Christian and "non-sectarian" organizations were invited to the preparatory meeting. In order to prevent jealousy and rivalry between the existing organizations, McDonald explicitly declared that there was no intention of curtailing the activities of the existing agencies in any way. The aim was "to coordinate the activities and to advise agencies abroad, as well as agencies and individuals in this country". This declaration did not satisfy Max Kohler, chairman of the Committee on German Jewish Immigration Policy, and John L. Bernstein, the representative of HIAS. They believed that the establishment of another coordinating committee would only increase the duplication, as "there are enough agencies organized, so that there is no need for a new coordinating group".[4] Despite their opposition, it was decided to found the new body. HIAS did join the NCC and its representatives took part in its deliberations, but rivalry and competition were to spoil the relations between the two organizations.[5]

3 Minutes of a meeting called by James McDonald and Joseph Chamberlain for "a discussion of possible coordination of the work of various organizations in the United States in connection with the German refugees", March 9, 1934 (MP : H), p. 1.

4 *Ibid.*, pp. 1, 3.

5 Minutes of the meeting of the Executive Committee of the NCC, June 29, 1934; Minutes of Special Meeting of the Executive Committee of the NCC, July 23, 1934 (MP : H); Cecilia Razovsky to Joseph Chamberlain and Joseph Hyman, June 8, 1936 (NCC papers, JDC). See above, pp. 251—252.

After some tentative preliminaries, the Committee laid down the guidelines for its work and its institutional procedures. Joseph P. Chamberlain, professor of Public Law at Columbia University and United States representative on the Governing Body of the High Commission for Refugees, was elected chairman. He was not put at the head of the Committee merely to decorate its letterhead with a Protestant name. Professor Chamberlain, in fact, guided the affairs of the Coordinating Committee throughout the early years of the organization. The executive director was Cecilia Razovsky, an expert in the field of refugee care, who had good contacts with the Administration in Washington. According to the Committee's regulations, it was to serve as the coordinating office in America to which the High Commissioner for Refugees could apply in all matters concerning the issue of entry visas. The Committee was also to serve as the central agency for collecting information and providing guidance on refugee questions and was to arrange the placement of refugees through the appropriate organizations. It was also empowered to initiate steps that would enable refugees to emigrate to South America, as well as to help immigrants in their search for work and to find sources for financing and maintaining those who had not been taken care of by existing organizations.[6]

These aims were gradually realized. A central card index of all refugees was set up in the NCC offices and it included not only those who had already reached the United States, but also those in Germany who had registered for immigration. By means of this card index it became possible to prevent duplication in handling the cases of some 700 refugees who had applied to two or three different welfare organizations. The Coordinating Committee issued circulars to all its affiliated bodies with the latest information on matters concerning immigration and absorption. Warnings regarding Nazi spies or impostors posing as refugees

6   Cecilia Razovsky, "Report of the Situation of German Refugees in the United States", April 18, 1934; NCC, Report of the Executive Director, November 13, 1934 (NCC papers, JDC).

were also circulated to the various agencies. Leaflets with advice, information bulletins and the like were issued for the use of the agencies affiliated with the Committee.[7] Within a few months there were already eighteen Jewish, Christian and "non-sectarian" organizations affiliated with the Committee.[8] The requests of various organizations to have their names put on the official letterhead of the Committee constitute additional evidence of the success of the NCC. At the suggestion of William Rosenwald, vice-chairman of the NCC, however, it was decided that "no additional names of agencies be added to our letterhead at the present time . . .", since they do not add to the importance of the Coordinating Committee.[9]

While the central aim of the NCC was coordination and liaison, circumstances forced the organization to go beyond the limits it had originally set for itself and provide assistance for refugees.

7 William Rosenwald, "Report of the Activities of NCC", May 14, 1937; Circular, "To All Cooperating Agencies", October 25, November 30, December 14, 1938; "Manual on Immigration"; *Bulletin of the Coordinating Committee*, no. 1, February 1939 (NCC papers, JDC).

8 Eventually, twenty agencies were affiliated with the NCC: The American Committee for Christian German Refugees; The American Friends Service Committee; American Jewish Committee; American Jewish Congress; American Jewish Joint Distribution Committee; Emergency Committee in Aid of Displaced Foreign Physicians; Emergency Committee in Aid of Displaced German Scholars; Federal Council of Churches of Christ in America; German Jewish Children's Aid; Hebrew Sheltering and Immigrant Aid Society; Hospites; Independent Order of B'nai B'rith; International Migration Service; International Students Service; Musicians Emergency Fund; National Council of Jewish Federations and Welfare Funds; National Council of Jewish Women; Zionist Organization of America; Catholic Committee for Refugees; YWCA.

9 Minutes of the Executive Committee of NCC, October 12, 1938 (Chamberlain papers, p. 1697, YIVO). Among the organizations that wanted to join the NCC were the American Association of Universal Women, the National Institute of Immigrant Welfare, and the International League for Peace and Freedom, *ibid.*

The ever-increasing flow of refugees from Europe, their concentration in the New York area and the fierce competition for jobs due to the economic recession, created difficulties in the absorption of the refugees. A large central organization like the NCC could not stand idly by. Gradually it began granting loans to refugees, finding them jobs, initiating courses for vocational retraining and even devoted its attention to resettlement outside the New York area. As early as June 1934 James McDonald indicated that the NCC should also function as a placement bureau, which would, without publicity, find jobs for thousands of refugees annually.[10] Since the NCC had been set up hurriedly, it was prepared neither financially nor organizationally to implement this plan. In a letter written in early 1935 to Cyrus Adler, president of the American Jewish Committee, Joseph Chamberlain noted that "We are not ourselves in a position to handle the individual case". Nonetheless, in 1936 the Committee handled 1251 new files, 92 welfare cases and 1159 cases of counseling and service, and its expenses amounted to $337,000.[11]

The increase in the scope of the Committee's activities was not accompanied by any expansion of its administrative machinery. The result was a loss of efficiency, which led to constant and repeated criticism of the working methods of the NCC.[12] In mid-1936, therefore, the reorganization of the Committee on a more efficient basis and under more vigorous leadership was under consideration. The participants in the discussion, Jewish leaders involved in refugee work — Paul Baerwald, Alfred Stein, David Sulzberger, Dr. L. Farmer and Joseph C. Hyman — indirectly criticized Professor Chamberlain for being unable to devote himself to the Committee. They decided to appoint an energetic vice-chairman who would do the work and be responsible for carrying out the policy of the Committee. Chamberlain, who was

10   Minutes of the NCC Meeting, June 7, 1934 (MP : H).
11   Chamberlain to Cyrus Adler, April 10, 1935; "NCC Activities, 1936—
     1938"; NCC Information, n.d. (c. March 28, 1939); (NCC papers,
     JDC).

not invited to participate in the preliminary discussions, admitted that there were serious faults in the functioning of the organization, and he also came to the conclusion that "the NCC ought to enter the second stage of its work".[13]

Following William Rosenwald's assumption of his duties as vice-chairman in the summer of 1936, the Committee's Executive Committee and working procedures were reorganized. During this period, all the services which provided welfare, loans, social absorption, and vocational retraining were expanded, but the Committee's chief priority was the resettlement of the immigrants outside of New York. Using the slogan, "New York is big, America is bigger", Committee member Jacob Billikopf went out to the smaller towns of America in search of places where immigrants could be absorbed.[14] From year to year, the scope of the NCC's activities expanded as well as its expenses. In 1939 the budget reached $2,470,393, as opposed to $804,258 in the previous year. The NCC, who employed four hundred and forty-one workers, offered welfare in $1,316.702. Whereas 1256 refugees were settled in 150 locations in 1938, 3546 were settled in 300 communities in 1939.[15] Despite the criticism leveled against the Committee, it became the largest and most professional organization for the absorption of refugees functioning in the United States at that time. Thus, it truly deserved the praise accorded by James L. Houghteling, the Commissioner of the Immigration and Naturalization Service, for the "splendid work being done by the NCC".[16]

---

12 Hyman to Razovsky, July 10, 1936 (NCC papers, JDC).
13 Memorandum, "Re Meeting to Consider Program for German Refugees in this Country", June 25, 1936; Memorandum from Joseph C. Hyman to Paul Baerwald, October 1, 1935 (NCC papers, JDC).
14 Billikopf to Rosenwald, December 1, 1937 (NCC papers, JDC).
15 Lyman C. White, *300,000 New Immigrants*, Appendix A, p. 397; NCC Information: "What We Have Achieved", n.d. (March 28, 1939); NCC papers, JDC). See below, Tables XII—XIII.
16 James L. Houghteling to Cecilia Razovsky, December 28, 1938 (NCC papers, JDC).

The reorganization of the NCC structure in mid-1936 also led to a change in the status of the Christians in the organization. At this point it is necessary to examine the "non-sectarian" character of the Committee. Upon its foundation as a "non-sectarian" organization in 1934, a suggestion was made to invite fourteen Catholic, Protestant and "non-sectarian" organizations to join the Committee. At the meeting of March 9, 1934, at which the decision was made to establish the Coordinating Committee, eight of the twenty-two persons present were non-Jews. The initiators of the organization were James McDonald and Joseph Chamberlain, both Protestants. Chamberlain was chosen as chairman of the organization, and due to his influence Raymond B. Fosdick, a Protestant who worked for the Rockefeller Foundation, was appointed vice-chairman. Fosdick did not attend the meetings of the Committee and had no real connection with it, but Chamberlain participated in all important discussions. Another Protestant, George L. Warren of the International Migration Service, also took part in the discussions as a member of the administration and Executive Committee of the Coordinating Committee. He was appointed head of the sub-committee whose function was to propose a plan of action for the Greater New York area. (As one of the four senior members of the Committee, Warren had power of signature on the checks along with the chairman, treasurer and executive director.) In addition, as early as 1936, Frank Ritchie, the secretary of the American Committee for Christian German Refugees, Francis Henson, secretary of the Emergency Committee in Aid of Political Refugees from Nazism, and Clarence E. Pickett, executive secretary of the American Friends Service Committee, served on the NCC together with Chamberlain, Fosdick and Warren.[17]

17   Razovsky, "Suggested Set-Up . . .", January 3, 1934 (NCC papers, JDC); Minutes of the Meeting of the Executive Committee of NCC, June 29, 1934 (MP:H); Razovsky to J.B. Lightman, June 23, 1936 (NCC papers, JDC).

What was the nature of the relations between the NCC and its affiliated organizations? The twenty agencies that were connected with the NCC can be divided into four groups: a) service agencies, which provided welfare, placement and rehabilitation,[18] b) immigration organizations, which dealt with the admission of refugees and their absorption,[19] c) committees concerned with more general questions of immigration policy and the creation of public opinion sympathetic to the refugees,[20] and d) Christian committees.[21] The budgets of the service agencies were covered either partially or entirely by the NCC, but the rest of the bodies were independent and did not receive financial support. In the words of Joseph C. Hyman, executive secretary of the JDC, a leading worker of the NCC, "The list of affiliated organizations concerned was more imposing than real, the relationship of the NCC to these organizations was one of mere sponsorship and its functions were actually limited. The NCC ... had had a nebulous and vague sort of contact with these organizations".[22]

In spite of the loose ties between the NCC and the nine Christian and "non-sectarian" organizations, there was room for cooperation between them. Thus, for example, the NCC referred Catholic and Protestant refugees to the appropriate committees.

18 This group includes the Greater New York Committee for Aid of German Jewish Refugees; Emergency Committee in Aid of Displaced Foreign Physicians; Emergency Committee in Aid of Displaced German Scholars; Emergency Committee for Musicians, and German Jewish Children's Aid.

19 National Council of Jewish Women and HIAS.

20 American Jewish Committee, American Jewish Congress and B'nai B'rith.

21 American Committee for Christian German Refugees; American Friends Service Committee; Catholic Committee for Refugees; International Migration Service; Hospites, and Federal Council of Churches.

22 Minutes of "Informal Meeting of the Sub-committee to discuss reorganization of the NCC", June 12, 1936; Memorandum of conversation between Joseph C. Hyman and William Rosenwald, July 8, 1936 (NCC papers, JDC).

(However, in cases of mixed marriages where the husband was Jewish, the NCC took care of the family as well — a procedure which did not conform with Jewish religious law.[23] The emergency committees for physicians, scientists and musicians, which provided services for persons of all faiths without distinction, received most of their funds from the NCC. The financial support given to these committees, which were considered "non-sectarian", constituted a significant contribution toward the placement and absorption of the Christian refugees who were members of the liberal professions. There was also cooperation in the field of publicity. The offices of some of the non-Jewish organizations, among them the American Committee for Christian Refugees, were situated in the offices of the NCC and their maintenance expenses were covered by the latter. This proximity strengthened the relations between the organizations and led to closer cooperation.[24] Christian refugees were entitled to the vocational retraining and placement services of the NCC, and to its loan fund for Jewish refugees, which was financed by the JDC. The NCC also assisted in bringing Christian students from Germany to the United States.[25]

In spite of all these activities, relations were not as close as they might have been. Representatives of the Christian organizations were not invited to most of the NCC meetings, and after 1936 the only Christians left on the Executive Committee were Chamberlain and Warren. From time to time appeals were made for greater cooperation, but they did not yield any results.[26] Moreover, an

23 Circular, "Names to Whom Clients Can Be Referred in NCC", February 3, 1939 (NCC papers, JDC).

24 Report by William Rosenwald, April 19, 1939; Report on the Activities of the NCC and Affiliated Organizations for the year 1937, p. 4 (NCC papers, JDC).

25 Minutes of the Board of Directors of NCC, October 11, 1935; Cecilia Razovsky to Evelyn M. Morrissey, February 4, 1936 (NCC papers, JDC).

26 William Rosenwald to Paul Baerwald, September 21, 1938; Minutes of "Meeting on Cooperation", December 29, 1938 (NCC papers, 15, YIVO).

examination of the NCC's activities raises doubts as to whether the Committee was really "non-sectarian". While it is true that James McDonald convened the meeting at which the NCC was founded, the main initiative, the actual work and the financing came from the American Jewish Joint Distribution Committee. The assessment made by Joseph Hyman, who was a member of all the NCC bodies and whose advice was sought on every issue, to the effect that: "It was the JDC which labored in this endeavor (setting up the NCC), which brought people together, which pressed them into service, which stimulated the organization, which paid for its initial expenses, which continued to support it...", is accurate.[27] Hyman, the executive secretary of the JDC, and Baerwald, its chairman, devoted a great deal of their time to the NCC. Furthermore, when five names were originally suggested as possible candidates for the chairmanship of the NCC, not one of them was a Christian. The idea of appointing Chamberlain only arose later. Moreover, it was not until November 1934 that the need "to stimulate non-Jewish interest" was put forward as one of the aims of the NCC.[28]

Throughout the existence of the NCC, its budget came exclusively from Jewish sources. As stated above, the main supporter was the JDC. (In the years 1934—1937, about 60% of the entire budget came from the JDC; in 1938 the JDC contributed $ 523,000 of a yearly budget of $ 813,300.)[29] Moreover, the JDC was entitled to supervise the use of the funds it contributed, and it was only natural that there would be a certain degree of intervention on the

27 Hyman to Rosenwald, March 22, 1938 (NCC papers, JDC).
28 A paragraph which had been erased but was still legible read: "As a possible chairman for this American or Emergency Joint Bureau, the names of Dr. John H. Finley, Stephen Wise, Judge Proskauer and Judge Brandeis have been suggested", Cecilia Razovsky, "Suggested Set-Up...", January 3, 1934, p. 5 (MP:H); Report of the Executive Director of NCC, November 13, 1934 (NCC papers, JDC).
29 Louis Rosner to Edwin Goldwasser, n.d.: "NCC Activities, 1938—1939", n.d. (NCC papers, JDC).

part of the JDC.[30] Indeed, this was the policy which was adopted —
the leaders of the JDC played a decisive role in the deliberations
of the NCC. Another important contributor to the NCC was the
United Jewish Appeal (UJA). While the UJA gave $35,000 in
1934 and $45,000 in 1935, as a result of the merger of its fund
raising and distribution with that of the JDC their combined
allocation to the NCC amounted to millions of dollars by the
end of the decade. Thus, for example, in March 1939 Chamberlain
asked the UJA for four million dollars.[31]

Other Jewish philanthropic agencies also contributed funds to
the NCC. Special mention should be made of the New York
Foundation, the Baron de Hirsch Fund, the Hofheimer Foundation, the Rosenwald Family Foundation and the American Philanthropic Foundation. In order to increase the involvement of
these private funds in the work of the NCC, and especially in
the resettlement of refugees outside of New York, their representatives were appointed members of the Board of Directors.[32]

As a result of the dependence on UJA funds, it was decided
that appeals to contributors should stress that the money was
going to help Jewish refugees. In every respect, in fact, the NCC
functioned as a Jewish organization. The refugees it cared for
were Jews; Christian refugees were referred to appropriate agencies.[33] In view of the fact that the refugee problem was especially

30 Yehuda Bauer, *My Brother's Keeper: A History of the American
    Jewish Joint Distribution Committee, 1929—1939* (Jewish Publica-
    tion Society of America: Philadelphia, 1974), p. 26.
31 Rosner to Goldwasser, n.d.; Joseph Chamberlain to Jonah B. Wise,
    March 25, 1939; "Notes on Budgetary Requirements of the NCC
    Fund Inc. and its Supported Organizations", 1939 (NCC papers,
    JDC).
32 Hyman to Lowenstein, August 26, 1936; "NCC Activities, 1938—
    1939"; Memorandum by E.M. Morrissey, December 21, 1934 (NCC
    papers, JDC); Minutes, Board of Directors of NCC, August 19, 1936
    (Chamberlain papers, p. 1669); Memorandum on Conference with
    Hyman and Chamberlain, August 5, 1936 (NCC papers, JDC).
33 Meeting, present: Solomon Lowenstein, H.L. Glücksman and Joseph

acute in New York, a special committee, called the Greater New York Committee for Aid of German Jewish Refugees, which was headed by David Sulzberger, was established under the aegis of the NCC. The committee was given this name since it was decided that "the name should include the word 'Jewish' and the funds should be applied to Jewish aid".[34]

The NCC staff was almost entirely Jewish. Apart from Chamberlain, all the heads of departments, the treasurer, the secretary and other officials were Jewish. This tendency became even more pronounced following the reorganization of the agency in 1936. The intention had been to dispose of Chamberlain by giving him the dubious title of "Honorary Chairman", and appointing Rosenwald as chairman. In the end, Chamberlain was allowed to retain his title in order to spare his feelings, but the responsibilities were assumed by Rosenwald, who ran the organization with a firm hand and soon rose from vice-chairman to co-chairman. While the structure of the NCC was being changed, the Board of Directors was also being expanded. However, only two Christians were added, Clarence Pickett and George Warren. Chamberlain remained the only non-Jew on the Executive Committee.[35]

In 1938 the National Coordinating Fund was created in order to enable the NCC to organize campaigns and collect contributions from the Federations and Welfare Funds. The management of this Coordinating Fund, which supervised the expenditures of the NCC, was placed entirely in Jewish hands, and even Chamberlain's

C. Hyman, October 9, 1934 (Chamberlain papers, p. 1748), William Rosenwald, "Report of the Activities of the NCC", May 14, 1937 (NCC papers, JDC).

34 Meeting, present: Lowenstein, Glücksman and Hyman, October 9, 1934 (Chamberlain papers, p. 1748).

35 In JDC archives there is a chart of the activities of the NCC and its affiliated and supported bodies. It includes the words: "Chamberlain — Honorary Chairman", but the word "Honorary" has been erased in pencil. Beside the name of the person intended as chairman is added "vice", written by hand. Memorandum on Conference with Hyman and Chamberlain, August 5, 1936 (NCC papers, JDC).

name was removed.[36] In fact, the more the NCC engaged in practical work, the less the Christian presence was felt at its meetings. In 1938 and 1939 there were no representatives of the American Committee for Christian Refugees or the AFSC on the Coordinating Committee. Only on rare occasions did a Catholic representative participate in the deliberations. The only person who occasionally took part was George Warren, but from 1938 on he participated not as the representative of the International Migration Service, as L.C. White contends,[37] but as executive secretary of the President's Advisory Committee on Political Refugees. Thus, it is no wonder that Catholic circles viewed the NCC as "the Jewish Committee" or "the Jewish Coordinating Committee".[38] Cecilia Razovsky's claim that her organization was "non-sectarian" and that members of all faiths enjoyed its services was inaccurate and tendentious. Her whole purpose in making this declaration was to secure rebates from the shipping company that transported the refugees. (Nonetheless her claim was accepted and the NCC was accorded the right to "charity rate tickets" for the refugees.)[39]

THE NATIONAL REFUGEE SERVICE (NRS)

The annexation of Austria to the Reich in March 1938 and the terror campaign following *Kristallnacht* altered the dimensions

---

36 William Rosenwald, president; David H. Sulzberger, vice-president; S. Marshall Kempner, treasurer; Paul F. Warburg, secretary; Eustace Seligman, chairman of the Board of Directors. See National Coordinating Fund Inc., n.d. (NCC papers, JDC).

37 White, *300,000 New Americans*, p. 40.

38 Bruce M. Mohler (National Catholic Welfare Conference) to McNulty, January 14, 1938; Mulholland to Mohler, March 16, 1939 (the archives of National Catholic Welfare Conference, Box 82); Zosa Szajkowski, "The Attitude of American Jews to Refugees from Germany in the 1930s", *American Jewish Historical Quarterly*, 61 (Dec. 1971), pp. 128—129.

39 Razovsky to Hunter (Truck Line Association), January 3, 1939; Razovsky to Harold Harding, December 30, 1939 (NCC papers, 39, YIVO).

of the problem. The pressure to emigrate increased and the refugee organizations operated under a tremendous burden. Efficient management of a team of 450 workers and a budget of three million dollars was beyond the capacity of the NCC leadership. There were many complaints about inefficiency, duplication of functions and a rigid attitude toward the refugees.[40]

In early 1939 Harry Greenstein, executive director of a Jewish welfare fund in Baltimore, was asked to prepare a survey of the structure and operational procedures of the NCC. In the detailed report presented in May 1939 Greenstein recommended that the Committee be reorganized and that its name be changed to the National Refugee Service (NRS). Tasks should be clearly delineated, and operational procedures and spheres of activity established. Greenstein severely limited the non-sectarian character of the organization. In his original proposal he noted that "There may be some difference of opinion with regard to the extent to which NCC, or its successor, should be completely non-sectarian in every phase of its work". He called for the creation of "the closest possible cooperation and understanding"[41] between the various religions, but in practice the Christian organizations were not meant to be included in the activities of the new organization. Instead, he proposed that "provision should be made for some form of effective liaison among the responsible groups". There is of course a considerable gap between these two formulations. In practical terms, the recommendation was to establish a Refugee Consultative Council, composed of representatives of the religious

40 Memorandum by William Rosenwald, May 17, 1938; Israel Goldstein to Rosenwald, n.d.; Memorandum from Kohn, June 28, 1938; Memorandum of meeting, May 19, 1938; I. Bettmann to Samuel C. Kohn, June 23, 1938 (NCC papers, JDC); Summary of the Proceedings of the First Regular Meeting of the Board of Directors of the NRS, July 21, 1939 (Chamberlain papers, p. 1856).

41 Harry Greenstein, *Reorganization Study of National Coordinating Committee and its Affiliated Agencies*, May 1939; Harry Greenstein to Joseph Hyman, April 17, 1939 (NCC papers, JDC).

bodies, which would coordinate the policies to be adopted concerning the refugees.[42] Although the Council was established in 1939, preliminary questions, such as the aims and functions of the Council, its official status and the persons who should be invited to its meetings, were still under discussion in March 1941. While the members of the Council met a number of times, the body did not justify the hopes of its founders. Eight representatives of Christian organizations were invited to join the Board of Directors of the National Refugee Service, but they did not take part in the actual management.[43]

There were still areas in which the NRS could cooperate with non-Jewish organizations and extend significant aid to Christian refugees. The various emergency committees for physicians, scholars and musicians continued to receive the majority of their budgets — tens of thousands of dollars annually — from the NRS, as they had previously received financial assistance from the NCC. The American Committee for Christian Refugees enjoyed the direct and indirect financial support of the NRS, which paid the rent for its offices as well as for their renovation. When the American Committee's financial position deteriorated, the NRS enabled the Christian refugees to obtain loans from a Jewish fund and allowed the Protestant organization to use its various departments.[44]

Extending aid to Christians and cooperating with non-Jewish organizations do not, however, make a relief agency non-sectarian.

42 Greenstein, *Reorganization Study*, p. 29; see also, Greenstein, "National Coordinating Committee, Recast", *Notes and News*, June 5, 1939 (JDC, Refugees, General).

43 Agenda for the March Meeting of the Consultative Council of NRS, March 12, 1941 (Chamberlain papers, p. 1766); "Strictly Confidential" Memorandum, "Non-Jewish Representation", June 19, 1939 (Chamberlain papers, p. 1484); Rosenwald to Cavert, June 8, 1939; Cavert to Rosenwald, July 12, 1939 (NRS papers, 52, YIVO).

44 Minutes, Executive Committee of NRS, March 11, September 9, 1941 (Chamberlain papers, pp. 1930, 1983—1984).

The Red Cross agreed with this appraisal and therefore refused to grant financial support to the NRS.[45] One can therefore accept the assertion of the American Committee for Christian Refugees, who received quite a bit of assistance and counseling from the Service and who had no intention of casting aspersions on the NRS, that the relief agency was an organization that dealt with Jewish refugee affairs.[46]

Although the NRS was not a non-sectarian organization, its record is nonetheless impressive. In the peak year of 1940, the Service spent $3,467,832 and employed 449 paid workers, who helped settle 5113 persons outside New York. During the first five years of its existence — from 1939 to 1944 — it allocated aid to 33,050 persons, placed 31,601 persons of different professions in jobs, retrained 1891 refugees, resettled 11,674 single individuals, granted loans to 4990 persons and answered 345,605 queries on matters concerning immigration. Perhaps the most important contribution made by the NRS was the high standard it established in providing professional assistance and social and cultural absorption — standards which other refugee bodies tried to maintain.[47]

---

45 Henry Baker to Arthur D. Greenleigh, May 23, 1941; see also the unconvincing reply of Greenleigh to A.L. Schafer, June 30, 1941 (NRS papers, 1075, YIVO).

46 American Committee for Christian Refugees, "Report of Service for the Year 1940" (FCC, Box 150); White also was of the opinion that the NRS was a Jewish organization. White, *300,000 New Americans*, p. 51.

47 White, p. 397; see below, Tables XIV—XV. "National Refugee Service, June 1939—June 1944; Five Year Period", NRS, Division of Statistics, July 12, 1944 (NRS papers, 369, YIVO). It was not only the National Refugee Service that was Jewish in character; its heir and successor, the United Service for New Americans, also remained essentially a sectarian organization. See United Service for New Americans, n.d. (Chamberlain papers, p. 2094), "Should USNA provide a Non-Sectarian Service?", March 6, 1947 (USNA papers, 193, YIVO).

PROFESSIONAL COMMITTEES:
THE EMERGENCY COMMITTEE IN AID OF
DISPLACED FOREIGN PHYSICIANS

One group of refugees whose situation was a source of concern
from the beginning was the physicians. Between January 1, 1933
and June 30, 1943, 6160 physicians entered the United States, 72%
of whom came from Germany and Austria.[48] In view of the fact
that 5500 doctors graduated annually from American medical
schools and that in 1939 there were about 170,000 physicians
throughout the country to provide medical care for a population
that was steadily increasing, the entry of a few hundred immigrant
physicians every year should not have presented a problem. Nevertheless, there was an urgent need to help the refugee doctors.
Besides the usual difficulties experienced by immigrants in adjust-
ing to a foreign country, the physicians were faced with additional
obstacles. In the United States there were substantial differences
in the attitude to the patient, methods of treatment and use of
medication. Thus, for example, sinusitis, which was widespread
in the United States, was virtually unknown in Germany and
Austria.[49] A more serious problem, perhaps, was the concentration
of refugee physicians in New York. Four out of every five doctors
preferred to settle in New York and go into private practice as
they were attracted by the professional and cultural advantages
offered by the large metropolis. Moreover, the regulations of the
New York State Board of Medical Examiners were far more
lenient than those of the medical institutions in other states. These

48 United States, Department of Justice: Immigration and Naturaliza-
    tion Service, "Immigrant Physicians Admitted to the United States"
    (NRS papers, 487, YIVO); David L. Edsall and Tracy J. Putnam,
    "The Emigré Physician in America, 1941", *The Journal of the Ameri-
    can Medical Association* (*JAMA*), 117 (Nov. 29, 1941), pp. 1881—
    1888, Tables, 1, 3.
49 Interview with Harry D. Biele, formerly executive secretary of the
    National Committee for the Resettlement of Foreign Physicians,
    April 19, 1974.

latter had very strict regulations regarding the acceptance of new members and this contributed to the doctors' refusal to leave the Greater New York area, despite the serious difficulties in finding work there.[50]

The concentration of hundreds and even thousands of refugee doctors in one city aroused the wrath of the local physicians who feared competition — fears which intensified due to the fact that America was in the throes of an economic crisis. When it became obvious that the great majority of the refugee physicians were Jews, the atmosphere of hostility toward the refugees became tinged with anti-Semitism. A single mistake by a refugee doctor was enough to set off a whispering campaign which left its mark on all the refugees. As the heads of the National Committee for Resettlement of Foreign Physicians observed in 1941: "Much gossip and false generalizations can be traced to prejudice, unfriendliness and an unwillingness to make allowance for the period of adaptation". Although the number of individuals submitting complaints was small, and in spite of the fact that the majority proved baseless on investigation, the Emergency Committee saw fit to remove 180 physicians from its list and to advise them to change their profession.[51] Even the organ of the American Medical Association published an editorial which complained that "some of the refugees are poorly trained or of low ethical standing... (and) some find it difficult to adapt themselves to American ways in the practice of medicine".[52]

During World War II patriotic arguments were also presented —

50 Minutes, Executive Committee of NCC, November 13, 1934 (MP:H); NRS, "A Study of the Adjustment of 282 Emigré Physicians Living in Greater New York, March 1945—August 1945" (NRS papers, 740, YIVO).

51 Edsall and Putnam, "The Emigré Physician", *JAMA*, 117, November 29, 1941, pp. 1881—1888 (Reprint, pp. 5—6, 10).

52 Editorial, "The Problem of the Refugee Physician", *JAMA*, 112 (Feb. 25, 1939), p. 735. Joseph Chamberlain asked the chairman of the Physicians' Emergency Committee to appear at a convention of refugee doctors "to explain to them the ethics of physicians here

the fear that refugees might take away the jobs of young doctors who joined the armed forces. In 1938 and 1939, 37 states adopted strict measures regarding the issue of licenses to practice medicine, which ranged from the obligation to work as an intern for a year to the condition that a candidate had to become an American citizen before he could apply for examination by the local medical association.[53]

As a result of these restrictions, which sharply reduced the prospects of finding work, the number of physicians living on welfare steadily increased. As early as mid-1934 there were already five organizations assisting physicians.[54] Naturally those who suffered the most from this duplication were the refugees themselves.

in New York". Chamberlain to Bernard Sachs, November 1, 1934 (NCC papers, 36, YIVO). It appears that there was a basis for complaints about the ethics of some of them, otherwise what was there to explain at the convention? A number of refugees, mainly from Austria, were indeed qualified as doctors of medicine, but had not actually practiced medicine for a number of years. This is the explanation of the low professional level. Interview with Biele, April 19, 1974.

53   "Proposed Plan with a View towards Loosening Restrictions on Emigré Physicians", n.d. (AJC, Refugees, Medical Profession); Edsall and Putnam, "Emigré Physicians", *JAMA*, 117, November 29, 1941 (reprint, p. 13); "Regulations Governing the Admission of Foreign Physicians to the Medical Licensing Examinations in the Various States of the Union", December 14, 1938 (Chamberlain papers, p. 2795).

54   The five organizations were: Emergency Committee in Aid of Displaced Foreign Physicians, Bernard Sachs, chairman; Physicians' Committee of the American Jewish Congress, Benjamin Jablons, chairman; German Jewish Physicians' Committee, Ernst Gundelfinger, chairman; Physicians' Committee of the Conference on Jewish Relations, Reuben Ottenberg, chairman; and another committee under the chairmanship of Dr. Auslander. Memorandum, Cecilia Razovsky, "Refugee Physicians in the United States", July 1934; Razovsky to Chamberlain, July 6, 1934 (Chamberlain papers, pp. 2762, 2765—2766); George Baehr to Razovsky, July 3, 1934 (NCC papers, 34, YIVO).

Therefore Cecilia Razovsky of the NCC arranged for the division of the spheres of responsibility and the different functions among the various organizations. The only agency which continued to function throughout the period, however, was the Emergency Committee in Aid of Displaced Foreign Physicians, which received funds from the NCC and accepted its authority.

The Committee was established in November 1933 on the initiative of a "non-sectarian" group in order "to facilitate the placement of a limited number of specially qualified foreign medical men in non-competitive positions".[55] From the beginning it limited its activities to finding work for outstanding physicians in research institutes, laboratories and universities. An additional aim was to set up a central card index with comprehensive data on the refugee physicians. This card index was made available to hospitals, universities and research institutes, which were thus able to choose the research worker most suited to fulfill their particular needs. The Committee's work, it should be noted, was not confined to the United States. It also helped resettle refugee doctors in Honduras, Paraguay, Mexico and Bolivia.[56]

From the beginning, the Committee was careful to deal with the physicians regardless of their religion or origin, but since the decisive majority of the refugee physicians were Jews, most of their beneficiaries were Jews.[57] Due to the extreme sensitivity of

55 Circular, Emergency Committee... Physicians, December 22, 1933 (MP:GC).
56 George Bachr to John A. Hartwell, November 1, 1933 (NCC papers, 94, YIVO); Baehr to Razovsky, March 26, 1935 (*ibid.*, 36); *Emergency Committee in Aid of Displaced Foreign Physicians* (10 pp. pamphlet), 1934, pp. 1, 9 (NCC papers, 34, YIVO). George Baehr to James McDonald, December 29, 1934; January 7, 1935 (MP:GC); L. Farmer Loeb to Cecilia Razovsky, March 14, 1935 (NCC papers, 36, YIVO).
57 Sources do not agree on the percentage of Jews among refugee physicians. According to government statistics, about 4070 of the 6160 doctors who immigrated into the United States in the years 1933—1943 were Jews. That is to say, about 34% of them were Christians. (U.S. Department of Justice, Immigration and Naturalization Service [NRS papers, 487, YIVO].) Another source went further still and as-

the American physicians on this subject, an effort was made to camouflage the work on behalf of the Jews behind the façade of a "non-sectarian" organization. Jewish circles issued and circulated leaflets repudiating the false views popular among the public and would find a "prominent Christian physician" to appear as the author.[58]

While several Christian members of the Committee were both active and influential, the organization's funds came, as already stated, from Jewish sources, such as the JDC, the Hofheimer Foundation, the Rosenwald Family Foundation and the New York Foundation. These funds were transmitted via the NCC. In other words, the Physicians' Emergency Committee was affiliated with the NCC, through which it received its budget of tens of thousands of dollars annually. When the Physicians' Emergency Committee was in danger of having to stop its work, the NCC assumed responsibility for its clients.[59] The Emergency Committee in Aid

sessed the proportion of Jews at 60% and Christians 40%. ("Report of the National Committee for Resettlement of Foreign Physicians, 1938–1940". [AJC, Refugees, Medical Profession].) As against this, a study made on the initiative of the National Refugee Service found that of 3429 doctors about whom particulars were known, 89.4% were Jews. (Central Index of Refugees, Physicians, Dentists and Medical Scientists, August 31, 1944 [NRS papers, 675, YIVO]); George Cohen to H. Schneiderman, March 3, 1939 (AJC, Immigration, 1939). It appears that the ratio between Jewish and Christian doctors was not very different from the ratio among the refugees as a whole. A similar conclusion can be found in "A Program for the Refugee Physician", *JAMA*, 112, May 13, 1939.

58   Louis Berg to Henry Levy, May 4, 1939; Frank Trager to Norton Belth, August 15, 1941 (AJC, Refugees); D.L. Edsall, "A Program for the Refugee Physician", *JAMA*, 112 (May 13, 1939), p. 1986; Edsall and Putnam, "Emigré Physician, 1941", *JAMA*, 117 (Nov. 29, 1941), pp. 1881—1888.

59   National Coordinating Committee, "Report, 1937"; Hyman to Baerwald, September 22, 1938; JDC, "Report: Sources of Income of Refugee Aid Organizations in the United States, Exhibit B" (NCC papers, JDC), Chamberlain to Baehr, April 8, 1935 (Chamberlain papers, p. 2772).

of Displaced Foreign Physicians was "non-sectarian" only in the sense that it provided assistance to persons of all faiths without distinction, although due to the nature of the immigration itself most of the aid went to Jews. There were some Christians on the Physicians' Committee who used their influence when this became necessary, but those who did the practical work, like the secretary, George Baehr, and the chairman, Emanuel Libman, were Jews. The articles that were published in the name of the Committee were written by Jews, whether members of the Committee or not. Thus it is doubtful whether the Physicians' Emergency Committee can truly be considered a non-sectarian organization.

The Committee, which limited its activity to research institutes and universities in order to find jobs for a small number of outstanding physicians, ignored the problem of medical students, young doctors and those physicians who were not research workers and had not achieved an international reputation. From 1934 to 1942 the Committee granted scholarships to 125 persons only and the total sum expended amounted to $294,075. An additional 100 doctors found work thanks to the Committee.[60] Thus, only about 225 of approximately 6000 refugee doctors benefited from the help of the Emergency Committee. This was indeed a very limited achievement in view of the serious dimensions of the problem. Nevertheless, the Committee informed the High Commissioner for Refugees that it "did not see its way clear to a modification of its function".[61] Consequently another body was needed to arrange for the placement of doctors outside New York and to find ways of employing them in private practices — tasks which were neglected by the Physicians' Emergency Committee.

Discussions which began as early as 1936 reached the decisive

---

60 About half of them received grants more than once. Report of the Emergency Committee in Aid of Displaced Foreign Medical Scientists, January 27, 1942 (NRS papers, 829, YIVO).

61 Memorandum from Emergency Committee ... Physicians to the High Commissioner for Refugees, n.d. (MP : GC).

stage on February 1, 1939 when a new committee, called the National Committee for Resettlement of Foreign Physicians, was established under the aegis of the NCC. Among the aims of this new body were the supervision of the qualifications and professional level of those who wished to practice medicine in the United States, help to those candidates considered qualified to pass the examinations of the medical associations, collecting of data on the regulations in different states and the restrictions on the employment of foreigners in medical practice, and resettlement of doctors outside of New York.[62]

A clear division of functions was made between the Emergency Committee in Aid of Displaced Foreign Physicians, now re-named the Emergency Committee in Aid of Displaced Foreign Medical Scientists, and the new Resettlement Committee. While the former continued to grant scholarships for the advancement of medical research and place scientists in hospitals and universities, the latter concentrated on resettling doctors. Two representatives of the new committee visited states in the south and the west of the United States in order to find jobs for doctors. They negotiated with medical school presidents to induce them to take refugee doctors into their institutions, and efforts were made to persuade medical authorities to relax the strict regulations governing the issue of licenses to practice medicine. They succeeded in the first of these endeavors, but failed in the second. Their survey revealed that general practitioners were in demand in rural regions, but very few refugees were willing to leave the big city, New York, and settle in rural surroundings far from the cultural centers of civilization. As late as May 1944, after five years of efforts, 1167 of

---

62 Summary of a Meeting of Representatives of Emergency Committee... Physicians, National Coordinating Committee and Greater New York Committee, December 5, 1936 (Chamberlain papers, pp. 2775—2776); Charles M. Jordan to Berg and Cohen, September 5, 1939 (NRS papers, 132, YIVO); *Report of the National Committee for Resettlement of Foreign Physicians, 1938—1940* (19 pp. pamphlet), p. 1 (AJC, Refugees, Medical Profession).

the 1802 doctors chosen for the National Resettlement Committee survey were still concentrated in New York and its environs. Between July 1939 and August 1943 the Committee helped set up 460 doctors in private practice and resettled 1345 doctors.[63] In 1944 alone, 155 physicians were placed in jobs — 60 in private practice, 82 in medical institutions and 13 in camps.[64] An interesting experiment was the project to send doctors and dentists to Indian reservations and to the territories of Alaska, Hawaii and the Virgin Islands. It is not exactly clear to what extent this project succeeded. The Committee even gave courses in pathology and other medical subjects, which were attended by hundreds of refugee doctors.[65]

Far from being an autonomous body, the National Committee for Resettlement of Foreign Physicians was an integral part of the National Refugee Service. Harry D. Biele, its executive secretary, who was a worker of the JDC, occupied a room in the offices of the NRS and wrote his letters on the official stationery of the relief agency. While it is true that David Edsall, chairman of the National Resettlement Committee, was a Christian, he did not participate in the internal discussions and consultations. He lived in Tyron, North Carolina, and his principal role was to sign articles written by members of the American Jewish Committee, or by Dr. Irving Graef, a Jewish member of the National Committee. The Committee's "non-sectarian" image was of importance in the discussions that were held with national and local medical authorities,

63 "Report of the Field-Work of the National Committee for Resettlement of Foreign Physicians, February 1, 1939—February 1, 1941", April 17, 1941 (NRS papers, 829, YIVO), "Tabulation of Information on 1802 Physicians' Division Cases", May 10, 1944" (*ibid.*, 675).
64 "Placements of Physicians in Private Practices" (NRS papers, 828, YIVO); National Refugee Service, "Physicians' Division, 1944" (*ibid.*, 831).
65 Minutes, Executive Committee of NRS, January 7, 1941 (Chamberlain papers, p. 1915); Harry Biele to Bob Pasternack, May 6, 1941 (NRS papers, 828, YIVO).

and the non-Jewish members of the Committee were mobilized to prevent the passage of legislation directed against the refugees. In spite of the statements by Harry Biele, it is difficult to label the National Resettlement Committee a non-sectarian organization.[66]

THE EMERGENCY COMMITTEE IN AID OF DISPLACED GERMAN SCHOLARS

German scholars and scientists who were forced to leave their country fared no better than the refugee physicians. By mid-1934 there were already 7500 academicians, teachers, and students who were in need of assistance. Some had already left Germany, while others, some of whom were practically starving, remained in the Third Reich.[67] Many of those who had succeeded in reaching America, moreover, had still not found employment. The fear was that the American institutions of higher learning would be swamped by German scholars — terms like "European invasion" were bandied about — and this led the American Association of University Professors to set up a Committee of Inquiry on the subject of foreign lecturers in universities. The High Commissioner for Refugees, James McDonald, remarked that "there was some evidence in college circles of resentment at the increase in foreign teachers".[68] The proportion of non-Jews, which was relatively higher among scholars than in the other professions, in fact aggravated the problem of dealing with this particular professional group, since "Aryans" refused to turn to Jewish organizations for

---

66 *Ibid.*; NRS, "Tabulation of Information on 1802 Physicians' Division Cases", May 10, 1944 (NRS papers, 675, YIVO); Robert Dolins to Resettlement Consultants of NRS, August 1, 1941 *(ibid.,* 829); Frank Trager to Norton Belth, August 15, 1941 (JDC, Immigration); Interview with Harry Biele, April 19, 1974.
67 High Commissioner for Refugees, Press Release, July 7, 1934 (MP : H).
68 Memorandum, McDonald to Walter Kotschnig, December 26, 1934 (MP : H).

help. Thus, the need arose for a non-sectarian committee to provide assistance for this group of refugees.[69]

The Emergency Committee in Aid of Displaced German Scholars
was founded in May 1933 long before the establishment of other
refugee committees. Its organizational framework and its policies
were firmly established due to the dedication and perseverance of
Stephen Duggan, former director of the Institute of International
Education. He served as secretary of the Committee from its
inception until it was disbanded in June 1945. He had good ties
with international foundations, such as the Rockefeller Foundation
and the Carnegie Corporation, and this partially explains his Committee's success in securing wide support from non-Jewish sources
as well.[70]

The Scholars' Committee, like the Physicians' Emergency Committee, restricted its activity to helping a limited number of outstanding scholars, whose placement did not involve competition
with American professors. Thus, the Committee decided to aid
only those scholars whose research could serve the advancement
of American civilization. Duggan compared the exodus of scholars
from Germany to the alleged flight of men of learning westward
after the fall of Constantinople in 1453 and to the expulsion of the
Huguenots from France on the revocation of the Edict of Nantes
in 1685. He maintained that just as Western civilization was the
major beneficiary of the Turkish conquests, so, too, the United
States would reap the fruits of absorbing the scholars from Germany.[71] The Committee abstained, however, from providing ma-

---

69 H. Jordan, "Remarks on the List Circulated by the Emergency Com-
    mittee . . . Scholars", January, 1934 (MP : H).
70 Laura Fermi, *Illustrious Immigrants: The Intellectual Migration
    from Europe, 1930—1941* (Chicago University Press: Chicago, 1967),
    p. 78.
71 Report of the Emergency Committee . . . Scholars, as of January 31,
    1942 (NRS papers, 838, YIVO); Stephen Duggan and Betty Drury,
    Rescue of Science and Learning (New York: Macmillan, 1948), pp.
    1—2.

terial assistance in any form whatsoever, in order to help the scientists maintain their self-respect. In the academic world the accepted practice is that universities invite foreign scholars to give lectures, but professors usually do not actively seek a place of employment. The Committee therefore distributed a list of unemployed scholars who had sought its assistance, along with their *curricula vitae* and lists of their publications. Thus, each university could then select the most qualified candidate in the field in which it was interested. The Committee allocated a grant to each institution which invited a scholar, on the assumption that after a trial period of a year or two the lecturer would be offered a permanent job. In this way, the scholar maintained his self-respect and at the same time was given an opportunity to find employment in a respectable institution.[72]

The stringent rules of the Scholars' Committee and its punctilious procedures were intended to forestall criticism from universities. However, academically qualified individuals who were not helped by the Committee or were harmed by its policy, objected to the line adopted. Those who suffered most were young scholars who had not yet made a name for themselves. The fact that they could not apply directly to academic institutions extremely limited their prospects of finding work. The Committee made what it called a "realistic" appeal to these people and suggested that they rebuild their lives by changing professions. The Committee held the view that all the efforts being invested were only worthwhile in those few cases where there was a reasonable prospect of success.[73] In

72 Confidential Report of the Emergency Committee... Scholars, as of February 1, 1935 (NRS papers, 838, YIVO); Annual Report of the Emergency Committee... Scholars, December 1, 1938, p. 1 (NCC, 35, YIVO); Report of the Emergency Committee ... Scholars, January 1, 1934, p. 15 (NRS, 838, YIVO).

73 "A scrupulous effort must be made ... to call only those individuals who are likely to succeed", Emergency Committee... Scholars, "Confidential Report as of February 1, 1935" (NRS papers, 838, YIVO). See also Yakov Malkiel to Thomas, August 15, 1941 (HIAS–HICEM papers, XXXIII, Carl Schurz Foundation, roll 41, YIVO).

spite of all the various precautions taken by the Committee, resistance to the employment of foreign scholars increased. In 1939 Duggan reported to Frederick P. Keppel, president of the Carnegie Corporation, that the universities were not capable of taking in any more foreigners and were not interested in doing so.[74] Sharp criticism of the policy of the Scholars' Committee increased to such an extent that in 1941 it decided to set up an advisory body, and as a result "the Committee ... reappraised its former policies and made more flexible the regulations it (had) hitherto followed".[75]

The Emergency Committee in Aid of Displaced German Scholars was set up as a non-sectarian organization. As Stephen Duggan wrote to Secretary of State Cordell Hull: "we have aided displaced Christians and Jews alike — for the problem, contrary to popular belief, is of course anything but a strictly Jewish one".[76] At the beginning of 1934 15% of the scholars were "pure Aryans". If "non-Aryan" Christians are also included, the number of non-Jews helped by the Committee is much larger, perhaps even twice as large. There was a particularly large increase in the number of non-Jews dealt with in the wake of the increased pressure put on Church circles in Germany and Austria. In all, approximately one-quarter to one-third of those aided by the Scholars' Committee were non-Jews.[77] The Committee purposely refrained from inquiring as to the origin or religion of the scholars on its lists and

74 Stephen Duggan to Frederick P. Keppel, April 15, 1939 (MP:P); for complaints by professors regarding the unpleasant attitude toward them in the universities, see Duggan and Drury, *Rescue of Science*, pp. 123, 131—132.

75 Report of the Emergency Committee ... Scholars, as of June 1, 1941 (NRS papers, 838, YIVO).

76 Stephen Duggan to Cordell Hull, April 9, 1938 (National Archives, 840.48, Refugees/140).

77 Chamberlain to McDonald, April 10, 1934 (MP:GC). The precise number of Jewish professors is hard to ascertain, because these intellectuals were more opposed than any other group to identifying themselves as being of Jewish nationality or belonging to the Jewish faith, and many refused to declare themselves as Jews. See above, p. 70.

the sole criterion for providing assistance was that of professional qualifications. Thus, the first report of the Scholars' Committee stated that, "The words Jew and Gentile, Liberal and Conservative, have had no meaning in the course of its (the Committee's) deliberations".[78] The fact that the majority of the members of the Plenary Committee and even of the Executive Committee were Christians, points to the non-sectarian character of the Scholars' Committee, and Stephen Duggan made use of this argument as proof that the organization was, indeed, non-sectarian.[79] However, the Jews, who constituted a minority on the Executive Committee, were the organization's officials and its most dedicated workers. Alfred A. Cohen, Fred M. Stein, Bernard Flexner and Stephen Duggan made up the organizing committee that initiated and established the Scholars' Committee and they constituted the most active element throughout its existence. The chairman, Livingstone Farrand, former president of Cornell University, and Nelson Mead, acting president of the City College of New York, were added to the list more for their status than for their activities on behalf of the Committee.[80]

During the first years of its existence, the Committee was financed entirely from Jewish sources. The New York Foundation, the Nathan Hofheimer Foundation, the Rosenwald Family Foundation and, especially, the JDC contributed the lion's share of the budget. From 1934 to 1936, for example, the JDC allocated $297,000. Over the entire period of the Committee's existence, the New York Foundation contributed a total of $339,851 and the Hofheimer Foundation $67,000. All the funds were transmitted through the NCC and afterwards through the National Refugee Service. In other words, the Scholars' Committee, like the Emergency Committee in Aid of Displaced Foreign Physicians, was considered

78 Emergency Committee... Scholars, Report as of January 1, 1934, p. 5 (NRS papers, 838, YIVO).
79 Emergency Committee... Scholars, Report as of June 1, 1941, p. 2 (NRS papers, 838, YIVO).
80 Duggan and Drury, *Rescue of Science*, pp. 6—7.

an affiliate of the NCC.[81] Unlike the Physicians' Emergency Committee, however, the Scholars' Committee was able to preserve its independence in spite of its financial dependence on the NCC. When Jacob Billikopf, head of the NCC's refugee resettlement department, tried to bypass the Scholars' Committee and appealed directly to the universities to employ Jewish professors, the Scholars' Committee protested vigorously. After the issue was discussed by representatives of the two bodies, it was agreed that "the NCC would no longer consider the placement of refugee scholars as part of its activities".[82]

The Scholars' Emergency Committee not only succeeded in conducting an independent policy but even managed to secure wide financial support from non-Jewish sources. Thus, for example, the Rockefeller Foundation, which specialized in helping scientists all over the world, supported its activities from the very beginning. Besides advice and guidance, the Foundation also provided substantial financial help, and it participated in the Scholars' Committee scholarship program matching and, on occasion, even surpassing the sums allocated by the Emergency Committee. Besides these contributions, which did not go directly to the Emergency Committee but to the universities, the Foundation allocated a sum of $ 10,000 a year for two years to cover the administrative expenses of the Scholars' Committee. It also contributed toward financing the establishment of the central card index of scholars ($ 5000 a year for a period of five years). Throughout this period the Rockefeller Foundation supported a total of 303 refugees with

---

81   Besides the annual reports of the Committee during its years of activity, assembled in NRS papers, 838, YIVO, see Evelyn M. Morrissey to Jonah B. Wise, March 4, 1937 (JDC, NCC papers); Duggan and Drury, *Rescue of Science.* p. 188.

82   Duggan and Drury, *Rescue of Science*, p. 184. See also, Jacob Billikopf to William Rosenwald, February 10, 1938 (JDC, NCC papers); Edwin Goldwasser to M. Fainberg, April 20, 1934 (NRS papers, 58, YIVO).

aid amounting to $1,410,778.[82] During the years 1934—1940 the
Carnegie Corporation awarded 20 grants to scholars, most of whom
were living in Canada, which totaled $110,000. With the increase
in the number of refugee scholars needing assistance, the grant
awarded by the Committee decreased in size. Thus the assistance
given from 1939 on by the Oberlaender Trust was of crucial importance. This trust, which was set up in 1931 in order to foster
goodwill between Germany and the United States was administered
by the Carl Schurz Memorial Foundation and the secretary of
both these bodies was Wilbur K. Thomas. In the period until 1945
the Oberlaender Trust awarded grants to scholars which totaled
$300,000.[84] In addition, the trust had excellent ties with Christian
organizations for refugees, and cooperated with such bodies as the
American Committee for Christian Refugees, the American Society
of Friends and the Catholic Committee for Refugees.[85]

The cooperation of non-Jewish foundations in the placement of
hundreds of displaced scholars, at least two-thirds of whom were
Jews, is an exceptional phenomenon and hence noteworthy. The
Rockefeller Foundation and the Oberlaender Trust together contributed over $1,700,000 to help refugees, the majority of whom
were Jews. The relationship with these Christian foundations somewhat strengthened the non-sectarian framework of the Scholars'
Committee and this cooperation found expression in the invitation
to representatives of these foundations to serve on the Board of
Directors of the Emergency Committee.[86]

83   Duggan and Drury, *Rescue of Science*, pp. 77—79; W. K. Thomas to
      George W. Gray, October 25, 1939 (HIAS–HICEM papers, XXXIII,
      Schurz Foundation, roll 44, YIVO).
84   Duggan and Drury, *Rescue of Science*, pp. 87—88, 86.
85   Janet Seabold to W. K. Thomas, May 14, 1944; Thomas to Alice
      Waldo, February 9, 1938 (HIAS–HICEM papers, XXXIII, Schurz
      Foundation, roll 25, YIVO); Emil N. Komora to Thomas, December
      3, 1941 (*ibid.*, roll 28, YIVO).
86   Stephen Duggan to Wilbur K. Thomas, September 17, 1940 (HIAS–
      HICEM papers, XXXIII, Schurz Foundation, roll 29, YIVO).

The Scholars' Committee cooperated with Christian organizations in exchanging information and in guidance work. Displaced Christian scholars were referred to the Committee in the hope that it would find jobs for them. At the same time, Christian refugee organizations concerned themselves with helping scholars. Thus, for example, on the initiative of the Christian organizations, the AFSC placed more than 20 professors in colleges. When the budget of the Christian organizations increased after 1943, a "Clearance Committee for Scholars" was established which included representatives of the Scholars' Committee to deal with the applications submitted to these bodies.[87] In addition, the Emergency Committee contributed funds and helped create a coordinating committee for scholars under the aegis of the High Commission for Refugees, which was to collect information on refugees as well as on jobs available in universities all over the world, in coordination with the various national committees for scholars.[88]

The achievements attained by the Scholars' Committee in the dozen or so years of its existence were limited. The Committee succeeded in getting the National Association of University Professors to pass a resolution condemning the abrogation of academic freedom in Germany, and it secured the signature of 281 American scientists on a petition to President Roosevelt asking him "to speak and to act" on behalf of Jews in countries occupied by Germans.[89] Although the Committee slightly assuaged the bitter resentment against the foreigners that prevailed in the uni-

87 Minutes, American Friends Service Committee, Refugee Committee, February 3, 1939 (AFSC, Minutes File); A. Benneyan to Thomas, May 24, 1943 (HIAS–HICEM papers, XXXIII, Schurz Foundation, roll 25, YIVO).

88 High Commission for Refugees, Press Release, July 7, 1934 (MP : H). See also Confidential Report of the Emergency Committee . . . Scholars, as of March 1, 1936 (NRS papers, 838, YIVO).

89 Duggan and Drury, *Rescue of Science*, p. 182; "Petition of Scholars and Scientists to the President of the United States on Behalf of the Jewish Population in the Nazi-Dominated Countries", March 22, 1943 (Chamberlain papers, p. 1721).

versities, it was precisely because of its approach to this matter that it was compelled to turn away the majority of those who sought its help. Of the 6000 scholars listed in the central card index, only 288 were allocated grants from the Committee, while another 47 research workers received assistance from the Rosenwald Foundation.[90] Among the noteworthy recipients of grants were a half dozen Nobel Prize winners, headed by Albert Einstein.[91]

Despite the fact that the Emergency Committee for Scholars was less Jewish and more independent than the Physicians' Emergency Committee, one must keep in mind the Jewish initiative in creating the body, the decisive Jewish financial support for its work, the fact that the majority of those it helped were Jews and its affiliation to a Jewish organization. Its limited achievements did not permit it to influence the American public or to serve as the prototype of a non-sectarian organization. However, due to the illustrious personalities it aided and their contribution to the United States, the Scholars' Committee became one of the best known of the "non-sectarian" organizations dealing with refugees and the one on which the most research has been done to date.

PLACEMENT COMMITTEE FOR GERMAN AND AUSTRIAN MUSICIANS

Another group of immigrants which encountered difficulties in settling in the United States was the musicians. As in the case of other refugees, most of the musicians were concentrated in the New York area. Only the most outstanding musicians succeeded in finding work, while those with only average talent were forced

---

90 Duggan and Drury, *Rescue of Science*, p. 62.
91 Emergency Committee ... Scholars, "List of Grantees and Fellows", June 30, 1944 (NRS papers, 838, YIVO).

to turn to a different type of musical occupation. Many tried to join orchestras, but the Musicians' Union placed obstacles in their way.

There was a need for an organization to regulate the market for musicians, evaluate their professional level and try to lessen the competition by settling musicians outside New York. These were among the tasks of the Placement Committee for German and Austrian Musicians, which was established in June 1938 on the initiative of the NCC.[92] The Musicians' Committee, as it was called, consisted at first of a chairman and a part-time secretary, and it tried to find at least single engagements for its clients in schools, synagogues and churches. It organized concerts for pupils, offered private lessons, opened a conservatory, placed refugees in existing orchestras and choirs, found jobs for musicians as lecturers on music in colleges and even provided welfare assistance to artists during their first six months in the country. In 1940, the second year of its activity, the Committee found temporary or permanent employment for 534 musicians, and presented 1097 concerts by 263 different performers; 17 persons received a total of $7095 toward their resettlement, while 15 were awarded grants totaling $1112.[93]

Unlike the Scholars' Committee or the Physicians' Committee, the Musicians' Committee was considered an integral part of the NCC and later of the National Refugee Service. Its chairman, Mark Brunswick, had the status of a department head in the NRS. He was required to report on the work of his Committee to the NRS Statistical Section, and his Committee's achievements were credited to the NRS. At first Brunswick tried to free himself of his

---

92 Memorandum from Mark Brunswick to Greenstein, March 7, 1939 (NRS papers, 238, YIVO); Eni R. Jaspersen to S. Baruch, August 12, 1940 (*ibid.*, 414).

93 Placement Committee for German and Austrian Musicians, "Report on Second Year's Activity, September 1, 1939—September 1, 1940", November 1, 1940; National Refugee Service, "Musicians, 1942" (NRS papers, 827, YIVO).

absolute dependence on the NCC. When the *Survey Graphic* did
not even mention the Musicians' Committee in a survey it published
on the various refugee organizations, Brunswick commented bitterly: "While we are a part of NCC, I think it would be greatly to
our advantage if our autonomy were somewhat more stressed.
I believe it to be desirable that we be named specifically on the
letterhead of the NCC, along with the other affiliated refugee
organizations".[94] His request, however, was refused.

The Musicians' Committee did not discriminate between artists
of different religions in providing assistance to refugees, but the
Christian musicians among its "clients" were no more than 11 to
12% of the total.[95] Thanks to the secretary, Eni R. Jaspersen, who
coordinated the Committee's welfare work, close ties were created
between the Musicians' Committee and Christian organizations,
like the American Committee for Christian Refugees and the
American Friends Service Committee.[96] Despite efforts to present
the Musicians' Committee as a "non-sectarian" body, it is apparent that due to the nature of its work, its sources of income, its staff
and its dependence on the NRS, it was more of a Jewish organization than the Scholar's Committee or even the Physicians' Committee. When Brunswick wanted to note the difference between his
organization and a parallel body called the Musicians' Emergency
Aid Fund (directed by Yolanda Mero-Irion), he argued: "Her
connections and financial supporters are largely Christians and
represent an entirely different group from those connected with
our organization".[97] In other words, Brunswick's Musicians' Com-

94 Brunswick to Cecilia Razovsky, February 3, 1939 (NRS papers, 412,
    YIVO).
95 See Placement Committee... Musicians, "Report on Second Year's
    Activity", November 1, 1940 (NRS papers, 827, YIVO).
96 Mark Brunswick to M. Kovarsky, July 2, 1940 (NRS papers, 411,
    YIVO); Kurt Adler to Eni Jaspersen, July 13, October 5, 1940 (*ibid.*,
    953).
97 Mark Brunswick, "Memorandum on the Relationship of Our Com-
    mittee's Work with that of the Musicians' Emergency Aid Fund"
    September, 1938 (NRS papers, 827, YIVO).

mittee, unlike the Musicians' Emergency Aid Fund, was essentially Jewish and was financed by Jews.

ORGANIZATIONS TO AID REFUGEE CHILDREN

One of the tragic aspects of the destruction of European Jewry was the problem of children whose parents had been deported to concentration camps and who were dependent on the mercy of strangers. There were also thousands of children living in refugee camps in France, Spain, Belgium and Switzerland, whose parents could not care for them. The projected Wagner–Rogers Bill, that 20,000 refugee children be admitted outside the official quota, met with sharp opposition from anti-Semitic and nativist circles.[98] Many Jews agreed with Lotte Marcuse, a worker of the German Jewish Children's Aid (GJCA), who was of the opinion that the passage of the bill depended to a large extent on the amount of support it received from non-Jewish personalities and organizations.[99] Indeed, in March 1939 the Non-sectarian Committee for German Refugee Children was created and among its members was a group of distinguished Christian personalities and heads of Churches.[100] Clarence E. Pickett, executive secretary of the Ameri-

98 Circular, John B. Trevor (President of American Coalition), February 20, 1939 (Chamberlain papers, p. 1334); Lotte Marcuse to Eleanor F. Schwartz, May 12, 1939 (GJCA papers, 110). For the cause of the opposition to the project, its history and the reasons for its failure, see Wyman, *Paper Walls*, pp. 75—98; see above, pp. 62—63.

99 Lotte Marcuse to A. Nyle, n.d.; Hannah Hirschberg to Lotte Marcuse, April 28, 1939 (GJCA papers, 110).

100 Co-chairman: His Eminence George Cardinal Mundelein (represented by Bishop Bernard James Sheil of Chicago); Canon Anson Phelps Stokes of the Washington Cathedral; Governor Herbert H. Lehman of New York; William Allen White of Emporia, Kansas; Dean Helen Taft Manning of Bryn Mawr College; and president Frank Porter Graham of the University of North Carolina. Circular, Non-sectarian Committee for German Refugee Children, March 31, 1939 (GJCA papers, 109).

can Friends Service Committee, who was nominated acting director of the Non-sectarian Committee and was the moving spirit of the new organization, declared that the aim of the Committee was "to support the movement to give sanctuary in this country to at least some of the child victims of Germany".[101] It should be noted that in practice this Committee, which was unrivaled as regards the prestige of the Christian personalities listed as its heads and the number of Christian organizations which supported it, did not concern itself with bringing in children nor did it provide the refugees with material help. It was not even able to raise money for the children, and its entire activity was confined to leading the campaign for the passage of the Wagner–Rogers Bill.[102]

The new committee issued a "Newsletter", appealed to the public to send telegrams in support of the bill, encouraged the creation of non-sectarian committees in the different states to arouse public opinion, asked public figures to write letters to the editors of leading newspapers, and its members testified before the Congressional Sub-committee on Immigration which reviewed the details of the bill. A complete program for the absorption of the 20,000 children was worked out by a prestigious non-sectarian committee of social workers under the chairmanship of Dr. Marion E.K. Kenworthy, director of the Mental Hygiene Section of the New York School of Social Work. The proposal could have provided a sound basis for activating the Childrens' Committee, had the Wagner–Rogers Bill been passed.[103]

The failure of the attempt to bring 20,000 refugee children into the United States outside the quota was the kiss of death for the Non-sectarian Committee for German Refugee Children. The or-

---

101 Pickett to Lotte Marcuse, April 8, 1939 (GJCA papers, 110).
102 Memorandum on the meeting of Lotte Marcuse, William Haber, George L. Warren, Judge Polier and Dr. Viola Bernard, August 2, 1939 (GJCA papers, 111).
103 Non-sectarian Committee for German Refugee Children, "Newsletter", May 22, 1939 (GJCA papers, 110); Marion E. Kenworthy to Clarence Pickett, March 20, 1939 (*ibid.*, 109).

ganizers, however, continued to try and save refugee children and they founded another body, the Non-sectarian Foundation for Refugee Children. This foundation was an incorporated body empowered to raise funds. Its president was Clarence E. Pickett and its acting director Owen R. Lovejoy. The first task it sought to achieve was to bring fifty children to the United States. However, since it lacked the appropriate government authorization for corporate affidavits, it was obliged to turn to the German Jewish Children's Aid and ask that body to assume responsibility for bringing the children to the United States.[104] Following the outbreak of war and the occupation of Western Europe, Lovejoy decided to resign, since, as he said, "the possibility is so remote of accomplishing ... the major program for which this organization was founded".[105] After Lovejoy's resignation, the Non-sectarian Foundation handed over the responsibility for the ten children it had managed to bring in to another organization and it ceased to function.

The Non-sectarian Committee for German Refugee Children, like the Non-sectarian Foundation for Refugee Children, was an outstanding example of Christian support and clearly demonstrated the desire of non-Jewish circles to identify themselves with the efforts to rescue children in desperate straits, most of whom were Jews. The initiative and the actual activities were the work of well-known Christian personages, among them heads of Churches, but their goodwill was not translated into deeds and both organizations failed. The Non-sectarian Committee did not succeed in getting the Wagner–Rogers Bill passed, while the Non-sectarian Foundation brought only ten children into the United States.[106]

104 Memorandum from L.M. (Lotte Marcuse) to C.R. (Cecilia Razovsky), May 15, 1940 (GJCA papers, 113).
105 Minutes of Special Meeting of Directors of Non-sectarian Foundation for Refugee Children, May 27, 1940 (GJCA papers, 113).
106 Memorandum: from the United States Committee for the Care of European Children to the Department of Justice, n.d. (c. December 7, 1942, GJCA papers, 113).

The massive bombing of the cities of Britain by the *Luftwaffe* in the summer of 1940 left thousands homeless. The United States was swept by a wave of sympathy for the children of Britain, and the refugee organizations were flooded with thousands of emotional appeals along the lines of: "Are You Doing Anything to Save Children from Pagan Forces in Britain?".[107] Under the influence of Eleanor Roosevelt, who was anxious to direct this sympathy into practical channels, a new body called the U.S. Committee for the Care of European Children was created in July 1940. This non-sectarian committee, whose president was Marshall Field, decided to raise five million dollars in order to bring British children to America. The Committee officially declared that the rescue of children of "the victims of the war in Europe" was one of its aims. It sought to bring young people out of the war zones, but, because of the restrictive immigration laws, the only youngsters who could legally be brought into America were children from Britain. More-over, there was a readiness in government circles and in Congress to seek solutions for the legal difficulties hindering the entry of British children into the United States.[108] In fact, the striking difference in the attitude of the American public toward children from England, who were not in danger of extermination, and toward refugee children from the countries occupied by the Nazis, most of whom were Jewish, is particularly noteworthy.

The sinking of the ship, *The City of Benares*, with 77 children aboard in the fall of 1940 brought the evacuation from Britain to a stop. In all, the Children's Committee was responsible for 861 children from Britain aged 5 to 16, whom it brought to America.

---

107   Cable of L. Peabody to the Federal Council of Churches, July 12, 1940. See also Ruth H. Parker to Federal Council of Churches, July 8, 1940; C. Byrd Harbour to George A. Buttrick, July 8, 1940 (the archives of Federal Council of Churches, Box 11).

108   U.S. Committee for the Care of European Children, "Preliminary Information", July 1, 1940 (NRS papers, 407, YIVO); Minutes, Executive Committee of NRS, July 2, 1940 (Chamberlain papers, p. 1875). See also Feingold, *Politics of Rescue*, pp. 152—154.

Of these, only 89 had to be cared for by the Committee. The rest were taken care of by local groups in the United States, such as the Kodak Company, professors of Yale University, and others. The evacuation of the British children can hardly be classified as a brilliant achievement. Out of 200,000 children who were registered in England for transfer, only about 1000 reached the United States, whether with the help of various organizations or by private means. Many agreed with the conclusion of one of the heads of the U.S. Committee that, "As it turned out, the British children probably didn't need to come".[109]

If the evacuation of the children from Britain was not very successful, the rescue of refugee children from France was a complete failure which ended tragically. More than 8000 children of foreign nationality were stranded in un-Occupied France. In August 1942, when the Germans began deporting Jewish adults and children from the un-Occupied zone of France to the death camps, the U.S. State Department, under pressure from Jewish and Christian organizations, secured the consent of the Vichy Government to the emigration to America of 5000 refugee children. The children's Committee undertook to carry out this project with financial help from the JDC and the aid of the Quakers in France. Bureaucratic red tape in Washington and deliberate delaying tactics on the part of the Vichy Government resulted in the closing of the French frontiers two days before the first convoy of 500 children was due to leave for Lisbon. Thereby the fate of the majority of the children was sealed and they were later deported to extermination camps. The 28 persons who were to have accompanied them and had already left Baltimore to bring over the group, returned with only 31 children. From August 1942 the Committee brought over 87 refugee children from France. In the words of Katheryn Close,

---

109 Katheryn Close, *Transplanted Children: A History* (the U.S. Committee for the Care of European Children: New York, 1953), pp. 5, 7, 22.

who recorded the story of these refugee children, it was "too little and too late".[110]

The American Government granted the U.S. Committee for the Care of European Children an exclusive license to bring children into the country on the basis of group affidavits, and thus all children brought into the United States were put under the supervision of the Committee. In May 1943, when the U.S. Committee for the Care of European Children was recognized by the War Relief Control Board as "the single responsible agency..." and all the funds for this purpose were transmitted via its channels, the Committee became influential and it supervised all the relief agencies dealing with children.[111] It was only natural, however, that those organizations which had been bringing in children for a number of years, headed by the German Jewish Children's Aid, should refuse to give up their independent status. The GJCA, which was founded in 1934 to rescue Jewish children from Germany and settle them in private homes, was financed by the NCC; after 1938, the responsibility for financing its activities was undertaken by the National Council of Jewish Women. When the U.S. Committee for the Care of European Children was firmly established, it "indicated a desire to take over and absorb the project" of the GJCA, but the latter did not accept its fate. At a meeting of its Executive Committee in August 1941 the GJCA resolved that it would "maintain its identity as a corporate body", in order to go on caring for the 554 children it had brought over between 1934 and 1941.[112] The dispute over spheres of responsibility was ended by a com-

---

110 *Ibid.*, p. 26. See also U.S. Committee for the Care of European Children (U.S. Committee). "Report of the Executive Committee to the Board of Directors", May 12, 1943 (GJCA papers, 174).

111 "U.S. Committee became the single responsible agency in the United States for assisting Agencies..." U.S. Committee, "Report of the Executive Committee to the Board of Directors", May 12, 1943 (GJCA papers, 174).

112 "Statement on German Jewish Children's Aid Inc.", August 19, 1941 (GJCA papers, 10).

promise reached in June 1941, according to which the U.S. Committee would concern itself with the immigration and transportation of the children from Europe to the United States, while the GJCA would care for the children from the time they reached the port of New York. The GJCA received $25,000 a year, but these funds were in fact transferred to the U.S. Committee by the National Refugee Service. The U.S. Committee was also given permission to conduct a separate campaign on behalf of the children, in spite of the fact that this would harm the UJA — which participated in the maintenance of the GJCA.[113] Another agreement was needed in 1943 however, as during the two years following the first agreement nothing at all had been done to transfer responsibilities to the U.S. Committee.[114]

The U.S. Committee for the Care of European Children served in effect as a non-sectarian coordinating committee for the care of children of different religions. It concentrated on collecting and transmitting information on the situation of the children in France. The Committee was empowered to bring children to the United States, distribute them among the respective organizations and was responsible for them vis-à-vis the Administration. Prior to May 1943, 1193 children from Britain, France and Spain were brought into the United States under the aegis of the U.S. Committee. Of this group 735 were Protestants, 113 Catholics, 320 Jewish, and the rest either children of mixed marriages or unaffiliated.[115] The high ratio of non-Jewish children among those cared for by the U.S. Committee was due to the fact that the figure included the 861 children evacuated from Britain, the great majority of whom were

113 Robert Lang to Ethel Wise, October 16, 1941 (GJCA papers, 287); Minutes, Executive Committee of NRS, June 3, 17, 1941 (Chamberlain papers, pp. 1946—1947, 1963—1964).
114 U.S. Committee, Report of the Executive Director, May 12, 1943 (GJCA papers, 174); Robert Lang to Blanche Renard, April 22, 1943 (ibid., 288).
115 U.S. Committee, Report of the Executive Committee, May 12, 1943 (GJCA papers, 174).

Christians. After subtracting the 861 British children from the total of 1193 youngsters under the care of the U.S. Committee, we see that the percentage of Jews among its charges was quite high. Of the 336 children brought to America from France via Spain and Portugal under the aegis of the U.S. Committee between 1940 and 1943, 290 were Jewish.[116]

The U.S. Committee's budget also came mainly from Jewish sources. The JDC and the NRS covered the cost of the children's upkeep, since the current expenses had to be borne by the private organizations responsible for the children. The JDC also paid for the traveling expenses of all the children who were brought from Europe. In May 1943 it was agreed that for every nine dollars of expenses, the U.S. Committee would pay five dollars and the JDC four dollars. In addition, the JDC undertook to provide other help "to the best of its ability". Altogether, the JDC paid over half the expenses, but insisted that its assistance be kept secret. If we add the fact that the UJA consented to a separate campaign being conducted on behalf of the U.S. Committee, it becomes clear that the greater part of the latter's budget came from Jewish sources. Unlike the other "non-sectarian" committees (with the exception of the Scholars' Committee), however, a considerable portion of the U.S. Committee's funds did in fact come from non-Jewish or governmental sources. The American Red Cross contributed $100,000, and the National War Fund annually allocated hundreds of thousands of dollars to cover the administrative expenses of the Committee and for children in need of special care. In 1943, for example, the National War Fund allocated $334,000 for this purpose.[117]

The U.S. Committee for the Care of European Children expanded the scope of its activities over the course of the years. After the

116   U.S. Committee, Report of the Executive Director, May 12, 1943 (GJCA papers, 174).
117   U.S. Committee, Report of the Executive Committee to the Board of Directors, May 12, 1943 (GJCA papers, 174); Close, *Transplanted Children*, pp. 69—70.

war it concentrated on finding children wandering about in war-torn Europe and helped 3000 of them to emigrate. This task was completed in 1953, and its completion marked the end of the activities of this Committee, whose Christian members excelled in humanitarian action on a non-sectarian basis.[118]

SELF-HELP OF EMIGRES

An organization of a different sort, with different scope and aims, was the body called Self-help of Emigrés from Central Europe. Founded in December 1936 by a group of immigrants from Germany who had come to the United States before Hitler assumed power and had attained a certain status, its members knew from their own experience how difficult it was to settle down in a new country. Being well acquainted with the problems of new immigrants, they formed their organization in order to provide the refugees with advice and guidance, find them a night's lodging, a job, a kindergarten for their children and, above all, extend psychological assistance to those in need of it. Even without substantial financial resources, Self-help could at least provide words of consolation and encouragement to a refugee who had not found work or friends. The organizers' aim was to complement the work of the other welfare agencies and not to compete with them.[119]

Since the organization strictly adhered to the principle of self-

---

118 Close, *Transplanted Children*, p. XI.
119 The organizers included Paul Tillich, president of the Protestant Theological Seminary of New York; Dr. Erna D. Ball; Martha Bergmann; Else Braendstroem-Ulich; Jacob Billikopf of the NCC; Hertha Kraus, professor of Social Work and counselor to the AFSC on refugee affairs; Frank Ritchie, secretary of the American Committee for Christian Refugees; and Alice Waldo, also of the Committee for Christian Refugees. Memorandum Self-help of Emigrés from Central Europe, March 22, 1939 (NRS papers, 70, YIVO).

help and its income came only from former immigrants and refugees, its budget and the scope of the assistance it could provide were naturally limited. From its establishment in 1936 until March 1940 it collected only $ 36,000. Small sums of money were disbursed to refugees by authorized agents from among the personnel of the JDC and the Quakers in Czechoslovakia, France, Italy, Belgium, Austria and Spain.[120] From 1940 to 1942 the organization concentrated on assisting refugees in France and Spain. It distributed clothing, food parcels and medication worth $ 22,379 in un-Occupied France. It also found ways to transmit funds to France, Spain and Portugal, and in this manner helped 5431 persons.[121] In 1941 more than half of its annual budget of $ 55,457 was expended on welfare services and aid to refugees in the United States. Its office, which was located in the office of the NRS (rent-free), was visited by an average of 150 persons a day, and its placement section found work for 900 persons. Nine hundred and ninety-six children were sent to summer camps — a project organized with the help of NRS and the American Friends Service Committee. Together with the NRS, Self-help also provided 5000 persons with lodging for short periods.[122]

The expansion of the activities of Self-help apparently caused resentment in NRS circles. The placement section of Self-help, as well as other services which it provided in an unprofessional manner, constituted a duplication of the services provided by the NRS. In order to overcome this "painful complication", NRS decided to make Self-help part of the NRS. Self-help, however, firmly refused to surrender its independent status. Eventually Self-help's independence was preserved, and the organization

---

120 Self-help, "Report", n.d. (FCC, Box 150). See also, Self-help, "Condensed Report, 1937—1939", January 1939 (NRS papers, 70).
121 Self-help, "Help for Refugee Internees in Unoccupied France, November 1940—November 1942", December 1942 (NRS papers, 310).
122 Self-help, "Report for the Years 1940 and 1941", March 30, 1942 (NRS papers, 312).

promised to consult the NRS workers regarding professional matters.[123]

While most of the organizers of Self-help were Christians, the key posts of treasurer and secretary were in Jewish hands. Close cooperation between Christian and Jewish organizations in the United States and Europe, as well as the help of the personnel of the JDC and the NRS on the one hand, and the American Committee for Christian Refugees and the Quakers on the other, led to the creation of this small non-sectarian organization — four paid workers in 1940 — which continued to exist and even to expand in the years following World War II.[124]

"NON-SECTARIAN" ACTIVITIES TO FIGHT ANTI-SEMITISM

The hostile attitude vis-à-vis immigration in general and Jewish refugees in particular produced feelings of frustration among American Jewry. Jewish leaders were gripped by a sense of helplessness in spite of the fact that a large number of Jews held key positions in the Administration at the time, such as Secretary of the Treasury Henry Morgenthau Jr., Supreme Court Judge Felix Frankfurter (who was one of Roosevelt's close friends), presidential adviser Bernard Baruch, Samuel Rosenman (another trusted supporter and close associate of the President who was also the

123   Hanna Ziegler to William Haber, June 29, 1939; Jacob Kravitz to
       William Haber, July 26, 1939; "Relations of Self-help with the
       National Refugee Service", 10 pp. memorandum, n.d. (Nov. 1939);
       Goldman to Greenleigh, December 18, 1939 (NRS papers, 70).
124   President, Paul Tillich; vice-presidents, Frederick Pollock, Else Stan-
       dinger, and Toni Stolper; treasurer, Moritz Straus; executive secretary,
       Fred. S. Weissman. Weissman to John W. Pehle, October 17, 1944
       (the papers of the War Refugee Board, Box 20, FDRL); Self-help,
       "Statements of Receipts and Disbursements", January—April, 1948
       (NRS papers, 311).

President's speechwriter), as well as such influential Congressmen as Samuel Dickstein, Chairman of the House Committee on Immigration and Naturalization, Emanuel Celler, and Sol Bloom.

Many people agreed with the assertion of the Viennese Pastor Forell that "Jewish handling of the refugee work offers justification for anti-Semitism".[125] Thus, for example, when James McDonald considered creating two separate advisory councils for the High Commission, one for the Jewish institutions and the other for the Christian organizations, James N. Rosenberg of the JDC protested to McDonald, ". . . question advisability of separate Jewish Advisory Council for reason that Jewish separatism in this non-sectarian work should be avoided as far as possible". A Joint Council of Catholics, Protestants as well as Jews would prevent "undue Jewish emphasis".[126] The view generally held in Jewish circles was that the participation of Christians was the primary precondition for success. When the question of establishing a High Commission for Refugee Affairs at the League of Nations was being discussed in September 1933, Joseph Chamberlain wrote to Samuel M. Cavert, secretary general of the Federal Council of Churches of Christ in America: "I am sure that a message from so important a Christian organization as yours will have very great influence", and asked him to use his influence with the State Department to recommend the establishment of the High Commission.[127]

A typical example — and one of importance for our theme — is the advice given by Emanuel Libman, chairman of the Emergency Committee in Aid of Displaced Foreign Physicians, to a hospital director in Denver, Colorado, regarding the establishment of a local organization to help refugee doctors: "I would urge that you have as many non-Jewish members as possible. In Boston, a strong group has just begun to function. The organization there is headed

125　James McDonald to André Wurfbain, July 8, 1934 (MP:H).
126　Cable of James N. Rosenberg to James McDonald, November 28, 1933 (MP:GC).

by prominent Christian men. ... It is to be expected that groups constituted in such fashion will meet with less opposition than such as are headed by Jewish men, or such as are composed of Jews only. It is important that all the groups work quietly ...".[128]

Another example that reinforces the doubts about the "non-sectarian" character of the supposedly non-sectarian organizations is the case of the social workers. The Committee for Displaced Jewish Social Workers was an exclusively Jewish Committee which helped Jewish refugees and which operated under the aegis of two Jewish organizations. In February 1939 it was decided that this Committee should become "non-sectarian". The reason for this step is to be found in the Committee's record: "This is particularly desirable, it was felt, because we expect to get our funds from the NCC". Since the NCC was "non-sectarian", or so they mistakenly thought, the new agency also had to be "non-sectarian". For the sake of "non-sectarian" appearances, it was decided to include Joanna Colcord, representative of "Hospites", a Protestant organization of social workers. The new body, which was created in March 1939, was in essence nothing more than a Jewish institution camouflaged as a "non-sectarian" one.[129]

Did non-sectarian activity increase cooperation and understanding between the religious groups in America? Cooperation was one of the aims of working together, but the achievements in this respect were limited. Some scores or perhaps even hundreds of Christian personalities were found who did do a great deal for the refugees. However, it is hard to point to any great successes achieved as a result of their efforts. The gates of the United States were not opened to refugees, Congress did not abolish the quotas and the Administration did almost nothing to ease the stringency of the immigration regulations. The hostility toward refugees did

---

128 Emanuel Libman to Charles J. Kaufman, August 10, 1938 (NCC papers, 32, YIVO).
129 Minutes, Committee for Foreign Social Workers, February 16, 1939, Minutes of the meeting of the Committee for Displaced Foreign Social Workers, March 6, 1939 (NCC papers, 33, YIVO).

not diminish nor was anti-Semitism substantially weakened. The Christian public was not aroused out of its apathy, and the argument that the refugee question concerned Christians as well as Jews was not generally accepted.

Nonetheless, it may be that if not for Christian help and "non-sectarian" activity the situation would have been even more serious. Cooperation paved the way for greater understanding toward the Jews on the part of some heads of organizations, and thus the basis was laid for more fruitful cooperation in the calmer atmosphere after the war.

10

CONCLUSIONS

"It is my deep disappointment over the failure of American Christendom to bestir itself to arise against the brutal foes", Rabbi Stephen S. Wise reprimanded his American countrymen in 1949.[1] The American people, preoccupied with their country's own economic crisis, were reluctant to offer a haven to victims of Nazi persecution, particularly when they mistakenly considered almost all of the refugees to be Jewish. With few exceptions, not excluding the Jewish leadership, Americans failed at first to grasp the gravity of the situation. Only when it gradually became evident that a considerable proportion of the refugees, approximately 30%, were Aryan and non-Aryan Christians, did some Christian leaders voice the need to establish relief agencies for the care of such refugees. It was a long, disheartening campaign, laden with disappointments, to persuade Christian communities to assume moral and financial responsibility for their co-religionists. The American Committee for Christian Refugees, the first major Christian relief agency to be established, had to struggle for long years from its inception in

1 Stephen S. Wise, *Challenging Years: The Autobiography of Stephen Wise* (New York: Putnam's Sons, 1949), p. 295.

1934 for its existence against the tide of nativism, anti-alien sentiments and apathy. The Catholic Committee for Refugees was
founded in 1936, but only began to operate effectively around
1938—1939. After *Kristallnacht* the American Friends Service
Committee and the Young Women's Christian Association each
formed a committee on refugees. There were agencies, like the
Unitarian Service Committee and the Emergency Rescue Committee, that were only stirred to action after the fall of democratic
nations of Western Europe.

Despite the fact that these agencies were operated by Christians
on behalf of Christian refugees, the great majority of the American
people maintained a largely apathetic attitude to their cause. In
1939—1940, the peak period of immigration, the combined expenditures of the major Christian refugee agencies, excluding the
AFSC, amounted to less than half a million dollars, while that of
the National Refugee Service, which was responsible for Jewish
refugees, came to three and a half million dollars during the same
period. It employed 450 paid workers compared to 20 of the
Catholic Committee and 33 of the ACCR.[2] The lack of funds and
other forms of support from Christian sources reflected the mood
of the American people, even though America was recovering from
the Depression in 1940.

There was a considerable gap between the leaders and the rank
and file Christians. Heads of Churches and prominent politicians,
who supported the refugee cause and sometimes actively participated in the committees' directorship, found themselves with almost
no followers. Even the generally disciplined Catholic Church members were reluctant to follow the directives of their Church hierarchy. The challenge of the refugee issue seems to have been too
heavy for the Christian leadership.

2 NRS, Division of Statistics, July 24, 1944, "NRS, June 1939—June
   1944; Five Years Period" (NRS papers, 369, YIVO); Mohler to Mulholland, August 6, 1940 (NCWC, 80); Maurice Davie, *Refugees in
   America*, p. 98.

The change in the Roosevelt Administration's approach toward the rescue and relief of victims of the war, in 1943—1944, opened a new phase in the activities of the private agencies. Between 1943—1947 the National War Fund distributed the sum of $ 315,504,806 among the relief organizations.[3] UNRRA expended more than four billion dollars during that period. Since American shores were almost unreachable at this stage of the war on account of strict immigration regulations as well as the lack of transport facilities, this help came too late to help refugees emigrate to this country. Overseas relief, however, was meaningfully expanded. This was the heyday of the American private agencies, which extended their various services to liberated and neutral countries in Europe, North Africa, Latin America and the Far East. With effective governmental support, Christian organizations provided crucial aid to those most in need, sometimes on a non-sectarian basis.

Interfaith cooperation was a positive outcome of the struggle to cope with the refugee problem. Jewish agencies, like the JDC, were instrumental in founding the ACCR and extended financial support in its crucial stages. The American Friends Service Committee, the Catholic Committee for Refugees, the Emergency Rescue Committee and the Young Women's Christian Association also enjoyed Jewish contributions. The National Coordinating Committee and, later, the National Refugee Service provided services to Christian refugees and organizations. In Europe, the JDC and HICEM helped many non-Jewish refugees. Such aid was by no means one-sided. Christian committees extended relief to and saved the lives of not a few Jewish refugees. Thus, for example, 75% of the beneficiaries of the International Relief Association were Jews. Leaders of the Quakers, the International Migration Service and the Unitarian Service Committee played key roles in rescue operations and in conciliatory missions to German, French, Spanish, Portuguese and American authorities. Because of their

---

3   Harold J. Seymour, *Design for Giving*, pp. 70—71.

impartial status they had access to places and could act among circles which Jews had no hope of entering. "Non-sectarian" committees also operated successfully. Interfaith collaboration among refugee activists was particularly significant in the area of American anti-Semitism.

The multiplicity of relief organizations, along with the inexperience of their staff members, who, however, lacked neither devotion nor goodwill, led to inefficiency, maladministration and duplication. Refugees complained of "indifference, laziness and incompetence" on the part of relief agencies. Sometimes major organizations extended their services in a routine manner, failing to show any real understanding for individual problems.[4] Despite justifiable criticism, Maurice Davie rightly observed that, in general, the refugee relief services in the 1930s and the 1940s were "more comprehensive and more scientifically planned and coordinated than previous services to immigrants", constituting "a new chapter in the history of immigrant aid in this country".[5] Due to the large proportion of well-educated and talented individuals among the refugees, their process of Americanization was easier than that of earlier waves of refugee immigrants. In the 1944—1945 edition of *Who's Who in America*, 91 refugees were listed, including twelve Nobel Prize winners.[6]

Despite a prevailing apathy among Christian Americans toward the refugee problem, particularly on the part of the rank and file, a great deal of refugee work was done by Christian individuals and organizations. While, out of hundreds of refugee committees, only a few major agencies have been discussed, their activities clearly illustrate what was accomplished by a relatively small group of devoted Christian humanitarians. Several hundred staff members of various Christian denominations offered services to thousands of refugees in the United States and overseas, disbursing

---

4 See Kent, *Refugee Intellectual*, pp. 237—238; see also Davie, *Refugees in America*, pp. 117—118.
5 Davie, *Refugees in America*, pp. 93—94.
6 *Ibid.*, pp. 432—435.

more than twenty million dollars. They provided affidavits, extended relief, secured employment, provided vocational guidance and training, immigration services and scholarships, helped in social and cultural adjustment, located relatives, carried out mass feeding, clothing and medical aid projects, fought malnutrition, rescued anti-Fascist political and intellectual leaders and encouraged resettlement.[7] No refugee was deported from the United States on account of becoming a public charge. Thomas Mann, writing in 1945 to the American Committee for Christian Refugees, "out of feelings of admiration and gratitude for the great, stirring and memorable humanitarian accomplishments", remarked as follows: "Our national conscience would be much more heavily burdened if it were not for the activity of the ACCR, which actually functioned ... as the conscience of America".[8] These words could aptly be extended to the aid given to refugees by other Christian bodies as well. The experience of dealing with refugees made these voluntary agencies much more sensitive to the overall world needs and strengthened these organizations so that they were in a position to respond more fully and competently in the postwar years, when the generosity of Americans, both private and public, was in even greater demand and was to a remarkable degree forthcoming, and indeed still is.

Table I

ANNUAL QUOTA
IMMIGRANTS
ADMITTED TO THE
U.S.

1925—1944

COUNTRY	Quota immigrants admitted 1925–1944	Annual quota 1930–1944
All countries	1,280,716	153,879
Europe	1,264,884	150,501
Northern and Western Europe	1,006,984	127,266
Belgium	8,117	1,304
Denmark	17,207	1,181
France	30,876	3,036
Germany	405,842	27,370[4]
Great Britain and N. Ireland	254,816	65,721
Iceland	454	100
Irish Free State (Eire)	165,653	17,853
Luxembourg	945	100
Netherlands	17,372	3,153
Norway	37,593	2,377
Sweden	52,134	3,314
Switzerland	15,975	1,707
Southern and Eastern Europe	257,900	23,235
Albania	1,488	100
Austria	8,310	[4]
Bessarabia	16	[5]
Bulgaria	1,314	100
Czechoslovakia	33,361	2,874
Danzig, Free City of	1,757	100
Estonia	1,335	116
Finland	5,883	569
Greece	4,994	307
Hungary	11,035	869
Italy	52,779	5,802
Latvia	2,398	236
Lithuania	5,118	386
Poland	70,664	6,524
Portugal	6,824	440
Rumania	9,044	377[6]
Spain	4,408	252
Turkey	3,606	226
Union of Soviet Socialist Republics	24,291	2,712[7]
Yugoslavia	8,841	845
Other Southern and Eastern Europe	634	400
Asia	9,276	1,528[8]
Africa	2,710	1,200
Pacific	3,846	650[9]

(From: U.S. Immigration
and Naturalization Service,
in NRS papers, folder 475,
YIVO.)

Quota immigrants admitted

30-944	1932	1933	1934	1935	1936	1937	1938	1939	1940	1941	1942	1943	1944
,C94	12,983	8,220	12,483	17,207	18,675	27,762	42,494	62,402	51,997	36,220	14,597	9,045	9,394
,497	12,410	7,922	12,125	16,820	18,244	27,235	41,637	61,535	51,141	35,316	14,147	8,714	8,983
),152	6,368	3,831	6,829	8,849	10,102	16,481	25,383	41,135	34,313	23,748	8,934	4,608	4,793
,456	117	60	106	175	190	215	279	307	444	1,172	416	204	128
,091	209	123	101	146	135	192	324	282	255	318	107	132	106
,617	299	261	325	432	490	579	749	850	770	1,858	1,084	504	220
,479	2,086	1,324	3,515	4,891	6,073	11,127	17,868	32,759	26,083	13,051	4,883	1,276	1,324
),365	2,315	1,274	1,882	2,071	2,035	2,584	3,365	3,426	3,141	4;257	1,495	1,724	2,303
154	5	2	2	2	5	3	6	5	6	9	10	10	26
,938	452	282	322	301	367	447	1,100	1,418	966	331	161	196	123
450	7	4	2	12	5	10	18	24	24	85	97	23	2
),467	196	133	143	259	262	379	365	670	1,140	1,175	235	222	259
7,258	260	141	155	208	197	330	518	465	456	448	100	102	176
7,285	290	105	153	160	154	303	364	324	411	285	111	94	80
5,292	132	122	133	192	189	312	427	605	617	759	235	121	46
) 345	6,042	4,091	5,286	7,971	8,142	10,754	16,254	20,460	16,828	11,568	5,213	4,106	4,190
,016	102	75	57	74	107	98	106	97	88	7	1	3	10
,097	187	121	229	641	569	409	-----	-----	-----	-----	-----	-----	-----
16	10	6	-----										
805	11	11	17	52	63	57	106	105	92	102	14	8	20
3,693	304	171	389	610	766	1,519	2,853	2,716	1,079	1,787	568	362	323
692	6	10	8	13	16	41	89	177	100	40	13	6	9
723	15	17	36	28	34	30	40	107	98	63	27	18	27
3,320	69	72	114	105	72	215	496	461	282	355	58	99	63
4,257	141	108	200	324	347	370	351	381	346	232	199	301	287
8,590	329	187	209	399	515	739	962	1,087	1,432	584	284	163	212
4,390	2,013	1,109	1,363	2,129	2,470	2,906	3,435	4,161	3,971	690	59	67	160
1,644	43	29	48	49	60	114	154	223	184	171	105	62	62
3,290	181	96	124	190	151	221	397	365	294	232	126	117	93
1,504	917	961	1,138	1,682	1,250	1,855	4,218	6,512	4,354	4,406	2,203	1,533	1,338
4,371	201	70	168	304	276	236	323	404	417	316	143	263	380
5,261	318	236	199	295	282	371	407	499	460	286	282	220	230
3,602	191	164	228	252	250	244	264	253	225	265	175	255	241
2,927	217	221	224	226	204	184	243	213	186	167	115	107	178
4,016	533	318	425	370	409	592	942	1,772	1,647	1,612	732	426	389
5,760	252	105	110	215	291	527	852	850	651	238	107	90	167
211	2	4	-----	13	10	26	16	17	13	15	2	6	1
3,769	331	189	223	202	234	295	584	587	549	532	257	191	214
1,309	72	20	33	41	40	64	74	78	99	162	97	63	47
2,459	170	89	102	144	157	168	199	202	208	210	96	77	150

Table II

THE AMERICAN COMMITTEE FOR CHRISTIAN REFUGEES

ACTIVITIES FOR 1940

I. *Statement of Operations, January 1, — December 31, 1940*

A.	Income from Foundations and Organizations	$ 102,750
	" " the Churches	$ 35,551
	" " other sources	$ 87,913
	Total Income	$ 226,214
B.	Total Expenses of Operations	$ 62,676
	Service Division Expenditures	$ 83,437
	Relief and grants	$ 100,637
	Total of all expenditures for 1940	$ 246,750
	Excess of expenses over income	$ 20,535
	(From Moss Papers, FCC, Box 142)	

— — —

II. Migration Department handled 4413 cases, comprised of 9047 individuals in the U.S. and abroad.

Vocational Department provided careful advice and vocational guidance to 678 people.

38 scholarships obtained for students.

256 people received jobs directly through Vocational Dept.

127 people received retraining.

(From : *Our Story For 1940*, pp. 1, 7.)

Table III

THE AMERICAN COMMITTEE FOR CHRISTIAN REFUGEES

ACTIVITIES FOR 1941

Service Division : handled 3798 cases (involving 7786 individuals).

Case work Service : served in the U.S. to 1281 cases.

Change of Status (from temporary to permanent visa) — completed for 55 clients.

Work permits granted to 72 cases, 5 denials and 29 still pending.

939 cases closed during 1941.

Cash-relief — amounting to $ 35,232 — was given to 427 cases (involving 854 individuals).

Vocational Services rendered service to 721 cases.

Placement secured for 309 refugees.

Loans granted to 65 persons.

93 people resettled in 23 communities.

Scholarships granted to 19 students.

Summer vacation opportunities were found for 223 children and adults.

Guest houses in New England accommodated 98 persons.

(From : "Facts and Figures from 1941 Annual Report", *Newscast*, 2 [February 1942], p. 3.)

Table IV

THE AMERICAN COMMITTEE
FOR CHRISTIAN REFUGEES

CONDENSED SUMMARY OF OPERATIONS
SEPTEMBER 1935—DECEMBER 31, 1945

Total Income $ 1,531,153

Disbursements

Finance Division :
Publicity and production expenses $ 173,363
Administration expenses $ 112,535
                                                  _____
                                  Total $ 285,898

Relief and Welfare
Salaries of executives and workers $ 304,466.91
Administration $ 64,471.74
Relief work in the U.S.A. $ 473,538.79
Relief work outside the U.S.A. $ 353,054.80
                                                  _____
                                  Total $ 1,481,532.24

Total Expenditures $ 1,481,431.06
                                                                    _____
Excess of income over disbursements $ 49,722.12

(From : ACCR, *Toward a New Life : Ten Years of Stewardship,* 1945.)

Table V

THE COMMITTEE FOR CATHOLIC REFUGEES FROM GERMANY

STATEMENT OF INCOME AND EXPENDITURES
for the Period from Inception [1.1.1937] to September 30, 1939

R E C E I P T S

Contributions from Dioceses	$ 204,814.65
Donations from Individuals & Organizations	48,752.11
Concerts, Entertainments & Assemblies	16,767.77
Bank Interest	74.80
	$ 270,409.33
From Coordinating Committee	10,125.47
Loan and Relief Refunds	4,951,32
TOTAL RECEIPTS TO SEPTEMBER 30, 1939	$ 285,486.12

E X P E N D I T U R E S

Relief to Refugees	$ 41,894.80
Loans to Refugees	24,846.18
Transportation and Travel for Refugees	1,306.48
Subsidies to European Committees	10,200.00
Total Direct Refugee Expenditures	$ 78,247.46
Administration and Office Expenses	59,622.55
TOTAL EXPENDITURES TO SEPTEMBER 30, 1939	$ 137,870.01
Balance on Hand — September 30, 1939	$ 147,616.11

(From : *Annual Report of the Committee for Catholic Refugees from Germany,* January 1, 1937—September 30, 1939, p. 18.)

Table VI

THE COMMITTEE FOR CATHOLIC REFUGEES FROM GERMANY
STATISTICS ON SERVICES RENDERED
October 1, 1938 to September 30, 1939

	Jan. 1-37 to 9-30-38	Oct.	Nov.	Dec.	Jan.	Feb.	Mar.	April	May	June	July	Aug.	Sept.	Year's Total	GRAND TOTAL
Immigrated (Units)	60	7	12	9	10	14	8	6	9	5	8	11	4	103	163
Total No. of persons who immigrated	60	13	29	15	12	29	15	8	11	7	14	15	9	177	237
Affidavits supplied	190	26	65	46	92	45	55	49	32	40	28	31	22	531	721
Affidavits worked on-average 100 monthly	301	301	349	346	365	395	340	290	340	345	270	259	115	—	—
Secured employment	143	16	21	23	20	6	28	20	30	35	17	18	24	258	401
Scholarships supplied	9	—	—	1	5	1	6	2	4	2	2	4	11	38	47
Free room and board supplied	28	—	1	1	1	1	—	2	3	2	—	—	1	12	40
Free medical assistance	14	—	—	2	—	—	—	2	—	1	1	1	1	8	22
Letters incoming	9008	1103	1400	1702	1616	1598	2122	1737	1830	1608	1050	984	1078	17828	26836
Letters outgoing	16287	1026	1462	1982	3896	2121	5697	3744	5300	5829	2650	3509	3535	40751	57038
Office Interviews	1936	174	195	211	152	208	304	292	272	298	368	423	553	3450	5386
Trying to secure work-average 100 monthly	97	97	106	87	114	104	145	149	176	180	151	168	180	—	—
Circular letters	129	1	—	2	7	8	11	10	26	28	9	14	24	140	269
Outside contacts	311	7	8	18	19	8	5	8	10	7	1	—	8	99	410
Assistance from Emergency Comm.	5	—	—	—	—	1	—	—	—	—	—	—	—	1	6
Assistance from Rockefeller Foundation	—	—	—	—	—	1	—	—	—	—	—	—	—	1	—
Assistance from Rosenwald Foundation	—	—	—	—	—	—	—	—	—	—	—	—	1	1	1

(From: Catholic Committee, *Annual Report, 1937—1939*, p. 13.)

Table VII

THE CATHOLIC COMMITTEE FOR REFUGEES

STATEMENT OF CASH RECEIPTS AND PAYMENTS
For the Period from Inception 1.1.1937 to September 30, 1946

RECEIPTS : —

Diocesan Contributions	$ 237,707.76
Donations	94,651.18
Concerts and Entertainments	18,565.08
Pius XII Refugee Fund	20,000.00
N. C.W. C.	117,000.00
Bank Interest	637.56
Refugee Coordinating Committees	25,541.90
National War Fund	232,391.34
War Relief Services	4,230.00
Refugees Refunds	45,568.88
Designated Gifts	3,624.00
International Catholic Office	303.79
Mass Stipends	12,242.00

TOTAL RECEIPTS					$ 812,463.49

LESS PAYMENTS : —

Refugee Relief	$ 340,701.21
Refugee Loans	75,628.01
Refugee Scholar Fund	54,105.95
Refugee Relief in Toronto	4,291.00
Refugee Relief in Oswego	12,192.74
Designated Gifts	3,402.00
International Catholic Office	260.77
Refugee Coordinating Committees	25,459.90
Mass Stipends	10,886.00
Administration	233,263.59

TOTAL PAYMENTS					$ 760,191.17

Balance of Cash — September 30, 1946			$ 52,272.32

(From : *Tenth Annual Report of Catholic Committee for Refugees*,
October 1, 1945 — September 30, 1946 ; "Summary : 1936—1946", p. 35.)

Table VIII

THE CATHOLIC COMMITTEE FOR REFUGEES

BASIC SERVICE CHART

January 1, 1937 to September 30, 1946

Incoming Mail	75,413
Outgoing Mail	143,481
Office Interviews	33,667
Outside Contacts	1,231
Immigration Service	6,967
Affidavits Secured	3,776
Employment Service	1,846
Employment Secured	1,052
Relief Service	1,226*
Scholarships	168

* Excludes relief cases serviced abroad by foreign Catholic Committees with our funds.

(From : *Tenth Annual Report*, p. 34.)

Table IX

REFUGEE SECTION

AMERICAN FRIENDS SERVICE COMMITTEE
Financial Statement — December 31st. 1941

	To 12/3/41	December	Total	Balance
Balance 1/1/41				42745.74
RECEIPTS				
General Contributions	83349.08	12938.86	96287.94	
Sale of REFUGEE	18.50	1.00	19.50	
Sale of REFUGEE FACTS	.48		.48	
Sale of THEY STILL DRAW PICTURES	1.00		1.00	
Interest Earned	462.05		462.05	
	83831.11	12939.86		96770.97
DISBURSEMENTS				
Administration	27833.50	3184.73	31018.23	
Publicity	1304.16	246.46	1550.62	
Service	30615.33	2673.28	33288.61	
New York Office	6845.01	482.81	7327.82	
Aid-Philadelphia Office	1006.37	1.90	1008.27	
Relief-General Funds	1627.00		1627.00	
	69231.37	6589.18	75820.55	

	To 12/3/41	December	Total	Balance
Cuba Hostel				
Operating Receipts	1180.61			
Operating Disbursements	2663.92			
Cost to AFSC	1483.31		1483.31	
Quaker Hill Hostel				
Operating Receipts	5389.84		5389.84	
Operating Disbursements	12227.32	95.86	12131.46	
Operating Deficit	6837.48	95.86	6741.62	
Less : Contributions	265.05		265.05	
Cost to AFSC	6572.43	95.86	6476.57	
Scattergood Hostel				
Operating Receipts	8797.88	987.99	9785.87	
Operating Disbursements	17947.84	2059.16	20007.00	
Operating Deficit	9149.96	1071.17	10221.13	
Less : Contributions	93.91		93.91	
Cost to AFSC	9056.05	1071.17	10127.22	

	To 12/3/41	December	Total	Balance
American Seminar				
Operating Receipts	6527.00			
Operating Disbursements	7952.42			
Operating Deficit	1425.42			
Less : Contributions	401.79			
Cost to AFSC	1023.63		1023.63	
Sky Island Hostel				
Operating Receipts	1960.54	1960.54		
Operating Disbursements	2368.83	2391.06		
	23.23	23.23		
Operating Deficit	408.29	430.52		
Less : Contributions	167.10	167.10		
Cost to AFSC	241.19	22.23	263.42	
Co-Operative College Work Shop				
Operating Receipts	8973.24	8973.24		
Operating Disbursements	10115.23	12391.08		
Operating Disbursements	2275.85	1141.99	3417.84	
Total Disbursements-General Funds	89883.83	8728.71		98612.54

(From : AFSC : GF : 1941 : Ref. Sec.)

Table X

THE AMERICAN FRIENDS SERVICE COMMITTEE : RELIEF DIVISION

STATEMENT OF AVAILABLE CASH, ELEVEN MONTHS, ENDED NOVEMBER 30, 1944

Total Income	$ 2,106,512
Total Expenditures	$ 1,975,101

Expenditures

General	$ 392,311
France	$ 294,663
Great Britain	$ 93,018
China	$ 278,280
Portugal	$ 42,889
Switzerland	$ 113,808
Italy	$ 23,415
Spain	$ 124,354
Latin America	$ 2,031
India	$ 500,767
Miscellaneous Operations	$ 100,000
Sweden	$ 36,363
North Africa	$ 11,011
Cairo (UNRRA)	$ 12,185

(From : AFSC : FS : 1944.)

Table XI

THE AMERICAN FRIENDS SERVICE COMMITTEE

FOREIGN SERVICE BUDGET FOR YEAR
JANUARY 1, 1944 — JANUARY 1, 1945

	Gross operations	cash from AFSC
EXPENDITURES OUTSIDE THE UNITED STATES		
(Total brought forward)		$ 1,911,300
EXPENDITURES IN THE UNITED STATES		
Service performed in Philadelphia for beneficiaries abroad		15,500
SERVICES TO REFUGEES IN U.S.		
Philadelphia office	14,000	
Powell House and N.Y. refugee office	14,000	
Hostels	1,000	
Direct payments to refugees from designated funds	8,000	
Other services	1,300	38,300
SERVICES TO INTERNEES IN U.S.		
APPROPRIATIONS		5,000
Clothing offices (N.Y., Wash., Chicago)	7,000	
Work of Caroline Norment	2,500	
Central Registry Bureau	5,000	14,500
ADMINISTRATION AND PUBLICITY		
Salaries	52,650	
Other administrative expense	3,025	
Publicity	14,500	
New York relief office	6,100	103,500
CENTERS		
Administration	1,800	
Service, travel, maintenance, etc.	3,800	
Centers abroad	12,000	17,600
		$ 2,105,700

(From : AFSC : FS : 1944 : Finance.)

Table XII

THE NATIONAL REFUGEE SERVICE ACTIVITIES

Year	Total Immigration Jewish and non-Jewish	Jewish Immigration	Personnel employed	Total expenditures	Relief expended	Average No. persons given relief	Resettlement individuals
1933	23,068	2,372					
1934	29,470	4,134					
1935	34,956	4,837					
1936	36,329	6,252					
1937	50,244	11,352				250	460
1938	67,895	19,736				398	1,256
1939	82,998	43,450	441	$ 2,470,393	$ 1,316,702	4,925	3,546
1940	70,756	36,945	449	$ 3,467,832	$ 1,987,762	8,175	5,113
1941	51,776	23,737	NA	$ 3,056,015	$ 1,479,007	6,688	3,169
1942	28,781	10,608	299	$ 2,420,573	$ 1,190,466	4,590	770
1943	23,725	4,705	NA	$ 1,530,947	$ 492,482	2,105	293
1944	28,551	2,400	"	$ 1,103,656	$ 384,225	872	95
1945	45,603	5,000	"	$ 989,012	$ 249,598	222	NA

(From: White, *300,000 New Americans*, p. 397, Appendix A.)

Table XIII

THE NATIONAL COORDINATING COMMITTEE

Summary of Activities for 1938

Cash income	$ 702,307.12
Expenditures	$ 804,258.52
Deficit	$ 101,952.35

Physicians Committee	$ 50,000
Scholars Committee	$ 68,000

Case-work and relief	6,332 cases
Immigration	19,512 "
Employment (asked 11,605) secured	2,500 "
Resettlement secured (in 150 communities)	1,256 individuals
Staff for NCC and Greater NY committee	308 persons

(From : NCC, Report of William Rosenwald, "Summary of NCC Fund Activities, Jan. 26, 1938 [NCC papers, Folder 1, JDC].)

Table XIV

THE NATIONAL REFUGEE SERVICE

ACTIVITIES FOR 1940

Total Income	$ 3,174,886
Total Expenditures	$ 3,476,693
Deficit	$ 301,806

Traffic count department	321,295	
Employment applications	20,322	
Migration Services rendered	78,370	
Special committees and projects, interviewed	64,640	
Central reception, interviewed	68,979	
Resettlement 2,826 units	5,113	individuals

From : NRS, *Annual Report for 1940*, p. 25 ([NRS papers, folder 369, YIVO].)

Table XV

THE NATIONAL REFUGEE SERVICE

Summary of Five Years' Activities, 1939—1944

Individuals afforded relief	33,050
Placement secured	31,601
Vocational retraining	1,891
Individuals resettled	11,674
Number of loans granted	4,990
Immigration services provided	345,604

(From : NRS, Division of Statistics, July 12, 1944 [NRS papers, folder 369, YIVO].)

BIBLIOGRAPHY

1. PRIMARY SOURCES

A. MANUSCRIPTS

The papers of the American Committee for Christian Refugees, the archives of the Presbyterian Historical Society, Philadelphia, Pennsylvania.

The papers of the American Friends Service Committee, Philadelphia.

The papers of the American Jewish Committee, AJC's Record Center, New York City.

The papers of the Bureau of Immigration of the National Catholic Welfare Conference, the archives of the U.S. Catholic Conference, Center for Migration Studies, Staten Island, N.Y.

The papers of the Catholic Committee for Refugees, the archives of U.S. Catholic Conference, Staten Island, N.Y.

Joseph P. Chamberlain papers, YIVO, New York City.

Records of the Department of State, National Archives, Washington, D.C.

The papers of the Federal Council of Churches, the archives of the Presbyterian Historical Society, Philadelphia, Pennsylvania.

The papers of German Jewish Children's Aid, YIVO.

Carlton J. Hayes papers, Butler Library, Columbia University, New York City.

HIAS–HICEM papers, YIVO.

The papers of the International Migration Service, the offices of the International Social Service, New York City.

The papers of the American Jewish Joint Distribution Committee, the JDC archives, New York City.

James G. McDonald papers, the School of International Affairs, Columbia University, New York City.

Leslie B. Moss papers, the archives of the Presbyterian Historical Society, Philadelphia.

The papers of the National Coordinating Committee, YIVO and JDC.

The papers of the National Refugee Service, YIVO and JDC archives.

F.D. Roosevelt papers, FDR library, Hyde Park, New York.

The papers of the War Refugee Board, FDRL, Hyde Park, N.Y.

The papers of the YMCA, YMCA Library, New York City.

The papers of the Refugee Committee of the YWCA, the archives of the National Board of YWCA, New York City.

The papers of Felix M. Warburg; the American Jewish Archives, Cincinnati, Ohio.

B. PAMPHLETS, BULLETINS AND REPORTS ISSUED BY PRIVATE ORGANIZATIONS

The American Committee for Christian Refugees

Newscast, a bi-monthly bulletin, March 1941—March/April 1947.

An Outcast (New York, 1938).

12 Questions and Answers (New York, n.d.).

Out of the Darkness (New York, n.d.).

The Church and the Refugee (New York, n.d.).

Our Story for 1940 (New York, 1940).

Toward a New Life: Ten Years of Stewardship (1945).

Periodical and Annual Mimeographed Reports, 1934—1947.

The American Friends Service Committee

Mimeographed "Bulletin on Refugees Abroad and at Home", 1943—1944.

"The Powell House Crier", a mimeographed monthly bulletin, 1944.

Refugee Facts (Philadelphia, c. 1939).

A Friendly Service for Refugees (Philadelphia, n.d.).

Services for Refugee Scholars and Teachers (Philadelphia, n.d.).

Haverford Cooperative College Workshop, 1941 (Philadelphia, 1941).

"Quaker Hill: A Friends Service Center" (1941).

American Seminar for Refugee Scholars, Teachers and Artists (Summer 1942).

Mimeographed Annual Reports of the Foreign Service Section, as well as of the Refugee Division, 1938—1945.

The Catholic Committee for Refugees

Report of the Catholic Committee for Refugees Coming from Germany, Covering the First Fiscal Year, January 1, 1937—September 30, 1937.

Report of the Catholic Committee for Refugees Covering the Period January 1, 1937—September 30, 1938.

Report of the Catholic Committee for Refugees Covering the Period January 1, 1937—September 30, 1939.

Annual *Reports* of the Catholic Committee, 1940—1946.

"News Service", mimeographed bulletin of the National Catholic Welfare Conference.

The Committee on Displaced Foreign Psychologists

"Progress Report", by Barbara S. Burks, *Psychological Bulletin*, 36 (March 1939), 188—190.

The Committee of Ten

Asylum for Refugees Under Our Immigration Laws (New York, n.d.).

The Emergency Committee in Aid of Displaced German Scholars

Annual *Reports*, 1933—1945.

The Emergency Committee in Aid of Displaced Foreign Physicians (in 1940 it was renamed the Emergency Committee in Aid of Foreign Medical Scientists)

Reports for 1934, 1942, 1947.

The Episcopal Church, Committee on Refugees

Diocese of Southern Ohio, *Aid the German Refugees: A New Diocesan Project* (1938).

Episcopal Committee for European Refugees

In the Name of These Refugees: Aid All Refugees (n.d.).

The Emigrés Among Us (n.d.).

Resettlement of Refugees: A Program for Parish Committees (New York, n.d.).

The Federal Council of Churches

Monthly *Bulletin*, 1933—1945.

Annual *Reports*, 1938—1945.

Mimeographed "Press Service" of the Home Missions Council, 1940.

The International Migration Service

Typed Annual "Memorandum on Work and Finances", 1934—1945 (ISS).

The International Rescue and Relief Committee
Two Years Against the Gestapo (n.d., c. 1942).
Report of the International Rescue and Relief Committee (n.d.).
"The International Rescue and Relief Committee in 1944" (WRB).

The Lutheran Refugee Service
Refugees Are People Like Us (n.d.).
What About Refugees? (n.d.).
Who Says I'm an Enemy Alien? (n.d.)

The National Coordinating Committee
Bulletin of the Coordinating Committee (February 1938).
Refugee Immigration: Facts and Figures (n.d.).
Notes and News (April 1939).
Reports on the Activities of the NCC and Affiliated Organizations, 1937, 1938—1939.
Harry Greenstein, *Reorganization Study of National Coordinating Committee and its Affiliated Agencies* (May 1939).

The National Refugee Service
Dividends for New Immigrants (May 1941).
They Can Aid America (1943).
Periodical and Annual Mimeographed Reports, 1939—1945.
"The National Refugee Service, June 1939—June 1944: Five Year Period" (NRS, July 1944).
"Reports of the Meetings of the Board of Directors", 1941—1944 (mimeog.).
Quarterly Report, 1940—1941.

The National Committee for Resettlement of Foreign Physicians
Report for 1938—1940 (AJC).
David L. Edsall and Tracy J. Putnam, "The Emigré Physician in America, 1941: A Report of the National Committee for Resettlement of Foreign Physicians", *The Journal of the American Medical Association,* 117 (November 29, 1941), pp. 1881—1888.

Placement Committee for German and Austrian Musicians
Mimeographed "Report on Second Year's Activity, September 1, 1939— September 1, 1940" (NRS).

Self-help of Emigrés from Central Europe
"Report", n.d.
Mimeographed "Condensed Report, 1937—1939" (NRS).
"Report for the Years 1940—1941" (March 1942, NRS).

The Unitarian Service Committee
Standing By (a monthly bulletin, 1942—1944).
"The Second Mile, May 1941—May 1942", mimeographed (AFSC).
Saving the Future in Europe (n.d., c. 1942).
"Unitarian Service Committee, 1939—1944", a mimeographed report.
Reporting for Service (n.d., c. 1945).

The United States Committee for the Care of European Children
Preliminary Information, Bulletin no. 1 (July 1, 1940).
We Are Standing By (1941).
Mimeographed Annual Reports (YIVO).

World Council of Churches: Ecumenical Committee for Refugees
Church Refugee Work in War Time (Report, January 1942).

Young Men's Christian Association
Manley J.E. "Administration and Relationships of War Prisoners Aid of the YMCA in the United States During World War II" (typescript, c. 1947).

Young Women's Christian Association
Woman's Press (Bulletin of the National Board of the YWCA).
Refugees (1938).
Refugees (December 1939).
Meet the Refugees (New York, 1940).
Refugees in War-Time (New York, February 1943).
Report of the National Board for the Biennium, 1938—1940.
Mimeographed "Final Report, Committee on Refugees", February 1, 1946 (YWCA).

C. B O O K S (Memoirs, Reports)

Bentwich, Norman, *Wanderer Between the Two Worlds.* London : Kegan, Paul, Trench, Truber & Co., 1941.
— —, *My Seventy Seven Years: An Account of My Life and Times, 1883—1960.* Philadelphia : Jewish Publication Society of America, 1961.

Close, Katheryn, *Transplanted Children : A History.* New York : The U.S. Committee for the Care of European Children, 1953.

Detzer, Dorothy, *Appointment on the Hill.* New York : Holt & Co., 1948.

Dodd, William Jr. and Martha (eds.), *Ambassador Dodd's Diary, 1933—1938.* New York : Harcourt, Brace & Co., 1941.

Duggan, Stephen and Betty Drury, *The Rescue of Science and Learning : The Story of the Emergency Committee in Aid of Displaced Foreign Scholars.* New York : Macmillan, 1948.

Fry, Varian, *Surrender on Demand.* New York : Random House, 1945.

— —, *Assignment : Rescue.* New York : Four Winds Press, 1968.

Hayes, Carlton J.H., *Wartime Mission in Spain, 1942—1945.* New York: Macmillan Co., 1948.

Hirschmann, Ira A., *Lifeline to a Promised Land.* New York: Vanguard Press, 1948.

— —, *Caution to the Winds.* New York: David McKay Co., 1962.

Israel, Fred L. (ed.), *The War Diary of Breckinridge Long: Selections from the Years 1939—1944.* Lincoln: University of Nebraska Press, 1966.

Lowrie, Donald A., *The Hunted Children.* New York: W.W. Norton and Co., 1963.

Pickett, Clarence E., *For More Than Bread.* Boston, Little Brown & Co., 1953.

Seymour, Harold J., *Design for Giving: The Story of the National War Fund Inc. 1943—1947.* New York: Harper & Brothers, 1947.

Vulliet, André, *The YMCA and Prisoners of War During World War II: Preliminary Report.* New York: International Committee of YMCA, 1949.

Waldman, Morris D., *Nor by Power.* New York: International Universities Press Inc., 1953.

Wise, Stephen S., *Challenging Years: The Autobiography of Stephen Wise.* New York: G. P. Putnam's Sons, 1949.

D. PERIODICALS AND NEWSPAPERS

The American Jewish Year Book
America (Jesuits' organ).
Christian Century (liberal Protestant).
Commonweal (liberal Catholic).
Congressional Record (organ of the AJC).
Contemporary Jewish Record (AJC).
Congress Weekly (American Jewish Congress).
Forum

Jewish Social Service Quarterly
The Nation
National Jewish Monthly (B'nai-B'rith).
The New Republic
The New York Times
Survey Graphic
Brooklyn *Tablet* (Catholic, conservative).

E. CONTEMPORARY ARTICLES WITH SPECIAL EMPHASIS ON
CHRISTIAN RELIGIOUS PUBLICATIONS

"American Christian Committee for German Refugees", *America* (February 22, 1936), 464—465.

"Aliens Have A Right to Work", *Christian Century*, 58 (July 9, 1941), 876—877.

"Anti-Semitism is Here", *Nation* (August 20, 1938), 167—168.

Atkinson, Henry A., "A Christian Problem", *Congress Weekly* (January 8, 1943), 7.

"Attempts to Help Jewish Refugees from Germany and Austria Largely Unsuccessful", *Catholic Digest*, ii (September 1938), 53—55.

"Anent the Olympics", *Commonweal* (July 17, 1936), 296.

Barton, Bruce, "Hitler's Loss Is Our Gain", *National Jewish Monthly* (1939), 314—315, 345.

Benedict, Libby, "Refugees and Red Tape: A Survey of Seven Years of Refugee Work", *Congress Weekly* (January 31, 1941), 9—11.

Bentwich, Norman, "The International Problem of Refugees", *Foreign Policy Reports*, xi (February 12, 1936), 306—316.

— —, "The Evian Conference and After", *Fortnightly*, 144 (September 1938), 287—295.

— —, "Minorities and the League of Nations", *The Menorah Journal*, 24 (Winter 1936), 8—14.

— —, "A Grim and Humiliating Story", *Midstream* (Spring 1968), 34—35.

Benziger, Marieli G., "The Nazi Dictators Steal Faith From Germans", *America* (March 26, 1938), 580—581.

Bernstein, Philip, S., "Hitler Dooms the Church", *Nation*, 146 (March 19, 1938), 329—331.

Bliven, Bruce, "Thank You Hitler", *New Republic* (November 10, 1937).

Boyd, Barrett E., "Pius XI and America", *The Christian Century* (June 5, 1935).

Boyd, Ernest, "As A Gentile Sees It", *Scribner's Magazine* (October 19, 1933), 242—243.

Brandt, Albert, "Hitlerism vs. Catholicism", *Catholic World*, 137 (September 1933), 641—651.

Browne, C.A., "The Role of Refugees in the History of American Science", *Science*, 91 (March 1, 1940), 203—208.

"By the Jericho Road", *Christian Century* (August 31, 1938), 1030—1031.

Chamberlain, Joseph P., "High Commissioner for Refugees", *Survey Graphic*, 23 (April 1934), 177—180.

"'Christian American' Jew Baiting", *Christian Social Action*, 4 (September 19, 1939), 101—115.

Clinchy, Everett, "The Church and Freedom", *Survey Graphic*, 28 (February 1939), 139—140.

Close, Kathryn, "A Place to Call Home", *Survey Graphic*, 30 (December 1941), 673—679.

C.O.C., "Germans in America Today", *Woman's Press* (October 1942), 410—411.

"Committee for Catholic Refugees from Germany", *Commonweal* (July 30, 1937), 336.

Conning, John S., "Highways for Christ in the Jewish World", HMC, Press Service", no. 15 (May 14, 1940), 1—4.

— —, "Beside the Golden Door: New Hope for Jewish and Non-Aryan Refugees", HMC, "Press Service", no. 16 (June 27, 1940), 7—9.

— —, "The Jews — A Christian Test", HMC, "Press Service", no. 15 (May 14, 1940), 4—8.

— —, "The Soul of the Jew", HMC, "Press Service", no. 16 (June 27, 1940), 3—7.

Davie, Maurice R., "Minorities, A Challenge to American Democracy", *Journal of Educational Sociology*, 12 (April 1939), 451—456.

Davis, E., "On the Gentility of the Gentiles", *Harper's Magazine*, 167 (July 1933), 147—155.

"Demonic Germany and the Predicament of Humanity", *Christian Century* (November 30, 1938), 1456—1458.

Dempsey, David, "The Jericho Road", *Christian Science Monitor*, February 10, 1940.

Dingol, Solomon, "How Many Refugees from Nazi Persecution Were Admitted to the United States", *Rescue*, 1 (February 1944), 1—7.

"Do We Want More Mouths to Feed?", *Saturday Evening Post*, May 19, 1934.

"Do You Care?", *Churchman* (May 1, 1939), 9.

Dodd, William E., "Germany Shocked Me", *Readers Digest*, 33 (September 1938), 102—105.

Edsall, D.L., "A Program for the Refugee Physician", *Journal of American Medical Association*, 112 (May 13, 1939), 112.

— —, "The Emigré Physician in American Medicine", *Journal of American Medical Association*, 114 (March 23, 1940), 1068.

Ellis, Mabel, "The Refugee Problem and the War", *Woman's Press* (November 1939), 452, 486.

— —, "Alien Registration Plans", *Woman's Press* (September 1940), 379.

— —, "Children in Flight from War", *Woman's Press* (September 1940), 391.

— —, "Before and After Taking", *Woman's Press* (June 1941), 279.

— —, "Women's Organizations and the Woman Refugee", *Woman's Press* (January 1942), 20—21.

Estorick, Eric, "The Evian Conference and the Intergovernmental Committee", *Annals of American Academy of Political and Social Science*, 203 (May 1939), 136—141.

"Evian Conference", *Catholic World*, 147 (August 1938), 618—619.

Fairchild, Henry Pratt and Frank Ritchie. "Are the Refugees a Liability?", *Forum and Century*, 101 (June 1939), 316—320.

"Father Coughlin and the Jews", *Commonweal* (December 9, 1938), 169; (December 30, 1938), 268—270.

Feige, G., "Anti-Semitism: Why Jews Are Hated?", *Catholic Digest*, 1 (March 1940), 24—39.

Fisher, Dorothy, "Keeping Normal", *Christian Herald*, March 1942.

"The Forbidden Theme", *Christian Century*, 58 (September 24, 1941), 1167—1169.

"French Protestants Side with Persecuted Jews", *Christian Century*, 58 (October 15, 1941), 1261.

Fry, Varian, "Our Consuls at Work", *Nation*, 154 (May 2, 1942), 507—509.

"German Catholic Bishops Protest Curbs on Church", *Christian Century*, 58 (July 23, 1941), 924.

"German Refugees", *America* (June 23, 1934), 243—244.

"German Refugee Commissioner Resigns", *America* (January 11, 1936), 338—339.

"German Situation", *Commonweal* (May 26, 1933), 87—88.

Gurian, Waldemar, "Hitler's Undeclared War on the Catholic Church", *Foreign Affairs*, 16 (January 1938), 260—271.

High, Stanley, "Star-Spangled Fascists", *Saturday Evening Post*, 211 (May 27, 1939), 5—7.

"Hitler vs. The Son of God", *Churchman* (October 15, 1936), 9.

Holborn, Louise W., "The League of Nations and the Refugee Problem", *Annals of the American Academy of Political and Social Science*, 203 (May 1939), 124—136.

Holmes, John Haynes, "Christian Refugees from Germany", *Christian Century* (April 18, 1937), 550—551.

"Hospitality of the United States", *America* (September 10, 1938), 531.

"Hunting Homes for the Refugees", *Christian Century* (December 7, 1938), 1485.

Hurblutt, Mary E., "The World Crisis and New Americans", *Woman's Press* (February 1939), 58—60.

"The Inner Forum", *Commonweal* (March 10, 1939), 559.

Irwin, Theodore, "Inside the Christian Front", *Forum*, 103 (March 1940), 102—108.

Isseman, F.M., "They Escaped", *Christian Century* (January 1, 1936), 14—15.

"Jewish Plebiscite", *Christian Century* (June 1, 1938), 688—689; (June 22, 1938), 793.

"Jewry and Democracy", *Christian Century* (June 9, 1937), 734—736; (July 7, 1937), 862—864; (August 4, 1937), 977.

Johnson, Alvin, "The Rising Tide of Anti-Semitism", *Survey Graphic*, 28 (February 1939), 113—119.

Jordan, "Center Party is not Hampered", *Tablet* (April 22, 1933), 7.

"Justice for Jews", *Commonweal* (April 5, 1933), 620.

Karpf, Ruth, "Displaced Persons; A USA Closeup", *Survey Graphic*, 34 (June 1945), 282—284.

Kazin, Alfred, "In Every Voice: In Every Ban", *The New Republic*, 110 (January 10, 1944), 44—46.

Keller, Adolph, "The Churches Under the Cross", *The Presbyterian*, January 1942.

Kellogg, Paul, "Team Play for Refugees", *Survey Midmonthly*, June 1939.

Keyhoe, Donald E. and John Jay Daly, "Hitler's Slave Spies in America", *American Magazine*, 131 (April 1941), 14—15, 120—121.

Kimball, Alice M., "Uprooted Children", *Woman's Press* (April 1941), 175, 197.

Kirchwey, Freda, "State Department Versus Political Refugees", *The Nation*, 151 (December 28, 1940), 648—649.

——, "While the Jews Die", *The Nation*, 156 (March 13, 1943), 366—367.

——, "Rescue Hungarian Jews", *The Nation*, 159 (August 26, 1944), 229.

Kramer, Dale, "The American Fascists", *Harper's Magazine*, 181 (September 1940), 380—393.

Kraus, Hertha, "The Plight of Refugees in a Preoccupied World", *Woman's Press* (July–August 1940), 321—323.

Kun, Anton, "These Are the Refugees", *American Mercury* (January 1940), 45—52.

Lasher, L.D., "Test for Civilization", *Survey Graphic*, 27 (December 1938), 601—603.

Lasker, Bruno, "An Atlas of Hope", *Survey Graphic*, 29 (November 1940), 583—590.

Lavine, Harold, "Fifth Column 'Literature'", *Saturday Review of Literature*, 22 (September 14, 1940), 3—4, 14, 16.

Leiper, Henry Smith, "The State of the Church", *Advance* (July 26, 1934), 332.

— —, "Three Years of Hitlerism", *Christian Evangelist* (January 30, 1936), 152.

— —, "Those German Refugees", *Current History*, 50 (May 1939), 19—22.

— —, "How Can We Help Europe's Churches?", *Christian Century* (May 24, 1944), 641—643.

Levmore, Bernard W., "A Stimulus for American Industry : Nonprofessional Refugees", *Annals of American Academy of Political and Social Science*, 203 (May 1939), 162—167.

Levy, H.W., "Good Will to Men", *National Jewish Monthly* (December 1938), 129—130.

Lundberg, Isabel, "Who Are These Refugees?", *Harper's Magazine*, 182 (January 1941), 164—172.

"Lutheran State Churches in Germany Unite", *Lutheran* (June 22, 1933), 6.

McAfee, J.E., "Jewish Solidarity in America", *Christian Century* (January 10, 1934), 52—53; Discussion: January 24, February 28, April 25, May 9, 1934.

McCulloch, Rhoda E., "The Dispossessed", *Woman's Press* (January 1939), 14—16.

McDonald, James G., "I Cannot Remain Silent", *National Jewish Monthly* (February 1936), 150—151, 162—164.

McMillan, L.K., "American Negro Looks At the German Jew", *Christian Century* (August 31, 1938), 1034—1036.

Mann, Erika and Eric Estorick, "Private and Governmental Aid of Refugees", *Annals of American Academy of Political and Soical Science*, 203 (May 1939), 142—154.

Mann, Thomas, "America and the Refugee", *The New Republic*, 101 (November 8, 1938), 38—39.

"Many Knotty Problems Face Evian Conference", *America* (August 13, 1938), 434—435.

Martinus, J., "Way of an Emigrant German Catholic in Exile", *Commonweal* (March 20, 1936), 572—573.

Moley, Raymond and C. Jedel, "About the Aliens in Our Midst", *American Mercury* (October 1941), 481—486.

"More Refugees: Same Questions", *America* (December 15, 1934), 220.

Moss, Leslie B., "Proceed With Courage", *World Call*, February 1942.

— —, "Christian Prepare", *The Evangel*, February 1942.

Mott, John R., "Steadfast Christian International", *World Call*, March 1942.

"Nazi Mentality", *The Catholic World*, 141 (April 1935), 3.

"No Room At the Inn", *Commonweal* (November 18, 1938), 86.

North, Eric M., "Wherever Hearts are Hungry", *Window of YMCA*, April 1942.

Ostrolenk, Bernhard, "The Economics of an Imprisoned World", *Annals of American Academy of Political and Social Science*, 203 (May 1939), 194—201.

"Palestine and the Refugees", *Christian Century* (March 29, 1939), 407—408.

Pell, H.C., "Immigration", *Commonweal* (May 26, 1933), 91—93; Discussion; (July 7), 269; (July 14), 288—289.

Perlman, K.B., "Refugees: Hazards or Opportunities?", *Woman's Press* (February 1942), 65—66.

Petrie, J.C., "Too Many Jews in Government? Anti-Semitic Charge Made at Human Relations Conference", *Christian Century* (December 28, 1938), 14—16.

Phillips, P.O., "Gandhi Speaks on Jewish Problems", *Christian Century* (January 18, 1939), 94—95.

Pickett, Clarence E., "Difficulties in Placement of Refugees", *Annals of the American Academy of Political and Social Science*, 203 (May 1939), 94—98.

"Plight of the German Catholic Refugees", *Commonweal* (March 10, 1939), 559.

"The Pope and the Jews", *America* (July 1, 1944), 350.

Popper, David H., "International Aid to German Refugees", *Foreign Policy Reports*, 14 (November 1, 1938), 186—196.

"The Problem of the Refugee Physician", a Letter to the Editor, *The Journal of American Medical Association*, 112 (February 11, 1939), 570—571.

"The Problem of the Refugee Physician", *The Journal of the American Medical Association*, 112 (February 25, 1939), 735, 737.

"Protocols: Replies", *America* (April 2, 1938), 617—618.

"Quakers and the Refugees: Delegation to Germany in the Interest of Jewish Refugees", *Christian Century* (January 18, 1939), 80—81.

"Reactions to Father Coughlin's Broadcasts in the Press", *Commonweal* (December 16, 1938), 213—214.

Reed, Douglas L., "The German Church Conflict", *Foreign Affairs*, 13 (January 1935), 483—498.

"Refugees and Ourselves", *America* (May 13, 1939), 108—109.

"Refugees and the Professions", *Harvard Law Review*, 53 (1939), 112—122.

"Refugees from Germany", *America* (April 28, 1934), 52.

"Refugee Problem", *Woman's Press* (December 1938), 561.

"The Refugees: What to Do With Them?", *Christian Advocate* (December 16, 1938), 1604.

Reynolds, Quentin, "Unwanted", *Collier's*, 103 (February 11, 1939), 12—13, 28, 30.

Ritchie, Frank, "America Needs Them", *Forum*, 101 (June 1939), 319—320.

Rocker, Rudolf, "I am an 'Aryan'", *Jewish Frontier* (February 1942), 11—15.

Roe, Clara S., "Some Go Abroad", *Woman's Press* (January 1942), 13.

— —, "And War Victims", *Woman's Press*, April 1943.

"Roman Catholic Bishops Define the Crisis of Christianity", *Christian Century* (December 3, 1941), 1493.

Rublee, George, "Refugee Settlement", *Commonweal*, 29 (February 24, 1939), 479.

Sachar, Abram L., "Jewish-Christian Relations", *Vital Speeches* (October 15, 1936), 2—7.

Seagle, W., "All Radicals Are Jews", *The Nation*, 135 (October 5, 1932), 307—308.

Shuster, George N., "Catholics in Nazi Germany", *Commonweal* (June 29, 1934), 234.

— —, "The Conflict Among Catholics", *American Scholar*, 10 (Winter 1940—1941), 5—16.

Solow, Herbert, "Refugee Scholars in the United States", *The American Scholar*, 11 (Summer 1942), 374—378.

Stewart, Maxwell S., "The Immigrant as a Worker", *Social Work Today*, 7 (December 1939), 39, 44.

Thompson, Dorothy, "Refugees: A World Problem", *Foreign Affairs*, 16 (April 1938), 375—378.

— —, "Escape in a Frozen World", *Survey Graphic*, 28 (February 1939), 93—96, 168—169.

Timoney, Alice, "Step-Children of the Fatherland: German Refugees", *Commonweal* (October 6, 1939), 531—533.

"Uprooted in 1939", *Commonweal* (February 3, 1939), 410—412.

Vallotton, A., "Christmas Eve in a Refugee Camp", *Woman's Press* (December 1941), 495—496.

Villard, Oswald Garrison, "Our Duty to Protest", *Jewish Forum*, 18 (July 1936), 161—162.

— —, "Issues and Men: Nazi Barbarism in Germany", *The Nation*, 147 (November 26, 1938), 567.

— —, "Our Moral Confusion", *Christian Century* (July 9, 1941), 881—882.

Wagg, Alfred III, "Washington's Stepchild: The Refugee", *The New Republic*, 104 (April 28, 1941), 592—594.

Waldeck, Countess, "The Great New Migration", *Foreign Affairs*, 15 (April 1937), 537—546.

White, William A., "A Voice from Street U.S.A.", *Survey Graphic*, 28 (February 1939), 133—135.

Williams, Michael, "Hitlerism and Religion", *Commonweal* (May 19, 1933), 69—71.

— —, "Blood and Tears", *Commonweal* (July 2, 1937), 258.

Woodsmall, Ruth F., "Refugee Problem: To the National Associations from the World's Council of the YWCA", *Woman's Press* (December 1938), 561.

"World's Refugees Costly to France", *Literary Digest* (February 6, 1937), 10—11.

F. MISCELLANY

McDonald, James G., *Letter of Resignation of James G. McDonald, High Commissioner for Refugees (Jewish and Other) Coming from Germany, Addressed to the Secretary General of the League of Nations, With an Annex.* London, December 27, 1935.

— —, *Palestine: The Primary Hope of the Post-War Era; A Record of a Quarter of a Century of Intergovernmental Efforts on Behalf of Refugees.* New York: United Palestine Appeal, 1944.

McDonald, James G., and Harry Emerson Fosdick, *Modern Christian German Martyrs.* New York: The American Committee for Christian Refugees, n.d.

Pehle, John, "Final Summary Report of the Executive Director of the War Refugee Board", September 15, 1945.

Randall, John H., Mrs., *The Voice of Thy Brother's Blood: An Eleventh-Hour Appeal to All Americans,* Washington D.C. International Women's League for Peace and Freedom, 1944.

The Voice of Religion: The Views of Christian Religious Leaders on The Persecution of the Jews in Germany by the National Socialists. New York: The American Jewish Committee, 1933.

2. SECONDARY WORKS

A. BOOKS

Abell, Aaron I., *American Catholicism and Social Action: A Search for Social Justice, 1865—1950.* Garden City, N.Y.: Hanover House, 1960.

Adler, Cyrus and A.M. Margalith, *With Firmness in the Right: American Diplomatic Action Affecting Jews, 1940—1945*. New York: The American Jewish Committee, 1946.

Avni, Haim, *Contemporary Spain and the Jewish People*. Hakibutz Hameuchad, Yad Vashem, 1975 (Hebrew).

Barth, Karl, *The Church and the Political Problem of Our Day*. New York, 1939.

Bauer, Yehuda, *My Brother's Keeper: A History of the American Jewish Joint Distribution Committee, 1929—1939*. Philadelphia: Jewish Publication Society of America, 1974.

American Jewry and the Holocaust: AJJDC, 1939—1943, Detroit: Wayne State University Press, 1981.

Boyers, Robert (ed.), *The Legacy of the German Refugee Intellectuals*. New York: Schocken Books, 1972.

Cantril, Harvey (ed.), *Public Opinion, 1935—1946*. Princeton: Princeton University Press, 1951.

Carter, Paul A., *The Decline and Revival of the Social Gospel: A Social and Political Liberalism in American Protestant Churches, 1920—1940*. Ithaca: Cornell University Press, 1954.

Cochrane, Arthur C., *The Church's Confession Under Hitler*. Philadelphia: Westminster Press, 1962.

Conway, John S., *The Nazi Persecution of the Churches, 1933—1938*. London: Weidenfeld and Nicholson, 1968.

Davie, Maurice R., *Refugees in America*. New York: Harper & Brothers, 1947.

Dawidowicz, Lucy S., *The War Against the Jews, 1933—1945*. New York: Holt, Rinehart and Winston, 1975.

Divine, Robert A., *American Immigration Policy, 1924—1952*. New Haven: Yale University Press, 1957.

Esh, Shaul, *Studies in the Holocaust and Contemporary Jewry*. Jerusalem: Institute of Contemporary Jewry, the Hebrew University, Yad Vashem, Leo Baeck Institute, 1973 (Hebrew).

Falconi, Carlo, *The Silence of Pius XII*, trans. by Bernhard Wall. London: Faber & Faber, 1970.

Feige, George, *The Church and the Jews*. New York: The Paulist Press, 1937.

Feingold, Henry L., *The Politics of Rescue: The Roosevelt Administration and the Holocaust, 1938—1945*. New Brunswick: Rutgers University Press, 1970.

Feldblum, Esther Y., *The American Catholic Press and the Jewish State 1917—1959*. New York: Ktav Publishing House, 1977.

Fermi, Laura, *Illustrious Immigrants: The Intellectual Migration from*

Europe, 1930—1941. Chicago: The University of Chicago Press, 1968.

Flynn, George O., *American Catholics and the Roosevelt Presidency, 1932— 1936.* Lexington: University of Kentucky Press, 1968.

Friedman, Saul S., *No Haven for the Oppressed: United States Policy Toward Jewish Refugees, 1938—1945.* Detroit: Wayne State University Press, 1973.

Gallin, Mary Alice, *German Resistance to . . . Hitler: Ethical and Religious Factors.* Washington, D.C.: The Catholic University of America Press, 1969.

Hilberg, Raul, *The Destruction of the European Jews.* Chicago: Quadrangle Books, 1961.

Hopkins, C. Howard, *The History of the YMCA in North America.* New York: Associated Press, 1951.

Kent, Donald Peterson, *The Refugee Intellectual: The Americanization of the Immigrants of 1933—1941.* New York: Columbia University Press, 1953.

Kubowitzi, Leon, *Unity in Dispersion: A History of the World Jewish Congress.* New York: World Jewish Congress, 1948.

Lewy, Gunther, *The Catholic Church and Nazi Germany.* New York: McGraw-Hill, 1964.

Littell, Franklin H. and Hubert G. Locke (eds.), *The German Church Struggle and the Holocaust.* Detroit: Wayne State University Press, 1974.

Maritain, Jacques, *A Christian Looks At the Jewish Question.* New York and Toronto: Longmans, Green, 1939.

Marty, M.E. (ed.), *The Religious Press in America.* New York: Holt, Rinehart, and Wilson, 1963.

Morse, Arthur D., *While Six Million Died: A Chronicle of American Apathy.* New York: Random House, 1967.

O'Brien, David, *American Catholics and Social Reform.* New York: Oxford University Press, 1968.

Robinson, Jacob and Philip Friedman (comp.), *Guide to Jewish History Under Nazi Impact.* New York: YIVO Institute for Jewish Research and Yad Vashem, 1960.

Robinson, Jacob and Mrs. Philip Friedman (comp.), *The Holocaust and After: Sources and Literature.* New York: YIVO and Yad Vashem, 1973.

Ruhm von Oppen, Beate, *Religion and Resistance to Nazism.* Princeton, 1971.

Simpson, John Hope, *Refugees: Preliminary Report of a Survey.* New York: Oxford University Press, 1938.

Snoek, Johan M., *The Grey Book.* Assen, 1969.

Stember, Charles F. and others, *Jews in the Mind of America*. New York, and London: Basic Books, 1966.

Strauss, Herbert A. (ed.), *Jewish Immigrants of the Nazi Period in the United States of America*, vol. I, New York, 1978.

Strong, Donald S., *Organized Anti-Semitism in America: The Rise of Group Prejudice During the Decade 1930—1940*. Washington, D.C.: American Council of Public Affairs, 1941.

Thompson, Dorothy, *Refugees: Anarchy or Organization*. New York: Random House, 1938.

Tull, Charles J., *Father Coughlin and the New Deal*. Syracuse: Syracuse University Press, 1965.

Voss, Carl Herman, *Rabbi and Minister: The Friendship of Stephen S. Wise and John Haynes Holmes*. Cleveland and New York: World Publishing Co., 1964.

White, Lyman C., *300,000 New Americans: The Epic of Modern Immigrant Aid Service*. New York: Harper & Brothers, 1957.

Williams, Michael, *The Catholic Church in Action*, rev. ed. Zsold Arady. New York: P.J. Kenedy, 1957.

Wischnitzer, Mark, *Visas to Freedom: The History of HIAS*. Cleveland and New York: The World Publishing Co., 1956.

Wyman, David S., *Paper Walls: America and the Refugee Crisis, 1938—1941*. Amherst: The University of Massachusetts Press, 1968.

Zahn, Gordon C., *German Catholics and Hitler's Wars*. N.Y. 1962.

B. ARTICLES AND PAMPHLETS

Abrahams, Olga, "The Catholic Church and Persecuted Jewry, 1939—1945: A Survey of Contemporary Press Reports", *The Wiener Library Bulletin*, 18 (January 1964), 4, 6.

Adler-Rudel, S., "The Evian Conference and the Refugee Question", *Yearbook of Leo Baeck Institute*, 13 (1968), 255—273.

Adler, Selig, "The United States and the Holocaust", *American Jewish Historical Quarterly*, 64 (September 1974), 14—23.

Ainsztein, Reuben, "The Failure of the West", *Jewish Quarterly* (Winter 1966—1967), 11—20.

Davie, Maurice R. and Samuel Koening, *The Refugees Are Now Americans*. Committee for the Study of Recent Immigration from Europe, 1945.

Diamond, Sander A., "The *Kristallnacht* and the Reaction in America", *YIVO Annual of Jewish Social Science*, 14 (1969), 196—208.

Dinnerstein, Leonard, "The U.S. Army and the Jews: Policies Toward the Displaced Persons After World War II", *American Jewish History*, 68 (March 1979), 353—366.

Esh, Shaul, "Between Discrimination and Extermination: The Fateful Year, 1938", *Yad Vashem Studies*, II (1958), 79—93.

Feingold, Henry L., "Roosevelt and the Holocaust: Reflections on the New Deal Humanitarianism", *Judaism*, 18 (Summer 1969), 259—276.

— —, "The Roosevelt Administration and the Effort to Save the Jews in Hungary", *Hungarian Jewish Studies* (1969), 211—252.

— —, "Who Shall Bear Guilt for the Holocaust: The Human Dilemma", *American Jewish History*, 68 (March 1979), 261—282.

Feldblum, Esther, "On the Eve of a Jewish State: American Catholic Responses", *American Jewish Historical Quarterly*, 64 (December 1974), 99—119.

Genizi, Haim, "American Non-Sectarian Refugee Relief Organizations, 1933—1945", *Yad Vashem Studies*, 11 (Jerusalem, 1976), 164—220.

— —, "James G. McDonald, High Commissioner for Refugees: 1933—1935", *The Wiener Library Bulletin*, 30 (Summer 1977), 40—52.

— —, "James McDonald and the Roosevelt Administration, 1938—1945", *Bar Ilan Studies in History* (Ramat Gan: Bar Ilan University Press, 1978), 285—306.

Gottlieb, Moshe, "The First of April Boycott and the Reaction of the American Jewish Community", *American Jewish Historical Quarterly*, 57 (June 1968), 516—557.

— —, "The Berlin Riots of 1935 and Their Repercussion in America", *American Jewish Historical Quarterly*, 62 (December 1972), 146—161.

— —, "In the Shadow of War: The American Anti-Nazi Boycott Movement in 1939—1941", *American Jewish Historical Quarterly*, 62 (December 1972), 146—161.

Grobman, Alex, "What Did They Know: The American Jewish Press and the Holocaust, September 1939—17 December 1942", *American Jewish History*, 68 (March 1979), 353—366.

Kent, George O., "Pope Pius XII and Germany: Some Aspects of German-Vatican Relations, 1933—1943", *American Historical Review*, 70 (October 1964), 59—78.

Lewy, Guenter, "Pius XII, the Jews and the German Catholic Church", *Commentary*, 37 (February 1964), 23—26.

Mashberg, Michael, "American Diplomacy and the Jewish Refugee, 1938—1939", *YIVO Annual of Jewish Social Science*, 15 (1974), 339—365.

Ludlow, Peter, "The Refugee Problem in the 1930s: the Failures and Successes of Protestant Relief Programmes", *English Historical Review*, 90 (July 1975), 564—603.

McDonald, James G., "Forewarned But Not Forearmed; The James Mc-Donald Letter of 1935", *The Wiener Library Bulletin*, 14 (1960), 55.

Norden, Margaret K., "American Editorial Response to the Rise of Adolf Hitler", *American Jewish Historical Quarterly*, 59 (March 1970), 290—301.

Parzen, Herbert, "The Roosevelt Palestine Policy, 1943—1945", *American Jewish Archives*, 26 (April 1974), 31—65.

Prinz, Arthur, "The Role of the Gestapo in Obstructing and Promoting Jewish Emigration", *Yad Vashem Studies*, 2 (1958), 205—218.

Robbins, Richard, "American Jews and American Catholics: Two Types of Social Change", *Sociological Analysis*, 26 (Spring 1965), 1—18.

Rosenstock, Werner, "Exodus 1933—1939: A Survey of Jewish Emigration from Germany", *Leo Baeck Institute Yearbook*, 1 (1956), 373—390.

Ruhm von Oppen, Beate, "Catholics and Nazis in 1933", *The Wiener Library Bulletin*, 16 (January 1962).

— —, "Nazis and Christians", *World Politics*, 21 (1969), 392—424.

Simpson, John II., "League of Nations and the Refugees", *Fortnightly Review*, 149 (February 1938), 225—230.

Snoek, Johan M., "Did the Non-Catholic Churches Keep Silent?", *Yad Vashem Bulletin*, p. 20 (April 1967), 30—34.

Strauss, Herbert A., "Jewish Emigration from Germany: Nazi Policies and Jewish Responses", part I, *Leo Baeck Yearbook*, vol. 25 (1980), 313—358.

Szajkowski, Zosa, "Disunity in the Distribution of Jewish Overseas Relief, 1919—1939", *American Jewish Historical Quarterly*, 58 (March 1969), 336—407; ibid. (June 1969), 484—506.

— —, "The Attitude of American Jews to Refugees From Germany in the 1930s", *American Jewish Historical Quarterly*, 61 (December 1971), 101—143.

— —, "Relief for German Jewry: Problems of American Involvement", *American Jewish Historical Quarterly*, 62 (December 1972), 115—145.

Tal, Uriel, "'Political Faith' of Nazism Prior to the Holocaust", in *Annual Lecture of the Jacob M. and Shoshanah Schreiber Chair of Contemporary Jewish History*. Tel Aviv University, 1978.

Warburg, G., "None to Comfort the Persecuted: The Failure of Refugee Conferences", *The Wiener Library Bulletin*, 15 (1961), 43—47.

Wilson, John P., "Carlton J. H. Hayes, Spain, and the Refugee Crisis, 1942—1945", *American Jewish Historical Quarterly*, 62 (December 1972), 99—110.

Wyman, David S., "Why Auschwitz Was Never Bombed?", *Commentary*, 66 (May 1978), 37—46.

C. UNPUBLISHED WORKS

Lewis, James Ford, "The Unitarian Service Committee". Ph.D. Dissertation, The University of California, 1952.

McCarthy, Edward, "The Christian Front Movement in New York City, 1938—1940". Master's Essay, Columbia University, 1965.

Murphy, F.I., "The American Christian Press and Pre-War Hitler's Germany, 1933—1939". Ph.D. Dissertation, The University of Florida, 1970.

Shafir, Shlomo, "The Impact of the Jewish Crisis on American-German Relations". Ph.D. Dissertation, Georgetown University, 1971 (2 vols.).

Schleunes, Karl A., "Nazi Policy Toward German Jews,, 1933—1938". Ph.D. Dissertation, University of Minnesota, 1966.

Stewart, Barbara McDonald, "United States Government Policy on Refugees from Nazism, 1933—1940". Ph.D. Dissertation, Columbia University, 1969.

Wetzel, Charles J., "The American Rescue of Refugee Scholars and Scientists from Europe, 1933—1945", Ph.D. Dissertation, The University of Wisconsin, 1964.

INDEX